PICK ONE INTELLIGENT GIRL:
EMPLOYABILITY, DOMESTICITY, AND THE GENDERING OF
CANADA'S WELFARE STATE, 1939–1947

During the tumultuous formative years of the Canadian welfare state, many women rose through the ranks of the federal civil service to oversee the massive recruitment of Canadian women to aid in the Second World War. Ironically, it became the task of these same female mandarins to encourage women to return to the household once the war was over. *Pick One Intelligent Girl* reveals the elaborate psychological, economic, and managerial techniques that were used to recruit and train women for wartime military and civilian jobs, and then, at war's end, to move women out of the labour force altogether.

Negotiating the fluid boundaries of state, community, industry, and household, and drawing on a wide range of primary sources, Jennifer A. Stephen illustrates how women's relationships to home, work, and nation were profoundly altered during this period. She demonstrates how federal officials enlisted the help of a new generation of 'experts' to entrench a two-tiered training and employment system that would become an enduring feature of the Canadian state.

This engaging study not only adds to the debates about the gendered origins of Canada's welfare state, it also makes an important contribution to Canadian social history, labour and gender studies, sociology, and political science.

(Studies in Gender and History)

JENNIFER A. STEPHEN is an assistant professor in the Department of History at York University.

STUDIES IN GENDER AND HISTORY

General Editors: Franca Iacovetta and Karen Dubinsky

PICK ONE
INTELLIGENT GIRL

Employability, Domesticity, and the Gendering of Canada's Welfare State, 1939–1947

Jennifer A. Stephen

UNIVERSITY OF TORONTO PRESS
Toronto Buffalo London

© University of Toronto Press Incorporated 2007
Toronto Buffalo London
Printed in Canada

ISBN-13: 978-0-8020-9146-8 (cloth)
ISBN-13: 978-0-8020-9421-6 (paper)

Printed on acid-free paper

Library and Archives Canada Cataloguing in Publication

Stephen, Jennifer Anne, 1959–
    Pick one intelligent girl : employability, domesticity, and the gendering
of Canada's welfare state, 1939–1947 / Jennifer A. Stephen.

(Studies in gender and history)
Includes bibliographical references and index.
ISBN 978-0-8020-9146-8 (bound)
ISBN 978-0-8020-9421-6 (pbk.)

1. Women – Employment – Government policy – Canada – History –
20th century.   2. Welfare state – Canada.   3. Sex discrimination in
employment – Canada.   4. Women – Canada – Social conditions –
20th century.   5. World War, 1939–1945 – Women – Canada.
6. World War, 1939–1945 – War work – Canada.   I. Title.   II. Series.

HD6099.S76 2006   331.40971'09044   C2007-900481-4

University of Toronto Press acknowledges the financial assistance to
its publishing program of the Canada Council for the Arts and the
Ontario Arts Council.

University of Toronto Press acknowledges the financial support for
its publishing activities of the Government of Canada through the
Book Publishing Industry Development Program (BPIDP).

To
Nordra Stephen
and in memory of Robert Garnett Stephen

Contents

Acknowledgments

This study has its origins in the regular struggles of ordinary life. Before taking up graduate studies, I worked alongside an extraordinary group of women and men associated with the Toronto Labour Council and the Metro Labour Education Centre. There, we witnessed the rollback of what so many of us had come to understand as the 'gains' made through the political struggle of the generations before us. The lives of many women and men with whom we worked during that period were profoundly disrupted by the devastating wave of job loss in the wake of federal government trade and macroeconomic policy decisions. These experiences profoundly altered my understanding of unemployment – as category, as condition, and as policy outcome grounded in deliberate political choice. As we fought to defend the unemployment insurance system, we also pushed for greater access to federally sponsored training for at least some of the nearly 1.5 million people counted among the 'officially' unemployed of Canada during the early 1990s. The question 'training for what?' ultimately prompted me to turn back, as historians do, to an earlier period, from which vantage the vexed relations of training, employability, unemployment, and domesticity could be pursued more directly, but certainly no less passionately.

This book originated as my doctoral dissertation. The research and writing could not have been completed without the financial support of the Social Sciences and Humanitieis Research Council of Canada. I would also like to thank the many archivists and librarians at various institutions, including Library and Archives Canada, the Ontario Archives, the City of Toronto Archives, and the John Robarts and Thomas Fisher libraries at the University of Toronto. At University of Toronto Press, I would especially like to thank Jill McConkey for her exceptional work as editor, and Barbara Tessman, together with Franca Iacovetta and Karen Dubinsky, for their assistance in guiding the manuscript – and me – through the publication process. I also wish to thank the anonymous readers whose insights and suggestions have helped me to produce a more readable and accessible narrative.

In the course of this work, I have continued to draw inspiration, focus, and commitment from a vibrant community of activists, artists, scholars, and good friends. I cannot name them all but would like to single out a few: Maureen Thompson, Margot Francis, Laura Mitchell, Shelly Gordon, Karen Charnow Lior, Jan Borowy, and Lillian Allen. From the book's origins as my doctoral dissertation onwards, Anne Healy shared in every concept, word, and challenge, just as she shared in the circumstances that prompted me to take it on in the first place. Ruth Roach Pierson, as thesis supervisor, guided me through the process with humour, rigour, and generosity. I do not know which had the more accelerated growth rate: her extraordinarily large goldfish or the chapter lengths of the thesis. I continue to draw inspiration from her exceptional standard of committed – and rigorous! – feminist historical scholarship. Kara Dehli first introduced me to many of the theoretical insights that remain a mainstay of my work. I would also like to thank Franca Iacovetta, James Struthers, and Margaret Little. Members of the Toronto Labour Studies Group provided feedback on various iterations of the present book, and I am grateful for their insight and support. As my partner, Chris Lee has provided unwavering emotional sustenance, love, and enthusiasm throughout this project. Rory has provided a companionship grounded in a uniquely peaceful sense of time and place. I would also like to thank some of the many people who have extended their support, friendship, and scholarly input: they include, again, Franca Iacovetta, together with Carolyn Strange, Ian Radforth, Craig Heron, Mariana Valverde, Cynthia Wright, Mercedes Steedman, Julie Guard, and Gary Kinsman.

Finally, as a young girl, my mother, Nordra Jean (King) Stephen, was among the many British children to be evacuated from a home to which they would never return, in person or in memory, in quite the same way. That, of course, would be to Canada's gain, not to mention my own and that of my brother, Bruce Stephen. Both she and my father, the late Robert Garnett Stephen, taught me the art of perseverance with humour, and it is to them that I dedicate this book.

PICK ONE INTELLIGENT GIRL:
EMPLOYABILITY, DOMESTICITY, AND THE GENDERING OF
CANADA'S WELFARE STATE, 1939–1947

Introduction

During the Second World War, women moved into the formal waged economy in record numbers, more than doubling the female labour force participation rate between 1939 and 1943. Civilian women quickly took advantage of newly opened spaces in the paid labour force and in the women's divisions of the three armed services – army, navy, and air force. Bureaucratic Ottawa opened up somewhat as well, admitting women such as Fraudena Eaton and Dr Mary Salter at the Department of Labour and Dr Olive Ruth Russell at the Department of National Defence. The national mobilization of Canada's womanpower was more than the push and pull of patriotism. It was also an unparalleled opportunity to test out new ideas about social and economic policy planning and to advance the professional aspirations of educated women who sought to consolidate their place in the expanding civil service. Occupying strategic positions within the federal war administration, these women actively contributed to public policy development, all within the ambit of the emerging Canadian welfare state apparatus. The Government of Canada was on record as supporting formal equality for women, including declarations issued by the International Labour Office, temporarily headquartered at Montreal for the duration of the war. Most policy staff and their community counterparts in the voluntary sector, however, proceeded on the view that women would not be inclined to pursue what were clearly understood to be men's occupations once the war was finally over. Instead, the wheels of public administration turned on the firm understanding that most women would marry and leave the paid labour force. Was it the task of these new female mandarins, then, to encourage women to abandon regular waged employment and return to the household once war was done?

This is a story about women, work, war, and peace, spanning the tumultuous period that also saw the formation of the welfare state. In the brief period between 1939 and 1946, Canada's women figured in public policy in three entirely distinct ways. Coming out of the decade-long economic collapse of the 1930s, women workers were viewed as a drag on employment, a threat to men's jobs. As the economy heated up in the opening years of the war, however, critical labour shortages started to emerge, threatening Canada's ability to meet its production quotas to the Allied Forces. The answer to Canada's 'manpower crisis,' it seemed, lay in its womanpower. Ottawa could not possibly hope to win the war without this newly discovered strategic economic asset, and so it proceeded to launch an unprecedented campaign designed to draw women into wartime production. By all accounts the recruitment drive was an outstanding success. According to official records of the period, the number of women in the labour force grew by nearly 700,000. But the drive was also short-lived. In fact, the term *womanpower* disappeared from use entirely by the war's end.[1] By 1944, with victory in sight, Canada's womanpower was expected to disappear, apparently back into the household, at war's end.

The story is familiar enough: how Canada's women traded aprons for coveralls only to change back to aprons just as quickly. Ruth Roach Pierson's ground-breaking 1986 study, *'They're Still Women after All,'* charted the continuities between pre- and postwar Canada, pointing out that, while there was a notable increase in average per-capita income, for the women of Canada life looked pretty much the same after the war as before it. Building on such earlier work, *Pick One Intelligent Girl* sets out to examine how the massive mobilization and then demobilization were accomplished. The following chapters look closely at the public policy measures that guided federal officials through the wartime mobilization, measures that also laid the foundation for the postwar consensus of the Canadian welfare state. I examine the elaborate psychological, economic, and managerial techniques that were used in the early years of the war to draw women into the labour force, to train them for wartime jobs, and to ensure that they were as efficient in their work as possible. I then show how *these same techniques* were used to achieve precisely the opposite effect during the postwar phase of demobilization and rehabilitation: to marginalize some women in low-waged occupations, and for the rest – in particular, married women – to move them out of the paid labour force altogether.

The federal government entered the Second World War with a piecemeal, ad hoc approach to labour-force planning and economic policy, well behind its fellow member states in the all-but-defunct League of Nations. When Canada joined the Allied powers and declared war against Germany in September 1939, the federal government under Prime Minister Mackenzie King rapidly moved into position, taking charge of a 'command economy' and of the labour market. Canadian industry lined up, hoping for the lucrative war contracts that were sure to follow. Production levels in essential war industries would need to accelerate rapidly to feed the gaping maw of the war machine. However, productivity levels lagged, and, of even greater concern, the nation was soon facing a serious shortage of labour. As the debate over Canada's 'manpower crisis' began to heat up, bureaucrats turned their attention to the 'quality' of the labour supply. Chapter 1 examines the almost frenetic efforts of the King administration and senior wartime officials to resolve the growing crisis of labour shortages in essential war industries. It would soon become clear that the country desperately required a massive infusion of workers. Great Britain's greatest ally, the Dominion of Canada, was in danger of reneging at a critical time in the war. And the problem was only going to get worse.

The only answer to the recurring labour shortages that threatened to derail the war effort was to mobilize the dormant 'female labour reserve.' Mobilizing Canada's women for wartime labour might have seemed a moderate, even sensible, proposition. Seeing the plan through was quite another matter. Government officials would have to prevail upon employers, trade unions, even women themselves to accept and respond to such an urgent call. Bringing thousands of women into the formal waged economy presented a cultural, political, social, and sexual challenge unmatched in government policy or, for that matter, Canadian history. Ottawa would embark on an uncharted course into industrial planning, labour policy, and regulatory intervention. But it would not set off alone. Federal Department of Labour officials enlisted the aid of a new generation of experts: industrial engineers, managerial consultants, industrial psychologists, and, of course, the 'intelligence men,' with their battery of mental-testing techniques.

Once women had been ushered through the factory gates, it fell to the National Selective Service Women's Division (NSSWD) to keep them there for the duration of the war. Chapter 2 takes up the work of the NSSWD between 1942 and 1945. This work reflected and was informed by that latest of corporate innovations, the personnel department. Women were thought ideally suited as both subjects and practitioners of the new personnel policies. The NSSWD went about its task through a combination of personnel supervision and a deeply gendered moral regulatory program of industrial welfare. These administrative and managerial practices sought to structure and modify social relations of work in order to secure the objective of the national enterprise – the conduct of war – while at the same time stabilizing the end goal of postwar policy – overseeing the peaceful withdrawal of women from the formal waged economy at war's end.

Women were needed in the armed forces as well, and they responded in thousands to the call to service – and the opportunity for a decently paid job. Chapter 3 follows the 'psychologist at war' to explore the mental-testing techniques encountered by women attempting to sign up in the Canadian Women's Army Corps (CWAC). As an army examiner for the CWAC, Dr Olive Ruth Russell would finally come into her own. I read Russell's contribution as a critical phase in the genealogy of intelligence within the scientific discourse of educational psychology. The repercussions were real enough: many women were dishonourably discharged from military service at the recommendation of the army examiner. In the service of a very modern war, this new science could also go far in averting the terrible debacle encountered during the First World War and the aftermath of its demobilization. In her assessments of CWAC recruits, Russell charted a well-defined course through the recruiting lines, assessing the best and the apparently most dangerous that Canadian womanhood had to offer, applying the litmus test of moral probity and sexual deviance, always in combination with IQ and personality. Russell's work demonstrated both the utility of and the potential for mass application of modern personnel screening, particularly among women, with enduring effect.

In chapters 4, 5, and 6, I examine preparations for the postwar period. 'Looking for a postwar job' became a familiar refrain among both civilian women and ex-servicewomen. No one could know for certain when the war would finally end – neither government personnel, whose job it would be to hasten the return to domestic stability, nor the more than 700,000 women whose wartime employment brought much-needed cash into the family economy. Chapter 4 returns to the NSSWD and the 1943 federal Report on the Post-War Problems of Women. Postwar planning was designed explicitly to secure the withdrawal of women war workers from the formal economy. Government advisers drawn from liberal and professional women's organizations rehearsed the twin rationales of domesticity and employability in their attempts to balance, in even a limited fashion, wartime gains against postwar domestic priorities – priorities that required the primacy of a household and formal economy ordered according to the principles of the male breadwinner model. Throughout the postwar planning phase, initiated while the war was underway and continuing into the postwar years, each and all were enlisted in the considerable challenge of converting home, community, industry, and workplace from the economic rationality of war to the domestic passivity of peace. This work enlisted scores of government administrators and community volunteers, organizations, and agencies.

In chapter 5, I turn to the work of postwar rehabilitation planning for ex-servicewomen to take up once again the work of Olive Ruth Russell, this time at her new post in charge of rehabilitation programming for women veterans. Under the veil of scientific objectivity, educational psychologists, particularly those associated with the National Committee for Mental Hygiene (Canada) (NCMH), diligently approached their goal of a national standard for mental health, one grounded in a model of ideal citizenship, domestic stability, industrial security, and national order. *Psychological security* and *individual adjustment*, the key terms in this model, were deeply inflected by notions of respectability and stability. The ideal-typical household anchored liberal democratic discourse as mental hygiene practitioners turned their gaze to a postwar social order of national stability and security. In this world, the shared national and cultural identity was white, middle-class, educated, and above all, organized around the male breadwinner-dependent housewife model.

Rehabilitation legislation contained formal equality provisions for the women and men who had sacrificed so much in the service of nation and defence of democracy. Ex-servicewomen were accorded equal rights under the Veterans' Charter. Nonetheless, women veterans were equally subject to the broader federal-provincial policy objective. The federal Department of Labour, in cooperation with the provinces, had one goal in mind and that was to orchestrate the massive withdrawal of civilian women and ex-servicewomen from the formal waged economy. Debates among veterans' organizations, business and employer organizations, the labour movement, and government about the most appropriate role for the National Employment Service clearly illustrate the gendered contours of the state's regulatory strategy in relation to employer rights, collective bargaining rights, and employment rights in the labour market. Even as women veterans were explicitly identified as equally entitled to all postwar rehabilitation programs and credits, there was little intention to intercede directly into the labour market or the workplace on their behalf. Simply put, there was no equivalent discourse of employment rights for women.

Finally, in chapter 6, I examine the federal government's postwar consensus for women: the return to postwar domesticity. By 1945, women war workers found themselves directed into the household as home-makers or labourers in other women's homes, or into a narrow range of acceptable occupations. For those women who insisted upon waged employment, the NSSWD turned to pre-employment vocational training as a strategy to direct women into those occupations for which they were deemed suitable. I look at a selection of occupational groups – domestic labour, the needle trades, and hospital service – to consider the multiple ways in which pre-employment training and related personnel tech-niques were deployed to counter labour shortages, stabilize the labour supply, and suppress women's resistance to entering these 'traditional female' occupations. In each case, the 'quality of labour' was the central problem to be addressed through policy.

Stabilizing the household and averting postwar unemployment were the twin goals informing government policy for women during this period. A strategic economic asset during the war, by war's end women were regarded as a potentially disruptive force, one capable of destabiliz-ing the wage-setting mechanisms of the labour market. The policy chal-lenge lay in how government might secure women's peaceable withdrawal from the formal waged economy while at the same time upholding the gender-equality provisions to which Canada was signatory through inter-national convention and within domestic rehabilitation legislation. Women were accorded formal equality through a discourse of liberal choice within the framework of contract theory, eliding the material effects of oppression grounded in race/ethnicity, class, gender, and sexuality. Within the emerging social security state, then, women's first, only, and true vocation lay within the household. Women's employabil-ity had been widely scrutinized during the war as a key factor in averting the labour shortages emerging in essential industries. By the war's end, women's postwar employment was to be shaped by discourses about domesticity and employability. The household, meanwhile, was posi-tioned as the primary social unit and the primary unit of social policy. The official consensus was that a healthy democracy depended upon happy homes.

The Veterans' Charter in Canadian Welfare State History

The Second World War has been characterized as a watershed in the formation of the welfare state in Canada. The Veterans' Charter, a compendium of rehabilitation programming for ex-service personnel, is singled out by Canadian historians as a path-breaking legislative initiative designed to secure and promote equality and universality, complementing the social security initiatives that accompanied the postwar reconstruction program.[2] Rehabilitation legislation was certainly indicative of that broader convergence of interests across the country, culminating in the drive for a postwar era of peace, prosperity, and national social security.[3] Included among its many provisions were elements of income support, education, training, housing, and employment security. Military historians Peter Neary and Shaun Brown aptly characterize this omnibus of social and economic legislation as an important building block of the Canadian welfare state, even as they acknowledge its limited application to women.[4] Certainly, the elaboration of state regulation during the war intersected with the growing chorus of demands for social security, permanently altering the purpose and scope of state activity by the postwar period. Social security measures, including unemployment insurance, the family allowance, and old age security provisions, are the hallmarks of the welfare state, the class-based postwar consensus between labour and capital that underscores welfare state models generally. By mid-century, the formative pieces of social security legislation were in place, although notions of entitlement remained closely informed and regulated by a convergence of political objectives of concern to the Liberal government between 1943 and 1945, in particular that of wage stabilization. Welfare state historian James Struthers points out that family allowances and old age security provisions introduced during the period are more accurately read as the collective product of a strategic compromise to meet the economic and political challenges confronting Canadian federalism in the 1940s rather than a broad endorsement of social democratic principles, as claimed by so many defenders of the welfare state then and now.[5]

The history of state formation in Canada is also a history of the emergence of 'the social' as an arena – a field – for the administration of identities thought to bolster or to threaten the social body, the Canadian nation. Public policy is a rich field for historical analysis of this sort. This is true of those studies that adopt a more critical scrutiny of unemployment and poverty in order to examine how social problems are reworked as administrative categories within state policy. So, for example, residualism remained deeply entrenched within the design principles of social security, notwithstanding rhetorical gestures towards universality, just as the principle of 'less eligibility' was – and still is – an enduring feature of income support provisions as forms of wage replacement and subsidization.[6] Discourses about responsible citizenship framed questions of postwar rehabilitation and civilian readjustment as techniques of the self. That is, they placed a strategic emphasis on what were increasingly taken up as allegedly innate abilities and inherent qualities of individual women and men. Subjectivity, as Joan Scott has suggested, is constructed through experience, such that we see as subjective ('originating in oneself') the string of interpersonal, material, and economic relations 'which are in fact social, and in a larger perspective, historical.'[7] Indeed, recent historical investigations have yielded a rich literature documenting the formation of the postwar social security state and its impact on identity formation and citizenship norms in postwar Canada. Recent Canadian historical scholarship shows how Cold War policies scrutinized and screened out those deemed unfit for national citizenship within the polity. Discourses of citizenship intertwined with those of domesticity, as Julie Guard convincingly demonstrates in her study of women consumer activists regarded as potentially 'dangerous foreigners.' Similarly, Franca Iacovetta and colleagues consider practices of internment during the Second World War and the treatment of displaced persons (DPs) after the war.[8] In either case, the ways in which the state and a range of gatekeepers scrutinized, screened, and deported enemy aliens or prospective newcomers served to reify normative standards for postwar citizenship.

The period 1939 to 1947 is characterized as much by patterns of profound continuity as by transformative change in the direction of universality and equality. Moreover, both the changes and the continuities were grounded in enduring gender, class, and race-based relations and subsequent inequalities. It is a cherished element of the national Canadian imaginary to retrospectively cast the Second World War as a historical marker signifying a critical turning point for Canadian women. As feminist historians have argued, the war did not dramatically alter women's substantive economic and social equality. Ruth Roach Pierson's *'They're Still Women after All,'* a study of the experiences and state practices confronted by women war workers and service personnel, broke considerable new ground, tracing the continuities linking material conditions of postwar society to those obtaining during the pre-war period. As Pierson and Marjorie Cohen suggested in their collaborative study of federal labour market policy during the Second World War, Ottawa's position on the matter of gender equality was deeply contradictory, if not ideologically inconsistent. Postwar gender equality amounted to little more than a rhetorical device of greater import on the international stage than it was for domestic policy. The federal government proceeded to implement social and economic policies that gave short shrift to arguments favouring the consolidation of the wartime social and economic gains made by women.[9] A close reading of this period suggests the further need to reassess both the basis of equality claims and the alleged universality of such claims. Claims to universality often risk obscuring how different material conditions and lived experiences of women are collapsed into, and therefore subsumed by, the universalizing category of 'woman' as the subject of historical study.[10] As recent feminist and race-critical scholarship makes clear, these universalizing narratives cannot take us very far in tracing the multiple tracks followed by welfare state policies nor expose to view the class, gender, and raced relations that such policies have helped to construct and transform. Like liberal discourses generally, and liberalist ideology as it has infused such feminist equality claims, official recognition measured by frequency of government appointments illustrates just that: the official recognition of some women, by virtue of their membership within the dominant culture, but not all women. Even more, accepting numerical representation on government committees of inquiry or state agencies as a mark of gender progress restates the original elision of women who are not of the dominant culture by positioning the hegemonic interests of dominant culture women in liberal choice discourse as universalizing and truly representational and viewing gender as a unifying and unitary category uninflected by race, class, and sexuality. This mode of analysis also positions 'individual' freedom as fundamentally opposed to 'government,' another accomplishment of liberalist discourse.[11]

Equity versus Efficiency: Theories of the Welfare State

This study demonstrates how liberal state formation projects and techniques of governance work through the articulation of 'personal' interests and private interests of organizations – community and other – to represent the claims and interests of the dominant culture. Nowhere was this more apparent than in the workings of the voluntary advisory committees instituted as techniques of governance during the Second World War, including the subcommittee appointed to 'investigate' the postwar problems of women. The women practitioners whose work I examined concentrated their attention on culturally appropriate forms of labour among working women. Factors such as class, race, ethnicity, education,

and marital status influenced assessments of legitimate need and, therefore, the legitimacy of waged labour. Whether the subject was training
for household domestic service or stenography, vocational training was
the order of the day. But 'skill,' as I demonstrate, was a highly contested,
deeply racialized, class-based, and gendered category grounded in employability discourses. Such policy discourses were reflective of, and
worked through, notions about proper citizenship and about appropriate forms of domesticity and acceptable representations of employability
for women. Skill, moreover, worked discursively to organize and stabilize
the gendered and racialized division of labour, shoring up the boundaries of the formal waged economy. Skill, aptitude, and intelligence were
deeply embedded within citizenship discourse, code for women's status
within and capacity to make claims upon the broader social polity, of
which the labour market was one facet.

The Second World War witnessed an extended and considerably elabo-
rated role of the Canadian state, particularly in the area of labour
market regulation, a development that is frequently cited in support of
claims that this was a formative period for the construction of welfare
state forms. The emergence of modern forms of labour market regulation was signalled in particular by the acceptance of collective bargaining
as a legitimate practice – and domain of governance – and of trade
unions as legitimate representatives of workers, after a long struggle that
finally culminated in the institution of compulsory dues check-off following a ninety-nine-day strike at the Ford Motor Company Windsor facility
in 1945.[12] Labour historians generally point to the actions of the National Selective Service, the Wartime Labour Relations Board, and the
federal Department of Labour as evidence of the increasing role played
by government in building the regulatory state.[13] Historians disagree on
the question of how extensive such regulatory control was, or ideologically could ever be. Certainly, the federal government sought desperately to assume control of a wartime 'command economy.' Department
of Labour administrators did not entirely succeed in developing, let
alone successfully implementing, any such master plan. Prime Minister
Mackenzie King's war administration was regularly criticized, even lam-
pooned, for its inability to respond to what was clearly shaping up to be a
major 'manpower' crisis by 1943. Recent studies document the considerable opposition to the NSS, positioned as it was in between veterans'
organizations arguing for the preferential placement of returning enlisted personnel (primarily men) on the one hand, and, on the other,
unions attempting to secure recently won collective bargaining rights by

enforcing seniority provisions as the central vehicle for exercising rights under negotiated collective agreements. For example, Michael Stevenson observes how 'NSS failed to find a satisfactory compromise between the positions of the unions and the veterans' organizations. This failure illustrates the practical limitations of government interference in the labour market in Canada at the time.'[14] However, when the gendered and racialized dimensions of NSS regulatory measures are placed under the microscope, the impact of NSS practice on women can be seen as profoundly influential.

Pick One Intelligent Girl considers two interdependent questions central to the historical study of welfare state regulation: (1) What are 'human resources' in the context of historically contingent 'efficiency' measures and discourses of nation? (2) How is the 'labour market' conceptualized historically for the purposes of state-based regulation as an articulation of state, of nation, and of human productive capacity? A dilemma often posed in studies of welfare state formation is the incapacity of central regulatory measures to enhance full efficiency and productivity. At the core of this critique lies the ongoing tension between states and markets – the alleged trade-off between the equity objectives presumed to under-score welfare state forms and the alleged efficiency objectives of so-called free markets.[15] As Ann Porter has documented in her study of postwar federal labour market policies, building upon Ruth Pierson's study of the deployment of gender as a central organizing strategy in the development of the unemployment insurance program, the labour market is itself a social institution deeply informed by relations of gender (in addition to those of class and race).[16] Earlier critiques of classic liberal and Marxian labour market theorists make much the same point, drawing attention away from structural predeterminants of market operations and towards their constitution as social institutions. In their classic study, Bowles and Gintis challenged the then-prevailing Marxist theory of labour markets for its inability to examine and come to grips with how women were differ-entially located in and by labour markets. While there is no necessary correspondence between capitalism and patriarchy, capitalist employers readily followed a divide-and-rule strategy along the lines of gender. Public patriarchy, in the form of state-provided income support programs, was key to the extension of consciousness, identity, and transformative social action: 'What Marx thought the accumulation process would do for work-ers – create the conditions for the transparency of capitalist exploitation and thus promote a common working-class identity and consciousness – "public patriarchy" may well do for women.'[17]

This study looks at the labour market as a key constituent feature of welfare state formation and takes the analysis one step farther to challenge conceptualizations of markets as ontologically distinct from government and, therefore, from governance. For the vast majority of women, the public policies of the federal government and its agencies were profoundly influential, even in the presence of an administrative apparatus that was far from the 'well-oiled machine' its overseers purported it to be. The need for concerted intervention and diligent community involvement – for social order – was often made through pointed allusions to sexual danger, immorality, and excessive and unwholesome leisure activities among women whose taste for such activities was unhealthily whetted by their inflated wartime incomes. Suitable vocation, aptitude, measures of intelligence: these concepts were drawn upon as part of a growing apparatus of 'manpower policy' intended to facilitate the smooth transition into the postwar period. As it happened, such 'career' terms applied readily to men. The question of women's employment was framed quite differently and reflexively in relation to men's right to work. As Margaret Hobbs has indicated in her study of women's employment experiences during the 1930s in Canada, the solution to men's unemployment was women's unemployment.[18] The ideal-typical citizen who was the subject of emerging rights discourse was white, male, and capable of consolidating his employment rights through his skilled capacity. For a woman, whatever else might be demanded of her within official policy discourses concerning the war effort and postwar reconstruction, domestic vocation – in her own home or someone else's – was all. In the face of postwar fears of recurring depression, unemployment was framed in terms of economic democracy and the rights of citizenship.

Welfare state regimes that adopted policies of full employment, as Jane Lewis has demonstrated, incorporated women's economic dependency on men as a given.[19] These gendered assumptions formed the conceptual bedrock underpinning theories and subsequent policies about unemployment and the employability of groups within the population during the period in question. The demobilization of women war workers took the form of 'clearing' the labour market of women. The strategy of choice was one of moral regulation involving practices of normalization that disciplined specific groups of women as subjects of employment policy. The vast majority of women were encouraged – and, as subjects of employment policy discourses, positioned as 'choosing' – to withdraw from the paid workforce altogether in order to take up their rightful place within the so-called private household. This stood in direct contrast to the articulation of men's employment rights around which veterans' organizations and trade unions were actively organizing. For the thousands of working-class women, immigrant women, Native women, and racial/ethnic women whose future paid employment was very much in question, there would be no such political space within which to organize and through which to mobilize similar citizenship claims and entitlements.

Towards a National Standard of Mental Health: Canada's Mental Hygiene Movement

Studies of the Second World War period rarely subject the activities of educational psychologists, industrial psychiatrists, and various other self-styled mental hygienists to historical inquiry.[20] Mona Gleason has studied the multiplicity of ways that psyche-experts sought to shape the 'normal' family through middle-class, heterosexual, and Anglo/Celtic cultural and sexual norms. Gleason demonstrates the considerable scope of psychological practice in the policy activities of the Canadian welfare state in the postwar period. In a similar spirit, *Pick One Intelligent Girl* scrutinizes the activities of the principal federal departments concerned with mobilization for the services and essential war industries. Consider, for example, the following excerpt, a description of the psychological screening techniques deployed within the personnel selection practices of the RCAF, developed by Edward Bott, University of Toronto psychologist and associate of the National Committee for Mental Hygiene (Canada): 'The first difficulty arose over selection procedures. How was aircrew potential to be assessed? Physical failings were easy to spot and it was possible to make fairly accurate judgements of mental stability, but intellectual capabilities were harder to pin down.'[21] The Second World War provided a critical opportunity to apply new policy approaches and ideas in building the apparatus of the Canadian welfare state.[22] The science of mental hygiene was not without its critics. The burden of a psychiatrist or, for that matter, a psychologist was a heavy one to bear, as not everyone appreciated the value of this body of professional expertise. Veterans' organizations and military officials alike contended that what male veterans needed most was a job: it was jobs not minds that needed to be adjusted. The distinction, as it turned out, was far less precise than officials may have hoped or more strategically made it out to be. As the quality of the labour supply became a central concern for the Dominion government during the course of the war, driven as it was by the need to achieve optimum productivity in essential war industries, administrative effectiveness was increasingly understood in terms shaped by psyche-discourses regarding human capacities. Mental testing promised an efficient method for screening military as well as civilian populations. Once applied to matters of labour policy – to diagnose problems of high turnover, absenteeism, and manifestations of 'labour unrest' such as strikes or union organizing, or to design and deliver vocational training in an effort to enhance productivity – the promise of mental testing seemed limitless. Unlocking the productive potential of intellectual capacity was tantamount to locating the map to King Solomon's mines, and modern psyche-science promised to lead the way into the uncharted territory of individual psychology.

The psyche-sciences took centre stage during the Second World War, their practitioners moving into top posts in government departments to oversee personnel selection for industry and the military and advising on appropriate policy measures to reduce absenteeism and ensure stability. Personnel planning transformed the economic 'fact' of employment – the need for and the act of securing paid employment – into a psyche-based register for calibrating 'employability' along a continuum of alleged individual capacities, based on the study of individual psychology. Diagnostic assessments of human capacities were grounded in, and intensified the effects of, racialized and gendered conventions of the period, revealing innate potential and pathology, speaking the truth about the individual to whom they were applied.[23] In this way, the inability to find or keep a job of any sort was a function of intelligence, skill, or poor vocational choice, driven by an understanding of who the job seeker was understood to be: lunch counter server, stenographer, domestic worker, or manual labourer. Such totalizing practices marked out groups within the population according to what was thought most culturally appropriate. With these activities as vectors for the norm – the average – all others fell into or out of place. The maladjusted worker, the man or woman out of place, was to become both a new challenge and a new rationale, demonstrating the utility of and pressing need for a comprehensive employment policy.

Psychological techniques would have enduring effects into the postwar period, as practitioners deliberated over the most appropriate rehabilitation programs for women and men seeking to take up their private lives in a peacetime economy. I examine these practices as instances of the 'conduct of conduct,' a practice of governance that drew upon the psychology of the individual evident in the development and application of intelligence testing. How was intelligence considered a marker of social and economic efficiency? By what techniques was 'intelligence' taken up within economic space, as both a linear scale by which to define and administer subject populations and the key to unlocking the individual's allegedly hidden, unique capacities as worker, mother, student, or soldier? In what different ways were groups of women both encouraged and compelled to understand themselves in these terms and to submit themselves to the techniques developed by the psyche-experts, whose battery of tests and self-help manuals held out the promise of everything from suitable vocation and clear occupational choice to healthy and well-adjusted children? Personnel assessment was a rich and promising new area of expertise. Postwar rehabilitation plans drew specifically upon the work of Canada's foremost industrial psychiatrists and education psychologists, in particular those associated with NCMH. Leading academic institutions, such as the University of Toronto and Montreal's McGill University, supplied a range of vocational experts, educational practitioners, psychiatrists, and psychologists to both the men's and the women's services. Dr Olive Ruth Russell and her colleague Dr Jack Griffin of the NCMH felt mental hygiene was a neglected but vital area of public policy. As a senior bureaucrat whose responsibilities included the development of rehabilitation policy for women veterans, Russell was also an advocate for economic and social equality for women. Her work as an army examiner with the Canadian Women's Army Corps provided her with a wide field for the application of mental testing and examination techniques and the development of personnel policy for the Department of National Defence. She saw the potential for extending practices developed during the war well into the postwar period in a manner that she hoped would consolidate the wartime gains enjoyed by women like her. At the same time, management engineers such as the Montreal firm of Stevenson and Kellogg, along with industrial psychiatrists such as Montreal-based McGill psychiatrist Dr Ewen Cameron, worked closely with National Selective Service personnel during the war, busily advancing themselves as leading practitioners in the field of personnel management. The interior of the subject – the allegedly innate, hidden capacities – was intensified as a field for governance by psyche-experts eager to place their specialized areas of expertise at the service of the wartime and postwar policy regime of the Canadian state. 'Am I intelligent enough for this job?' – this was the question ex-servicewomen and men were invited to ask themselves. The question embodied the techniques and technologies – the matrix of knowledge practices – that practitioners hoped to make the new common sense of postwar planning.

'I Want You to Pick One Intelligent Girl': Mobilizing Canada's Womanpower

By 1941, Canada had still not resolved the labour chaos that had plagued it since the war's beginning. Canada's role as a junior member of the Allied Forces was to supply troops and materiel to the hard-pressed British forces stationed in Europe. Canadian industry was not really up to the challenge of meeting the high military production quotas needed to feed the increasingly voracious appetite of total war. The federal war cabinet designated key industries as essential to the war effort. Essential industries were under orders to suspend all production for civilian markets and concentrate instead on feeding the war machine. The King administration had assumed the extraordinary powers available under the War Measures Act, yet still Ottawa failed to demonstrate any capacity to meet its military production commitments. The problems were as numerous and as critical as the barbs flying in Ottawa's direction. The federal government lacked a comprehensive manpower plan. Relations between unions and management were increasingly fractious, and productive capacity was lagging. In response, Ottawa's senior mandarins convened a study. Their goal – solve the manpower crisis. Their method – expedite recruitment of a body of labour that had been consistently ignored, if not denied recognition altogether – Canada's womanpower.

So began an expansion of the federal bureaucracy that would in time lay the groundwork for the labour policies of the Canadian welfare state. For now, Canada lacked any national coherence, at least where its labour power was concerned. Canadian industry had largely remained unhindered in its labour dealings, blocking union organizing, hiring, and firing at will and following practices that could not in any way be described as either modern or enlightened. In the few short years between 1939 and 1945, Canada would develop the scaffolding of a national employment service. Canadian industry would benefit from the insights of modern personnel practice. Canadian workers would be channelled through a complex process of personnel assessment, training, and deployment to areas where they were needed most: staffing the machinery of war, and then rebuilding for the peace. Canada's womanpower would respond to the most serious challenge of all: leaving the household to join the ranks of the gainfully employed. But what then?

On 28 July 1941, a group of worried bureaucrats assembled to discuss what the press would soon openly dub Canada's manpower crisis. The group was to oversee the Labour Supply Investigation Project (LSIP) and report on its findings directly to Prime Minister Mackenzie King's war cabinet.[1] Those attending the committee's first meeting constituted a who's who of the newly minted – and newly powerful – Ottawa elite. The group included Dr Bryce Stewart, deputy minister of labour; Dr W.A. Mackintosh, a senior official in the Department of Finance; Alex Skelton and John J. Deutsch of the Bank of Canada; Dr W.J. Couper from the Department of Labour; and Pierre Waelbroeck of the International Labour Office, temporarily headquartered in Montreal for the duration of the war. This was no standard government study. The LSIP drew together individuals who would ultimately be responsible for drafting and marshalling Canada's employment policy regime through the trying years ahead. There was no disputing that the National Employment Service was inadequate to the task of harnessing productive labour power, and certainly not in the limited time available.[2] This was to be an investigation of the national labour market and a prescriptive conceptual map of its proper functions. But it was also a problematization of market operations. Who had rights in the labour market? In what ways ought the federal power to intervene in the array of employer rights to hire, to fire, and to train – or not? Federal officials certainly anticipated opposition from the provinces, forced by the War Measures Act to cede powers to the central state. Private industry would likely object to direct state intervention in the operation of the labour market itself. Nevertheless, the bureaucrats contended, matters such as whom, when, and in what quantity an employer would hire could no longer be exclusively an internal business affair. The central government was in charge of a command economy and thus required the power to direct labour to where it was most needed, at least in time of total war. During the war and into the postwar period as well, government bureaucrats argued the necessity of a comprehensive national employment service, an agency of the state operating in a disinterested but efficient capacity, presiding over the allocation and balancing of labour supply and market demand.

Employers remained wary of relinquishing to the state the power to hire and recruit – traditional private rights of contract. Trade unions and central labour bodies were also ambivalent about this move. Members of King's cabinet were not so ready to lend their support either. Cabinet remained split, with Labour and the armed services both in competition with the grand war production plans of C.D. Howe, the 'Minister of Everything,' and his associates in government and industry. Classical economic theory was still the wisdom of the day in this debate. Competition between war and non-war industry, between armed services and production, such theory predicted, would see scarce manpower resources allocated to the most efficient enterprise. This was fine in theory. However, efficiency was not the primary goal of this operation. In a time of war, the objective was as crucial as it was incalculable: securing the national interest.[3] And in case anyone needed to be reminded, the national business at hand was war, not profit.

When the LSIP tabled its confidential report to cabinet in October 1941, Mackintosh and his colleagues insisted that the only way through the manpower crisis would be for the federal government to take control of the labour market. The civilian army of labour would be conscripted into the service of the federal state. The Department of Labour would lead the way, planners argued, helping industry to develop the managerial function over, if not necessarily in place of, the market function. Markets might allocate, but they did not necessarily allocate well. Modern personnel planning, assessment, and management, and not the market, should be deployed as the primary mechanism determining the allocation of labour – human capital. The experiment may have seemed straightforward on paper, but it promised to be an exercise of unparalleled complexity. This was a battleground upon which the varying rights of citizenship and property would be contested by employers, veterans' organizations, trade unions, and individual men and women. Indeed, in the end the debate converged on the employment rights of returning male veterans against those of women.

'It Is Not to Be Wondered That Aggressive Employers Produce Aggressive Unionists'

As the authors of the LSIP report made all too clear, the road ahead would be full of new challenges. Labour relations were fractious at best. Employers followed old methods of hiring and even more antiquated methods in resolving labour disputes. The economy was overheating, and the search for new workers brought many to the plant gate who really had no business being there. Adding women to such a volatile mix seemed impossible, and so the first objective was to get employers to cooperate. On this point, officials were surprisingly candid in their critical assessment of the current industrial relations climate. Employers and labour unions came in for equal criticism for their antagonistic roles in the recent wave of strike action that was plaguing industries across the country. Stubborn employers and aggressive unionists were characterized as intransigent adversaries whose disruptive practices posed a threat to production schedules. To substantiate these claims, the LSIP had conducted a national survey of firms deemed essential to production. Very few followed progressive managerial practices, leading the committee to conclude that there was no administrative basis for an effective labour management policy, one that might see smooth implementation of the federal plan. Industrial relations languished at the 'master' and 'servant' stage, backward by any modern standard. 'It is not to be wondered at,' officials mused, 'that aggressive employers produce aggressive unionists.'[4] The individual bargaining capacity of workers was insignificant compared to the strength of employers, and so it ought to surprise no one that workers were banding together to bargain collectively through unions. Unions were social institutions, sharing with industry the same evolutionary path towards economic modernization. But left alone, the industrial relations climate was threatening the legitimate interests of both parties, not to mention the now paramount interests of a nation at war. Clearly this was a precarious environment into which to introduce so many new women workers. But if addressing social prejudice against hiring women workers was a problem, the evidence suggested that such prejudice diminished as employers gained more experience with the new workforce.[5]

Absenteeism was another serious problem. Accelerated turnover and mobility were caused by workers whose wayward habits disrupted regular work routines and production planning. Firms could easily resolve this problem through comprehensive personnel policies, still largely unknown to Canadian industry. The quality of the labour force was addressed through careful inquiry into the employability of Canada's workers, especially new entrants attracted by the enormous numbers of job vacancies. It was regrettable that so many new hires, pulled in to Canadian industry because of the labour shortage, were of inferior 'physical' and 'mental' capacity. In selecting these key policy areas for discussion, the LSIP redefined and deepened government scrutiny of labour supply and demand in an exercise that sought to rationalize the labour market as governable economic space. In so doing, government officials developed a template for the future investigation and regulation of workers in Canada.

The major thrust of LSIP research was directed towards a perennial issue in the federation: federal-provincial responsibility. Labour relations fell within provincial jurisdiction. Economic development was a shared responsibility, although many of the levers of the national economy were in federal hands. Where did this leave specific responsibility for cultivating a skilled supply of workers? There was simply no comprehensive federal-provincial agreement governing funding of and responsibility for the development of a skilled labour force. For now, the matter was temporarily resolved when Ottawa assumed complete control of labour force training, now considered the key to resolving the current crisis. Training of both sides, workers and employers, it was thought, would utterly transform the industrial relations system. For employers, the LSIP recommendations stressed the importance of advanced personnel policies. 'Short practical courses in personnel management' provided by the Department of Labour would slowly but surely turn the tide on industrial unrest. Plans had to be developed to address the many issues implicated by the tremendous transformation of the anticipated role of women as workers. Officials were well aware that employers might oppose this move. They also were concerned about meeting the responsibilities now falling to the government as regulator of not only the labouring capacities but the welfare of these new entrants to the workplaces and factories of the nation. In any case, such reforms were long overdue.

Confronting the Challenge of Full Employment

As part of their investigation into the quality of labour, the LSIP critically assessed the existing labour supply. Unemployed women and men were, of course, the first potential source to be drawn upon by war industries. However, this was a labour pool of doubtful quality. The unemployed were able to find work only because of the current tight conditions obtaining in the labour market. It was for once a worker's and not an employer's market, a challenging prospect indeed. An important dimension of this analysis was the apparent inverse relation between total employment and productive efficiency. That is, as the economy neared full employment, the quality of available workers deteriorated. Training could only go so far to remedy the problem since this was also considered a question of inferior human capacity among workers drawn into the labour market by the sudden increase in jobs. Echoing the point made in the 1935 census report on unemployment of the Dominion Bureau of Statistics (DBS), officials confirmed that the unemployed pool, for the most part, possessed 'inferior physical and mental qualifications. This condition,' they concluded, 'must, of course, be expected as the economy approaches full employment.'[6]

Looking for a job in 1939 was a relatively straightforward proposition. Workers lined up at the plant gate and waited while the designated foreperson patrolled the queue, selecting from the available stock. The technique may have worked in the past, but it had no place in modern industry. Employers who clung to traditional methods of hiring at the plant gate on a whim and a sight contributed to the wandering habits of inefficient workers. In the absence of a trained personnel expert or, better yet, an employment officer associated with one of the public exchanges, employers were fated to stumble through the hiring queue haphazardly selecting candidates who would continue their inefficient careers at the employer's expense. The toll in lost production time and spoiled goods would continue to rise unless government took the lead by ending this wasteful and unscientific practice.[7] Labour turnover was rampant as workers moved from job to job in search of higher wages and better terms, while employers – many of whom were not even manufacturing essential war supplies – freely poached the best workers from their competitors. The problem was therefore framed as one of compromised employability combined with the ineffectual method of hiring 'at the plant gate' without the aid of a comprehensive personnel policy or, better yet, a centralized public employment service.

Matching workers and jobs haphazardly, that is to say, leaving the market function to do the job, contributed to diminished productivity. Part of the problem lay in workers who were branded unemployable. Employers were helpless to deal with those whose alleged mental deficiency rendered them of little use, unsuited for the task at hand, in jobs well beyond their capacities – the 'square peg in a round hole' syndrome. Such individuals were maladjusted and therefore unstable, wandering from one job to another just as they pleased. Physical incapacity was only part of the problem. More troubling were those whose deficiency was internal, whose delinquent work habits were only revealed once they were on the job, or had wandered off, as they were apparently so prone to do. Here was one of the reasons why full employment was such a mixed blessing. Hundreds of people were flooding the tight market, drawn from the rural and less industrialized regions. Under normal conditions, these itinerant individuals would have been unlikely to find work at all. Hiring critieria based on simple availability could not identify those workers who were able and potentially productive. The solution lay with the new technique for investigating and regulating labour supply: aptitude testing.

LSIP researchers drew on a growing body of employment and personnel research to make their case, commenting, for example, on a large Montreal manufacturer that had its own personnel department. The hiring process involved medical, intelligence, and aptitude testing of all 'new recruits.' The tight labour market was clearly attracting less desirable applicants since, as the Montreal firm in question reported, 'new employees are testing lower than one year ago.'[8] Fortunately, the new personnel selection technique meant that new recruits could be monitored and the less efficient be systematically weeded out. Personnel technique added a new dimension to the calibration and subsequent administration of employees based on their degree of conformity to the emerging norm of mental, as well as physical, capacity. Evidence of an undesirable attitude, revealed as wandering habits (or labour turnover), absenteeism, or poor performance on the job might now be diagnosed according to a new grid of intelligibility: the cumulative results of employee aptitude tests. The statistical capacity to measure labour quality through aptitude and intelligence testing was a breakthrough in modern personnel administration. Imagine what it might do for Canadian enterprise.

The Ottawa men enthusiastically endorsed this 'scientific' calibration of Canadian workers. Labour force quality could be measured and cultivated through assessments of 'mental equipment,' skill, and aptitude. Aptitude testing became the hallmark of modern economic enterprise, with enduring effect. The LSIP thus drafted a blueprint for federal regulation of the labour supply. The 'manpower problem' would be resolved by a massive recruitment of women, combined with the new insights and methods of personnel administration, vocational assessment, and training. The work would be guided by close investigations of the labour supply, with an eye to quality as defined by the principles of employability assessment. These new managerial techniques centred increasingly on a single administrative site: a national employment service linked directly to Canadian industry, charged with the responsibility for regulating Canada's national labour force.

The National Selective Service

On 24 March 1942, Prime Minister Mackenzie King rose in Parliament to defend his government's handling of the manpower debacle. 'We have been criticized (and I do not deny that criticism has been merited in some instances),' King magnanimously acknowledged to his parliamentary colleagues, 'but I want to assure this House that every complaint which has come to us has been fully investigated.' Such complaints had nothing to do with the government's efforts, of course, and everything to do with ignorance of government regulation or, worse, unpatriotic sentiment. After all, lurking out there across the Dominion were those who insisted that, despite Ottawa's best efforts, 'personal welfare should be placed above that of a nation at war.'[9] Still, Ottawa was moving on the home front, taking important steps to strengthen the war effort. But Canadians would have to do their part – Canadian women, above all. King moved to announce the government's ten-point program. The newly inaugurated National Selective Service (NSS) was poised to launch a massive campaign that would attract women into essential war industries. Women applicants would report to offices of the NSS Women's Division (NSSWD) – offices that were equipped with modern facilities and run by skilled professionals. Women would receive advances to cover costs as they travelled to their new postings in essential war industries. Housing would be available, in women's dormitories or approved billeting assignments. Day nurseries or other means of caring for children would be provided, and paid for from the public purse. Women would have full access to medical and recreational facilities. The federal government would provide job training specifically designed for women, both directly through industry and in government training schools. Civil service and industrial restrictions on the employment of women, particularly married women, would be eased.[10] Never had the federal government committed itself to such broad and sweeping measures as these. The workplace and the home were becoming ever more closely intertwined as matters of public policy – at least as far as women were concerned. Ottawa was clearly ready. Officials fervently hoped that the present state of disorder would change in the wake of the series of orders-in-council just passed by the War Committee of Cabinet. Only one question remained: would employers cooperate? On that issue, King vowed to exert unyielding pressure upon recalcitrant employers who baulked at the prospect of opening the gates to the anticipated flood of female labour.

With Prime Minister King's announcement, Canadians were introduced to what would become a very familiar agency. The National Selective Service was established in March 1942 as a division of the Department of Labour, thereby assuming full control of the Unemployment Insurance Commission / National Employment Service apparatus by July 1942. The combined UIC/NSS apparatus rapidly expanded from a total of 1,500 staff and 95 offices in July 1942 to 5,200 staff and 242 offices by 1944, including five regional and four district offices, 202 local offices, sixteen branches, and fourteen suboffices. NSS soon launched the massive recruitment campaign to mobilize women and men for the war economy. It would also oversee demobilization and adjustment measures in preparation for the postwar peacetime economy. All workers were required to register under the national Unemployment Insurance scheme. All the old National Registration machinery introduced piecemeal through 1940 would be transferred from the Department of National War Services to the Department of Labour. To ensure a balance of labour supply between military service and production, the NSS issued a series of regulations designed to stabilize supply and, hopefully, end competition between the two equally vital aspects of war labour planning. All men employed on farms as of 23 March were to be frozen in their current stations, a measure intended to end the practice of abandoning the farm to seek out more lucrative employment in industry. All farmers and essential farm labourers were exempt from compulsory military training, but, in a nod to the military, approval would be granted to those volunteering to sign up. The NSS issued a list of 'restricted' occupations and industries into which no male person of military age and fitness might enter without the permission of the local National Selective Service officer. The draft age was increased from twenty-four to thirty (then raised to forty) for men who were unmarried as of 15 July 1940. A series of further provisions involved special treatment for technical and professional persons, reconditioning of recruits designated unfit for military service, and the training of personnel managers for private industry.[11]

Ottawa was desperate to project the image of a well-oiled NSS machine operating at peak efficiency, supplied with and capable of generating all the information necessary to move labour from one point to another – a central watchtower that could identify problems in even the remotest corner of the economy. King's war cabinet had been heavily criticized for mishandling the 'manpower' problem to date. Shortages and disorganization were common. Estimates of available labour resources varied widely, often missing the mark entirely. The whole story made its way to the pages of *Maclean's* magazine in September 1942. Six months after King's headline announcement, Canada stood on the threshold of a fourth year of war and had yet to resolve its most 'muddled problem.' Why was it taking so long to come up with a systematic 'manpower' program that could accommodate the needs of both the armed services and vital war industries? Part of the problem lay in competition between the two sectors for increasingly fewer men. But the larger problem was the absence of any central plan, for which the increasingly beleaguered 'manpower boss,' Elliott M. Little, a former industrialist appointed to head the newly created NSS, was blamed. To date, the only action coming out of Ottawa was a flurry of futile efforts of government officials working in isolation and at cross purposes as they 'sharpened their pencils to solve their own little manpower problems.'[12] Building a bureaucracy and passing orders-in-council was all well and good. But the absence of central authority produced instead a poorly organized system that relied on voluntarism where perhaps compulsion was needed.

Identifying the 'Female Labour Reserve'

Elliott Little, a CEO from industry, was soon replaced as head of the new agency by a more appropriate choice: former Manitoba deputy labour minister, Arthur MacNamara. By then federal deputy minister of labour, MacNamara understood industry and government equally well. He preferred to run NSS not like a private corporation but as a decentralized bureaucratic structure guided by the protocols of 'compromise and conciliation.'[13] Better still, MacNamara was an expert in labour policy. Two months after taking the helm, he was joined by Fraudena Eaton, newly appointed director of the NSS Women's Division. The importance of this division in federal labour policy was underlined when Eaton was promoted to the position of associate director of the NSS in August of the following year. The NSSWD effectively ran the massive mobilization of women during the war, overseeing all recruitment, training, and placement efforts across essential industries. Fraudena Eaton worked closely with MacNamara and a field staff that extended across the country, supervising the work of NSSWD staff as employment placement, welfare, and personnel officers, together with a network of industry and community-based practitioners.

MacNamara and Eaton got to work immediately. Deciding to target untapped reserves of women was one thing. But how was the Department of Labour going to find them? How many women were available for employment? The department scrambled to measure a workforce whose existence had hitherto been consistently denied, or at the very least ignored, as a matter of state policy. And this was the point. Assuming control of the labour force meant developing the institutional infrastructure to produce a detailed rolling tally of the labour supply. The technical means were available in the form of new 'tabulating equipment' at the Department of Labour and the DBS. But when it came to counting women as a potential labour supply, the conventional method of counting heads was not entirely productive. The 1940 national registration of men had turned up useful estimates but excluded women. The most comprehensive data came from regular surveys conducted by the DBS on behalf of the Unemployment Insurance Commission. The bureau's figures represented insured workers covered under the new Unemployment Insurance program and were considered 'typical of all persons working.'[14] This method was also flawed since the program excluded a large proportion of the labour force through occupational and hours-of-work criteria, thus cutting out many women. Estimating the numbers and predicting the movements of women workers – employed and unemployed alike – proved a challenge of an entirely different order.

The problem of locating women was partially resolved when labour analysts decided to conduct a national registration of women between the ages of twenty and twenty-four, an age range in which it was assumed women were most likely to be single, least likely to have children and related domestic responsibilities, and therefore most likely to be available for waged labour. Estimates of available labour among the rest of the female population would simply have to proceed through other means. The registration took place in September 1942, marking the first time women had been formally canvassed by the federal government in this way, apart from the regular census. It was also the first occasion upon which women were compelled to report their employment status. The results were confused and confusing. Women were reluctant to report either as already employed, or as unemployed – the only options provided in the registration. Clearly, economic chaos combined with a distinctly different attitude on the part of women baffled bureaucratic officials, casting doubt on the reliability of the resulting data.[15]

Women had never been asked to think of themselves as regular members of the workforce. Declaring one's status as 'unemployed,' as labour officials assumed they would, was beyond women's experience, at least in their relation to the remote federal government. Officials working on the national registration were therefore at pains to explain why 'hundreds' of women presented themselves at 'Employment Offices throughout Canada ... in order to avoid being registered as unemployed.'[16] When the registration results were compared to the regular NES reports of job applicants to vacancies, researchers acknowledged a glaring incongruity. More women registered as available for work through the National Registration in September 1942 than were listed as 'unplaced applicants' by the NES. In total, 63,133 registered as available for full-time employment in September 1942, compared to 46,000 registered as 'unplaced applicants' from the NES tally for the same period. Another way of reading the national registration tallies is as documentation of the tremendous need for paid work and evidence of regional concentrations of dire poverty. For example, the Maritimes reported a 583 per cent surplus of job applicants over vacancies. Quebec reported only a 49 per cent surplus. British Columbia had a surplus of 497 per cent, the prairies 257 per cent, and Ontario 138 per cent. Labour analysts at the Research and Statistics Branch dryly observed that the Maritimes surplus might suggest a 'certain amount of frustration among women' who could not find jobs in war industries. The DBS hastened to add that the figures were 'affected to some extent by variations in the proportion of employable women who apply for jobs at the employment offices.' For example, Quebec women might be available to work, although cultural difference would render them less likely than Ontario women to report for work. The challenge was to encourage women to identify themselves as available for work without also identifying themselves as unemployed. The tremendous disproportion of applicants to jobs might well be attributable to the regional concentration of war industries, but there can be little doubt of its testimony to the devastating impact of the Depression on regional economies. The disruption and destabilization of individual, familial, and community survival strategies wrought by the Depression drove many women to find paid work. The promise of jobs in wartime Canada was strong, and women were anxious to meet the challenge.

Economic necessity, however, did not figure in any of the official narratives recounting Canada's wartime appeal to women. In her 1943 address to the National Council of Women in the year following the registration, Fraudena Eaton explained that the labour shortage was best understood as more cultural than economic. The relatively limited industrial development of the Dominion meant that women did not see themselves as regular workers. The domestic tug was still strong, more-

over, and women preferred to attend to maternal responsibilities as their
primary vocation. Eaton was appealing to an audience of the solid
middle class, and so her approach as head of the NSSWD reflected a
narrative that subsumed all women war workers within the same universalizing discourse of domesticity and nationalism. If women were to
respond to the call of their government by taking up positions in essential war industries, they would do so as an act of self-sacrifice, temporarily
putting aside family and self to serve the paramount interests of their
country in the desperate fight against fascism. Noting Canada's lower
level of industrialization in contrast to that of Great Britain and the
United States, Eaton stressed that the challenge ahead lay in overcoming
the 'natural indifference on the part of women to the needs of industry.'
Here, indeed, was a new twist to the notion of 'female reserve.' It was up
to government to enlist the twin sentiments of nationalism and maternalism, 'to change the attitude of the women of Canada toward industrial work,' without entirely unhinging the doors of domesticity in the
process.[17] Eaton described the registration of young women as having
had the desired effect, testimony to the prodigious capacity of government to identify and respond to a need with dispatch and accuracy. Not
only did it generate 'a good sound list of names and addresses with
something of the training and experience of each woman,' but the
National Registration drive was also provoking the necessary attitudinal
shift. Women were now coming to identify themselves as workers. As
Eaton said, 'It immediately made women think in terms of employment.
It brought us a success that almost caused us discomfort. We were
embarrassed by our own success.'[18]

Behind the scenes, Eaton took a very different position, sharing the
view of employment experts whose experience of tackling unemployment
during the Depression had left them rather jaded on the subject of female unemployment. The policy position adopted by all levels of government in the decade just past was emphatic: no woman need ever be
unemployed, not where there was an option of domestic service. For this
reason, analysts approached the National Registration with strong scepticism. There was 'less social pressure on women to enter gainful employment than on men,' and so the resulting head count would be skewed.[19]
Registering women who did think of themselves as unemployed was
equally unlikely to yield significant results. The category of female unemployment was subject to an intensely class-based, racialized, and gendered
rationale. First of all, unemployed women exhibited qualitatively different features from unemployed men, given their very different experi-

ences in the labour market. The DBS Social Analysis Branch reflected the official policy position, arguing that unemployed women could always find work in domestic service. Such work was inherently female in its nature, requiring no technical skill. Put another way, the domestic household – together with the women who were seen to be its principal occupants – was reified in policy as a 'natural' space existing outside rational economic space and therefore beyond the sphere of the formal economy except as a site of consumption, and a limited one at that.[20] Any woman who could not find paid work as a domestic servant could not be considered employable. This rationale found its way into the confidential LSIP report as well, when analysts concluded that, since unemployed women were more able than men to find work as domestic servants, women designated unemployable were thus 'likely to be a larger proportion of the total of unemployed women than is the case of men.'[21] Fraudena Eaton was doing no more than stating the conventional wisdom of official policy circles in suggesting that, while a national registration of unemployed women was a good idea, she doubted if the exercise would reveal a 'substantial number of employable women.'[22] This conceptual approach to the relationship between female unemployment as an economic category and women's employability as a vector for their efficiency, discipline, and desirability as workers had important implications for how women would be viewed during the war and beyond.

As these attempts at defining the female labour supply illustrate, policy practitioners were finding many of their ideas about conventional labour market practice inadequate for the task at hand. Government planners confronted a complex matrix of relations surrounding women's employment and unemployment. Women constituted a special problem for policy precisely because they were not workers. The problems women were thought to pose were identified as originating in culture and in the social. It was for this reason that the 'female labour reserve' was identified as a distinct population in the minds of policy experts. The term 'female reserve' therefore appealed directly to notions of domesticity, drawing specifically on maternalist discourse. Women had to be habituated to the routines of the workplace as productive economic space. The NSSWD recruiting campaign drew on the trope of domesticity, speaking through audiences of solidly middle-class women. Eaton's public utterances addressed the prescriptive identity of the white, middle-class, female subject, whose claims in the social were grounded in her domestic and reproductive capacity not in her paid labour. This figure of feminine respectability was unfamiliar with and out of place in the formal waged economy, save for a slight window in the early years before marriage. Such a conception of the 'female reserve' could not coexist with the reality of those whose waged labour was a regular, if unstable, feature of daily life. Women who knew the pressures of unemployment and regionalized poverty – for example, the thousands of Maritime women who would make their way to munitions plants across southern Ontario – were even less likely to figure in the imaginings of government statisticians.

'I Want You to Pick One Intelligent Girl': Industrial Engineers Tackle the Job

'You will realize that to keep a machine of this size operating requires close and constant supervision,' commented Labour Minister Humphrey Mitchell. The minister was not among the strongest in cabinet, and for this reason was probably even more committed to defending the considerable achievements of his department in resolving the crisis of 'manpower.' The mobilization of 'womanpower' was proceeding with as little disruption as possible to the 'home life of the nation.' Calling up thousands of women and men would not alone solve the labour problem; only training and careful assessment of each individual worker would ensure an appropriate match between the person and job. To those who failed to grasp its significance, the labour minister publicly defended the manpower strategy by pointing out that jobs could not be filled by just matching supply and demand. 'As the records of any employment office will show ... you cannot fill 100 vacancies with [just] any of the 100 applicants on your books. The skills of the applicant must satisfactorily match those required of the job. If they do not, there is a wall created between employer and worker which can only be broken down by training.'[23] Wartime employment training, under the federal War Emergency Training Programme (WETP) held significance for the postwar period of readjustment as well, according to Mitchell, in proving once and for all that unemployment was not a simple disjuncture between supply and demand so much as a deficiency *of the worker* that could be corrected through job training. This was welcome news indeed. As Minister Mitchell confidently declared, nothing would stand in the way of full employment after the war. Recent experience showed that 'a partnership of management, workers and the community can make useful work available in time of peace no less than in time of war.'[24]

Assessing worker capacity was now a top priority for labour mobilization. In this work, NSS officials relied on the diagnostic and prescriptive expertise of a burgeoning industry of professionals: psychologists, psychiatrists, employment researchers, vocational guidance experts, industrial engineers, and management specialists. These experts tackled the job of devising personnel and training policies to integrate the female reserve into the war economy. The process became known as 'skills dilution,' a strategy designed to boost productivity through work reorganization. Deskilling was the inevitable by-product of economic and technological modernization. But women's differential skills were conceptualized according to an explicitly gendered rationale. LSIP researchers had earlier commented that improvements in production technology were already contributing to the deskilling of production tasks such that 'improved mechanical operations have added to the possible uses of female employment since the last war.' In this way, job training designed for women proceeded in tandem with work reorganization through job analysis and 'decomposition' on the one hand, and the practice of 'skills dilution' on the other. Skills dilution was broached as a purely technical matter by job analysis experts. As a radically new managerial technique, skills dilution was thus stripped of any gender, class, or racialized content, reduced to a function of economic modernization and technological change.

The marriage of psychology and industry found a particularly receptive audience during the war. 'Psychologists Go to War' was a feature article published in the popular women's journal *National Home Monthly* in 1943. There could be no doubt that 'applied psychology' was responsible for strengthening the British war effort. The feature article described a government-operated munitions plant where the work and the workers had been completely re-engineered by the National Institute of Industrial Psychology in Britain. 'Psychology has come out of the lecture theatre and taken its rightful place in everyday life' was the enthusiastic view of the article's author, Luscombe Whyte. Surely such expertise would benefit Canada's war effort as well? Job analysts were the new priests of industry. These trained psychological experts understood that workers needed careful guidance. Employees had to be encouraged to understand that the old way of doing things had to give way before the expert advice of 'the professor,' who entered the plant, closely observed existing work practices and habits, and then presented a new plan for how the work would get done and by whom. Job analysis worked by consolidating and systematizing work routines, eliminating individual variation in favour of a plant-wide 'standard procedure.' This method, once developed by the analyst, was transferred across the workforce through on-the-job training. As Whyte put it, 'I want you to pick one intelligent girl to learn it and teach the others.' Boredom and fatigue were always a threat to efficiency on the job, and so attention to details of the work routine such as psychic comfort, rest breaks, and optimum hours of work were introduced as scientific techniques designed to achieve maximum efficiency. There was no room in this program for individual variation or other disordered routines of the past. With so many inexperienced women entering the manufacturing environment, system and order had to be imposed immediately, before poor work habits were picked up in the 'old haphazard ways.' Novices who learned 'by watching comparatively old hands at work' gained poor attitudes as well as inefficient habits. Scientific instruction would instil obedience to 'standard procedure.' As the best experts put it, no worker ought to be permitted, or tempted, to 'go his own way.'[25] Once inducted into the new, scientifically designed regime, the female worker would have only one thing on her mind: the job at hand.

Keeping workers' attention focused on the job required that they actually report for work in the first place. One of the greatest challenges in the early years of the war, after the labour shortage, was absenteeism, a problem LSIP analysts thought serious enough to warrant lengthy discussion in the report to cabinet. The Department of Labour decided to tackle the issue head on and enlisted the industrial engineering firm of Stevenson and Kellogg to assess the situation and recommend appropriate action. The Montreal-based firm was given broad terms of reference: to assess any labour problems that might be hindering the war effort. Job analysis worked as a prescriptive program, informed by vocational adjustment, guidance, and training. The job engineers measured each job for its mental and physical requirements, level of skill and responsibility, and general working conditions.[26] In the end, Stevenson and Kellogg associates concluded that the least necessary jobs in the entire production process were in office and clerical work. They did not want to suggest that office and clerical work was unnecessary, but said that the work 'must be viewed as essentially non-productive.' In general, plants would be well-advised to keep such work 'to a minimum under wartime conditions.'[27] Women could be readily substituted into these jobs, thus freeing up vital male workers for more useful and productive labour. The industrial engineers also targeted the unique problems presented by women workers. Efficiency and discipline were the watchwords in this exercise. Absenteeism and job turnover were out of control, unchecked as a result of inadequate personnel procedures, problems of morale, and 'the use of female help.' Women responded differently than did men. For example, married women were more prone to certain 'illnesses.' They were thus more vulnerable to industrial accidents. Women in general developed 'personal factors' brought on not only by general factory conditions but also by their 'domestic burdens.' The former could be dealt with directly, especially industrial fatigue. Women could not sustain the long hours to which men were accustomed. The resulting condition of industrial fatigue took its toll in lower morale and subsequent productive inefficiency. The twelve-hour shift had become a norm in many plants, but management engineers now recommended ten-hour shifts in plants employing women. In sum, modern personnel practice promised the most comprehensive solution for vital war industries across the Dominion.

The centrepiece of personnel research was mental testing. However, the Stevenson and Kellogg report argued that aptitude testing was of limited use when assessing women. Women's exposure to the knowledge content embedded within the testing instrument was limited, and so would be their aptitude for the tasks the testing instrument was designed to measure. More important to measure were women's learning ability and 'dependability,' rather than the innate capacity of aptitude. Instructors were instead encouraged to see women as passive agents who needed to be taught. It was the *attributes* and not so much the aptitudes of women that were seen to provide the material for vocational assessment and training. To illustrate, the Stevenson and Kellogg engineers included a section headed 'Work at Which Women Excel,' itemizing the physical characteristics of jobs best suited to women's more limited physical capacities. The list would be familiar to the modern reader: 'work requiring care and constant alertness,' good eyesight, limited physical exertion, manipulative dexterity, and speed, and 'work requiring considerable skill but little strength.' Height, weight, and physical attributes all found their way into this intensified gendering of the female labouring body, remade as a site for potentially productive labour once its inherent limitations had been accommodated through work reorganization and related engineering strategies. Skill and mental capacity were approached as separate categories for analysis. Skill was a function of mental requirements: formal education, special education, mathematical ability, type of instruction – oral, visual, written, or through the use of blueprints and sketches. Mental effort on the job was calibrated according to such factors as task repetition and variety. Did the job require memory, reasoning, and imagination? What were the written, oral, and reading requirements in either English or French? Skill was also approached as a function of mechanical aptitude, including the layout, set-up, and use of templates and power tools, gauges and measurements. In addition to the physical requirements of the job, the Stevenson and Kellogg questionnaire investigated certain personal qualities: 'Does the job specifically require any of the following characteristics? Unemotional; deliberate; quick; dynamic; tact; patience.'[28] Skill was rational and fixed, stable and calculable. Capacity, on the other hand, was personally variable, capable of being thwarted by the psyche of the individual subject. Emotion, impatience, and limited self-confidence were all irrational attributes: that is, all inherently ungovernable, disruptive, and potentially incalculable. This provided the material upon which the personnel expert had to fix her/his remedial expertise if the worker was to be successfully integrated into the industrial enterprise, to become a normative subject, the trainable and self-governable worker. The end result of job analysis and skills dilution, once adopted as regular managerial practice in the organization of work, seemed the product of neutral technological innovation. The female body was thus opened up to the prescriptive gaze of industrial management engineers, produced anew through the rational and rationalizing conceptual framework of capitalist modernity, now a site for regulation.

Conclusion

The Labour Supply Investigation Project directed its attention to the pressing question 'Is the individual a potential national asset worth developing?' This question contained the seeds of an approach to labour force regulation that linked the worker more closely to the national economy. Human capital would be approached, and increasingly so into the postwar period of reconstruction, as a national resource in which the state was prepared to invest. In a climate of war and reconstruction, the interests of individual women and men would come to be defined through those of nation, community, and family. Federal officials and employment experts understood that the solution to the labour problem involved more than simply matching supply with demand. Once attention turned to recruiting women in mass numbers, the NSS took on the task of increasing the quantity and managing the quality of the labour force. As war production intensified, new challenges developed: the manpower shortage was taken up and reorganized as a campaign to eradicate absenteeism and excessive labour turnover. In the next chapter, I examine how these issues converged in a much closer scrutiny of the work and labour force habits of women. Employability discourses mobilized gender, race, class, and sexuality, contributing to categorical expert knowledge about 'female labour' and the unique challenges posed by women workers. Managerial personnel strategies designed to bring women into war production constituted enduring notions of differential skill and human capacity, setting the foundation for training policies that would cultivate and improve the quality of labour in the national interest. Women were strangers to the modern workplace, unfamiliar with the disciplines and routines of economic modernity. Personnel techniques drew upon the psychology of the individual, opening up the interior spaces of the female labour reserve to fashion the identity of the woman war worker whose patriotic spirit drew her into the national community to do her part for the war effort.

chapter two

The National Selective Service Women's Division and the Management of Women War Workers

On 26 August 1942, National Selective Service Women's Division head Fraudena Eaton reported to Labour Minister Humphrey Mitchell on the progress of the female mobilization campaign. Her report, while generally positive, struck a note of concern for the moral conditions confronted by women war workers. The situation at the Cockshutt Plow Company was particularly disturbing. Indeed, conditions at the Brantford, Ontario, plant teetered dangerously on the brink of anarchy. Eaton was especially concerned about the 'lack of supervision and discipline' at the munitions plant. Women were free to wander away from their work stations whenever they felt the urge, 'loitering and lounging' willy-nilly on the job, hanging about the washrooms in gossipy klatches when they ought to have been at their workstations. 'The cloak rooms serve as lunch rooms and as there are no lockers or racks, clothing lies and hangs all over. These rooms and the washrooms are in bad condition and are not kept clean,'[1] Eaton declared. If the minister thought the National Selective Service Women's Division (NSSWD) was responsible only for finding and placing women in war work, he was quite mistaken. The NSSWD was entrusted to safeguard the moral status of these young women, for their own sake as well as the nation's.

There was good reason for concern. War work drew women from every province. From farms and hamlets women flocked to the major industrial districts, at this time concentrated around Toronto and Montreal, eager for the high wages promised by jobs only now open to the female wage earner. The wage and employment picture changed dramatically once women joined the war effort, with both wages and employment more than doubling in the brief span of five years. Long years of depression made particularly welcome this opportunity to add to one's own and the family purse. When Canada entered the war in 1939, more than 400,000 women and men were unemployed, according to official estimates.[2] At that time, women's average industrial earnings were just 54.1 per cent of men's, an average that had increased to 69.3 per cent by 1944. Average weekly wages, meanwhile, rose from $12.78 in 1939 to an astounding $20.89 by 1944, while for the same period women's labour force participation rate climbed from 24.4 per cent to 33.5 per cent.[3] The hourly wage gap was closing: in 1939 women earned 47.9 cents for every male dollar, a figure that rose to 71.2 cents by 1944.[4] Employment patterns shifted significantly as well. In 1939, domestic service was the largest occupational sector for women. By war's end, manufacturing was. The percentage of women working in domestic service plummeted from 18.6 per cent in 1939 to only 9.3 per cent by 1943, while for the same period, as a proportion of women in the labour force, manufacturing employment rose from 27 per cent to 37 per cent.[5] Finally, the number of women working in the formal waged economy doubled from 600,000 in 1939 to 1.2 million by 1943. Of this total, approximately 250,000 were working in essential war industries; 439,000 in the services sector; 373,000 in manufacturing; 180,000 in finance and trade; 31,000 in transportation and communications; and 4,000 in construction.[6]

The campaign to recruit women was by all accounts an outstanding success, due in no small measure to the diligent efforts of Fraudena Eaton and her colleagues at the NSSWD. Eaton pressed for clear policies to ensure the rapid movement of women from all parts of the country to the industrial manufacturing centres in Ontario and Quebec. The NSSWD oversaw the implementation of comprehensive personnel measures to integrate women into unfamiliar workplaces, to ensure appropriate training and vocational guidance on the job, and to provide some measure of supervision off the job. Women's Division staff, many of whom were policy experts in female labour force patterns, understood that the current federal initiative would be short-lived. Whatever their views on the question of women's right to work, they were determined to demonstrate that female labour was as viable, productive, and reliable as that of the traditional breadwinner.

From her appointment in 1942, Eaton worked closely with the federal deputy minister of labour, Arthur MacNamara.[7] From the start, the Women's Division was guided by two key objectives: through employment policy came the national enterprise – fighting the war – and through domestic policy, securing the peaceful withdrawal of women workers from the industrial workforce once the war was finally ended. How did the Women's Division take up the challenge of mobilizing and managing Canada's womanpower? Training and the special Industrial Welfare program worked in tandem to accommodate the 'special needs' of women, if only for the duration of the war. Because the call to women was temporary, to last only as long as the war, Women's Division staff had to narrow the campaign's focus, knowing that they would soon need to redirect thousands of workers from war employment across the industrialized economy into a limited range of occupations, waged and unwaged. In this context, I approach postwar planning in much the same way as did the policy practitioners whose work is considered here; that is, as an integral part of the organizational approach to planning for the war itself.

Managing war workers, both men and women, was difficult enough. Never before, it seemed, had the country seen such labour strife. The labour market was volatile. Clearly, establishing peace on the home front had to be a top priority. The federal department heeded the advice of policy experts from the International Labour Office through to its own Economic Advisory Committee. MacNamara pushed employers to adopt an enlightened industrial relations regime, a deeply gendered approach steeped in anti-Communist ideology. The department's Labour–Management Co-operation Section of the Industrial Relations Branch actively encouraged the development of labour-management productivity committees, enlisting the cooperation of the organized labour movement with the promise that unions would be able to secure and consolidate their position as recognized bargaining agents in the workplace.[8] But some unions would be excluded – for example, those associated with the organized left.[9] The same climate of anti-Communism gripped many of Canada's trade unions, whose leadership claimed their positions through U.S.-based international unions. Industrial relations policy was organized through a masculinist framework, drawing on discourses of employment rights, the family wage, and collective bargaining. Fraudena Eaton pressed for a similar regime of industrial welfare to oversee women war workers, most of whom were excluded from the ranks of organized labour. Industrial welfare was a gender-based program of personnel planning anchored by the principles of moral regulation. Both married and young single women needed careful supervision if the wartime recruitment was to be considered a success.

'Keeping Workers in Their Jobs'

Eaton certainly had her hands full. Women came from as far as Newfoundland to work in war plants scattered across southern Ontario and
Quebec. Getting them to the workstation was a complex task that had to
be accomplished quickly. Keeping them there was a further challenge.
When women objected to conditions on or off the job, they made their
views known, sometimes through direct protests such as work refusals
and related collective job action. Even harder to address were the individual acts of resistance as women quietly drifted away one by one,
draining vital national labour resources. The obvious policy response
was direct supervision through personnel programming. Thus began a
concerted effort to convince the male bureaucrats that the needs of
women war workers had to be taken seriously. Eaton addressed her
concerns directly to the minister of labour, reporting in detail on the
substandard conditions faced by the new recruits. She selected three war
plants, each of which epitomized just how bad things were in these
essential industries under contract with the federal government. Defence Industries Limited was contracted to supply the war effort, and
thus enjoyed generous terms and a regular infusion of federal subsidies.
The Pickering plant suffered a chronic labour shortage, despite the fact
that the NSSWD regularly sent women there. The reasons were not hard
to understand. Workers had to deal with inadequate housing and limited public transportation. These problems were serious enough, but the
underlying issue was negligence. Meals provided by this and other employers were regularly described as poorly prepared and inadequate.
Women had to pay for this substandard fare whether or not the meals
were consumed. Eventually, the 'girls' at Defence Industries took matters into their own hands, staging mass demonstrations to protest the
unpalatable meals served up by an indifferent management. If ever
there was a case for the introduction of progressive personnel policy, this
was it. In some cases, a company might have a personnel manager, but it
was evident to Eaton that the position existed in name only. For example, one offending plant had a personnel manager, 'Mr Russell,' who
was clearly delinquent. So great were the problems in this plant that
production was all but derailed. It appeared that the hapless personnel
manager had failed to take the concerns of women recruits seriously.
'Mr. Russell,' Eaton stated, 'unfortunately adopts the attitude that "if
they don't like it, they don't have to stay."' It appeared that they did not
like it. In one month alone, of the 350 young women sent from Nova

Scotia to work at the plant, 90 insisted that they be placed in jobs elsewhere.[10]

The Women's Division extended its attention to women's leisure time as well. Was it unreasonable for young women to expect steps to be taken to provide recreational facilities? The issue cut both ways. Attention to leisure activities contributed to safeguarding the young women's morality as well as their morale. NSSWD staff were concerned that young women, unaccustomed to urban life, should be supervised during off hours, directed towards wholesome recreational activities such as bowling, roller skating, and similar innocuous pursuits. The Women's Division fielded numerous reports recounting 'sordid details of events that had occurred amongst women in war industries' and was as concerned about protecting the reputation of the NSS as it was that of the woman war worker.[11] Bad publicity was to be avoided at all costs, especially in Quebec. Early in 1943, Eaton received an urgent appeal from Mme Martel, NSSWD's Quebec representative. Ottawa was grappling with wide-ranging opposition to the female mobilization campaign. In Quebec, the Catholic Confederation of Workers led the charge, arguing that industrial labour was 'incompatible with the French Canadian philosophy of family life.' Not only that, but the hard physical labour and indiscriminate intermingling of the sexes such work entailed posed 'physical and moral dangers' to women.[12] Officials worried that the intervention of the Quebec press might succeed in discouraging women from signing up at NSS offices. A strong counter-offensive designed to meet critics head on – for example, through the Wartime Information Board (WIB) – was ruled out as too 'argumentative.' The Department of Labour preferred to counter with a low-key approach – at least until it appeared that the hostile press campaign against women's employment was having an impact. In the meantime, the department circulated a report prepared by the U.N. Information Center in New York, detailing how the Nazis were recruiting women from occupied territories for war work. The race to arms, it seemed, hinged on the labour of a nation's women, free or conscripted.[13] NSS quietly stepped up its training of personnel workers in Quebec industry, while intensifying its efforts on the industrial welfare front.[14]

Given the obviously delicate political situation in Quebec, reports of moral delinquency were precisely what NSS wanted to avoid. And so, whenever such a report came to the Women's Division's attention, it was immediately investigated. Such was the case in Brownsburg. Several hundred young women had been sent from New Brunswick to work at the plant, mingling with male workers on the job and, it seemed, off the job as well. At least some of the female workforce were said 'to seek solace in alcohol' at a village beverage room during their off hours, there being 'few amusements' with which they could occupy their leisure time in more appropriate (that is to say, feminine and wholesome) pursuits. Eaton called on Renée Morin, NSSWD officer and women's employment specialist, to conduct a discreet investigation, being careful not to advertise the reason for her visit. In March 1943, Morin reported back to Eaton and the chief commissioner of the UIC, Mr L.J. Trottier, 'on the moral situation of men and women workers.' There was scant evidence of the morally deleterious conditions recounted by the opponents of women's employment, she observed. 'From what people have told me,' Morin advised, 'it seems that the conduct of the employees of the two sexes in the factory is irreproachable.'[15] The mere suggestion that women were engaging in any morally delinquent behaviour in the local village was enough to arouse the ire of the local curé, notwithstanding Morin's painstaking attempts at investigative 'tact.' 'Brownsburg,' she concluded, 'does not present a more sombre picture than other industrial municipalities.' Moral inquiries by federal officials were clearly unwelcome, having left the local curé 'a little offended by the very fact that there was some suspicion about the conduct of his parishioners. Personally, he seemed very satisfied with the situation at the factory.'[16] The company in question treated its employees with care, maintained a recreation room, and conducted its business appropriately. Such problems as had occurred were addressed and readily resolved. What the workers, men and women alike, did during their own time might be the business of the local church but was clearly considered off limits to NSS snoops.

Concern for the welfare of the young women working in Brownsburg did not end there, however, as the matter was again the subject of discussion at an NSS industrial relations conference at Dalhousie University three months later. Renée Morin was scheduled to speak on the issue of women's employment at war plants. The chief employment officer for Moncton, identified only as Miss Mary, confronted Morin on the Brownsburg case. Word had reached her of the problems in Brownsburg, and she was gravely concerned for the girls and, likely, the reputation of the Women's Division. The problem was not what happened on the employer's time or property, since 'the company sees that employees follow discipline in the shops and in the residences.' Rather, once left to their own devices, 'girls are entirely free; leadership and counselling is [sic] lacking.'[17] Perhaps more to the point, many of the Brownsburg women were agitating to return home to Moncton to get jobs at a recently opened aircraft plant just outside the city.

Having made their way through the factory gates, women asserted their right to be accorded the freedoms traditionally enjoyed by their wage-earning fellows. If conditions were poor, some women exercised such rights by refusing NSSWD assignments. The Women's Division arranged accommodations for out-of-town workers, but such efforts were not always enough to entice young women with a newly independent turn of mind. This was the situation in the Ontario town of Belleville. Although Women's Division officers reported no shortage of female labour, the women in the small city refused work at the nearby Bata Shoe Company plant. Accommodation was available at a new 'staff house,' but only a few had taken up residence since it was little more than a building with beds. The recreation room doubled as the entrance hall. Women complained that there was nothing to do in the off hours, not even 'a game room where they can play even simple table games.' The local moving picture theatre had been closed for more than six weeks. As though this were not enough, the plant cafeteria provided an uninspired selection of food described as 'badly cooked and of inferior quality.'[18] The situation was described in terms that made obvious the only solution: women required proper health, welfare, and recreation facilities to attend to their unique needs as workers in an unfamiliar and inhospitable environment. Proper meals had to be provided, along with wholesome recreation and properly supervised accommodations. The workplace environment itself required careful organization and supervision under the expert guidance of trained women personnel specialists whose assignment was to safeguard the femininity of their charges.

In contrast, progressive managerial techniques had succeeded in solving the absenteeism problem at the John Inglis Company in Toronto and at nearby Small Arms Limited in Long Branch. The minister of labour's office publicized the commendable example set by the John Inglis Company, obviously hoping that others would follow suit and so deal with their absenteeism and turnover problems. For example, Inglis employed a female welfare supervisor plus a recreation supervisor. Women employees enjoyed access to the nearby community swimming pool and gymnasium. The neighbourhood roller-skating rink had been converted into a recreation club, reserved for the exclusive use of the women at the plant. Never before had women received such careful attention to their needs as workers, inducted into a leisurely worker-centred culture that was usually the exclusive preserve of working men. Organized recreational activities and other forms of entertainment, together with the collegiality of fellow women at the plant, must have provided a crucial camaraderie to help relieve the stress of high-paced production on the job, not to mention a world at war, when there was time to think of such matters.

Comradeship also provided an opportunity to compare notes in the articulation of grievances. For the NSSWD, supervised recreation was welcomed, but collective action was not. Eaton, along with her fellow women bureaucrats, regularly pointed out the structural causes of high turnover, and not only in lower wage industries. In the absence of central collective bargaining strategies and in the presence of a tight labour market, workers usually voted with their feet and left in search of jobs with better wages and working conditions.[19] Even though women were but temporary sojourners in the labour market, ministry officials were well advised to heed their demands as they exercised new-found power in their wage-earning capacities. The NSSWD promoted Industrial Welfare as a way to deal with both concerns. Women's needs as workers had to be attended to and their leisure hours turned to useful purposes. The Industrial Welfare program had solved the problem of labour instability at Inglis and would be sure to do the same for other war plants. Expense was a poor excuse for inaction, as this case made all too clear: the community, when asked, had willingly pitched in and made available several facilities in an excellent example of local community and private industry coming together to eradicate absenteeism, the number one threat to the war effort. Labour Minister Mitchell coined yet another pithy slogan to remind Canadians of their duty: 'absence makes the war last longer.'[20]

Federal labour officials took steps to get their provincial counterparts on side with the female mobilization campaign and in early 1943 invited all provincial labour ministers to a conference in Ottawa to discuss the problems women workers might be experiencing. Mitchell broached the 'conditions under which women are employed,' hoping that the provinces would cooperate in the federal push to reduce absenteeism among the female labour force.[21] The best way to do this was to improve hours of work. The 1943 federal-provincial labour conference would not result in concrete action, and no incursions were anticipated in such a clear area of provincial jurisdiction. Mitchell acknowledged the temporary nature of federal emergency powers. His government had no legislative authority with respect to working conditions and no intention of moving into that area of regulation. Conference delegates debated the question of working hours, trying to get consensus that the provinces would reduce shifts worked by women from the customary twelve hours to a standard of ten hours, the optimal level needed to maintain efficiency. Officials closest to the ground, including Eaton, knew that women might oppose this move, especially in industries paying low wages. In the end, two resolutions were passed out of the conference. One called for a federal committee to study the hours-of-work issue, the results of which would be passed over to the provincial authorities. The second resolution called for the appointment of a National Safety Committee to investigate safety in war industries.[22] At the same time, conference delegates confirmed the need to address conditions for the worker outside as well as inside the workplace, attending to recreation, health, and living conditions – anything deemed pertinent to maintaining a healthy and productive worker.[23]

Studies of absenteeism were informed by the work of industrial experts in Britain, notably a recent study conducted on behalf of the British Department of Labour by the Medical Research Council Industrial Health Research Board. The Research Board's 'Emergency Report No. 4' looked at the amount and distribution of absenteeism among women working in ordinance factories. But it is the mode and effects of the report that are of particular interest here: the study provided a template for other employment researchers to follow, one that investigated causality as an individual and not a structural phenomenon. Among its general observations was perhaps one of the key insights that would influence how the problem came to be organized, investigated, and remedied until well into the future. Absenteeism was seen as an action of the individual worker herself.[24] The study proceeded by searching for any pattern that might reveal statistical regularity. Finding none – except for the taken-for-granted category of gender (i.e., the study found that married women lost more time than single women, and that the rate was lowest on payday and highest on Saturday) – researchers at the Medical Research Council were forced to conclude that, since women were absent for varying lengths of time, the reasons for such absences were 'as varied as individual needs and desires.' This led invariably to the remedy: while some attention ought to be devoted to the 'general conditions of work,' this preliminary investigation called for 'a study of the personal causes of absenteeism, and for an individual method of treatment.'

These findings were confirmed by a further investigation conducted in 1943 by the Stevenson and Kellogg firm.[25] The report created the category of 'vocational instability,' a condition caused by two problems:

ineffective vocational guidance and the 'condition of vocational instability (casual labour) or a "work dodging" attitude on the part of the person.' To these two distinct sources – the one a matter of administrative governance and the other a condition of the psychology of the individual – the NSS could trace most of its 'manpower' problems.[26] The NSS needed to increase the efficiency of its local offices if it ever hoped to institute a comprehensive plan to keep people in their jobs: instilling good work habits was opened up to the local techniques of governance of the public employment office.[27] The experts at Stevenson and Kellogg were confident that 'labour drift' would be easily corrected through a national employment system, a network of employment offices that could continuously track and direct labour. MacNamara liked what he heard and, relying increasingly on the expertise of the Montreal firm, wanted to bring Stevenson and Kellogg back to update and extend the Welland study they had conducted the previous year. John Grierson, then at the Office of War Information (OWI) objected, arguing that the Department of Labour should develop such expertise internally. Grierson explained that it was important to show that the department 'was intensifying its initiatives and interest in industrial relations matters.'[28] What may have seemed a minor issue carried broad implications for the agenda and scope of Department of Labour activities. After all, the provinces had just received assurance that the federal government would not implement any lasting action and would withdraw and leave matters to the provinces as soon as it was feasible to do so. When the return of Stevenson and Kellogg was proposed to the Advisory Committee on Absenteeism Studies, the ensuing discussion revolved around two sets of arguments, both moving towards the same outcome. The department would take on the work as part of a broader industrial welfare promotion and research program. Adjusting the behaviour and work patterns of individual workers, it seemed, really was a legitimate domain for the federal government. After all, labour research was a service, whereas Stevenson and Kellogg was a private enterprise, and business might not want to impart confidential information of a potentially proprietary nature to private firms. Business managers would probably not mind sharing such information with government. Furthermore, some committee members speculated, organized labour might resent the idea that the Department of Labour was enlisting the services of a firm of industrial engineers.[29]

True to his conciliatory style, MacNamara got his wish and so did Grierson. Stevenson and Kellogg conducted another investigation for

the NSS, while the Department of Labour took up the issue of absenteeism through an investigation of its own.[30] The internal study laid the
basis for the productivity-boosting campaign of 1943, publicized through
Grierson's Office of War Information.[31] The campaign institutionalized
the Industrial Welfare program as the solution to lagging productivity,
while low production levels were blamed on absentee workers. Every
plant was advised to establish fact-finding missions to root out absenteeism. Unions and labour-management committees were enjoined to take
leadership in the workplace, enlisting workers' support and confidence.
Day nurseries and extended store hours would considerably ease the
burden on working mothers. Grierson was also keen to launch a major
campaign aimed directly at improving bad plant conditions, such as
poor heating, inadequate locker and washroom facilities, and slow and
insufficient medical attention for accidents. At the very least, a publicity
campaign would assure workers that government was keeping a watchful
eye on the workplace. For its part, government would see to it that
adequate housing, transportation, and recreation were provided. Management had to do a better job of convincing its employees that the
company was all out for production and did not discriminate in promotion and upgrading. Safety rules and faithful use of safety devices were
everybody's responsibility. Workers deserved hot, nourishing meals at
reasonable prices. Employers were again encouraged to improve in-
plant training, intended to facilitate workers' adjustment to new jobs
and communities. And finally, perhaps the most central element in the
newly enlightened approach, 'Prevention and remedy are better than
punishment.'[32] Lest employers be put on the defensive, dangerous health
and safety conditions would be 'improved' but would not be subjected to
penalty and/or eradicated. Finally, the principles of modern personnel
planning enlisted individual identification with goals and objectives,
routines, and rituals of the enterprise, the pursuit of which were held to
satisfy everyone – the worker, the company, and the national interest.

Developing Women's Personnel Work

In 1942, the NSSWD convened its first Women's Personnel Conference
in Montreal to plan precisely how the movement of women into war
production would proceed. It was an opportunity to educate delegates
on the finer points of worker assessment and job placement. Placement
work was a professionalized body of knowledge, and much depended on
the initial interview with the applicant. Placement efforts were chal-

lenged from all sides, not least on account of 'wide discrepancies in the general field of employment.' Finding potential labour recruits was hard enough. Experienced workers openly criticized the work assignments handed to them by beleaguered NSS staff. Even worse, raw recruits might be brimming with enthusiasm, but eagerness to earn did not compensate for lack of qualifications. NSSWD employment officers were beset by organizational problems that were as prosaic as they were integral to efficient labour deployment. The list was a long one: 'controlling distribution of workers, bringing together the right applicant and the right job, setting up suitable offices for placement, obtaining competent staff.' Employers were digging in their heels at the prospect of having women descend upon their territory. Government bureaucrats outside the Women's Division did not always appreciate the different challenges posed by the employment of women. And, of course, the women themselves held ambitions that did not always match NSSWD priorities. Where all else failed, however, authorities could at least appeal to patriotism and 'the constant feeling on the part of the employee that there is first a war to be won.'[33]

The 'problems of placement' were addressed through screening and selection, a technique that aimed to look beyond external credentials to address the innate capacity of each woman applicant. Eaton explained this approach to her colleagues at the Department of Labour, pointing out that counting heads through endless labour force estimates was only part of the challenge facing the NSSWD. Global statistics were all well and good, she pointed out, but 'in the matter of supplying women for industry, we are interested in the individual.'[34] NSSWD staff expanded the public employment office as both a conduit and a point of convergence at the local level, an official public space bringing together state, community, employer, and worker. These efforts built upon and complemented job placement efforts overseen by the Department of Veterans' Affairs (DVA). The Army Course on Veterans' Rehabilitation described the new employment service as a considerable improvement over the bureaucratic nightmare faced by veterans of the First World War. The modernized national service had made great strides since its days as a provincial patronage machine that in fact worked, and poorly at that, as a revolving door for allegedly unskilled, casual labour and domestic workers. Now it was run much like the most efficient personnel operation in a modern corporation. Like a stock exchange however, it was impossible to trade in unlisted securities, and so it was incumbent upon employers and job seekers alike to register with this new public service.

Gone was the inefficiency characterizing the hit-and-miss lottery that saw potential workers wandering from one factory to another, 'looking for a job which may or may not exist.' Employers would benefit, too, as only the most suitable applicants would be referred to them.[35]

Throughout the Depression, middle-class white women's organizations such as the Young Women's Christian Association (YWCA) and local chapters of the National Council of Women had expanded the women's employment bureau through a sponsorship approach to maternal supervision over their less fortunate sisters. NSS Women's Division staff were able to tap into this organizational network of local community and women's organizations and, increasingly, professional associations of women's personnel practitioners. The Women's Division constructed a sophisticated network for the recruitment and referral of women from across Canada, based on the existing array of women's organizations that had been called into service over the past decade to deal with female poverty and unemployment. The Toronto council president, a Mrs Stephens, was enthusiastic about the task her chapter was now called upon to accomplish. Stephens welcomed close collaboration with the NSS Women's Division, placing the chapter's extensive network of contacts and organizational capacities at the division's disposal. The NSSWD Toronto supervisor, Mary Eadie, reported this satisfactory arrangement to Eaton, noting how important the local council's support would be during the war and 'for whatever experience we can gain to help us with post war employment difficulties.'[36]

Eaton also devoted considerable time to investigating the structure and operation of the modern science of personnel practice. She wrote to Mary Anderson at the U.S. Department of Labor Women's Bureau, inquiring about guidelines for U.S. companies interested in setting up internal personnel departments. Although the Women's Bureau did not issue firm guidelines, Anderson was pleased to refer Eaton to International Harvester in Chicago, and to AT&T's former personnel department, now absorbed into the U.S. War Department. Eaton also corresponded with Laura Smith of the Civilian Personnel Division at the U.S. War Department, explaining that such work in Canada 'has not been developed to the extent that we have sufficient trained and experienced people to meet the present demands.'[37] Smith provided an organizational chart depicting the 'set-up of a typical personnel department,' a plan for employee counselling that was used with great effect throughout many government offices, a collection of studies of 'Women in War Industries' from the Industrial Relations Section at Princeton University, and, finally, a study conducted on behalf of the U.S. government by Industrial Relations Counselors.[38] This was the managerial consulting firm with which Bryce Stewart, deputy labour minister in Canada, had worked as director of research throughout most of the 1930s, cooperating closely with the Roosevelt New Deal administration to develop the U.S. Employment Service and Manpower Commission. Finally, Smith informed Eaton, the Metropolitan Life Insurance Company was at that very moment 'engaged in making a very comprehensive study of the principal personnel problems in connection with the increased employment of women.' The focus of these efforts lay in encouraging industry to establish personnel departments to oversee recreation, housing, day nurseries, and health and welfare services for women workers – the same roster of policies that Eaton had championed for the NSSWD Industrial Welfare program.

The insights provided by the U.S. Department of Labor supplemented recommendations from MacNamara's favourite industrial engineers, the team at Stevenson and Kellogg. These experts readily drew from a burgeoning field of research. The blueprint consisted in the following: a management-employee committee to act as buffer between supervisory personnel and workers; clear personnel plans based on job analysis and careful engineering of tasks; vocational guidance and industrial training; close monitoring of the workforce to chart turnover and absenteeism rates; and finally, provision for workers' social security related to health, welfare, and safety on the job. In what is here viewed as an exercise of pastoral power, the personnel expert invited the employee to enter a confessional relationship. The management consultants explained this aspect of the personnel program in the language of paternalism, only now in the service of psychology. Paternal counsel sought intimate contact with the troubled employee-as-patient: 'Let each and every employee in the organization realize that he has the right to discuss his own particular personal problems, without prejudice, with the Personnel Manager,' stated the guidebook. The adept manager was one who proceeded gradually, as would 'a good father confessor.' Above all, effective counselling probed beyond the factory walls, and so it was in the managerial interest to 'keep a close watch on the health, safety, security and financial worries' of one's employees.[39]

The paternalist bent favoured by the Stevenson and Kellogg engineers, however, was adapted to the maternalist model that favoured women as best placed to supervise other women. Not all employers could be counted on to see the benefit of this work, of course, but such recalcitrance could not stand in the way of progress. Sara Southall of International Harvester in Chicago had earlier warned Eaton that, no matter what size the company, some employers remained obstinate in their attitude towards women staff generally, and would continue to discount the importance of personnel work. Government-owned corporations and private companies across the United States were all bringing women into their personnel divisions to oversee the hiring process. This was an encouraging sign, suggesting that women were making headway in the new profession. Some employers, Southall noted, insisted on marginalizing trained female professionals, seeing it as 'a kind of function where the girls can come and cry on someone's shoulder.' 'I, personally, have tried to discourage the counsellor being used simply as a "weeping wall,"'[40] Southall advised her Canadian colleague. Eaton clearly saw the benefit of such work and proceeded to incorporate the science of modern personnel development into the industrial welfare program. Once fully integrated into all areas of production work and leisure, this policy would prove the answer to labour problems – from Brownsburg, Quebec, to Belleville, Ontario.[41]

With MacNamara's backing, Eaton encouraged the formation of women's personnel associations, such as the Women's Personnel Group of Toronto. Personnel planning was a new professional outlet for graduates of the women's business colleges and provided a valuable contribution to the overall war effort. 'I think we should give further service to industry in connection with personnel departments,' Eaton argued, consolidating the presence of women's personnel work as a regulatory device – a measure supported by the considerable resources and educational expertise made available by the NSSWD.[42] Women, at least those conforming to the criteria of British origin and middle-class location, were looked upon as particularly well suited for personnel work. Women possessed a special expertise, one they might apply to the problems women workers were most likely to face. Women were best left to supervise other women, particularly in matters of moral guidance and guardianship. For instance, physical and mental examinations required greater discretionary and interventionary powers. Medical examinations were required of all women recruited by the NSSWD. Typically, employers were becoming far too lax on the subject, loosening standards in order to fill job vacancies as quickly as possible. What better evidence of the need for hands-on female supervision by trained personnel experts?

NSS regional women's division heads, the National Council of Women of Canada (NCWC), and the Toronto Welfare Council held an emergency conference in June 1943 to develop a more appropriate response. They agreed that close monitoring of all travel and accommodation was necessary, in keeping with the broader moral regulatory measures instituted through the campaign against venereal disease.[43] Employers clearly could not be relied upon to enforce mandatory medical inspections of all women employees. Moreover, it would be a difficult measure to implement with any tact or discretion, and discretion was the watchword, given the close scrutiny of morality generated in the heat of the VD panic. Eaton advised her lieutenant, Mary Eadie, to put the case to NSS Women's Division supervisors, suggesting that medical examinations be made mandatory and that they be conducted 'before the girl leaves her own community,' no matter how strenuously employers agitated for any general relaxation of medical examination standards. Moreover, each woman would be required to have 'twenty dollars in her possession.' As a further safeguard, no young woman under the age of eighteen would be transferred from her home community.[44]

In this way, the NSSWD steadily built up a parallel system of women employment officers, personnel experts, and industrial welfare officers through the NSS apparatus. The YWCA, the local welfare councils, and women's personnel staff from industry and local councils of women – all were in place to oversee the activities of women war workers. Building on the sponsorship model that had worked so well in the previous decade, this matrix of women experts sought intimate contact with the female worker, monitoring, supervising, and guiding women throughout their tenure as war workers. The same network was to perform a crucial function in the postwar program of rehabilitation and demobilization. This was by no means a compensatory measure filling a perceived void in a government-run employment service. Local councils of women worked in close collaboration with community welfare agency workers as part of a web of localized governance, in concert with the centralized NSS Women's Division network of offices and regional staff. Local formations such as these were one of the many ways that state and 'community' established coextensive, overlapping networks. Women personnel supervisors worked with welfare officers, and the YWCA cooperated with employment placement staff from the NSS, with each consolidating the other's position.[45]

The NSSWD soon found that its hard work was beginning to pay off. The National Association of Manufacturers might ridicule women as making poor supervisory staff – given their greater propensity to 'throw their weight around' – but a trained female supervisor could accomplish a great deal with the 'girl munitions workers' in her charge. *Maclean's* magazine ran a lengthy article about Canada's new womanpower in 1942, lending much-needed publicity to the Industrial Welfare program, and to the professionalization of women's personnel work. Thelma LeCocq, the author of this exegesis about the new industrial 'woman power,' explained how the featured personnel supervisor cheerfully lobbied for improved wages and working conditions at her plant: .

> The manager of [an aircraft manufacturing] plant has women draughtsmen on his staff and says they're swell. As personnel manager he has a cheerful, competent woman who worked the floor herself for three weeks so that she knows what it's all about. It is she who got the girls a fifteen minute break both morning and afternoon and proved to the management that they work better for it. It is she who encourages girls to fit themselves for men's jobs and is going to get them men's pay for it if it's humanly possible.[46]

Like the coach of a sports team, the female supervisor cultivated group identity, obedience, and a sense of fair play – good qualities for both workers and citizens.

'She Has No Chance to Develop Poor Work Habits': Training and Personnel Management

When the minister of labour rose in Parliament to report on the success of the new War Emergency Training Programme (WETP), he drew explicitly upon the image of the 'unemployable man.' This figure of the Depression was not a victim of economic upheaval or the collapse of financial capital markets. The unemployable man symbolized personal failure, the family breadwinner whose masculinity was compromised by deficiency. That spectre of uncertainty and social dissolution could now, however, be remedied through a coherent program of training and vocational guidance. Training promised a measure of stability, regularity, and order. Skill would become a stabilizing force, a vector linking the individual to the market. Mitchell heaped praise on the 'fine achievement' of the new wartime training apparatus: 'Over 68,000 persons have been trained in industrial classes in the last year to man the thousands of machines in the factories making the tools of war.'[47] These were the same workers, Mitchell stated, whose skill had been entirely lost to the Dominion during the Depression through prolonged unemployment. Mitchell's words would have found a receptive audience, as the recent

Depression was never very far from the minds of government planners, let alone ordinary women and men. Propelled by these vivid recollections, women responded eagerly to the opportunity of immediate employment in a job that paid a decent wage. This was the key message promoted through popular media, as the following snippet illustrated: 'Apart from their innate enjoyment of their new work, and blithely innocent of what it may prophesy for their reluctance to give up their big place in industry when the war ends, Canada's girl munitions workers are undoubtedly delighted by their fatter pay envelopes.'[48] What should not escape the reader was the allusion to what might lie in store for women once the war was over.

Training was integral to the government's mobilization plans. Vocational training for women was deeply informed by understandings of differential skill and learning capacity, guiding principles for the 'skills dilution' approach to work reorganization. Vocational or 'pre-employment' training was designed to convert the female reserve into a viable and productive labour force. It was also conceived of as a second tier within the federal training and employment strategy – a second tier that would be instrumental in the postwar employment settlement.

Senior officials at the Department of Labour realised that the WETP had to be expanded dramatically, whatever their minister told Parliament. More workers had to be trained, women in particular. In the absence of provincial cooperation, federal bureaucrats wanted stronger control of labour force training. The argument was familiar enough: since the federal government assumed a greater share of fiscal responsibility, it should also get to control the cost-shared program. But this was only part of the story. By far the more controversial question lay in an issue of equally long standing: federal responsibility for employment and that more contentious policy issue, unemployment. Embedded within this question was an even more vexing one: female employment. To what extent was any level of government, in particular the federal government, prepared to recognize and 'normalize' the continuous labour force attachment of women while at the same time assuming managerial control over the labour market? Ottawa could not have it both ways: taking control of employment – as part of the labour policy envelope – meant assuming responsibility for women, and for unemployment.

The War Emergency Training Programme was conceived under the authority of the Youth Training Act (1939) and provided that the federal government would pay up to 50 per cent of the cost of provincial programs for the training and 'rehabilitation' of unemployed youth. As

soon as the WETP came into effect in September 1940, the federal
government assumed control of all designated technical schools and
plant schools and, through war appropriations, increased its coverage to
85 per cent of WETP implementation costs.[49] While this cost-sharing
arrangement gave the Department of Labour the lion's share of the
control, there was a catch. In an effort to consolidate backing from the
business community, Ottawa promoted the WETP as a boon to employers. NSS would diligently supply workers to be trained to company
specifications. The program did not signal any fundamental change in
the division of powers over labour policy, a point made somewhat emphatically by WETP director A.W. Crawford. Responsibility for training
policy was only temporarily assumed by Ottawa. Its primary purpose,
advised Crawford, 'is to serve the needs of war industries, not to educate
individuals.'[50] Of course, individuals were apparently benefiting from
training. The value accruing in vocational training could not be ignored,
and government was keen to emphasize its salutary economic effects.
Individuals would certainly become better workers at the same time that
the national interest in securing a technically skilled workforce would be
met. A new spirit of efficiency and cooperation had 'taken hold' of men
and women 'of all classes, adding a greater degree of skill and education
that contributed not only to the war effort, but to the technical value of
the labour force itself.' As a measure of federal policy, wartime training
benefited all parties: the worker, industry, and the state as overseer of
the wartime economy.

The WETP trained workers up to the semi-skilled or skilled level to
meet the demands of war production. Program content was intended to
maintain employment fitness or to enable the individual 'to obtain
better or more suitable' employment, according to the terms approved
by the labour minister.[51] As a national strategy, vocational training
aimed at producing a productive labour force of war workers in the
shortest amount of time possible. It was an ambitious policy, the results
of which were truly impressive. In the early years of the war, at least to
1941, policy practitioners and employers alike assumed that women's
training would be minimal and short term. 'Up to the present time
occupations for which women are being used in war industries are of a
nature which require very little training and this training is being given
in industry rather than in pre-employment classes established under the
War Emergency Training Programme,' Minister of Labour Norman
McLarty explained to his cabinet colleague, Minister of Pensions and
National Health Ian Mackenzie, in May 1941.[52] Similarly, the *Labour*

Gazette reported that women did not require formal training for the limited tasks they would be expected to perform.[53] By 1943, this approach would change dramatically, in direct response to the deepening labour crisis.

The new push for female recruitment drove the NSS and industry into a complex campaign to reorganize production tasks on the plan recommended by the engineering experts, known as 'skills dilution.' In the Fordist model of industrial production, all knowledge and production technique was embedded within the technology itself, both in the physical machinery and the managerial technologies organizing the work of production: for example, through time-motion and engineering studies. Engineers designed the equipment and organized production schedules and sequential job tasks; workers executed assigned tasks. All of this work had been conducted long before the woman worker set foot in the workplace. The vocational training program also changed, in the new knowledge that women would now be channelled into jobs requiring greater skill. Plant instructors seemed flummoxed at the prospect of training the new recruits. In 1943, the Nova Scotia director of training for the Department of Labour described the scene as his department was called on to train a group of women as machine operators. His report proved a familiar narrative of problems instructors encountered as they tried to figure out how they might possibly deal with this unique group of 'workers.' It is worth citing at length:

> The instructors who had had no previous experience with women in productive shop work were inclined to be sceptical of their capacity to learn to run machines and were loath to take on the job of teaching them. Advertisements were inserted in the daily papers asking for applicants and a ready response brought out a large number who were eager to enter the training course. They were subjected to the same psychological tests for intelligence and mechanical aptitude as had been used previously with men. It was found that the latter was of little significance when applied to female applicants probably because they had not become familiar with common tools and mechanisms as they grew up. Through critical interviewing those were selected who seemed to possess outstanding qualities of teachability and dependability.[54]

Training for men proceeded smoothly on the basis of mass testing and instruction. The limited exposure and differential capacities of women required an individuated approach, organized around the 'teachability' of the female trainee in the absence of any innate propensity for the work at hand. Women simply possessed no mechanical 'aptitude,' or so the story went.[55] But did they have the capacity to be taught? The answer to this question cut to the core of women's identity as workers. Given their limited labour force attachment, women were observed to possess an equally limited desire to learn the whole trade. The narrative neatly complemented the managerial strategy of work reorganization through 'skills dilution': female recruits were best instructed on a task rather than a trade basis, an approach that embedded the segmentation of apprenticeable trades within the overall training strategy. The narrative from the Nova Scotia director of technical education cited above made a convincing argument for this approach. Women were deemed more timid in the use of machining tools – given their exposure to mechanical instruments no more complicated than a sewing machine. They were also characterized as less inclined to respond to skilled trades training, having no aspiration to continue working in an apprenticeable trade once the war had ended. This apparent lack of 'long-term ambition' reinforced the view that women had only a transitory attachment to the labour force: 'Their general attitude showed that they felt their effort was directly connected with war activity and [was] based on a keen feeling of patriotism,' wrote the Nova Scotia director of technical education, describing the progress made by his department in training women as electric welders in the Nova Scotia shipyards, where they were to work installing gun mounts and related military weapons systems.[56]

Training the woman worker became a task of instilling good work habits as the new work routines were learned. As a reporter for the business press explained, 'One of the big advantages of this training is that the new employee starts off on the right foot and learns how to be a good operator from the beginning. She has no chance to develop poor working habits.'[57] Training was a process of orientation to routines, rules, and procedures of work. Absenteeism and turnover could be prevented from the outset in a program greatly enhanced by mental testing. *Canadian Business* reporter Mary Oliver investigated conditions at the Small Arms Limited facility in Long Branch, on the outskirts of Toronto. Management at the plant was so impressed by the results of the new program that they intended to make these methods a regular feature of all personnel work:

When, on the third morning, Mary graduates from the school and takes her place on the production line, she doesn't feel at a loss. Nor is she left to the tender mercies of the foreman – two 'patrolling instructresses' watch new operators at their work, offer suggestions, and, if more instruction is needed, give it on the spot. This supervision continues until Mary and her friends are quite able to carry on alone. Occasionally a girl can't make the grade; she goes back to school again and an attempt is made to find a job for which she is better suited. As time goes on, the management plans to branch out into job placement and aptitude tests for all their workers.[58]

A key focus of progressive managerial technique, therefore, became the capacity of the individual worker. Employers were encouraged to follow the example of the Great Western Garment (GWG) Manufacturing Company in Edmonton. Faced with the same high turnover rates that plagued the low-waged needle-trades industry generally, GWG brought in a program of regular aptitude testing and vocational training. The program was favourably noted by Eaton. In December 1944, in her regular report to MacNamara, she greeted the GWG initiative as one of the most promising developments to cross her desk in recent months. Aptitude testing worked both as a screening mechanism to weed out women deemed unsuitable and as a method for monitoring the developing work capacities instilled through the occupational training program. These measures worked in combination with a regular wage increase tied to successful completion of training. The result was described by the company as a comprehensive employment policy that upgraded the occupation in order to stabilize the labour pool. 'The management is trying to improve the 1st aptitude tests in order to reduce the nos. who do not make good during training,' Eaton observed approvingly. She went on to add that Mrs Lyons, supervisor of the Edmonton Women's Division, had 'taken a keen interest in this development and I believe that some of the smaller firms in the area are making inquiries concerning the experiment.'[59]

Surveillance and inspection were the signature of modern personnel development, in stark contrast to the haphazard and unscientific practice of hiring at the plant gate. The training infrastructure built up around the war effort ushered in an entirely new approach to Canada's working classes, now cast as a national resource. The theme of surveillance was a central feature in descriptive and prescriptive narratives detailing the advantageous effects of training and personnel planning. Articles appearing in the popular media keenly promoted the government plan: the surest route to workplace order and stability was a close system of scrutiny and monitoring that began at the level of the individual worker. Such was the routine at Central Technical Collegiate in Toronto.[60] The school operated on a twenty-four-hour schedule, turning out war workers ready to take up their positions in essential industries, all the while under the 'watchful eye' of a battery of personnel planners, plant superintendents, inspectors, and instructors. The classroom was a microcosm of the developing continuum the NSS was so keen to replicate within its own regulatory infrastructure: screening, training, recruitment, employment placement, and continuous tracking. The classroom was transformed into a transparent public space of order and predictability, its internal routines open to public view, its occupants displayed as potential labour, and its techniques readily transferable to other locations, provided that the carefully developed knowledge practices around which it was organized were closely adhered to. Educational psychology had left its bold imprint. Remedial vocational instruction replaced the disciplinary ordering of workers' bodies; the interior of individual 'trainees' was made available to governance in classroom, the workplace, even the community, through assessment, calibration, and regulation. The new vocational training integrated the best insights of personnel development, now techniques for the development of the 'self' – the trained worker. 'Personnel executives, shop foremen and plant superintendents are constantly inspecting classes sponsored by their firms, seeing for themselves the progress made by each individual – or the absence of it,' explained Frederick Edwards, a feature writer for *Maclean's* magazine. In his article 'Night and Day School,' Edwards recounted how the trainee might 'at any given moment ... find himself under critical scrutiny by the man he expects and hopes to be working for in a few weeks' time.' Sponsoring firms would get regular reports on their charges and, best of all, 'slackers or misfits are eliminated ruthlessly – something that cannot happen to regular students.'[61]

Mingling among the potential misfits and slackers were 'baldish oldsters,' 'dignified white-haired matrons,' and 'pert misses': those groups specifically identified as the potential labour reserve. Skill capacity was a central theme in these gendered narratives. Where men might receive up to twenty weeks of instruction on 'some highly technical subjects,' three weeks was considered sufficient to instruct most women in machine operation or assembly-line work. But the real bonus came in the detailed work for which women appeared ideally adapted. 'Meter assembly,' according to one report, 'requires the accurate weaving of twenty-six strands of wire, each wrapped in a different coloured covering. No men need apply here. The male sex, it seems, is affected with colour

blindness to a much greater degree than are women.'[62] Women's training requirements could still be characterized as minimal, given their
'natural' proclivity for such mundane but precise tasks and their apparent tolerance for boredom and fatigue. The message carried through
popular media, likely designed to encourage women to sign up and
employers to welcome the new recruits, minimized the complexity of the
work at hand: a few days' training was all that was needed, provided that
the 'natural qualifications of dexterity, patience and keen eyesight' were
present and intact.[63]

The special aptitudes women were deemed to possess, if not monopo-
lize, were instead described as attributes, more a function of gender than
of innate intelligence to be developed as skill. Indeed, any interest in
machinery at all was characterized as 'queer,' and queer, as everybody
knew, was most certainly not feminine. *Maclean's* feature writer Thelma
LeCocq implied as much. The average woman might not possess any
'passion for machinery,' but her 'deft fingered' ways made her an ideal
candidate for assembly-line work. Assembling the machinery of war was
no more complicated than assembling a new housedress, even if it was a
bit dirtier. Some women, however, readily took advantage of the rare
opportunity afforded by war production work. LeCocq described the
typical experience of this atypical female type: 'Being a stenographer
wasn't her idea of a career, so she got a job with a typewriter firm doing
repairs. That was the best she could do in a world where a woman
interested in machinery was regarded as queer. Then the gun plant
called for women workers.'[64] In narratives like these, femininity was
unlikely to survive intact unless the closely delineated standards of normative gender identity were adhered to. It was the task of industrial
welfare and pre-employment training to ensure that they were.

The 'Housewife's Shift': A Case Study of Work Reorganization

As part of the mobilization campaign, Eaton and her staff at the Women's
Division engineered another innovative strategy: the housewife's shift,
modelled on the Victory Shifts in Britain. By 1943, part-time employment
was an important focus of NSS policy in a campaign that targeted older,
married women with children in order to free younger single women for
regular war work. Senior officials hoped this strategy would draw workers
to fill the gaps in less remunerative work such as domestic employment
in hospitals.[65] As a financial incentive, women were reminded that they
would only be required to pay UI contributions if they worked more than

four hours per day and that they were exempt from paying income tax if annual earnings were $660 or less.[66] Employers were advised that women had to be made to 'feel' that they were regular employees. It was best to defer to the expertise of personnel supervisors (and if they did not have such staff, the implication was that they most certainly ought to) whose task would be to encourage the part-time worker to 'feel welcome and a necessary part of your organization.' There remained the ever-present danger that this woman might degenerate to the status of the transient worker whose interests were increasingly removed from those of her employer; that she might treat both job and employer in the 'off-hand inconsiderate manner of a casual or temporary employee.' A note of challenge pervaded the prescriptive policy literature on this question: the women whose aid was to be solicited were also described as far more independent and therefore more likely to resist poor treatment. For such women, the tug of patriotic duty was strong but unlikely to withstand employer indifference or exploitive working conditions. Supervision by trained, preferably female personnel was crucial to the successful deployment of this segment of the female workforce, given their stronger identity as older women with home, family, independence, and responsibilities. Together, these factors made such women unused to the subordinate status of the regular employee. NSS employer advice literature explained that the part-time mature woman was 'serious of purpose,' and for that reason all the more likely to criticize carelessness on the job. Any sign of 'bullying' or 'nagging' would be 'keenly resented by the older women.' Unlike regular employees, these women would be more likely to quit 'than to stand their ground and fight it out.' The Women's Division addressed the matter head on: 'As a rule, these older women know exactly why they are working and what for and their purpose is usually an unselfish and self-sacrificing one.'[67] Thus, at one and the same time, the older woman as part-time worker was both driven by self-interest and compelled by her natural patriotic duty, itself a function of her role as mother, wife, and guardian of the middle-class home. She was more responsible, imbued with an agency that permitted greater freedom of movement to come and go, to enter the labour force but just as readily to leave rather than 'stand her ground and fight.' Identification with national purpose through patriotic spirit, an unselfish attitude of self-sacrifice, and 'sound commonsense' were all pointed to as advantageous features accompanying the introduction of the older part-time woman into the workplace, where she might provide a good example for younger and more impressionable women to follow.

Conversely, the autonomy that was so important to the maintenance of a healthy household was here a hindrance to that other subject of industrial welfare policy discourse: the productive worker capable of submitting to the sterner realities of the workplace. In fact, on closer examination, the individual household was seen to be more removed than ever from the structured space of the modern workplace. The part-time worker was more likely to request time off for 'trivial matters,' to which supervisors had to respond with a firm but sympathetic attitude. Workers on the housewife's shift had to be taught that responsibility to employer and nation demanded unflagging personal sacrifice and commitment. All regulations, those of the employer in the workplace and of the NSS, constituted an undifferentiated, continuous field of procedure and obligation that simply had to be adhered to. 'These women must be continuously reminded of their obligations,' according to NSS advice literature, and this could be done by 'constantly stressing the regular rather than the casual nature of their duties.' Supervision was essential to ensuring punctuality and regular attendance. NSS employment officers were advised to be vigilant and firm in dealing with the older woman, recognizing that 'her domestic obligations weigh heavily with her' and would likely affect work attendance and performance. 'Careful and sympathetic consideration' in helping her deal with such problems went firmly in hand with a close eye to her extreme individualism. According to the policy analysts at the Women's Division, home management was a matter of individual caprice and whim, and 'if the discipline of fixed schedules and punctuality has ever been known, it is likely to have been forgotten.'[68] The average household, it seemed, existed in a state of extreme individualism, as far removed from the orderly workplace as it was possible to be.

The part-time worker posed an interesting challenge because of her identity as housewife and mother and her tangential relation to the waged labour force. She was unused to the patterns of authority and standards of compliant behaviour of the conventional employment relationship. Through personnel technique, the women who were the target of the 'housewife's shift' had to become imbued with a new 'worker-identity,' a form of 'labour as dressage.'[69] NSS policy directives drew on these conceptions to emphasize the unstable identity of the part-time worker, especially when compared to the stable male worker, whose attachment to the labour force was known and therefore calculable. As would become clear, the woman at the centre of this narrative was white and married, the autonomous figure of idealized middle-class domesticity whose labours were motivated by a sense of patriotic duty, an affinity with the national purpose. Personnel guidance eased the transition from domestic household to the unfamiliar space of economic modernity signified by the modern workplace. Discipline, power, agency, and identity were the operative terms in this discursive field. Domesticity and employability intertwined in the documentary practice of the NSS advisories, underscoring the temporary, marginal, and therefore ambivalent location of women workers generally and part-time workers in particular.

Conclusion

The NSS Women's Division was responsible for overseeing all areas of labour market policies and programming involving the employment of women. NSS training and employment strategies mobilized gender-based assumptions about female employability at the same time as they constituted women workers as moral regulatory subjects. As concerns about labour shortages intensified, so too did moves to institute a comprehensive program of 'industrial welfare.' The presence of women in the industrial workplace was, of course, not a new phenomenon. The 'manpower shortage' intensified scrutiny of workers' bodies as disciplinary subjects as well as potentially morally disordered subjects. At the same time, compulsion was to be avoided at all costs. Democracy and the fight to defend it was a central organizing precept in this total war against fascism. The Dominion government walked a very fine line on the issue of conscripted labour for either military or industrial purposes, in the case of women's employment even more than men's. Consent, compliance, and, better yet, a call and willing response to service closely informed the sentiments to which policy officials wanted to appeal as part of the fusion of individual interest and the national enterprise. On closer examination, policy practitioners would discover a disturbing rate of absenteeism and turnover in industries designated essential to the war effort.[70] Regulatory procedures had to be tightened considerably to ensure that working women, in particular, not only reported to work on time but actually stayed put in their jobs for the duration of the war. Something simply had to be done to discourage women from wandering off in pursuit of higher wages and/or more favourable working conditions elsewhere. Intensification of managerial technique became a key strategy for regulating this newfound, if somewhat unruly, labour supply. NSS officials drew on the diagnostic and prescriptive expertise of psychologists, psychiatrists, employment researchers, vocational guidance experts, industrial engineers, and management specialists to assist in the project of overseeing and adjusting the work habits of women alleged to be unused to the rigours and challenges of regular industrial employment. As a strategy of gender-based regulation, NSS officials launched a series of policy initiatives that effectively reorganized and intensified gender coding in the workplace through a program of skills dilution, a core organizing principle underpinning the pre-employment training strategy.

Employability discourses worked to organize the differential capacities of groups of women according to occupation and domestic affiliation, while conditioning women's access to what came to be constituted through these same discourses as the regular, formal, waged economy. Industrial welfare and personnel programming were drafted on the basis of the new expertise of employment researchers, psychologists, and management consultants – proponents of the new managerial techniques that would reorganize Canadian enterprise. Similarly, the public employment office gained new significance as a strategic public space for directing the flow of labour. As workers, women were constituted as capable of only partially achieving and maintaining desired productivity levels: as mothers, whether actual or potential, women needed careful scrutiny and regulation through industrial welfare programs. These policy discourses collectively articulated the boundaries of nation, of the labour market as the productive site of national strength and security, and of the differential citizenship capacities of those called upon to secure the interests of the nation on the domestic front of total war.

chapter three

The Psychologist at War: Assessing and Recruiting for the Canadian Women's Army Corps

In 1942, Dr Olive Ruth Russell found herself stationed in a tent on the very muddy grounds of the Toronto City Hall. She was accompanied by an army brass band heralding the presence of recruiters from the Canadian Women's Army Corps (CWAC). Russell was dissatisfied. After only two months as personnel selection officer in Military District 2 (Toronto), she fired off a detailed list of policy recommendations to her director of personnel selection, Col. William Line, at national headquarters in Ottawa. In the first in a lengthy series of exchanges, Russell outlined what she perceived to be the lack of comprehensive measures for screening out 'unsuitable' personnel. Russell would continue, in the months ahead, to record her grave concerns about the state of the women's services. Army selection methods might apply adequately to male personnel. But if Canada was to open its armed services to women, then an entirely different roster of criteria must be brought to bear. After all, the reputation of the CWAC was at stake. As a consequence, in defence of the reputation of the CWAC, military personnel brought the full weight of their powers – and they were considerable – to the task of devising techniques by which to locate, identify, and remedy 'problems' that were most likely passing undetected by the mass-testing techniques deployed throughout the regular and women's services.[1]

The war presented women such as Dr Russell with a tremendous opportunity to apply the latest techniques of educational psychology and personnel planning to the massive mobilization now underway. Russell was part of a team of experts who would usher in a new regime in state social policy. Russell began her war career as an army examiner with the military rank of captain. Her job, with only one other colleague to assist her, was to screen all applicants seeking to enlist with the CWAC. She would soon move to the Directorate of Personnel Selection at National Defence to head the program for the rehabilitation and reintegration of servicewomen discharged from military service. As an expert in vocational guidance, Russell knew all there was to know about personnel selection and assessment. As a scientist and a deeply committed liberal progressive, she was anxious to use her considerable expertise in the service of her country, and her country's women.

A Brief History of the Intelligence Test: Mental Testing and Nation Building during the Interwar Period

The technique of mass intelligence testing most in vogue in the United States and Canada shared its origins with mass testing procedures instituted by the U.S. Army during the First World War. The U.S. Army Alpha and Beta tests purported to measure such capacities as literacy, mathematical and spatial reasoning, and mechanical aptitude. R.M. Yerkes, hired by the U.S. Army to oversee the testing of recruits, had asked two colleagues, Henry Goddard, superintendent at the training school and social laboratory for alleged mental defectives in Vineland, New Jersey, and Lewis Terman from Stanford University, to collaborate in developing the Alpha and Beta tests between May and July 1917. Yerkes's subaltern, C.C. Brigham, would elevate mass testing to another level of application when, as secretary of the U.S. College Entrance Examination Board, he launched the Scholastic Aptitude Test.[2] As evidence of the considerable power mobilized through intelligence discourse, Terman's guide to IQ testing, *The Measurement of Intelligence. An Explanation of and a Complete Guide for the Use of the Stanford Revision and Extension of the Binet-Simon Intelligence Scale,* originally published in 1919, was still in wide circulation decades later, the leading authority on mental testing in educational, industrial, and military screening. As explained in the guide, IQ testing was a powerful tool. As state policy related to 'feeble-mindedness,' a key focus of concern in the interwar period, Terman predicted that 'tens of thousands' of high-grade defectives would fall 'under the surveillance and protection of society.' Systematic testing was enlightened population policy if the objective was to curtail the reproduction of defective persons, 'precisely the ones whose guardianship it is most important for the State to assume.'[3] It was also smart social and economic policy and would go far 'in the elimination of an enormous amount of crime, pauperism, and industrial inefficiency' – forms of social malaise caused by mental deficiency. National measures of intelligence were what mattered most to Terman and to later advocates of mental testing, such as University of Toronto professor of educational psychology Peter Sandiford. The only question that really mattered was the quality of the national population itself, not the particularities of individual defectives. Standardized tests promised to show the way. 'How high is the average level of intelligence among our people,' Terman wanted to know, 'and how frequent are the various grades of ability above and below the average?'[4] With testing, the answer at last lay within the practitioner's grasp, and both – the test and the practitioner – had received a massive boost during the First World War.

Educational psychology in Canada was just as vulnerable as it was in the United States to the fallacious conclusions drawn from U.S. Army testing data. On both sides of the border, psychologists used a racial template of intelligence, exhibiting this template as scientific proof that 'intelligence' varied according to the 'biological' fact of race. Peter Sandiford, head of the Ontario College of Education at the University of Toronto, was Olive Ruth Russell's adviser during her tenure as a research associate at the college. He was also one of the strongest proponents of race-based testing, drawing his material directly from the United States, in particular the work of Terman. Throughout the interwar period, Sandiford's reputation grew, both as a scholar and as a leading spokesperson on the subject of intelligence testing and immigration restriction. He drew considerable attention from the press as a leading educational psychologist and, by all accounts, as a dynamic public speaker. When the debates over Canadian immigration policy again heated up in the late 1920s, Sandiford waded in. His main theme, that intelligence and race were directly linked, found resonance in the conventional wisdom of the day. Now Sandiford could bring firm, scientific proof to the claim that intelligence levels conformed to a racial hierarchy, a reflection of the natural biological order. Social problems such as prostitution and venereal disease, unemployment and alcoholism – all these preventable problems were traceable to the 'inferior stock' of 'inferior races.'

When the International Council for Exceptional Children held its annual meeting in Toronto in 1928, Sandiford was invited to give the keynote address. Echoing his counterparts in the United States, he contended that stronger quotas and more stringent restrictions in Canadian immigration law were imperative. Citing the U.S. Army test results, along with his own research, Sandiford warned his elite audience that the very survival of Canada depended upon its capacity to attract and retain the right stock of white British 'settlers.' This familiar theme played on the apprehension that too many of this preferred group were leaving Canada to seek their fortunes in the United States while so-called inferior races thronged at the borders and ports, filling prisons, asylums, houses of correction, and relief lines. Sandiford's message, as the following makes clear, ran dangerously parallel to the genocidal, anti-Semitic, and racist claims at that time fuelling the Nazi mobilization in Germany:

> Whether or not a nation's intelligence, health and morals shall be permanently raised or lowered by the immigrant groups admitted to its citizenship transcends in importance the more transient difficulties connected with tariff, transportation or economic difficulties ... A mistake with these lesser problems can be rectified by subsequent legislation, but once an inferior people are settled as citizens nothing on earth short of extermination can remedy the state of affairs.[5]

Good immigration law was nothing more than sound population policy: this was the message Sandiford was so anxious to communicate in his public activism. Immigration was central to the racial identity of the nation and the quality and calibre of its labour force. The distance between biological and social heredity largely determined the contours of this heated debate, while at the same time illustrating the multiple ways in which 'race' was drawn upon as a conceptual strategy and nation-building practice. For example, when so-called 'inferior' races outperformed preferred 'superior' races on IQ tests, culture became a racialized category to account for the difference, thus stabilizing the racial superiority of white population groups. When Sandiford conducted mass testing among students in British Columbia, he found that Japanese and Chinese students ranked first and second, respectively. Undaunted, he concluded that such results confirmed that intelligence was universal but development and civilization were culturally contingent. One would expect to find individuals of purportedly high intelligence even among more 'primitive' cultures. As he explained in the popular university text *Educational Psychology: An Objective Study,* published in 1938, 'A Beethoven born in the depths of an African forest or in the wilds of Patagonia would never compose beautiful sonatas and symphonies, although he might, and probably would, become the best tom-tom beater of his tribe.'[6] In sum, Sandiford's work exemplified the foundational racialized discourses underpinning educational psychology during this period. Race-, gender-

and class-based typologies of intelligence and aptitude came into play wherever mental testing was conducted, and the well-connected members of the National Committee for Mental Hygiene (Canada) (NCMH) would ensure that it was.

Educational psychologists associated with the NCMH struggled through the interwar years to create a strategic opportunistic balance in the ongoing nature-nurture controversy. The outcome of this struggle would determine the future of the movement for mental hygiene in Canada. Sandiford's work conformed to the key tenets articulated by hereditarian biologists and their psyche-based colleagues in the United States and Britain. Biological science actively constituted the 'fact' of race as a central focus and critical object of analysis of scientific research. Environment was enlisted through the educational enterprise to remediate, direct, develop, and administer biological 'inheritance.' As an interventionary strategy for associates of the NCMH, educational psychology was to make an enduring contribution in this strategic compromise. For Sandiford, heredity and environment were 'correlative factors' that, taken together, produced the dynamic relation of 'social heredity.' As can be seen most clearly in Dr Russell's research, the new prescription for population policy saw the dismal claims of hereditarianism tempered by the liberalist project of education, while opening both domains to the expert interventions of educational psychologists. By the end of the interwar period, the debate could be neatly summarized: 'Children are born *with* a biological heritage. They are born *into* a social heritage.'[7] Education and parenting were the obvious cornerstones of social inheritance. Capacity and intelligence were the quantifiable dimensions of the biological contribution.[8] Dr William Blatz, Canada's leading expert in the psychological study of the child, popularized the compromise position: 'A child is born with a capacity that is high or low or intermediate; what he does with it depends on his motivation and persistence.'[9] Heredity had not entirely left the scene, however. As Blatz explained: 'One can never leave one's heredity behind; one can never remain unaffected by one's environment ... In so far as heredity, over which we have no influence whatever, is stamped upon us at birth, it is apparent that the individual reaches whatever heights and depths the future holds through environmental factors.'[10]

Gender, on the other hand, was a less stable category as constituted within mental testing discourse. Terman, in his 1919 *Guide,* encountered some difficulties in pinpointing the relation of sex differences to IQ scores. Analysing the results of tests conducted among school-age children, he found that there was a 'fairly constant superiority' of girls until the age of thirteen, after which the curve of boys' test results rose above that of girls. Other than this slight difference, the 'distribution of intelligence' appeared equal between the sexes and ages within both groups. There was little variation to report. When looking at results from individual tests, practitioners claimed to note more specific aptitudes – boys were better at 'arithmetical reasoning, girls at aesthetic comparison and tying a bow-knot' – but these differences hardly substantiated claims of greater or lesser 'amounts' of intelligence between the sexes. So how to account for such tremendous variation in social *performance*, the subject matter to which testing was devoted? Terman was forced to admit that perhaps sexual differentiation could only be accounted for through 'wholly extraneous factors.' His speculative conclusions, of which there were four, are worth noting in full:

> (1) The occupations in which it is possible to achieve eminence are for the most part only now beginning to open their doors to women. Women's career [sic] has been largely that of home-making, an occupation in which eminence, in the strict sense of the word, is impossible. (2) Even of the small number of women who embark upon a professional career, a majority marry and thereafter devote a fairly large proportion of their energy to bearing and rearing children. (3) Both the training given to girls and the general atmosphere in which they grow up are unfavourable to the inculcation of the professional point of view, and as a result women are not spurred on by deep-seated motives to constant strenuous intellectual endeavour as men are. (4) It is possible that the emotional traits of women are such as to favour the development of the sentiments at the expense of innate intellectual endowment.[11]

Here was a case of grasping at straws if ever there was one. Gender difference was naturalized as a function of emotion and reproductive capacity, a biological 'fact' written on the bodies, and therefore the minds, of women.

Mental testing was to the administrative regime of congregate social institutions such as schools, armies, and factories what intelligence was to the psyche-based practitioner. Streaming in schools was just the first stage in what was to become a lifetime of endless sorting. Blatz encouraged parents to have children tested, thus alleviating disruption over the longer term by diagnosing differences before they could develop into social problems of maladjustment. The most modern schools systematically tested all pupils, ensuring that every student was directed into the most beneficial course of study and not slotted into a program that was either too difficult or not challenging enough. Blatz advised that streaming should begin when a child was seven, by which age all interests and capacities were known and could be directed into either academic or non-academic pursuits.[12] Under the tutelage of academics such as Sandiford, students at the Ontario College of Education were instructed in the three main applications of intelligence tests: calibration, or institutional organization of pupils according to alleged capacity and ability; diagnosis of mental deficiencies or 'feeble-mindedness'; and prognosis, or 'forecasting the intellectual or vocational future of young persons.'[13] Intelligence approached in this way was the 'raw material' on which the educational program worked. The test was not a crystal ball through which to forecast the destiny of its subjects. Parents and teachers alike were repeatedly told that they would do well to avoid overstating the significance of the test score. Sandiford was adamant on this point: 'Intelligence tests will not tell us which pupil will succeed at school, but only which pupils will succeed providing they work hard, and remain relatively free from disease, and from mental and moral degeneration.'[14] In this, Sandiford was once again echoing a point made repeatedly by Lewis Terman, that testing had no predictive capacity beyond the actual measure of intelligence. This was not some new phrenology dressed up to improve upon the vulgar measures of nineteenth-century cranium expert Caesar Lombroso.[15] On that point, Sandiford cautioned students against overestimating the capacity of testing. 'An intelligence test, like any other form of examination, is judged by its validity, reliability, objectivity, ease of administration and scoring, and by the satisfactoriness of its norms.' These were the standards by which to test the veracity of the truth claims made by any 'test.' But the foremost problems associated with such tests were twofold: their design and interpretation, together with the implementation and application of their results. Once again, the capacity to make truth claims, to establish one's authority to assert these claims to be true, and to assert the methods by which such claims were to be accepted as true were closely scripted and carefully guarded – to be appropriated only by trained practitioners within the discipline.

Through mental hygiene discourse, the test subject was caught up in a controversy that traversed both historical and evolutionary time, emerging as the product of both culture and biology. This was the unstable terrain over which hereditarians and environmentalists would contest the meaning and significance of intelligence as an index for social planning and national productive efficiency. Testing, because derived from statistical norms, was seen as a 'neutral' tool assisting the practitioner in a scientific ordering of population: difference emerged as the distance between the averaged norm and apparent deviations from that norm. The rest – performance and development – was the domain of education, vocational training, and employment policy. For example, vocational tests according to Sandiford, were 'still in their infancy.' Many such tests failed to meet the required standard because the problem to be tested was not well-defined. Defining a problem along the psychological dimension was a matter of calculating its mathematical probability. As Sandiford explained, the calculation of chance explained all: 'Every known variable trait,' including mathematical ability, memory, 'general intelligence, general morality,' and even 'speed in typewriting, [and] ability in handwriting.' Across the entire breadth of the evolutionary continuum, trait variability was reducible to digital expression and amenable to calculation and, therefore, predictive control. The first principle to accept was the operation, not of divine providence, but of trait variability among members of a homogeneous group according to 'the curve of chance.'[16] Once again, environment and heredity were correlative factors that, in the measurement of traits, including intelligence, generated correlation coefficients distributed along the curve of chance with predictable ease and administrative grace. Taking a leaf from Mendelian genetics,[17] Sandiford contended that factors or genes were in fact the 'true unit-characters in inheritance' and, notwithstanding the fact that genes could not be visibly apprehended as concrete entities, 'the factorial hypothesis accounts for every known fact in heredity.'[18] Failure to understand this technique meant that the object to be tested – the social problem to be inquired into – would not be properly identified, rendering the test design inadequate and subsequent results flawed. In other words, this was an exclusive club of expert practitioners, a loyal company of experts committed to the science of mental testing.[19]

'To Help Johnny See Johnny Through': Olive Ruth Russell and the Vocational Guidance Movement

Russell brought a tremendous body of expertise to her work at the CWAC. She was a practised educator who specialized in vocational counselling. Throughout the 1930s, she had lobbied tirelessly for the introduction of vocational guidance in the Ontario public school system. The challenges of economic depression threw into question the wisdom of relying on the free market to allocate human capacity according to its best and most efficient application. A well and truly governed society demanded a comprehensive program of citizen-formation, commencing at the earliest stages of child development in the classroom and extending beyond that into the labour market through a program of vocational assessment and guidance. Teachers required a thorough grounding in the new principles of educational psychology, particularly since so much of their work went beyond the mechanics of academic instruction to include as one of its objectives the formation of self-regulating subjects or, in Russell's words, 'to help boys and girls to consider and develop their individual capacities to best advantage ... to develop in them the self-discipline and perseverance to perform necessary duties well, whether they like them or not.'[20] Penetrating and monitoring the 'psychology of the school child' ought to be as regular a part of the work day as grading tests and cleaning the chalk board; psychological techniques of administration would become as mundane a tool in the teacher's repertoire as pencil and textbook. Such techniques were developed to a large extent through child-study research that set out to define the formative principles and stages of personality development and, what was more important, to explore conditions affecting the adjustment of human personality in order to guide the child into normal, healthy, and efficient pursuits. The new psychological knowledge of the individual – of individual and normative subjectivity – promised an array of positive applications, redirecting effort from the disciplinary work of correction to the investigation and identification of causality and the constitution of 'normal personality.' The objective of these endeavours was in part to devise a program for rehabilitation, for cultivating responsible citizenship through the formation of self-governing subjects.

The genesis of Russell's approach to, and faith in, vocational counselling lay in her doctoral research findings, conducted under the direction of Dr Peter Sandiford at the Ontario College of Education. Her doctoral dissertation traced the shift from the single-factor measure of intelligence to multiple-factor analysis, a move that, she hoped, made possible the study of personality as a psychological matrix of individual – and quantifiable – human factors. Environment was now approached as a multiple set of relations to be assessed for discrete and cumulative effects upon the psychological subject. Individual personality could be mapped against the normative distribution of these effects within the broader population. In this way, social maladjustment was meticulously charted

as a manifestation of psychological deviations from the norm, abnormalities that, if diagnosed correctly, could be addressed through remedial measures. But the first order of business was to develop the
multiple-factor approach and, more importantly, the technology through
which this new approach could be deployed as a practical regime for
examination, assessment, and remediation in work and school, family
and community.

Russell's study investigated mental capacities as a function of age and
gender. In this way, she hoped to extend the predictive capacity of
multiple-factor testing, since 'attempts to differentiate mental abilities
are highly important from a practical standpoint of Educational and
Vocational Guidance.'[21] The problem, as Russell framed it, lay in assessing whether mental ability was reducible to a single factor or if it was
instead a composite of a variety of abilities, each requiring separate
measurement.[22] The contradiction in this approach lay in conceptualiz-
ing social categories such as gender. This work signalled the shift that set
the mental hygiene movement on an entirely new course during the
interwar years: from the investigation of individual pathologies to the
study of the conditions of 'normal' personality development. This represented a substantive change from the rigid classification of abnormality
and pathology that had so strongly characterized the eugenic focus on
mental degeneracy and 'feeble-mindedness' during the earlier part of
the century. Psyche-practitioners attempted to isolate those factors in
personality that might be classified as examples of maladjustment, or
newly diagnosed 'personality disorder.'[23] The potential of this new,
more positive approach encompassed and further implicated an array of
programs and policy areas governing human relations and human conduct. 'The emphasis on environmental factors,' as William Blatz and
Helen MacMurchy Bott explained in a standard text for the period,
Parents and the Pre-School Child, 'tended to break down the vicious and
artificial distinction between "normal" and "abnormal" ... No longer
could the community be thought of as divided into two great classes, the
normal and the abnormal, the former at large functioning in society, the
latter shut off by themselves and denied the activities of everyday life.'[24]
Studies of 'self development' opened up a strategic space for the expert
practitioner, raising as it did that pressing question – what was 'normal'?[25] The technique of adjustment encompassed the problem, its
diagnosis, and the remedy all within the same frame. As Blatz and
MacMurchy Bott confidently asserted, only the expert clinician could
develop the necessary technique: 'to define the range of deviation that

may be considered "normal" is a highly technical matter involving research upon numerous cases with due account taken of the possibility of modification in these trends.'[26]

Psychological expertise was indispensable to a well-ordered society, as such careful research demonstrated. Still, individual citizens could either secure or subvert the principles of liberal democracy. In what was shaping up to be a fight for the very lifeblood of democratically ordered society, the first line of defence surely lay in the careful work of forming responsible, self-governing citizens. In a 1936 article for the Canadian Girls in Training's official organ, *The Torch*, Russell outlined the central organizing principles that were to guide her work in the coming years. They included: a 'philosophy of individualism' to cultivate not 'mere automatons, but dynamic, creative personalities'; stronger social planning to prepare for 'a new social order'; a progressive internationalism and 'world-mindedness' among citizens and their governments; and finally, the study of education grounded in the principles of science, specifically those of educational psychology.[27] Such insights drew inspiration from the vocational education program developed under Germany's doomed Weimar Republic. Russell had the opportunity to witness this work at first hand in the summer of 1932, although she feared the threat posed by the Nazi frenzy that was rapidly consuming that nation. The 'splendid efforts of the socialist government' were soon to be jeopardized by the Nazi regime, although the successes of the vocational movement, it seemed, had already spread well beyond Germany.

The new pedagogy of vocationalism began with a rigorous regimen of intensive testing. The implementation of assessment and observation through a network of state employment boards and a central federal state board most impressed Russell and likely informed her commitment to having a similar program implemented in Canada. The centralization of this work through the federal employment office during the 1920s had permitted practitioners to achieve the 'highest peak of efficiency' in their work of occupational assessment and vocational guidance, both integral components within the interlinked educational and national employment systems. The subject of this policy discourse was, once again, the psychology of the individual, understood to be a composite of multiple factors with multiple effects. The difference was that the focus of such investigation was the 'whole person,' rather than the fragmented compilation of test scores so favoured by American behaviourist psychologists. 'The influence of Gestalt Psychology is felt practically every where [sic],' Russell commented. As German psychologists understood, indeed persisted in emphasizing, 'each individual is a dynamic unity, an integrated whole. The total personality could only be understood in relation to the total environment of which he forms a part.' No psychologist worth her or his salt would attempt 'to classify or guide human beings' otherwise.[28] Russell campaigned vigorously to have similar techniques implemented in Ontario, taking advantage of the open discussion of employability and unemployment of the pre-war period to advocate for a more comprehensive system of vocational guidance in education. But there were not enough trained practitioners to go around. Those who found themselves in the guidance chair too often had found their way there more because of a 'pleasing personality' than any professional training or expertise. In a 1939 lecture to the North Toronto Neighbourhood Workers' Local Council, Russell suggested that the day was not far off when every school principal would require at least minimal training in the techniques of vocational guidance and would, moreover, supervise such work as a routine part of the educational work of the school. In fact, all teachers would soon 'be trained in methods of psychology and mental hygiene' as an integrated practice of provincial educational policy.[29]

Counselling was a key dimension in the new psychological assessment of human capacities. 'Guidance should not be thought of as "an attempt to see through Johnny and to see Johnny through."' The point was 'to help Johnny see through himself and see himself through.'[30] This was a crucial development for the vocational counselling movement, devoted as it was to forging a social order based on responsible citizenship, a category already occupied by the 'preferred' white, middle-class, skilled male of British origin, as had been so passionately articulated by Russell's adviser, Professor Sandiford. In this framework, the focus was not skill or academic performance, those discrete quantifiable entities that so preoccupied the crude psychometric imaginations of 'charlatans' whose testing instruments promised so much but delivered so little. Russell's attentions were instead concentrated on the more difficult but infinitely more productive – albeit costly – assessment of personality, an exercise that, if implemented as a measure of public policy, would generate a longitudinal record of each individual compiled throughout their tenure at public and high school, and beyond.[31] The counselling function extended the case study/interview technique that had marked the earlier, clinical phase of mental hygiene practice. The study of personality was infinitely more promising, because more positive, than earlier preoccupations with pathological abnormalities such as 'feeble-mindedness' and mental defect.[32] Educational psychology had practical application in the rationalization of managerial technique, ordering a variety of social institutional relations devoted to the education and labour of the 'whole person,' educating children, to be sure, but also directing the future labours – paid and unpaid – of every individual, as worker, as mother, as 'incorrigible' or delinquent, or as citizen or soldier.

Russell was therefore following a general movement that studied ability and capacity as psychological categories, in an effort to better understand mental abilities and, more importantly, to refine the techniques necessary to act upon those findings across a range of policy areas. She argued for the replacement of the 'single score or IQ obtained from a heterogeneous battery of tests or test-items.' Since mental ability was influenced by multiple factors, the practice of single-factor measurement could no longer be defended, if ever, as she emphasized *'psychological diagnosis of the individual is to be worthy of the name.'*[33] The domain of the 'social' was problematized in such a way as to leave little doubt about the discursive field through which these techniques would circulate and the problems they would transform anew, now defined as social problems located within the psychology of the individual. Foremost among these were the 'tragedies of unemployment and vocational maladjustment.' The only real question was how much longer these issues could be left unattended and at what escalating cost? At the time of Russell's speech to the North Toronto Neighbourhood Workers' Council, the fear of rising fascist movements in pre-war Canada had added considerable urgency to the impetus for educational reform, given the ominous appeal such movements were thought to have for younger, unemployed people. Cost issues held little weight with Russell: 'Can we not afford it? Dare we go on year after year spending hundreds of thousands of dollars in training thousands of boys and girls in our schools, only to have them go out to be misfits or dependants?'[34] Think only, she urged, of the considerable costs already accruing to governments and society in general. The costs of a well-financed but enlightened educational policy, including vocational guidance, paled when measured against the 'tremendous amounts we have to spend now in providing for those on relief and in reformatories, prisons and mental hospitals, to say nothing of the vast waste due to labour "turn-over" and the inefficiency of workers who are unsuited to their tasks.' Such claims were a radical departure from those of the testing movement in the United States. They would also transform personnel assessment procedures in the CWAC.

Modernizing War through the Psyche-Sciences

During the Second World War, the professional disciplines of psychology and psychiatry were enlisted to modernize the work of personnel selection and placement in the military. 'The psychiatrist at war' became a highly visible figure, signifying the truly modern army. At the same time as psychiatry and psychology were seen to be benefiting industry, science was contributing substantially to military success as well. Everyone knew that the German army had made extensive use of psychologists and psychiatrists in order to reach its current strength. Military and therefore national superiority was based not so much on size as on the 'quality of human material' that could be drawn out of the broader population. In 1942, the *Washington Post* published an article about the Mental Hygiene Unit of the U.S. Army to publicize the importance of mental hygiene and the tremendous contribution of the psyche-sciences to the war effort in the United States. The Mental Hygiene Unit deployed psyche-techniques for assessment and treatment; but its main purpose, according to the news story, was preventive – to weed out those alleged to be mentally unfit for military service through regular use of aptitude and intelligence testing by psychologists and intensive interviewing and examination by psychiatrists. These practices were found to have increased efficiency and returned considerable financial dividends. Such techniques permitted much closer examination and more accurate diagnoses of those who, in the First World War, might have slipped through the net and into that vague category of doubtful masculinity 'mama's boy,' or that expansive and infinitely more challenging category 'outright psychopathic case.'

The critical distinction between the First World War and now was that so much of earlier psychiatric science had approached problems encountered in the military as 'shell shock' – a misnomer that attributed all cases of maladjustment to an organic condition, thus overlooking the 'mental side' entirely. This error was corrected by the Mental Hygiene Unit as science moved to occupy the interior of the individual, assessing social problems as a manifestation of maladjusted psyches, disordered personality, and defective character. Examples found noteworthy enough to recount to the press included 20 per cent 'drunk,' 20 per cent 'maladjusted,' 13 per cent 'worried about families,' and 10 per cent 'involved with a girl.' The article portrayed the clinic as an integral part of the military experience, having gained acceptance among enlisted personnel: 'A large number of the soldiers, nearly a fourth of all those seen at the mental hygiene unit, have requested help. This is significant, for it shows that the men do not look upon the clinic as an outfit that is searching for "nuts."[35] The larger issue, however, concerned the problems enlisted personnel were seen to bring with them into the modern army. The high rejection and discharge rates experienced in both Canada and the United States – although the *Post* article looked only at the United States – could be attributed not to the experience of military service but to lifestyle and problems of maladjustment that had occurred long before enlistment. Inadequacies of character, 'defects in adaptation,' or a questionable lifestyle might well escape notice in civilian life but certainly could not withstand the 'iron mould of discipline' that was the military norm.

The Canadian armed services benefited from the growing influence of these expanding disciplines. In fact, by this time, the military apparatus included a number of prominent academic experts who constituted the current leadership of the National Committee for Mental Hygiene (Canada). All recruitment fell under the jurisdiction of the Directorate of Personnel Selection within the Department of National Defence. Its director, Col. William Line, was a member of the NCMH and an associate professor of psychology at the University of Toronto. The list included Dr J.D.M. (Jack) Griffin, associate medical director, NCMH, who became consulting psychiatrist with the Royal Canadian Army Medical Corps; and Dr S.R. Laycock, professor of educational psychology, College of Education, University of Saskatchewan, now appointed director general of rehabilitation for the Department of Veterans' Affairs (DVA). As strong proponents of the mental hygiene agenda, these practitioners were convinced that the expansion of psychiatry and psychology within public policy and social planning would prove a boon to society, if not all humankind.

Vocational counselling provided a crucial conduit through which the mental hygiene program could merge with the liberal education project to promote good citizenship and social order, and to prevent mental illness, the source of social malaise. Much of Russell's pre-war work reflected the policy agenda of the NCMH, whose goal was to have a national standard of mental health accepted as a matter of national public policy, indispensable to social modernization and progress, the twin objectives of liberal industrial democracy. NCMH associates also dreamed of the day that citizens would embrace the pursuit of mental hygiene as desirable, which meant understanding social maladjustment as a 'normal' condition to be corrected, not feared. The merging of mental hygiene and education was most certainly the heartfelt desire of Dr Clarence Hincks, director of the NCMH, a vision he shared with readers in the foreword to a 1940 publication of the American Psychological Association, *Mental Hygiene: A Manual for Teachers*, written by his NCMH colleagues Griffin, Laycock, and Line. Mental hygiene discourse organized the category of intelligence as a key vector into personality. According to Griffin, Laycock, and Line, intelligence lay at the root of all manner of problems of the social: criminality, unemployment, delinquency, poverty. Delinquency was characterized as the product of poor guidance and inadequate guardianship, not the product of 'a criminally perverted moral sense.'[36] Griffin and his colleagues specifically targeted working-class parents, who were seen to be shunning the vocational training for which their children were allegedly best suited. A healthy attitude, in particular towards work, could not be maintained, let alone developed, unless a person felt satisfaction at his or her personal achievements. As a discursive category, 'intelligence' was constituted as a new site of intervention by these experts, a key site of regulation. Similarly, educational psyche-experts insisted that their definitions of 'intelligence' were not the dismal hereditarian-based theories of their predecessors. The mental testing promoted by NCMH associates was pure science: objective, rational, dispassionate, and above all true. Griffin, Laycock, and Line argued that general intellectual growth was predictable, peaking between the ages of fourteen and sixteen, at which time development ceased. Intellectual calibre was distributed fairly consistently across the population, tracing a regular pattern of distribution showing very few people at either end of the curve – that is, of either very high or very low intelligence. Diagnostic procedures such as tests of ability, intelligence, and aptitude would, the authors confidently asserted, generate not a 'mass of unrelated data' but a 'unified picture of a living person.'[37] Cumulatively, these measures charted an entire population, national and institutional.

Notwithstanding these claims, racial typologies were clearly evident in the teachers' guide. The words 'primitive' and 'emotion' in association with religion frequently denoted race. And yet 'race' was nowhere identified in the manual's case studies intended to guide teachers who might be confronted by racially motivated conflict. Instead, the authors implicated difference-as-deviance as a problem of the individual, one that the individual could surmount given the right intervention of expertise. Teachers were advised to address racial discrimination through individual psychology, thus reducing to the level of individual behaviour, belief, and attitude systemic and material manifestations of race/ethnicity.

Griffin and his co-authors also approached class as a source of personality maladjustment and disintegration of the home. They asserted that maladjustment was frequently the product of those 'qualities of mind that produce poverty.' Working-class parents were singled out as misguided guardians, prone to dispensing inappropriate advice to their children, guided by their 'pathetic belief in the efficacy of the formal high-school course.' Such parental insistence led children to pursue an education for which they were ill-equipped. Compulsory education, specifically the tendency for children to remain in school longer, exacerbated this trend, in the mistaken view that matriculation was 'the only gateway to business opportunities.' Griffin rounded out the critique by concluding that such parents would provide better guidance were they to cease over-reaching their lesser station and suppress such inappropriate aspirations. 'Sometimes,' he observed, 'in forcing a high-school education upon their children, they are really compensating for their long-since-thwarted ambitions for an education themselves.'[38]

Delinquency and mental disease were seen to be correlates of what the authors dubbed 'disorganized' sections of society, 'slums and areas of deterioration.' These experts did not want to be trapped in a fallacy of their own design, however: they had already pointed out that intelligence was normally distributed across the whole population. How, if that were the case, could all residents of such districts record a uniformly low IQ? Ever agile and in a manner reminiscent of Sandiford, Griffin and his colleagues contended that culture and social conditions were also determinants of intelligence in the 'broadest sense.' The example they provided introduced gender into the equation, and sexuality along with it. After providing an account of a young man embarrassed by the manner of dress, speech, and 'deportment' of his 'uncultured' parents, the authors turned to the tale of how such maladjustments were manifested in young women and girls: 'One young lady, as a direct result of such influences, transferred her filial embarrassment into an aversion toward motherhood, and so clouded an otherwise lively and generous life.'[39]

But this was not a call for the rigid application of mental testing solely in order to fit the child for his or her most appropriate vocation within industry. The authors were scathing in their criticism of this narrow application of vocational guidance, focused as it was solely on bending the public education system to meet the needs and interests of the 'industrialist.' Where education was conceived of narrowly as training for 'life after school, giving the pupil the right skills so that he may fit into a workaday world and make a living,' the results were only too apparent in individualism and extreme 'freedom of individual action.' Such a system produced competition, serving the brightest while neglecting all others. Instead Griffin, Laycock, and Line advanced their view of the school as a vital social institution linked to home and community as well as industry and church. Its role was to foster a 'sound mental outlook' in the child, to facilitate healthy adjustment within the community, and to encourage participation in 'social progress' and 'good citizenship.' The school as a social institution was a 'character-building agency' responsible for fostering human psychological development and adjustment, working alongside other social institutions including the family. In this way, leading proponents of vocational testing and guidance sought to constitute normative psychological standards for citizenship as a matter of sound public policy.

In Line and Griffin, Olive Ruth Russell found like-minded allies. Indeed, with Line at the helm of DND's Director of Personnel Selection, both would confidently set about to modernize the military recruitment process according to the insights of modern educational psychology. Russell's work extended well beyond the administration of mass tests to the hundreds of women presenting themselves for military service. She saw an opportunity to reform internal military procedures as well. Both Line and Russell were institution builders and, as such, would rewrite the policy book on personnel administration. Like so many of her colleagues in the discipline, Russell had an opportunity to apply innovative and increasingly powerful tools both during the Second World War and through the postwar program of veterans' rehabilitation and reconstruction for peacetime. I now turn to a closer consideration of her work at the Directorate of Personnel Selection in DND, assigned to work with the CWAC.

Army examiners administered the 'M' test to appraise the psychological calibre of enlistees. According to the departmental policy guide, the personnel selection process was designed to assess the 'total personality of the individual soldier – his abilities, capacities, and skills, his desires and worries, his attitudes and interests, his emotional stability and his social habits.'[40] The purpose of the M test, and one of the main tasks of the directorate, was to examine all recruits for any signs of susceptibility to 'battle exhaustion,' or what had in the First World War been labelled 'shell shock.'[41] The examination consisted of a series of tests designed to gauge everything from mechanical aptitude to vocabulary, arithmetical reasoning – then considered a proxy for 'intelligence' – and spatial reasoning. The results were compiled into a single score based on the linear-scale measure known as the M score. Whatever sophisticated methodology might have informed the overall design of the examination, the M score was customarily understood to denote intelligence and, therefore, learning capacity. Scores were ranked in a hierarchy of human capacity, from the lowest level of private through to the top tier – officer material.[42] The predictive capacity of the M score followed military personnel throughout their career, dictating everything from future placement and promotion right through to postwar civilian opportunities.

'Every soldier,' according to the policy handout that was required reading for all army examiners, 'has a different type of personality and an individualized approach is absolutely necessary for a true and useful size-up.' What other factors had to be taken into account? The handbook described characterizing signs to watch for, in the certain knowledge that intelligence alone was an insufficient guide. In particular, examiners were to be on the lookout for signs of 'language handicap,' 'illiteracy,' and illness.[43] Language and literacy were important ways of gauging individual capacity and efficiency, markers of potential individual and social productivity. As would become evident, a different social index from that used with men came into play when assessing women: appropriate standards of femininity. The women's services were under close watch, and therefore carefully guarded the moral disposition of their charges. As a careful reading of Dr Russell's field notes suggests, the personnel assessment examination was about more than measuring intelligence and aptitude. The M score could not begin to probe into what mattered most in the case of women seeking to enlist with the CWAC – 'personality.' Appraisals of intelligence were deemed incapable of penetrating through to the core of the individual to reveal the personality of the inner self – the interior of the subject. Personality – a dynamic quality not so easily captured by the unidimensional score generated by the M test – was what mattered most. And so, leisure and work activity, domesticity, and familial status were scrutinized for what they might reveal of inappropriate activities concerning dance halls, theft, alcohol consumption, and 'dependency.' As familiar signposts on the terrain of moral regulatory discourse, leisure, sexuality, work, and family habits were meticulously probed for signs of personal and social maladjustment.

'If She Was a Problem in Civilian Life': Recruiting for the Canadian Women's Army Corps

Any accurate and complete assessment of the hundreds of hopeful young women who queued up at CWAC recruiting tents had to take account of home, family, school, and community, the full range of environment and experience encountered by Canada's eager young women. Measures of intelligence alone were not sufficient, in Russell's view. She actively extended the range and scope of her investigations to scrutinize all dimensions of the social and emotional lives of the women appearing before her. Russell drew on the findings of practitioners at the British National Institute of Industrial Psychology (NIIP) who, unlike their counterparts in the United States, approached the full range of human capacities as quantifiable and categorical elements that were not amenable to reduction to a unitary linear-scale statistical measure. In her review of the Birmingham experiment conducted by Dr Myers of the NIIP through the London Advisory Council for Juvenile Employment between 1925 and 1929, Russell noted that data were generated across a variety of categories: home and physical conditions; 'mental conditions as revealed by intelligence tests and tests of special abilities'; assessment of interests, temperament, and character, 'including general appearance, manners and social poise'; and finally, educational achievement.[44]

These categorical knowledges, combining as they did the techniques of interviewing and mental testing to constitute a complete 'case study' of the individual, would closely inform the approach taken by Russell in her work for the Directorate of Personnel Selection. U.S. practitioners were roundly criticized for the practice of compiling results from series of disparate tests to generate standardized intelligence scores, which leading British psychologist Charles Edward Spearman had earlier dismissed as 'the acme of meaninglessness.'[45] The point, after all, was to discern correlations among various human capacities and, in aggregate, to establish the significance of any factors thought to underlie those correlations. When these two opposing techniques met in the context of mass army examinations during the war, Russell went to great lengths to argue that no single measure could accurately reveal, let alone diagnose, the subject for psychological maladjustments in all of their variety.

The Canadian Women's Army Corps was the most accessible of the women's services, since the educational requirements were the least stringent of those for the three military services open to women. Russell devoted a considerable proportion of her monthly reports to describing women who were rejected from the CWAC. Her narratives detailed the standards that would constitute the 'undesirable' female recruit. M score, the military recruiting standard, was not enough. Education, occupation, and the narrative case study constructed the prognosis and, therefore, confirmed the finding. Every recruit examination became an inquiry into the social, and every woman potentially an embodiment of all that was held to threaten the social order. So-called illegitimate pregnancy, venereal disease, poverty, drinking, dancing, and sex topped Russell's list of social and individual pathologies.

In one such case, Russell interviewed a woman whose education had reached grade ten. She had taken the military IQ test and her subsequent M score was high. But she had worked as a domestic, an occupation considered unskilled. Here was the evidence psychological experts would produce repeatedly: IQ quotients on their own were not enough to reveal underlying character. Russell described the former domestic worker as a 'little tramp' and a 'superb liar.' She was most suspect for having collected money – a total of $10 – from her mates before leaving her station without authorization. As it happened, several women, like this one, were described as having histories of 'continuous incorrigibility.' One such case was described as a 'possible pregnancy' who 'would probably be quite incorrigible.'[46] Another working-class woman, whose education had ended at the eighth grade, supplemented with attendance at 'special vocational school,' was diagnosed as undesirable. To Russell, the woman's lack of secure employment and housing indicated a 'flawed moral character,' as did her poor grooming and 'nails bitten to the quick.'[47]

Many of these 'problem women' ought to have been identified as such in civilian life, Russell alleged, and for this reason every effort ought to be made to implement comprehensive measures designed to ensure that, upon discharge, they not be permitted to slip back anonymously into the civilian stream, there to continue to pose a threat to society. The women in question were thought to be of 'undesirable character,' described as 'social and moral misfits' whose deviant ways all too often went undetected until it was too late. They exhibited no evidence of 'neurosis' or 'psychosis': no condition, that is, that would be readily identifiable as *psychiatric* in either its origin or manifestation. In many of these 'case histories,' sexual agency came together with physical appearance to expose a socially maladjusted character. Intelligence offered no certain guide in cases such as these. An IQ test might be generally thought an important index of capacity, but studies of character and personality required more sophisticated and probing techniques to generate an accurate 'personality' assessment.

Screening for the CWAC truly was screening for society. It followed that corrective steps taken within the CWAC could just as readily benefit civilian society. If a recruit constituted a problem – real or potential – in the armed service, Russell claimed, then surely she must have been a 'problem' in civilian life? Examinations of women drew on the infinitely elastic measures of social maladjustment and 'emotional instability,' categories invested with considerable diagnostic and proscriptive powers. A comprehensive screening policy extended into the recruit's civilian life history, compiling a documentary record of the subject. The longitudinal case history reconstituted the subject as a 'problem case.' A recruit's military file became a permanent public record – an official identity – that might well accompany her beyond discharge and into her 'private' life as a citizen. Work of this kind added a profound layer of regulatory intervention into the personal lives of women caught within its ambit, since such a 'case history' could easily condition access to public assistance, triggering greater scrutiny and regulation through state and community social welfare agencies.

Like so many of her contemporaries, Russell had become frustrated by the waste and wreckage of the 1930s, the crisis of unemployment, homelessness, and ensuing political instability. Careful social planning meant educated supervision by state and civil society. Now, total war presented an opportunity to demonstrate the administrative promise of educational psychology. If applied in the right measure of social policy, psychology extended the scope of government, of social agency, and of educational practices in the resolution of real social problems. Whereas the American testing movement claimed scientific authenticity through objective and efficient methods of mass testing, Russell argued instead that the objective of the psychologist was to obtain 'a more intimate knowledge' of the subject, an exercise in which the subject's participation was actively elicited. It is noteworthy that even Binet and Simon had drawn attention to this most crucial aspect of the exercise, commenting that 'in its last analysis, an examination of this kind is based upon the goodwill of the subject.'[48] As Russell advised, 'If Mary Jane does not behave well, the question for the teacher or the parent is not, "How shall I punish her?" but "Why does she not behave well, and how shall I help her to make adjustments that will cause her to want to be a co-operative citizen contributing her best?"'[49] 'Maladjustment' was more than a simple condition of deviance or defiance. Its origins were many, as varied as human personality.

Drawing on the research of her former supervisor at Columbia Teachers' College, Dr Esther Lloyd-Jones, Russell examined maladjustment in CWAC enlistees according to four distinct categories. 'Infants' were characterized as those who had 'never grown up.' 'Timid souls' were those who exhibited shyness and fear, who tried to escape the challenges of daily life in daydreams or alcohol, insanity or suicide. 'Frozen people' were paralysed by prejudice, convention, fear, and conflict, particularly in matters of 'religion' or 'sex,' driven to mental illness by their inability to resolve conflicting beliefs. Finally there was the 'fighter,' who was not necessarily to be deplored since such a type could be either an 'obnoxious and pathetic member of society' or, if her energy were turned to causes of social justice, 'a great social benefactor.' A good practitioner, meaning one who understood the forms maladjustment might take, could be of tremendous service to society in the prevention and treatment of mental ill health. 'It is now a well established fact,' Russell asserted, 'that most delinquency and crime and mental illness too could be prevented if only the normal, physical and psychological needs of the individual were understood and provided for early enough.'[50] Parental education would help to instil a newly enlightened regime of discipline. The regulated development of a child's personality was the most effective way of eliciting behaviour that conformed to broader societal aspirations. All agencies and institutions involved in the central task of educating children – or, for that matter, guiding workers – would benefit from a regular program of vocational guidance. After all, the standards of citizenship and democracy could be guaranteed only when girls and boys, women and men *wanted* to comply. Regulation from above might elicit outward obedience and compliance, but what mattered more was internalized regulation – through the cultivation of the self, whose aspirations, desires, and interests became consonant with those of the surrounding society.[51]

In 1942, the CWAC launched a general campaign of mass recruiting in an all-out effort to encourage women to sign up, thus making as many men available as possible for service in the fighting forces. The CWAC was accessible to women who did not have trades training, high school, or vocational education. It was the only one of the three services open to working-class women, promising good wages, training, and a measure of security, not to mention work experience in a range of occupations unavailable in civilian life. Still, hopeful applicants and successful recruits would find themselves the subject of intense scrutiny and investigation of their personal lives, experience, 'suitability,' and 'emotional stability,' both in their former civilian lives and, if they were accepted, in their military lives as well. As Russell's work indicates, the categories of 'suitability,' 'incorrigibility,' and a variety of related terms were deployed to single out as 'undesirable' women whose social locations were already marginalized through relations of class, gender, nationality, race, and ethnicity. Categories such as these were laden with conceptions about appropriately feminine behaviour, particularly among women who worked for pay. A young woman who rose up in defiance of the rigid standards of femininity and efficiency, who challenged parental authority, or who resisted an increasingly stringent code of moral and sexual respectability, might easily find herself labelled 'incorrigible.' In combination with legal misdemeanours, such a finding might be accompanied by a sentence of incarceration.[52] Russell's determined investigation of women applying to the CWAC was sparked in part by the 'whispering campaign' against women in the military. Armies were exclusively masculine preserves, certainly no place for women.[53] At the same time, the war effort was everybody's concern. The armed services turned to the women of Canada to fill thousands of vacancies in the work of transporting, feeding, and cleaning up after troops and equipment. As the women's services stepped up recruiting efforts in 1942, the whisper campaign intensified in corresponding measure. The women's services were anxious to project an image of feminine respectability, both to confound the critics, who would have been happy to rid the military of all women, and to ensure that detractors did not succeed in scaring away potential recruits. It was not long, therefore, before an all-out effort was underway to clean up the women's services, rooting out any woman deemed to be of 'undesirable character.' Predictably, sexuality soon became the central focus of the campaign. 'Illegitimate' pregnancy and/or venereal infection were identified as leading indicators of sexual immorality. So was 'incorrigibility.' By the 1940s, out-of-wedlock pregnancies among women were diagnosed as evidence of psychiatric maladjustment. In the United States, these narratives played out along race and class lines: black illegitimacy was cast as cultural pathology, white illegitimacy as individual pathology.[54]

Many of the women applying to join CWAC had grown up through the Depression. Because the corps had the least stringent entrance requirements, it seemed a good prospect for working-class women attracted by the promise of a job with decent wages and working conditions. But here Russell was caught in a double bind. On the one hand, she drew on the trope of patriotism and nationalism and welcomed women who were eager to serve their country and the British Commonwealth, while deploring the army's failure to draw on the considerable commitment and skill of CWAC women. On the other hand, she invoked a stringent moral standard that found signs of deviance in any behaviour or condition in life that did not conform to a rigid measure of appropriate sexuality, class, race, ethnicity, and culture.

The following entries illustrate the narratives Russell constructed in her regular reports. The narrative was itself a standard of psychological analysis, in which gender conformity was assessed against a series of social categories. The numerical entry is the M score. Social and sexual misdemeanours were juxtaposed with the intelligence score to illustrate the 'folly' of relying on test scores. After all, for every ten applicants subsequently rejected, six achieved an M score higher than 100.[55]

One case concerned a twenty-nine-year-old woman who had worked as a 'packer' in industry. Her low score of 89 suggested a borderline intelligence. That there was a five-year-old child in tow suggested loose morality, or worse. From Russell's case notes we find that this potential recruit appeared 'wearing fox furs,' projecting 'a general air of superiority.' More to the point, her personality exhibited a decidedly uncooperative attitude, a moral failing displayed by the fact that she was 'quite unwilling to do any work for which she might have been qualified.' That she 'was not truthful' sealed her fate.[56] Such women would find no place in Russell's CWAC. Wearing 'fox furs' or any other symbol of middle- or upper-class respectability challenged the standard of appropriate apparel for an Irish working-class woman. Nor was she compliant. Like many women seeking entry to the CWAC, she insisted on something more than the general domestic labours to which working-class women were assigned. This woman was, in the end, rejected as 'untruthful' and therefore unsuitable to the Women's Army Corps. Similarly, a young woman from Windsor was assessed on the basis of her class background. She had worked at 'various jobs,' a common enough circumstance; however, the nineteen-year-old woman 'seemed unreliable,' having provided 'a confused account of herself.' Her husband was in jail, although no more is known about his circumstances. In another case, an eighteen-year-old woman's M-score was well within the acceptable range, 134. She had recently come from the United States and had a clear idea about what she wanted to do in the women's services. She, too, 'seemed unreliable' and was suspected of 'trying to conceal some bad record.' Her only ambition was to drive trucks, but at a height of five feet, one inch, she was disqualified from such work. Refusal to accept any other

job assignment would mark her as undesirable, unfeminine, and potentially disruptive.[57]

In the majority of cases reviewed, nationality and ethnicity were not
identified. When they were, they were clearly a factor, evidence enlisted
to support a diagnosis of 'undesirability.' For example, in the following
case entry, Russell's narrative merged with taken-for-granted character-
izations of francophone women as less advanced – culturally bound by a
parochial religious conservatism. The fact that the woman had applied
and was conversing – and being tested – in a second language was
obscured. Instead, Russell described her in psyche-based terms: for
example, using the term 'shyness,' code for a 'personality' that was not
forthcoming – a sign of 'maladjustment.' In this woman's case, job
stability was seen as an indication of passivity, of a femininity that did not
meet CWAC standards of efficiency and productivity. Thus, the 'shy little
French-Canadian who has never done any work but sit as a packer ...
seemed to have nothing to condemn but little to contribute to CWAC.'[58]

When Russell examined a group of young women from Newfoundland, ethnicity and class worked through sexuality to position the young
women as potentially acceptable, but only with close supervision and
guidance. Their rural cultural origin, according to Russell, made them a
more likely prospect than their urban sisters of industrialized Ontario.

> I believe the Newfoundland girls will provide much good material if prop-
> erly handled. There are many in the group who are very lacking in initiative
> and will be easily led, but they respond to good influences as readily as to
> bad, and will likely serve well if wisely guided. There are fewer of the 'little
> flapper' or 'hard boiled' types who are unwilling to do the tasks for which
> they are qualified, than in Ontario centres where I have worked.[59]

In her personal correspondence, Russell wrote more openly about some
of the young women she found most 'undesirable.'[60] One such case
concerned a Native woman, considered 'unsuitable material' for the
women's services. This case stood out in Russell's mind, suggesting what
was plainly wrong with mass recruiting methods: 'I think the girl is an
Indian – appearance given which is not surprising [since she] has had
dirty jobs etc. [I] don't know what I'll do if she finally passes medical
board.'[61]

Russell drew on the classic convention of psyche-based examination:
the case study. Her reports were a narrative about femininity threatened
by potential deviance, always lurking just beneath the surface. Failure to

detect and root out any such problem cases could imperil the reputation the CWAC, indeed all women, had managed to build through wartime service. Like her predecessors, U.S. psychologist Lewis Terman and University of Toronto psychologist Peter Sandiford, Russell used intelligence testing and now the more sophisticated methods of personnel selection to consolidate a racial and class-based typology of intelligence, in this case working through gender and sexuality, in her investigations of 'problem cases.' Any indication of excessive interest in clothing or appearance suggested 'loose' standards and immorality. Sexuality was clearly the target, in particular when those scoring 'border-line' or 'low average intelligence,' were deceptively 'well groomed and smart in their appearance.' For these, Russell advised that 'they should be viewed even more critically than those with the same low "M" score who may have a less attractive appearance but seem good steady workers.' Her narrative reports targeted all that was seen to be wrong with modern young womanhood – the litany of pregnancy, dancing, sex, and drinking. The war only accentuated social problems that had existed well before the Allies finally stood up to the Nazi challenge. Women were vulnerable to the lure of incipient consumerism, indifferent to personal development, and, above all, selfish in their disregard of truth and personal responsibility. Russell held that the CWAC recruiting drive was attracting 'undesirable' women, anxious to escape 'the ordinary duties of living or the consequences of some misdeeds' under the shelter of the services. It was not uncommon for the 'professional thief and prostitute' to appear at army recruiting stations.[62] There would be no room in Canada's female army for the 'low grade flapper type.'[63] The women's services were no place for those seeking to avoid responsibilities in civilian life. On the contrary, the military was an extension of personal responsibility, now elevated to a higher level of service to nation. In this way, the incidence of 'maladjustment' encountered among military recruits reflected in microcosm the much greater challenges confronting modern urban society.

Russell's application of her selection criteria was proactive and thorough. 'It seems important,' Russell recommended, 'that we screen out social and moral misfits who would not normally likely be sent to the Psychiatrist.'[64] Women who 'tend to be of questionable character' should as a matter of course be referred for psychiatric examination, especially where their M score was above 70 (of a possible 211) and/or there was no evidence of neurosis or psychosis. As it was, Russell regularly referred women scoring below 70 on the M test for psychiatric assessment as a provisional measure. She went even farther, to propose that the names of women applying to the CWAC be cleared first by the Social Service Index (SSI) in their city of residence. Under this proposal, all CWAC applications would be cross-referenced against the records of relief and community agencies, local police, and 'mental' hospitals. This 'new experiment,' was soon underway, prompting Russell to report that she was 'delighted that any plans for follow up of the kind will apply to CWAC.'[65] A reference check with the Social Service Index would clearly establish whether any pattern of immorality, dependence, or – even worse – incorrigibility and criminal behaviour existed.

In January 1943, Mary Salter, Russell's superior officer, approved an informal inquiry with Toronto's clearing house of welfare agencies, the Social Service Index, 'about applicants considered to be of doubtful suitability for CWAC.' The plan was thought a good idea, but Salter cautioned that 'making the inquiries and making use of the information' would be governed by discretion.[66] In her investigations, Russell claimed that she had found many cases of women registered with the Toronto Social Service Index for relief or assistance from one of the many social service agencies in the city. Many women were identified as having a dependent child.[67] Russell recommended that a trained social worker be brought on staff to conduct a 'further enquiry and follow-up study.' The move, she explained, would more than pay for itself, since a routine check of police and mental hospital records would save the longer-term cost of having to deal with 'these problem people,' who would otherwise have been accepted into CWAC for training.[68] 'In view of the considerable number of seemingly unsuitable applicants with whom I had to deal, *but for whom there was no medical or psychiatric grounds for rejection,*' Russell explained, she approached staff who maintained the Social Service Index for assistance and follow-up investigation. 'Of the first 8 persons about whom I enquired I found 6 listed with the Index for one reason or another,' she reported. The inquiry turned up 'women who had dependent young children for whom they were responsible as well as some with a history of almost continuous incorrigibility.'[69] Social investigation of this sort confirmed Russell's suspicions: nearly 50 per cent of all women applying from Military District 2 (the Toronto area) were found to have registered for relief or other assistance at a social agency at some time prior to their attempted enlistment with the CWAC. Registering for relief was a sign of 'dependence,' even 'unreliability,' undesirable traits that constituted grounds for rejection. The investigation revealed a long list of misdemeanours. Some of the women had

court records, while others had dependent children born out of wed-
lock. Not surprisingly, records of incorrigibility were also uncovered, a
charge that proceeded under the Female Refuges Act. Finally, the names
of some applicants were registered 'merely because their families were
on relief.'[70] A potential recruit so listed underscored the suspicion that
she was unlikely moral material for the women's services. Appearing on
the SSI sent up a red flag, but should this automatically mean disqualification from the CWAC?

Department of National Defence officials were not so keen to proceed
with a program that would document the personal and intimate details
of the lives of potential recruits, at least not as official policy. The
'stigma' associated with psychiatric assessment proved sufficient to convince DND that it was better not to have on file information considered
'too confidential, discreditable or libellous.' Discretion was the preferred approach, reliance on the ability of commanding officers to 'read
between the lines' with potentially troublesome or 'problem' personnel.
At the same time as Salter advised Russell to proceed with the Social
Service Index check, she also outlined her position on the proposal of
expanding the scope for psychiatric assessments. Salter had discussed
Russell's recommendation with Dr Jack Griffin, consulting psychiatrist
with the Royal Canadian Army Medical Corps (RCAMC) and an NCMH
member, who thought Russell's proposal a fine and sound one. He
insisted that, 'in this day and age,' surely it ought not to be considered a
'disgrace' that a 'girl' had a psychiatric referral on her record.'[71] Griffin's
opinion notwithstanding, Salter reiterated her earlier position, explaining that DND did not want to commit itself in any way on the matter, and
most certainly not when it came to discharging recruits found to have
failed to meet a loosely defined psychological bar. 'If she doesn't get into
difficulties it does no good to have a report following her around which
may discredit her, despite her good behaviour,' Salter advised.[72] If trouble
were looming, surely the specifics of each individual case would generate
the necessary grounds for punitive action, if any were warranted?

But this was not entirely satisfactory. So many applicants were intro-
ducing problems from civilian life into the CWAC and, confidentiality
notwithstanding, the corps had to equip its personnel selection officers
with the means to document and act on the basis of their scientific
diagnoses. What was the point of all these endless examinations and case
interviews, after all, if not to act on sound insights generated by the
expertise of the army examiner and her staff? If written regulations were
one matter, practices associated with recruiting examinations were an-

other. Certainly, issuing 'dishonourable' discharges to already-enlisted personnel would be a sticky business, involving possible disentitlement to military rehabilitation benefits, credits, and pensions. The CWAC and its members were under intense scrutiny, and so public attention of this sort was to be avoided at all costs.[73] Canada's women were now in uniform as part of the fighting services of the Dominion. But it was precisely because of the sensitivity associated with the newly established status of the women's services that Russell deemed it necessary to press ahead. She argued specifically for 'a higher standard' for CWAC than for men 'in screening out unsuitable personnel' – in particular, to address the tendency of army psychiatrists to accept into the corps women whom the CWAC's own officers felt should have been rejected.[74] Difficult though the task might be, rejection of unsuitable applicants and the discharge of 'problem personnel' were deemed absolutely crucial to securing and maintaining the 'prestige of the Corps and the happiness of its members,' Russell insisted. This was a position with which many officers and others, including Mary Salter, agreed. The majority of CWAC company commanders would likely share the position that far too many 'potential problem cases' had been permitted to join the corps. The presence of so many 'undesirables' would only hinder diligent efforts to attract the very best of Canadian womanhood. The tragedy, mused Salter, with perhaps a note of commiseration for Russell's efforts to institute a more rigorous screening policy, was that this small percentage of troublesome cases might have been 'screened out without great difficulty.'[75] For now, however, the corps adopted the more cautious approach. According to the Directorate of Personnel Selection, the question of the 'rejection of unsuitable material' was dubbed a 'rather ticklish matter,' which the director – Col. William Line – wanted to enact 'with proper authority.'[76] Staff would await further instructions before taking any decisive action. In other words, the armed services would not commit to an explicit statement of policy that clearly instituted a differential policy for entrance and examination standards with the intent of searching out and discharging vaguely defined 'unsuitable material' – at least not as official written policy. Procedure in this area was seen to be based on administrative practice and not on verifiable, clearly articulated regulatory guidelines.

In December 1943, Russell conducted a survey of all CWAC personnel stationed at Halifax, a total of some 700 women, the results of which were very favourably received by Line and CWAC commanding officers.

The study built on the success of the Toronto investigation, confirming 'the desirability of obtaining specific information about the reliability of persons whom [army examiners] consider doubtful.'[77] The survey stood out from the rest of Russell's work as a reassessment of already placed personnel. Where her earlier work had concentrated on initial screening of CWAC applicants, the Halifax survey was an internal evaluation of army examination techniques, a test of the veracity of mass testing. The standard of assessment was now the 'happiness' of personnel, as demonstrated by their capacity to find personal fulfilment and satisfaction in their assigned work. Where Russell found dissonance and discord, such negative results were interpreted to mean a mismatching of occupation and test score results: individuals had been placed in occupations that were either too challenging, and therefore beyond personal capacities and aptitude, or not challenging enough. In focusing on such qualities as satisfaction, happiness, and individual interest, Russell opened up the category of personality and character – of subjectivity – while offering a means of systematic assessment and placement through a rigorous review of occupational requirements matched to a standardized and objective scale of human capacity and at the same time recalibrating employability on the basis of individual psychological attributes. This approach transformed occupational problems and work-related discord through a readily transferable administrative technique. 'Problem cases' were even further marginalized within the population of tested subjects: they had been problems in their civilian lives and were most definitely out of place within the military population. Line heartily endorsed this latest instalment in Russell's work. The Halifax survey report was circulated at the directorate, where it was read with considerable interest. 'It represents a very complete and thorough study, and should assist immeasurably in effecting more suitable placements,' he wrote. Russell's research initiatives consolidated her position as a key policy adviser whose expert knowledge would contribute substantially to DVA personnel assessment, guidance, and placement policies. The Halifax survey generated concrete empirical evidence that individual behaviour and work performance were not only linked but could be systematically assessed through the predictive and diagnostic capacity of testing and interviewing. Russell's recommendations for systematic assessment and regular follow-up to ensure that personnel assignments were conducted according to test-score results and case-study interviewing would become regular procedure at the directorate. These techniques were equally applicable in the reallocation of existing personnel, an area of expertise that informed the organizing principles of rehabilitation programming that would guide DVA during the challenges of demobilization.

Conclusion

Russell's advocacy work as an educational psychologist had a long lineage, informed by a growing disillusionment with a system of government and economy that had withstood the First World War only to plunge headlong into economic chaos and fascism – and now, total war. Faith in democracy was sorely tested by the rise of totalitarianism on the one hand and reckless individualism on the other. Like many of her contemporaries, Russell believed passionately that states had an obligation first to secure and then to safeguard the rights and responsibilities of individual citizens through enlightened social planning that spanned a broad spectrum of social institutions including community, family, workplace, and school. Individual choice was a vital component of progressive policy; however, uninformed individuals required expert guidance so that they too could be brought to understand and accept the responsibility that necessarily accompanied the condition of free choice. This was the essence of educational guidance, according to Russell. Responsible citizenship was central to a healthy democracy, and it followed that the cultivation of self-governing citizens ought to become a more prominent focus of social policy. Russell traced the lineage of individual rights as articulated within the broader cultural and political totality through the emerging educational program of the state, following a trajectory that extended in a seemingly linear descent from Plato's *Republic* through to Rousseau's *Emile*. There had been a time to defend the inherent promise of the new international order signified by the League of Nations, a promise that was challenged by the rise of totalitarian movements, in particular by the fascist states of Germany, Italy, and Spain. Her now renewed hopes looked to a revitalization of educational policy, translated into a blueprint for national citizenship in which all might share equally in the club of Western democracies, as part of an international movement for liberal democracy.

The Second World War offered a staging ground upon which such ideas might be tested. The war held out tremendous opportunities to the women of Canada, women like Russell, who might finally assume a position that mattered by answering the call to national service and making a commitment to professionalism in the service of country. However, CWAC officials were irked by young women of independent lifestyle and habit. 'Excessive individualism' was the real problem, a faddish pursuit of pleasure that led to the failure of so many young women to observe their proper place within society. Russell took aim at the indulgent proclivity for dancing and drink, evidence of 'selfish' and irresponsible behaviour that threatened to undermine both the war effort and democratic society. Excess of any kind, as the sound social planner knew, gave rise to all manner of social problems. Comprehensive social planning was the true purpose of sound public policy. And that meant ensuring that no woman, once identified by CWAC as a 'problem case,' would be permitted to return to a civilian life of independent anonymity.

Personnel assessment was a major focus of work within the armed services, providing an excellent career opportunity for educational psychologists such as Olive Ruth Russell and William Line. No longer focused on the 'human tragedies' of unemployment and juvenile delinquency, the task was now to establish sound procedures for vocational counselling and personnel practice in the military. Russell's early career as student and then educator encompassed a crucial period in the development of educational psychology as a distinct discipline in Canada. Assessment and counselling techniques, embodied in the practice of vocational guidance, gained greater prominence through the interwar period, especially once these methods were refined for mass application in schooling. The discourse of individual mental and emotional capacity found broad application in the military setting. When applied to problems of recruitment, placement, and training, educational psychology opened up limitless possibilities for this specialized expertise. But psychologists also looked to the project of civil re-establishment and reconstruction as matter of individual and social rehabilitation, an exercise in citizenship formation that extended well beyond school to include work, household, and community. As the practice of personnel assessment in the services became regularized, its strategic significance for the postwar rehabilitation of enlisted personnel emerged more clearly. Russell hoped that personnel assessment, from its inception as a practice designed to 'screen out' unsuitable recruits, would become a key technique guiding the placement of ex-servicewomen and -servicemen in civilian employment in the postwar period.

chapter four

Preparing for the Peace: The Demobilization of Women Workers

In the spring of 1944, the staff of the National Selective Service Women's Division (NSSWD) coined a new phrase to capture the mood on the home front: 'war weariness.' Living quarters were cramped, factory shifts were long, and rationing measures meant that even the simplest pleasures were often unattainable or, if available 'under the counter,' expensive. But 'war weariness' captured only part of the mood. After all, women across Canada had carried much of this burden and could take stock of their efforts with pride. Whether taking the lead in clothing collection drives, promoting recycling and conservation drives to stockpile materials desperately needed in essential war industries, or organizing consumer leagues to lobby for federal inflationary controls, women across Canada had played a vital role in deciding the nation's future – and had done so with enthusiasm. The image of the 'postwar woman' captured this newly optimistic spirit. Women had proved they were up to the challenge and could now look forward to consolidating wartime gains in the spirit of equality and freedom of choice. Still, there was another refrain on the minds of women war workers – 'I want to get a postwar job.'

Planning now began in earnest for what many anticipated would be a rapid demobilization of the war economy. In preparation, NSSWD field staff, women's and community organizations, and media flooded NSS headquarters with requests for direction. What should employment officers tell women who said they wished to find a postwar job? Would all occupations be open to women? When would NSS controls be relaxed? Would the National Employment Service (NES) be able to deal with the hundreds of thousands of war workers who had answered the NSS call? The supervisor of the Winnipeg NSSWD complained that the employ-

ment figures provided by the Department of Labour were neither satisfactory nor accurate. How was she to advise women now being laid off as
war production contracts expired? If NSS staff were to do the job of
demobilization, it followed that a more accurate knowledge of the normal economy would be needed. How many women would work in a
regular economy functioning under normal peacetime conditions? Was
there even such a thing as a natural rate of female employment? Fraudena
Eaton understood that the issue of female employment was not a straightforward policy question but was instead a matter for the political staff in
the minister's office. She informed division supervisors to hold off until
the minister of labour made Ottawa's position clear. The minister would
soon be announcing Ottawa's employment projections in a statement to
Parliament at least a portion of which would speak to women's place in
the postwar economy. Until that occurred, it would be 'impossible' to
state definitively what might happen to this new army of working women.[1]
NSS would have nothing to say until Ottawa spoke.

There was ample reason for caution. Women's employment after the
war was becoming a matter of serious concern. Just how far was the
federal government prepared to go in recognizing postwar employment
for women? The issue finally erupted with the release of the final report
on the Post-War Problems of Women, produced by a subcommittee of
the General Advisory Committee on Reconstruction. Margaret Mc-
Williams, as chair of the subcommittee, issued a press release outlining
the report's key policy recommendations. Here was the news everybody
had been waiting for. McWilliams soon found herself at the centre of a
political tempest on the question of women's labour force participation.
The press corps quickly picked up on the report's estimate that 1.2
million women were active in the labour market. The news of McWilliams's
statement to the press sent Eaton, MacNamara, and senior Labour
bureaucrats in Ottawa into a panic. The figure McWilliams cited was
indeed an accurate estimate of women's labour force participation as of
30 November 1943. But issuing a public statement to that effect was the
last thing Ottawa wanted to do. As Allan Peebles, director of the Research and Statistics Branch at the Department of Labour, explained to
MacNamara, the department was ready to go with a count of active
women as of February 1944, by which time many production contracts
had already wound down. According to ministerial staff, if Ottawa acknowledged how many women had actually been working at the height
of the wartime production boom, expectations for postwar female employment would be inflated to an extraordinary degree.[2] But this was
only part of the problem. The more women the federal government

estimated as employed, the higher would be the estimate of women Ottawa would have to count as unemployed. Given the prospect of returning male veterans for whom the government would be responsible, a female unemployment problem was not an issue Labour officials wanted to deal with. Better to make the problem go away now, while there was still time. But how? Peebles advised substituting the new table with its lower employment estimates. Some 'critic' might still compare the old and the new, but this was a risk the department would have to take. 'We think now is the opportune time,' Peebles wrote to his superior. Waiting another six months to a year would only draw unwanted attention from an already critical press.[3]

It was left to Eaton to set matters straight with subcommittee chair McWilliams and to rein her in by suggesting that she avoid making any public statements about women's employment prospects. 'So much depends upon the attitude of the National Selective Service to these lesser problems,' Eaton explained, that it was better to wait until 'sound policy for the postwar' was well in hand. Sound policy meant drawing the line on just what proportion of the current female workforce would likely remain in paid employment and what responsibility, if any, the federal government would assume for women's postwar employment. Senior levels of government were debating the postwar employment situation through the powerful Economic Advisory Committee, the General Committee on Demobilization and Rehabilitation, and the Inter-Departmental Committee on Postwar Employment.

By the summer months of 1944, war production contracts with the federal government had all but ended, and manufacturers began retooling for the peace. Mass layoffs sent waves of war workers back through the plant gates, a scene that was provoking concern among NSSWD staff. Women were already on the lookout for more permanent postings, knowing that their wartime jobs would be short-lived. In response, NSS staff were directed to encourage women to stay in their jobs by appealing to their patriotic duty of service and sacrifice. 'Try to change the attitude of mind represented in the words: "I want to get a postwar job." Or "I am tired of making munitions,"' Eaton instructed. 'We need to remind ourselves and others that the war has yet to be won and completed. It is too early to express other ideas. Service and sacrifice are yet the key words.'[4] 'Looking for a postwar job' was not an activity women seemed inclined to leave to the end of the war. This was a tendency Stevenson and Kellogg had noted in their 1943 report, so much so that they devoted an entire section to the subject of 'Keeping Workers in Their Jobs.' What employment researchers characterized as excessive labour

turnover and government officials understood as the shortage of personnel in key, low-waged industries was also an expression of the need of
many women to secure postwar jobs that afforded decent wages and
working conditions, at least at rates and on terms that were a considerable improvement over what had been available during the years immediately preceding the war.

If higher women's employment levels were posing a problem, high
wages also sparked concern among both employers and policy planners,
who feared that wage competition worked to draw women away from
industries that paid lower wages. The labour shortage that opened up in
the traditionally 'female' occupations presented NSS with a vexing problem. For example, the Chrysler plant in Windsor paid a general starting
hourly wage of $0.83, rising to $0.93 after a short probationary period.
Would not such wage rates attract women from as far away as Toronto
and from other lower-waged industries? Should women be paid the same
starting rate as men? Chrysler requested a ruling on the matter from the
Regional War Labour Board for Ontario, suggesting that while the
company would be 'satisfied to carry out any ruling of the Ontario
Board,' were the board to rule that the same wage rates ought to be paid,
company officials felt quite strongly that such a measure would most
certainly draw female labour away from other industries and geographic
locations where it was also needed in order to sustain the war effort.[5]
Certainly, the hundreds of thousands of women who moved into the
formal waged economy were able to earn a significantly higher wage
than had been obtainable in the pre-war period.

One thing was clear – many women wanted to find a job, but not just
any job. No more domestic postings at meagre wages, in poor conditions, labouring under the watchful gaze of a nosy employer. The demand now was for a job that paid comparable wages. The NSSWD office
wasn't much help, as it turned out. Government employment officers
insisted on directing applicants to the menial jobs of laundry work,
household labour, or, for the better educated, low-paying clerical work.
Staff on the public payroll complained that it was next to impossible to
get women to take these jobs. As the summer months dragged on,
officials noted that many women would likely enjoy a brief vacation and
then trickle out of the labour force through marriage. Perhaps in this
way they might finally reconcile themselves to the current situation and
accept the jobs offered by NSS? The stubborn insistence continued,
however, and by September the Toronto office reported that hundreds
of vacancies in finance, insurance, and real estate had been rejected by
applicants who were holding out for 'higher priced opportunities.' Many

women would eventually turn to traditional service-sector employment in laundries and restaurants; but not if better pay and conditions might be available elsewhere. Mary Eadie, supervisor for the Toronto NSS Women's Division, had no illusions about the difficulties of the task ahead. Women's expectations had to be adjusted. The postwar period would not reward the years of wartime service and sacrifice. Nor would it see a return to pre-war economic conditions. What Eadie was sure of was that women workers would have to understand that there would be fewer jobs, at the very least at a considerably reduced wage scale and in occupations considered more suitable for women. This was a trying task, indeed. As Eadie confided to Fraudena Eaton, NSS staff and workers alike had to understand the futility of 'trying to place a woman in a new job at her present high wage scale.' Experience of repeated failure would likely get that point across.[6]

The demobilization plan NSSWD was to follow required that women return to their domestic stations. Officials hoped to restore the pre-war pattern of employment in predominantly female occupations.[7] The road ahead was going to be rocky, since the actions of women workers directly contradicted the government approach. Internal research studies had already been conducted by the NSSWD the previous year. For instance, a 1943 survey by the Toronto office canvassed job applicants across Ontario to find out what women's postwar aspirations were, and to see how closely these might match job opportunities in the postwar job market. The study was not looking at young, unmarried women, since among that group there was a well-established demographic pattern of a brief stint of paid employment after which women customarily married and withdrew from the labour force. Instead, the questionnaire canvassed married women over thirty-five years of age, all applying for work through NSS. Typically, 95 per cent were solely responsible for carrying on domestic work, while 85 per cent reported husbands at home – that is, not on active service. The picture painted by the Ontario study did not match the poster image of the Canadian woman war worker. The study portrayed a disturbing demographic pattern of married women whose husbands had not enlisted and who wanted and needed to work for pay. Three-quarters of the women interviewed indicated that they had no children in the household; only 10 per cent reported supporting two children, and 5 per cent had three or more children. Women were asked the question, 'What type of work have you done before?' The following distribution was reported: factory – 30 per cent, domestic – 27 per cent, office work – 14 per cent, laundry – 5 per cent, sales – 12 per cent, and 'not previously employed' – 12 per cent. Women were asked to indicate the areas of employment they sought work in. Again, one-third put down factory work as their first choice, followed by hospitality, retail, office, and clerical work. Surprisingly, only 9 per cent wanted a job in munitions work, suggesting that permanent employment was the priority. It would have come as no surprise that none of the survey respondents expressed any desire to secure a domestic posting.[8] The survey confirmed the distance between official perception and the intent of women workers. NSS officials speculated that women would be reluctant to report to government employment offices, fearing compulsory service. Overwhelmingly, 94 per cent indicated that they were quite happy to accept a job through NSS. When the survey examined women's motivation for seeking paid work, the results fell into a clear pattern. Where NSS promoted war work as patriotic service, survey respondents identified a very different set of priorities: 59 per cent of the married women in the Ontario survey said they needed to work to supplement the family income, while another 32 per cent suggested 'personal reasons' as their motivation.

NSSWD held to the government line and continued to promote the theme of self-sacrifice and service to country. Eaton faced a motivated press corps that was becoming increasingly interested in quizzing government officials about the 'postwar woman.' 'Bold indeed would be the person who attempted to predict with any certainty the place of women wartime workers in a peacetime world,' was her reply. Women had 'earned the right' to full recognition of their needs in any planning for postwar adjustment. Government would do its part to safeguard women's wartime gains, especially against those who hoped women would 'gracefully withdraw and yield their places to men.' 'The place of women in employment must be made secure and dignified with the door of advancement wide open,' Eaton declared, and the NSSWD would attempt to do just that. Canadians could look to a future in which negative freedoms – freedom from want, fear, poverty, and frustration – would be secured as general human rights. But general human rights should not be confused with equality rights, and rights for women had limits. For example, the training and accumulated experience of hundreds of thousands of women in war industries was a temporary phenomenon, limited to the needs of the war economy. 'They cling to the thought that they would like to continue in the industry for which they have been trained,' Eaton noted, but cautioned that none could predict whether or not this hope would be realized. Certainly training and opportunity should be made available to permit postwar employment for all who wanted it. As if to signal where those opportunities might lie, Eaton pointed to the 'natural professions' of health, social services, teaching, and welfare where women's 'organizing genius' had a real opportunity to shine. And then there was the domestic service to which thousands would return, 'provided wages and hours were reasonable and all social stigma removed.' Still, Eaton shared the growing perception that women had earned the right to work, and to work at equal pay. Speaking to the National Council of Women, she endorsed a platform of equal pay for equal work, looking to the trade union movement to lead the struggle: 'The greatest hope is that organized labour with thousands of new women members will lead the average citizen to accept a fair and liberal approach to the future employment of women.'[9] But what would the postwar economy look like for women? To be sure, a variety of occupations had opened up, prompted by the war and by demographic changes already underway. But there was only so much Ottawa could do: the federal government would not intervene. Its hands were tied, since control over labour market policy would be handed back to the provinces once the war was ended.

The 1943 Report on the Post-War Problems of Women

Middle-class feminist thought during this period acknowledged the right of every woman to work at whatever occupation she might choose, in comparable working conditions with men and with equal pay and 'opportunity for advancement.' Such rights, however, had to be balanced against the postwar challenges confronting the rest of society. Years of sacrifice were recognized, and women had clearly earned the right to full citizenship. Having 'played their full part as responsible citizens,' the women of Canada now 'expect to be treated consistently as such in the coming years.' Service to nation meant the sacrifice of sons, husbands, and fathers. It was more than time that women were accepted as 'full members of a free community.'[10] So began the 'Report on the Post-War Problems of Women.' Committee members endorsed a rights-based argument for the recognition of women's position within the paid labour market. It was an even stronger bid to recognize the economic, social, and political identity of the married woman in the home and, moreover, the importance of her voluntary labour to community, state, and nation.

In January 1943, the General Advisory Committee on Reconstruction established the Subcommittee on the Post-War Problems of Women. The General Advisory Committee on Reconstruction, appointed in March 1941, was chaired by the principal of McGill University, Cyril James. It included the Hon. D.G. McKenzie, chief commissioner of the Board of Grain Commissioners for Canada; J.S. McLean, president of Canada

Packers Ltd; Dr E. Montpetit, secretary-general of the University of Montreal; Tom Moore, president of the Trades and Labour Congress of Canada (replaced by Percy Bengough in 1943); and Dr C.R. Wallace, principal of Queen's University. Leonard Marsh was the committee's research adviser. The subcommittee, finally appointed in January 1943 after intense lobbying, was given only eight months to prepare its report. Its members included subcommittee chair Margaret Stovel McWilliams, a graduate of the University of Toronto and wife of R.F. McWilliams, lieutenant-governor of Manitoba as of 1940. Other members included Marion Findlay of the Ontario Ministry of Labour and Grace McInnis, Co-operative Commonwealth Federation (CCF) member for Vancouver-Burrard, together with other representatives of professional and philanthropic women's organizations. The subcommittee issued its final report in November 1943. Through this initiative, middle-class and rural women's organizations came together to frame demands for social policy as part of the postwar reconstruction program. The report drew on the language and ideals of liberal maternalism, setting out a limited rights discourse but taking care not to disturb the bedrock of domesticity in which maternal claims were grounded.

Equal rights for women would have to be built into any successful program for postwar reconstruction. Canada's women were responsible for the rearing and education of healthy and productive future citizens. If they were not accorded the full rights of citizenship, how could Canada take its place in the club of liberal democracies as a free and democratic nation? Women's organizations looked forward to being included in the liberal roster of citizenship rights, balancing the rights of postwar citizenship against domestic and maternal obligations. 'Happy homes' were, after all, in the national interest. Who could oppose such a claim?[11]

Equality for the Postwar Woman

A major target of the McWilliams report was the prohibition against the employment of married women. The introduction of part-time work as a strategic measure during the war had proved an effective solution to the labour shortage, while providing married women with the opportunity to work outside the home without jeopardizing domestic obligations. Surely there could be no reason to continue discrimination against this group? In a revealing rationale, the report's authors argued that ending the bar against married women's employment was little more than an extension of the moral rights accorded to working-class women, trans-forming economic need into a right of citizenship for middle-class women, if not for all. 'This right has always been conceded to workers in the lower economic ranks, such as laundresses and charwomen,' but public opinion continued to weigh against 'the ranks of the better-paid women,' such as those in the teaching profession.[12] The 'postwar woman' emerged in the pages of the report as a middle-class vanguard of a stable postwar social order, a universal liberal category of the 'educated woman,' in whose name and interests employment rights discourse would now be mobilized.

Committee members avoided reducing home to mere household. On the contrary, the limited rights analysis stressed the social and political importance of mothering and caring work, thus opening up the endur-ing paradox: it was precisely this same valuation of mothering work within moral regulatory discourse that judged – and found deficient – women who worked for pay within the formal waged economy. The right to choose to enter the labour market did not diminish the considerable social, political, economic, and 'personal' value accruing to homemak-ing and the skills of the homemaker. Such arguments were conceptually distinct from those regarding household labour as paid work. In this way, the report mobilized a class-based defence of middle-class women's employment rights as consistent with the shared interests of democracy, community, and nation. Stable marriage contributed to healthy citizen-ship and democracy – concerns of the state, to the extent that family was a central category of citizenship discourse, expressed as healthier and 'happier' democracy. William Beveridge's recent report demonstrated that the market wage was only also a family wage where women per-formed unpaid domestic responsibilities in the household. This was, as the eminent British architect of the welfare state pointed out, the foun-dation for the male breadwinner wage. Women's work in the home was 'vital though unpaid.' Recognition of this reality was sufficient of itself, at least 'in any measure of social policy in which regard is had to facts,' suggesting that sound postwar policy would be well-advised to credit, but not necessarily remunerate, women's household labours.[13]

This was not, however, a policy argument for the remuneration of household labour. The labour market and the household were separate, and it was the task of state policy to ensure a clear line of demarcation between the two. There was no plan to alter the redistributive income policies of the state through a program of family allowances, tax credits, or day nurseries as entitlement-based measures. The objective of public policy was to secure the domestic sphere as a preserve of middle-class respectability and a site of consumption. The report strategically endorsed the social security measures in the Beveridge and Marsh reports, including public health insurance, but not as an articulation of citizenship rights, that is, as claims upon state-based entitlement provisions. For example, the subcommittee proposed a limited program of children's allowances, framed as a pro-natalist measure designed to support but not fundamentally alter the distribution of labour within the postwar household.[14] The children's allowance would be a non-contributory, graduated allowance to supplement the market-based family wage and designed to help maintain a minimum standard of health and education. The allowance would offset the loss of a second income that would result from the withdrawal of women from paid employment. Committee members argued that this was an opportune time to introduce the measure since it would provide a 'psychological' boost, an 'alleviating factor in the mental attitude which may result from the surrender of a double income.'[15]

Wartime day nurseries, as Fraudena Eaton had already made clear, were no longer going to provide day-long care. And so the report recommended replacing the wartime day nursery with a system of part-time nursery schools, a 'natural centre' through which women might learn how to be better mothers, guiding the progress of their children through successive developmental stages.[16] Nursery schools were seen as a service that would potentially free some women to perform their household responsibilities. They would provide part-time care for the children of women for whom it was necessary to work, but only on a part-time basis, and still other women who would be better able to perform 'valuable community service' and 'spend more time with their children.' In this way, committee members tried to straddle the gap between limited rights discourse and the prior claims of domesticity.

Consistent with maternalist dictates, domestic status figured centrally throughout the report's pages. Much of the report was taken up in an analysis of household labour, in a return to Depression-era proposals to improve the occupational status of domestic work. Recommendations for domestic training set out a prescriptive identity of the ideal household worker, one who gained 'craft pride' through scientific training in the economics of household management. The ideal household worker actually symbolized the stability of the middle-class household. But there was a new approach to the age-old conundrum of how best to resolve the chronic labour shortage in this much-maligned occupation. The 'reha-

bilitation of the household worker' may also be read as a policy intervention that tried to reallocate female labour made surplus by the cessation
of war production. This was, after all, the challenge facing the federal
government. The postwar employment issue preoccupied planners at
the Department of Labour, and these concerns clearly made their way
into the pages of the McWilliams report. In the months leading up to
demobilization, officials feared that women war workers would flood the
market, thus disturbing its wage-setting mechanism, a clear statement
that the 'reserve' of women formerly seen as a lucrative national resource was now a liability, a threat to the otherwise orderly operation of
the market and, implicitly, a socially disruptive force to be contained
through state policy. The answer lay in drawing as many surplus war
workers into domestic labour as possible, a move informed as much by
market-driven concerns as it was by moral regulatory objectives. Making
domestic labour seem more attractive was therefore a strategy to avert
female unemployment, a problem never identified explicitly in the
report.[17]

The shortage of domestic workers during the war had been keenly
felt. All domestic service placements had been frozen, a move that
apparently prompted a 'belligerent' response from the good citizens of
Toronto.[18] McWilliams and the rest of the subcommittee faced a difficult
challenge in finding an acceptable balance between the 'right to work'
discourse animating liberal equality claims and the need to respond to
the demands of working-class women for whom jobs also had to be
found. And so the problem was taken up within employability discourse:
attracting the 'right type of girl' to the traditional safety valve of domestic service. Household workers simply had to be better trained. Careful
screening and selection would increase the status of household work to
the 'dignity of a vocation' and thus attract only 'well-trained intelligent
girls and women.' Increasing the number of suitably trained young
women in the occupation would also enable 'highly trained professional
and business women' to return to the labour market to 'make an adequate return to the state for their expensive education' – thus apparently strengthening the occupational status of all women.[19] For those
choosing not to enter the labour market, having access to a reliable and
highly trained household worker would increase the capacity of middle-
class women to contribute to community and society through volunteer
work. This was both a pro- and an anti-natalist argument, one advanced
under the rubric of the 'postwar woman' whose agency was mobilized
through her white identity, class respectability, and heterosexuality, and

whose advancement, moreover, was held to signify progress for all women.

As social policy, stabilization of the domestic labour supply recast household workers as a 'reserve of unskilled woman-power' in need of upgrading, while also securing the racialized class interests of educated professional and business women. Domestic service had long been an occupation of last resort, and the subcommittee members knew that this was unlikely to change. Rapid expansion of the labour force in an overheated war economy had destabilized the supply of domestic labour. Occupations newly opened up to young women drained rural and agricultural communities, leaving behind those least capable, least desirable, and least skilled or adept as potential domestic employees. This at least was how the subcommittee members rationalized the problems associated with the chronic shortage of domestic workers. Improvements to the occupation through upgrading and wage enhancements might be enough to overcome the stigma associated with household work.

In the end, the Report on the Post-War Problems of Women adhered closely to the official line, adopting a conservative estimate of how many women might be expected to need jobs in the postwar period. Starting from the figure of 1.2 million on active service in the wartime economy, it determined that roughly 750,000 could be expected to find work without help. That left 450,000 for whom some government or community assistance might be necessary. It is at this point that the magic of official statistics took over. Of all women in the labour force, government officials had estimated that approximately 50 per cent, or 600,000, would likely withdraw, returning the balance to pre-war levels. The subcommittee raised that estimate somewhat, but calculated the number likely to withdraw as a percentage of the pre-war count of 600,000. In this way, 45 per cent of those women considered surplus to an economy operating under normal conditions, a total of 270,000, were expected to withdraw from the labour market. That left a much more manageable number of women workers potentially unemployed: only 180,000 in all.[20] The view that marriage and domesticity would accommodate the majority of women considerably narrowed the report's understanding of full employment and the question of stable access to the formal waged economy. Of course, some women would work on an intermittent, temporary, or part-time basis. And single women – lacking, if only temporarily, attachment to a male provider – would be expected to work. Women at the margins of the formal labour market failed to find any presence in the report's pages. In general, it was assumed that marriage would resolve many of women's postwar problems.[21]

Only a comprehensive program of vocational guidance geared towards a 'wise and efficient placement' by highly trained staff could address the many challenges that lay ahead. The NSS ought to be absorbed into the NES, the report recommended, and the Women's Division continue in its capacity as overseer of employment policies concerning women. The country was in dire need of more women trained in vocational counselling, personnel, and social work, women whose special expertise would enable the state to regulate and monitor working women.[22] On this point, committee members expressed disappointment that no plans had been announced for vocational training of women in the postwar period. Vocational training should be made available to women on equal terms with men, but not in the same occupations. Training should be available only in occupations 'attractive to women,' that is, that would lead to a job. Finally, the report shared concerns raised in the Marsh report about living conditions in wartime Canada: poor housing, overcrowding, deteriorating neighbourhoods, and child labour – a combination of factors that produced juvenile delinquency and social unrest.[23] In the search for stability and security among the ranks of the middle-class, self-contained working-class community life was a threat best remedied by sound social planning. Training, with its regulatory capacity and developmental content, promised order and self-improvement to the undisciplined ranks of young working-class women.

The report found its way into broader circulation as the only statement from Ottawa to consider what the postwar woman might want once the war was over. Would women happily trade their coveralls for aprons? Cede office desk and job to male veterans in exchange for cradle and kitchen? The 'postwar woman' was no fiction. Many feared a return to high unemployment, that the wartime economy would shudder to a halt and pre-war depressed conditions set in once again. The real challenge lay in changing expectations. This, at least, is how the debate about women's postwar employment played out in the popular and business press. For example, the article 'Situations Wanted: Female,' which appeared in the November 1944 edition of *Canadian Business*, took on the contradictory recommendations found in the McWilliams report. As she took her measure of the government study, author Janet Keith questioned the careful silence on the subject of women who would soon find themselves out of a job. Keith pointed out that the right to work was never disputed when applied to, as she described it, women in 'lower economic ranks, such as laundresses and charwomen.'[24] Did postwar

planners intend to include women in their calculations of full employment? Keith drew on recent International Labour Office (ILO) studies
of the issue, commenting that ill-advised government policies and employer attitudes served to 'drive women out of employment' during
economic recession. Such practices had only succeeded in concealing
actual levels of female unemployment. This was the real issue, as far as
Keith was concerned, one that she and others intended to monitor. As
planners deliberated in their committee rooms over the postwar problems of women, they would do well to remember that women's 'problems' were precisely the same as men's. It was about time that Ottawa
committed itself to jobs for women by including a women's division
within the National Employment Service and providing occupational
retraining, vocational counselling, and even 'low interest loans' to cover
training costs incurred by women war workers who now wanted jobs in
civilian industry. Women had now joined the 'workers' army,' and the
country only stood to benefit from the contribution of their proven skills
and productive energy, much as it had during the war.[25] While Keith
agreed in part with the subcommittee's recommendations, her position
recognized the needs of women-as-workers, a departure from the report's
positioning of the vast majority of women as mothers above all else. For
Keith, then, whether postwar jobs were plentiful or scarce mattered little
if the government really intended to guarantee that all who wanted to
work for pay could.

Preparing for the Peace

In March 1944, the NSS plan for civilian demobilization made its way to
the Committee on Postwar Employment. The draft policy explained
postwar employment preparations and reflected what the government's
priorities ought to be in the high-stakes game of job allocations.[26] First
on the list would be returning male veterans. Female civilian war workers
would bring up the rear, just behind those demobilized from the women's
services. Demobilization was anticipated to take place in three distinct
phases, contingent on action in both the European and Pacific regions.
The first phase, a transitional period following the anticipated German
and Japanese capitulations, would immediately result in 'substantial
reductions' in the production of war materials and in the numerical
strength of the armed services. The second phase would follow the
Japanese capitulation, by which time all war contracts would be completed and the armed services reduced to 'regular strength.' In the third

and final phase, the economy would undergo a full transition to the 'normal' postwar period following conversion of military-industrial production and services to civilian activity. Calculating actual, let alone permissible, unemployment levels would be an impossible task since so much depended on the production of goods and services for export, aimed at rebuilding the devastated former theatres of war through the work of the United Nations Relief and Rehabilitation Agency (UNRRA) and its many affiliated agencies. Then there was the question of personal decisions to consider. People might reasonably be expected to want a vacation after the long years of service in the armed forces or war plants.

In the absence of concrete production data, Department of Labour officials Allan Peebles and George Luxton proposed that employment planning be downloaded to the community level. As part of the transition of employment planning from the federal to the provincial level, community surveys would be overseen by local employment advisory committees, now identified as 'focal points for local planning on postwar employment.'[27] Interestingly, the Department of Labour was particularly keen to isolate the impact of conversion on the 'industrial distribution of women and older age workers.' Although the Research and Statistics Branch of the Department of Labour was to assist, supplying the local committees with intensive labour market surveys, all decisions would be left to the local employment advisory committees. The advantage to government was that these committees were composed of business, labour, and 'public' appointees. Any decisions made by them would therefore be a matter of local accountability and would not be viewed as policies imposed from the centre.

Federal oversight would continue, since training was again an integral component of the postwar employment program. Canadian Vocational Training (CVT) was established in early 1944 as the federal government's training agency. CVT provided the federal legislative authority for postwar employment and training provisions extended to both civilian and enlisted personnel. Where the War Emergency Training Programme (WETP) had been organized around a two-tier infrastructure, CVT closed the circle, narrowing women's access through a tightly organized system of vocational guidance and training for a limited range of occupations that were considered necessary for the postwar period – specifically, training for domestic service under the Home Aide Plan. This was on the advice of A.W. Crawford, WETP director, who had confirmed that plans should not be finalized until there was agreement on what the postwar employment situation might be and what level of government obligation to the employment settlement would be required. That is, government should commit itself through legislation only after plans for demobilization were settled and a blueprint for the employment strategy had been devised to address the job needs of returning veterans.[28] While unemployment was anticipated to follow in the wake of demobilization, the level of vocational training would be substantially lower than that required after the First World War, given the thousands already being put through training this time around.[29] These arguments directly informed the drafting of the Canadian Vocational Training Act of 1944.

By May 1945, NSS had begun to relax regulatory controls, moving from the permit system designed to keep workers in their wartime jobs to a reporting system requiring voluntary registration by both employers and workers at local employment offices. This was an ideal time to relax controls and allow workers to leave war jobs and seek other opportunities while there were still jobs to be had. But there was also a strategic reason for the timing: the controls on women were to be lifted first – 'just at that time when the war industries were well manned and were to be curtailed rather than expanded' – giving the NSS an opportunity to prepare its network for the lifting of controls on men.[30] As a confidential NSS circular described it, the 'purely administrative' rather than regulatory changes were entirely flexible, as befitted their 'experimental' purpose. The experiment would reveal how best to deal with the male employment situation.[31]

Would employers and workers alike cooperate with the local branch? Would employers see that their hiring interests were best served by a local employment office administered by the federal government? Perhaps most pressing of all, would individual women turn their employment futures over to be decided by a local employment officer? Certainly Eaton was leaving nothing to chance. Every effort was made through press campaigns, radio broadcasts, and the persuasive powers of NSS officers to encourage employers and women alike to trust in the expertise and guidance of the employment service, the most efficient system available for matching jobs to workers. As Eaton explained to the Women's Division superintendent in Vancouver, 'Our women's divisions and all the officers will have to make a good showing on what can be done when we are selling a "service."'[32] Early reports suggested that the experiment was a success, promising a smooth transition. Employers and workers seemed quite prepared to turn to the employment service for assistance. Or were they? J.S. Brown, supervisor of the Women's Division in Hamilton, brought news that suggested otherwise. The National Steel Car Corporation had just announced a massive layoff of 650 women. The NSS employment officer arrived at the plant just in time to find the workers organizing in protest at the sudden decision by the employer. The incident was a problem not just for the company but for the local community as well. An estimated 250 workers, Notice of Separation in hand, had gathered in the plant cafeteria, demanding information on the lifting of the regulations. Some of the women, according to the NSS report, 'were stating very loudly and emphatically that they would now do what they pleased in looking for new work.'[33]

The lesson of the Hamilton incident illustrated the strategic importance of the central service, channelling displaced war workers through the local employment office, thus containing any likelihood of mass action or the feeling that women were being callously abandoned by their government now that the wartime crisis had passed. So successful was the outcome to the Hamilton protest that any woman who wanted a job was placed in one. In fact, the former Steel Car employees organized a farewell party, inviting NSS officers as special guests. As this example made clear, the smooth transition back to a normal economy was facilitated when the NSSWD was in control and working in cooperation with business and workers alike. All Women's Divisions at local NSS offices were to collaborate with volunteer community advisory committees and to be guided by a single refrain: 'the careful selection of applicants to fill the requirements of the vacancies existing.'[34] Back at NSSWD headquarters, far from the field of direct action, Eaton directed the final phase of the female mobilization campaign, rolled out under the curiously dry title 'Pre-Employment Training Survey.'

Surveying for the 'Right Type of Womanhood': Employment Planning for Postwar Peace

The Toronto Junction area was a centre for aircraft production during the war. Thousands of women had found well-paid and fast-paced jobs in plants located throughout the working-class industrial district. Employment at Victory Aircraft reached a peak of 3,300 workers. DeHavilland Aircraft added another 2,500, while parts manufacturer Canadian Acme Screw and Gear carried a total of 430 workers on its payroll. Throughout the war, women had readily answered the call for war production. Now that the work was drying up, the Junction women faced the difficult challenge confronting all women war workers. Opting to stay in the workforce meant accepting jobs that paid less, jobs traditionally thought more suitable for the unskilled female worker. The women at Victory Aircraft, however, did not hesitate to assert that high wages were what they expected and high wages were what they would get. Nevertheless, the tide was turning on women at the Victory plant. Returning veterans demanded assurance that they would have jobs, and the major industrial unions insisted that pre-war conditions should resume, starting with the expulsion of the women. When attention turned to the question of jobs in the postwar economy, the same women who had been so highly praised for self-sacrifice in the service of Canada's war machine now found a less sympathetic audience. The NSS Toronto Junction office illustrates the change in the public mood and the challenge faced by NSS as government officials confronted a determined group of working women. NSS Junction staff painted a very different picture of a female workforce that was if anything overpaid, accustomed now to an inflated wage rate obtainable only because of the temporarily overheated conditions of a labour market operating at 'full employment.' Once the new reality sank in, however, these 'girls' were expected to drift out of the labour market altogether, given their tendency to shun low-waged work. Officials held to the common view that women neither needed to work nor were favoured as employees by most employers. Work at the plant was described as light, 'in some cases one might almost say leisurely, and the wages have been extremely high compared to other plants.'[35] The use of the word *leisurely* underscored the notion that taking a wartime job was a matter of individual choice rather than financial necessity. But that was not all. High wages and 'leisurely' conditions had clearly gone to the workers' heads. Pink slips in hand, Victory workers were all of a mind to enjoy 'a good holiday, survey the employment field at their leisure and only accept employment at a lower rate if compelled to do so.' There was an up side, however. Faced with the choice of hard work at low pay in traditional female occupations such as domestic service or the needle trades, women were more likely to withdraw from the job market, thereby reducing the size of the female labour force and, most importantly, lowering subsequent official measures of female unemployment. Employment experts seemed quite prepared to wait it out, anticipating that the problem of laid-off women war workers would largely resolve itself. The Toronto Junction employment office certainly shared this view, arguing that anywhere from 15 to 50 per cent of women who were about to receive their notice of layoff would most likely leave the labour market through marriage. Similarly, women who had moved into the area in order to work at the war plants would have no choice but to return to their home towns. Low employment levels would take care of the rest, since women would become discouraged and withdraw – or enter domestic service. In this way, employment planners reached the conclusion that only the 'least employable,' least productive, and least desirable women would remain, making up the ranks of the 'reserve of unskilled womanpower.'[36]

Faced with a flood of wartime layoffs, the Women's Division developed a coordinated policy infrastructure that would channel war workers through a systematic process of screening, testing, and training. This massive bureaucratic initiative marks the first attempt by any level of government to directly intervene in workers' job choices. The program, known as the Pre-employment Training Survey (PTS), was a national strategy that would see thousands of women move from jobs in war industry into a narrow range of female job ghettoes, or out of the paid labour force altogether. As a reading of regional survey reports suggests, PTS was a remarkably effective policy response, one that set the NES firmly on course for the postwar years. PTS was launched through the Committee on Postwar Training at the Department of Labour. The survey was distributed by the Unemployment Insurance Commission (UIC) in June 1945.[37] As committee chair, Eaton coordinated the strategy through the regional NSSWD network, while the National Employment Service gradually assumed control over the postwar redeployment program. Ontario NES head B.S. Sullivan assured the province's regional managers that the purpose of the survey was to review training opportunities 'which might be practical in relation to available employment in local areas.'[38] 'Being only a survey,' he commented, 'it does not commit the Department to any definite policy or action.' Each office was instructed to survey not jobs but 'pre-employment vocational training opportunities' in a prescribed list of occupations. While employment officers were welcome to provide a 'running commentary' on local conditions influencing employment, their real task was to report on suitable training opportunities related to a restricted group of occupations. S.H. McLaren, acting chief executive officer for the Employment Service and Unemployment Insurance Branch, argued convincingly that, given both the apparently high costs associated with establishing separate training facilities for women and the strong likelihood of limited employer participation, on-the-job training would seem a more 'reasonable' course of action. That is, the Department of Labour saw no need to invest in training women for postwar jobs in which women were naturally adept. The list of occupations was narrow by any measure: household employment – live-in or by the day; hotel and restaurant service; hospital ward aide; retail sales; stenography; needle trades and dressmaking; and, finally, hairdressing.[39]

The PTS worked to reorganize both the purpose and the anticipated outcome of pre-employment vocational training within this narrow range of occupations. Employability discourse scrutinized the suitability of women as employees in occupations demanding new protocols such as proper deportment, attitude, appearance, and personal hygiene. Occupations involving direct contact with the consuming public, in particular retail sales, called upon a dimension of 'feminine' respectability as integral to the production of 'service' as a gendered work routine. Employers told government officials that they needed sales staff trained in both the correct forms of 'feminine deportment' and 'personality' and skills related to serving customers and selling products. Women needed to understand the 'psychology' of the sale, according to the Ottawa Retail Trade Council. Here was a new career opportunity at which women might excel, provided they understood the 'psychological idea that selling was a job to do.' On that point, New Glasgow appeared to be suffering from a city-wide epidemic of less-than-courteous women sales staff: 'This area offers great opportunities for qualified Salesclerks but it is the opinion of employers and we might say the public in general, that the general run of salesclerks now employed lack greatly one essential need, which is courtesy.'[40]

On the one hand, the female labour reserve that had been such a vital concern and solution to the shortage of labour during the war was now represented as a 'flood of untrained workers,' much as it had been in the Report on the Post-War Problems of Women. On the other hand, the availability of so many trained women war workers heightened concerns among placement officers faced with unreasonable wage expectations and a refusal to accept lower-waged jobs in the female occupations. As a reading of the regional survey reports suggests, these contradictory discourses found an uneasy strategic balance in the remedial strategy of pre-employment training. Only the 'right type of womanhood' could be selected for upgrading, in the hope that such training might upgrade the occupation as well. The Saskatoon NES office reflected precisely this approach in its proposed pre-employment course on waitressing. The high occupational vacancy rate was expected to continue, at least 'until girls are compelled by necessity to accept such employment,' NES staff reported. The proposed course might do the trick. It would 'improve the quality of persons doing this type of work,' and so upgrade the occupation by transforming candidates while simultaneously transforming potential workers 'from an unskilled group into one with a definite occupation at their finger tips.'[41] In low-wage industries such as the garment trades, which had suffered throughout the war from a chronic shortage of labour and of production materials, employers and employment experts alike were convinced that the best workers had all gone elsewhere, leaving behind those who were ominously characterized as 'unfit.' According to Sherbrooke employment and counselling officer Annette Coderre, 'pre-employment training would be a good thing in that it would allow immediate elimination of those who are unfit, and would give a chance to others who are more favoured with skill to succeed better and more quickly.'[42] This view, not surprisingly, resonated positively among a wide range of employers. Pre-employment training was viewed by NES staff as a most excellent screening mechanism, a practical and innovative service government ought to provide. In this way, vocational training discourse looked upon a woman's 'quality' as a measure of individual employability.

Workers who had to be cajoled into an occupation were unlikely to make proficient employees. They needed to choose work for themselves, as a vocation. Thus, the language of choice was prominent throughout the new policy discourse, a pretext that both legitimized the market function and demonstrated this new technique of welfare state governance. For example, the Winnipeg employment office reported that if women there were dissatisfied with wages in the placements on offer, they would simply have to go elsewhere. 'A recent example may be cited,' wrote the supervisor of the Winnipeg Female Employment Division, Mrs E.W. Gerry, of 'two Discharged girls [who] received the Canadian Vocational Training course in Hairdressing.'[43] The trainees took the course free of charge, as Gerry noted, plus the allowance of $60 a month. On completion, no jobs could be found for them in their chosen vocation. When offered employment that actually paid less than the government training allowance, approximately $40 per month, the women instead took jobs at the T. Eaton Company. One received $15 per week as an office clerk, while her mate earned a princely $16.58 per week as an elevator operator. Such examples were common, illustrating both the pattern of low wages, and the limited employment options available, even in the government-approved female occupations.

The Women's Division of the NSS was keen to ensure a place for women in federal postwar employment policy. Miss McIrvine, local employment adviser for the Women's Division in London, Ontario, speculated that aptitude testing might be just the ticket to ensure that only the right type of 'girl' was placed in that district's textile sector.[44] A systematic application of testing through the NES would be a significant improvement of the service and an appropriate postwar role for the federal agency. The Kingston branch also endorsed personnel screening and assessment as the right approach for a public employment service. According to the Kingston PTS report, such a program would permit closer monitoring by the NES: 'Job interest would thereby be created, opportunities offered by each local industry would be made known, unsuited learners in each field could be eliminated by such pre-employment training to the advantage of both employer and employee.'[45] The PTS provided an opportunity to publicize and shape an ongoing role for the NES by canvassing the opinions of employers about how such a federal service might serve their needs. As recent experience demonstrated all too well, proper personnel planning involved the science of assessment, screening, and placement. Surely employers had enough to do without taking on this onerous task as well? Women's Division officials joined with NES staff in proposing systematic aptitude testing and regular screening through pre-employment training, a model that promised to transform NES into the efficient placement service policy planners had long advocated. Pre-employment training of this kind did not develop job-related skills and knowledge, but instead screened and sorted women workers, scrutinizing individual employability as a matter of public policy. In this context, employment policy was a matter of assessing worker aptitude, capacity, suitability, and personality, 'weeding out' those thought unsuitable.[46] Employers would be responsible for job training, as so many had suggested was their preference. Reports culled from the survey indicated that all employers wanted and welcomed from the NES was 'suitable material.'

Employers responded favourably to pre-employment training as a public policy that aimed at producing 'good' workers. The war had disrupted regular work routines and disciplines. As evidence, some employers pointed to absenteeism and high turnover – a barometer of the uninterested attitude many women workers were now alleged to share. Mr Grier of the British America Bank Note Company in Ottawa emphasized that 'some form of training in discipline and prevention of absenteeism' would go a long way towards remedying this apparent problem.[47] Approached in this manner, pre-employment training was well on its way to becoming a new condition of employment, inflating hiring criteria by imposing more rigorous standards for personnel selection. For example, both Dominion Rubber and BF Goodrich endorsed the policy as one that cultivated desirable qualities, including the correct 'attitude towards employment, individual responsibility, [and] sincerity of purpose.' The companies had extensive wartime experience as employers of women in the prairies, Newfoundland, Quebec, the Maritimes, and Ontario, and so added credibility to their observation that women, particularly the 'younger generation,' were simply not 'work conscious' enough. From Ontario's industrial heartland, St Catharines employers agreed that the NES should do the work of selection, thus saving them the time and expense involved in screening out 'unsuitable' job applicants or, what was worse, investing time and resources in training 'inferior' workers. Vocational guidance was already a major focus in the work of the St Catharines office, in collaboration with the St Catharines Board of Education director of vocational guidance. The practice was intended to 'get the right youngster for the job,'[48] and well captured the leading concerns of education and employment experts about 'juvenile delinquency' and unemployment. The solution, according to the educators and employment experts at the board, lay in cultivating a sense of personal responsibility, following a model of self-improvement based on potential capacity, measured aptitude, and personal limitations. In this way, unemployment and poverty could be presented as self-correcting conditions, in the same way as the material effects of oppression, themselves the result of social relations of class and race and gender-based relations of rule, were subsumed within the individualizing effects of employability discourse. The Hudson's Bay Company Personnel Department in Winnipeg lent its support as well, agreeing that the NES ought to test the aptitudes of all job applicants, as the Hamilton office was already doing, apparently with great success. Aptitude testing ensured that only the best workers would be hired, at considerable savings to employers.[49] Bell Telephone also liked the idea. 'They [Bell Telephone] were not criticizing our selections now as they realized we didn't have much from which to choose,' reported the St Catharines office.

If the survey was intended to identify ways of compelling working-class women into domestic labour, Eaton and her colleagues must have viewed the results with disappointment. One region after another sounded the familiar refrain: women simply were not interested in this type of work. Kitchener reported that employment officers had not even bothered to canvass household training opportunities in light of its unregulated status: 'Until the Provincial government brings in legislation with regard to hours and wages, we see no future for domestics in the home' as a viable alternative employment for women, let alone ex-servicewomen.[50] The principal of the London technical school held much the same view, singling out working-class parents whose aspirations for their daughters, however inappropriate, were nonetheless a force with which the Women's Division and the NES would have to contend. Even if young women were successfully counselled to select a training course of this kind, there was every reason to anticipate that parents would object, since they perhaps unwisely preferred to see their daughters enter office or sales occupations.[51] Mrs E.W. Gerry only just managed to contain her exasperation on the matter. The Winnipeg office had interviewed all women applicants but had failed to turn up a single candidate who 'would definitely commit' to domestic service. Kate Lyons, supervisor of the Women's Division in Edmonton went further. Far too many 'new Canadian settlers' required higher wages and better working conditions to support their larger families. Domestic work simply did not pay. Perhaps it was a good thing that women had been deprived of the services of domestics during the war, Lyons mused. The 'enforced simplicity of wartime housekeeping' might now convince the employer that improved wages and better working conditions were the only way to attract efficient and trained workers. Government could certainly amend the Unemployment Insurance Act to include this occupation; a negotiated federal-provincial labour code could include the occupation under provincial minimum wage legislation; and provincial workers' compensation acts could be similarly amended. Finally, taking a leaf from the Report on the Post-War Problems of Women, Lyons agreed that household training 'should develop a uniform standard of practice of proficiency and a craft pride comparable to that obtained in other skilled trades.'[52] These recommendations reflected a growing consensus that federal employment policy for domestics would have to operate in the same manner as apprenticeship training, based on a national standard of proficiency that would confer on domestic workers the same recognition as other skilled workers.

Employment officers and policy planners alike appeared to be scrambling for a legislative solution to overcome the obvious resistance from the intended subjects of domestic training policy. Legislation would, however, constitute a new dimension of state regulatory practice in the private domestic sphere, a move private householders manifestly opposed. Regulatory measures accruing to designated occupations were based on skill and worker status; the more closely a worker conformed to the ideal-typical skilled white male of British descent with ownership in his labouring capacity, the more clearly did regulatory enhancements secure the status and labour market attachment of the occupation itself. Such were the design principles of state-based measures such as inclusion as an insurable occupation for the purposes of the unemployment insurance act under workers' compensation, and – as a floor – inclusion in provincial legislation on the minimum wage and hours of work. Collective bargaining sought to provide more comprehensive, if privatized, means of regulatory direction and, on the part of workers, some means for improving employment security under reasonable wages and working conditions. None of these approaches was available to domestic workers, nor would they be. Legislative protection of domestic workers would regulate their place of work, making the private household a site of state regulation. This move, most agreed, was best left off the labour policy agenda. This dilemma was captured in an intriguing entry in the Winnipeg report about NSS attempts to place Canadian women of Japanese descent in domestic employment. The program was designed to supervise the placement of young Japanese women in household labour for the duration of the war. Residential placement and extended supervision in the community – under the guise of vocational training – melded well with the professional remedial aims of community services such as the Children's Aid Society or the Big Sisters' Association, adding another dimension to the vocational training of household workers. Such training implicated interwar programs designed to 'produce' worthy citizens from those whose family histories and sexually and morally dangerous ways had brought them to the attention of correctional and/ or social service agencies. Certainly this was the view of social agencies such as the YWCA. In the joint PTS report from the Maritimes, the YWCA responded enthusiastically to a proposed training centre for household workers. Such a scheme would provide an excellent placement program for girls under their care. The Children's Aid was equally keen to place its wards 'in good homes requiring trained household workers.' Miss A.M.S. Ward added, however, that it would be advisable to include domestic work as an insurable occupation under the UI Act and even, she added, consider organizing the young women into a 'union.'[53]

Before the Winnipeg training and placement scheme could go ahead, officials discussed what other legislative measures might also be needed. The catch was that the young Japanese women were the responsibility of the federal government under the provisions of wartime internment. Officials soon found themselves having to consider the prospect of provincial legislation to regulate wages, hours, and working conditions.

Federally, it would be necessary to amend the Unemployment Insurance Act to include domestic service as an insurable occupation. In the end, the plan was scrapped as the broader implications of the legislative scheme became apparent. 'This would involve inspection in the homes,' reported Winnipeg supervisor Mrs Gerry, 'and we understand that this was a decided obstacle in the satisfactory placement of Japanese girls in household employment.'[54] Labour legislation of any kind would by implication locate domestic employment within the formal waged economy and thereby profoundly alter the relationship between the household and the state. In the end, officials resisted any course that would so profoundly change the place of female domestic labour in relation to both the private household and the formal waged economy.

Could household employment continue to serve as a solution to women's unemployment? By August 1945, Eaton was far less certain that household employment would ever again constitute a major employment sector among women. Improvements in hours, wages, and related working conditions could be made only through provincial legislation. In any case, such matters were beyond the scope of local employment officers and the national employment service. 'Our officers' in the employment placement service, Eaton complained to MacNamara, 'are somewhat hopeless about the attitude of the applicant' towards household work.[55] Planners were sensitive to the public criticism that might come their way if the NSS were accused of forcing women – and former war workers at that – into an unregulated occupation without any government protection. At the same time, officials expressed serious reservations about investing in training for an occupation that paid so little. Canadian Vocational Training was the federal program responsible for all postwar employment training, including the pre-employment scheme for women. Eaton submitted the Women's Division program designed to train women as domestic workers for CVT funding. The Home Aide Plan would constitute the lead response at the regional level when women applied to NES offices for postwar work. CVT baulked at the idea of footing the bill. Why, Director R.F. Thompson wanted to know, was CVT expected to pay training costs in an occupation that paid so little? 'It is an open question as to how far the Government should go in spending public money to train anyone over a six-month period for an occupation which at the end of training might only bring in wages of $15.00 or $20.00 per month.'[56] Eaton did her best to defend the program, knowing how limited the options were for postwar employment. The Home Aide Plan was not going to dramatically change women's job situation, and would certainly not transform the occupation from one of last resort into a prized vocation. Still, she argued, 'it is definitely a first attempt to put household employment on a level comparable to other lines of work with regular hours and minimum rates of pay.'[57] Officials throughout the national service were well aware that occupational employment was to be considerably restricted and that public policy would facilitate this constriction of labour market access for women. This would undoubtedly translate into high levels of female unemployment. Having reached a new level in the public service and in their own careers as experts on women's employment, women policy and program officials were caught in a double bind. It was their responsibility to ensure that the actual effects of employment policy in the postwar economy did not explicitly contradict Ottawa's public pronouncements regarding the formal equality rights of the 'postwar woman.' One way around the dilemma was found in liberal 'choice' discourse. Pre-employment counselling and placement would guide women towards a reasonable, if narrow, choice of future employment, an approach that accorded well with formal equality provisions. As the next chapter investigates, this roster of 'suitable' occupations was extended to ex-servicewomen as well, although the challenge was greater still.

As Eaton would later explain, the framework for vocational training had been determined through the careful and impartial research of her department, guided by the results of the national survey. The survey purportedly reflected objective local and regional employment trends. Survey results were forwarded to CVT to provide the basis for further research and to inform the policy planning and decision-making process. Eaton's report was also sent to the UIC Training Committee in the same capacity. Thus the findings, the organizational approach, and the administrative priorities reflected in the PTS were the foundation for employment and training policy for both ex-service and civilian women. The survey organized the question of women's postwar employment as a regulatory matter of containment and control. Occupational categories and classifications of 'female employment' would be narrowly constrained. Racial, class, and gender-based prescriptions closely informed prescribed social location and labour market access. Moreover, even though the rhetorical device of 'choice' was repeatedly articulated in the policy and programming work of the NES Women's Division, for the vast majority of women who were the subjects of these policy discourses, choice figured little if at all. Material location and conditions were taken up and reconfigured as indices of individual deficiency or potential, measures of social, domestic, and economic worth. In this way, vocational training, counselling, and placement became vehicles for sorting the labour supply and for regulating the social order under the guise of measuring and calibrating individual employability. The 'market' for women's labour was approached as decentralized and regionally fragmented, with the result that any subsequent policy, while centrally developed and administered, would be local and not national in scope or implementation.

Conclusion

The direction for postwar employment and training policy for women was in part organized through the final report of the Subcommittee on the Post-War Problems of Women (1943)[58] and by the 'findings' of the Pre-employment Training Survey (1945).[59] These reports were used as significant planning documents. They defined the social and economic challenges women were alleged to confront – and in what measure – and purported to contain appropriate prescriptive policy responses to the realities the reports were alleged to convey, the problems they were held to identify. As investigations of employment activity and of domesticity, these reports were also critical institutional organizing and lobbying opportunities. As official inquiries and investigations, the reports provided both pretext and context for collaborative intersections among state planners and organizations representing the hegemonic elite of white, middle-class, professionally identified women. Included among them were, for example, the National Council of Women of Canada, the YWCA, and the Big Sisters' Association, along with social practitioners whose interests in social reconstruction were indelibly associated with a distinct approach to citizenship anchored in the principles of social and collective security of the emerging postwar state. As a reading of both reports suggests, the women's organizations that were drawn into and strengthened through affiliation with these exercises were exclusively made up of the social, political, professional, and economic elite.

Women's access to the formal waged economy was contextualized in domesticity and liberal equality discourse in the Report on the Post-War Problems of Women. The report worked through two competing rationales. On the one hand, the report's recommendations foregrounded the formal equality claims of women within employment, as rational agents in the labour market whose ownership rights in their labour were to be acknowledged and respected. This was a discourse of liberal choice, grounded in the individualizing frame of contract, a frame that worked through the elision of the material effects of oppression grounded in race, class, and gender. On the other hand, the household was positioned as the primary social unit, one in which the state had considerable interest. Happy democracy depended for its very survival on happy homes. In this domesticity discourse, the first and true vocation of women lay within the household. At the same time, the Pre-employment Training Survey deployed a narrow framework through which women's access to postwar training and, more importantly, the formal waged economy, would be organized. While some may have argued – motivated by either eager anticipation or fearful trepidation – that employment trends and social changes evidenced by the war would indeed endure, the PTS reflected persistent efforts among Department of Labour officials to hasten the return of women to what they saw as their prescriptive social and economic locations. The PTS was a survey of training opportunities within a clearly demarcated cluster of 'suitable' vocations. Its 'findings' provided the basis not only for postwar training policies and programming but also for labour market research, mapping exercises that purportedly charted the 'normal' patterns of female employment. As such, the survey shaped the activities and priorities of the Women's Division of the National Selective Service and National Employment Service, defining the 'problems' for which training was the apparent solution and restructuring women's access to security in employment, childcare, education, income support, unemployment insurance benefits, labour standards protections, and, finally, the formal waged economy.

The Pre-employment Training Survey was a stage in the planning process whose goal was to develop recommendations for CVT and the UIC regarding training and employment policy and programming for rehabilitation training for ex-servicewomen and training for civilian women. The survey transformed the question of women's postwar employment into a problematization of women's employability. That is, as women were further subdivided based on assessed capacity, aptitude, and suitability, the resistance encountered among women workers to low-wage postwar employment was taken up by policy practitioners as evidence of the need for intensive scrutiny of individual employment capacity, expressed as 'suitability.' This was work for which the NES was thought to be ideally suited. Training was envisaged as a screening and assessment technique, a process through which the best 'girl' might be identified based on her alleged aptitude, respectability, personality, and suitability. Resistance to low-wage employment in prescribed female

occupations would be overcome by a program of pre-employment training. Rather than upgrading employment conditions through regulatory
measures such as wage improvements, hours of work, workers' compensation, or even unionization, the preferred approach was occupational
upgrading through vocational training. Upgrading the worker would be
the best route to upgrading the occupation.

These reporting processes, and the activities generated through them,
brought community, volunteer, and lobbying organizations, as well as
social agencies and government planners, to problematize the social in
their assessment of the challenges allegedly posed for and by the thousands of women who had been drawn into the formal waged economy as
a result of the accelerated program of military industrial production.
Promoting a diversity of training for postwar employment was not the
answer. Too many young women were seen to be roaming the streets of
downtown cities, sipping cocktails and dancing with uniformed soldiers,
availing themselves of all the allurements and pleasures of modern
urban life. There were apparent dangers associated with providing a
range of training opportunities that might lure young women into 'city-
based factories' and away from the safety of the rural home. Given the
close association within policy circles between stabilizing the home and
averting postwar unemployment, and given the nominal formal equality
provisions contained within rehabilitation legislation, the question of
women's equality of access both to state programming and to the labour
market was consistently in the foreground of discussion. At the same
time, however, where the vast majority of women had been approached
in the early years of the war as a lucrative reserve of 'female labour' the
identification and deployment of which presumably held the key to
resolving the wartime labour shortage, by the postwar period, the challenge had become what to do with the massive reserve of 'unskilled
women workers.' The 'female labour reserve' had shifted in public
discourse from strategic economic asset to liability – a disruptive force
capable of destabilizing the wage-setting mechanisms of the formal
labour market. The rationale governing public policy, then, lay in encouraging women to withdraw from the formal waged economy without
at the same time overtly violating the gender-equality provisions to which
Canada was a signatory, through international conventions at the United
Nations and the International Labour Office, as well as domestic rehabilitation legislation.

chapter five

'An Aptitude Test Is in *Your* Best Interest': Canada's Employment Charter for Women Veterans

By V-E Day on 8 May 1945, demobilization of Canada's forces stationed in Europe was well underway. War continued in the Pacific region, although many expected that the Japanese capitulation could not be far off, even if the catastrophic circumstances surrounding the conclusion of that surrender remained the secure knowledge of a secretive political elite. Approximately 250,000 Canadian military personnel had already been discharged by V-E Day. That number climbed to 395,013 by the end of the year, and another 381,031 were discharged in the following year.[1] Canada's major port facilities and cities were overflowing with military personnel, all anxious to return home – but to what? The memories of the First World War, while perhaps outside the lived experience of many young women and men in service, were certainly not far from the minds of their elders and the government officials who would oversee the demobilization exercise. In the months to come, the lives of thousands of military personnel and civilians would be directed by the actions of government officials anxious to build a social and economic order that would avoid the tribulations that had followed the First World War. Servicewomen could only hope that their efforts would be recognized in equal measure with those of their brothers-in-arms.

The task of demobilization planning was overseen by the Department of Veterans' Affairs (DVA). Rehabilitation was the watchword. And everyone had a part to play. Veterans' rehabilitation blurred the boundary between official state and community. Canadians were advised that government was simply an 'instrument of the public.' The real work was up to employers working alongside trade unions, churches cooperating with service clubs, and so on. Private citizens would do their part, too, by looking out for the needs of returning soldiers as they went about day-to-day life and work in their communities. Government propaganda drove the message home: 'Each city, town and village must do its part to help provide for the economic and social re-establishment of the returning veteran so that they enter fully into the life of the community.'[2] Peace on the home front was now just as vital as the pacification of battle-ravaged Europe and the Pacific. As the country emerged from total war, restoring ex-service personnel to productive civilian and domestic life became the new national mission, smoothing the transition to a peacetime founded on domestic stability and a revitalized national economy converted to Keynesian objectives of increased domestic consumption and international trade. The home was a key site of governance in this equation. Existing in non-market space, the home emerged in public policy as a formative site for developing and ordering the practices of citizenship, and of economy. Healthy democracy depended upon happy homes.

This chapter examines the ideas behind rehabilitation planning, ideas that led to the Veterans' Charter, a compendium of legislation considered one of the hallmarks of the welfare state in Canada. This chapter also examines the little-known role of associates of the elite National Committee for Mental Hygiene (Canada) (NCMH) whose efforts profoundly shaped the direction rehabilitation planning would take. Broadcasts such as the CBC radio series 'The Soldier's Return,' developed by the NCMH for the interdepartmental Economics and Research Rehabilitation Information Committee, conveyed the message that responsibility for successful postwar social reconstruction extended well beyond the individual veteran. Retooling for the peace meant rebuilding home, community, and nation to permit the Dominion to assume its rightful position within the new international order. Capt. (and Dr) Olive Ruth Russell drew increasingly on these themes, often incorporating similar objectives, from her appointment to DVA in charge of women's rehabilitation programming until she left the department – and the country – in 1947. Throughout her tenure at DVA, Russell sought to consolidate the gains of the 'postwar woman' while struggling with the tension between the principle of equality for women and the intractable differences both among women and between the prospects for women and men. The chapter concludes with an examination of Russell's arguments concerning the equality of women and the legislative means by which women's wartime gains might be secured.

When the topic of Russell's transfer over to DVA arose in the spring of 1944, her boss at the Department of National Defence (DND), William

Line, confided that he shared the hope that the techniques Russell had developed within the Canadian Women's Army Corps (CWAC) might be preserved. While the army would miss her considerable contribution, her expertise would be readily applicable within the rehabilitation program, 'whenever the time is appropriate for you to swing into action on the civilian side of the fence.'[3] Russell was optimistic that the methods developed by military personnel experts would indeed be used for civilian purposes. 'I find myself venturing to hope that some progress will be made toward the realization of my dream for systematic personnel selection work for Canadians in peace time,' she told Line.[4] The time was at hand to realize well-founded professional aspirations as well as personal ambition. 'You see,' Russell confided to her superior, 'I still cling to some of my dreams even at the risk of being branded an idealist.' Line was himself an acknowledged employment and personnel expert, as committed as Russell to instituting a national program of mental hygiene improvement. Why should there not be a national standard of mental health paralleling that of physical health? Like his colleagues at the NCMH, Line saw a tremendous opportunity to use the largely untapped potential of psyche-based knowledge practices in the service of state, community, industry, and family life. No social institution had been more neglected in this regard than the modern workplace. The timing could not be more opportune. Line had taken a leave of absence from his position as psychology professor at the University of Toronto to assume his posting at DND during the war. As a member of the NCMH, he actively promoted the use of psyche-based techniques and the profession of psychology as a reputable science, the full benefits of which, he contended, had yet to be fully realized. In April 1944, he jointly initiated the Inter-Service Conference on Psychiatry.[5] He was also a founding member of the Canadian Psychological Association in 1945. Earlier that year, Line had joined a panel of experts assembled by Dr Ewen Cameron, as part of the lecture series 'Studies in Supervision' at McGill University.[6] The lecture series consolidated the results of employment research organized through the principles of educational psychology and industrial psychiatry, outlining the basis of these techniques as central to the successful readjustment of civilians and military personnel alike once the war was finally ended. McGill principal and chair of the General Advisory Committee on Reconstruction (GACR), Dr Cyril James, wrote the preface to the published collection of lectures. These lectures, James suggested, were compelling evidence that a successful program of national reconstruction had of necessity to begin by recognizing that most basic fact, that the goal of re-establishment was 'satisfactory personal readjustment for the individual.'[7] Line now wanted to seize the opportunity to consolidate the techniques developed under his command at the DND Directorate for Personnel Selection and transfer the same approach over to DVA for the postwar reconstruction and rehabilitation program.

Educational psychologists pushed the envelope of postwar rehabilitation policy and the definition of successful readjustment, arguing that personal satisfaction was the only measure of adjustment that mattered. What was rehabilitation for if not the successful reintegration of servicemen and women to civil life? Since jobs were at the top of everyone's agenda, private industry must now be seen in its proper light, as a social institution bearing an organizational responsibility to promote and cultivate the learning capacities and activities of its labour force. Industry, that is, had an important governmental role to play in the formation of responsible and satisfied citizens. Rehabilitation was concerned first and foremost with the 'learning process,' Line explained. Learning had become a 'time-honoured battleground' between psychologists and psychiatrists. Where the latter tended to concentrate more on problems of emotional maladjustment, psychologists approached learning as a mechanistic process through which 'intellectual learnings' were reduced to a functionalist level of mechanical skill, and industrial work to a series of segmented job tasks.[8] Like other Canadian psychologists, Line was critical of such narrow functionalism. Harnessing learning capacities was a remarkable achievement, to be sure. Even women had been brought into the production process as vital contributors to the war effort: 'The world can be spanned in forty seconds with John Doe, or even Mary Joe, doing the spanning.'[9] Despite the benefits accompanying production planning and personnel organization methods, however, this was not the route to follow if industry ever expected to see the peaceful and successful reintegration of demilitarized personnel. Psychologists were too ready to apply their knowledge in the service of an industry interested only in boosting productivity, rather than in cultivating a more productive – because more well-adjusted – workforce. Educational psychology had much more to offer, as recent war production experiences now demonstrated.

Postwar planners were gravely concerned with the potential for civil unrest to spread into industry in the form of militant strike action, industrial sabotage, and even open conflict between unionized workers and returning veterans. The responsibility and the opportunity to cultivate 'human worth' lay within the grasp of industry. Indeed, there was no such thing as private industry from a social and psychological perspective. Industry was as much a social organization as were church, family, community, and school. In its proper perspective, the factory became a 'learning environment,' and the learning that occurred within its walls was as much social as it was task-based. 'Learning,' Line concluded, 'is synonymous with living.'[10] Here was the essence of the successful modern corporation. Other techniques were so much trickery designed to 'sell' the company to its employees. Joint labour-management productivity committees might have toyed with gimmicks – profit sharing, company picnics, 'non-directive counselling,' and 'bull sessions' – during the war, but these fads were unlikely to earn the respect of men who had returned to the production line from the line of battle. 'Industry really has the greatest of all possibilities and responsibilities in cultivating human worth; for, for most of the life span, you are given that opportunity in the case of the majority of our citizens.' In fact, citizenship training lay directly within the purview of the corporation as a social institution, 'a university of citizenship training.'[11] So far, however, it had not borne up at all well. 'The general manager must become the father figure and behave as such; the enterprise must be his, the worker's, and not something he does for you, for which in return you give him wages.'[12] The general manager stood in relation to the worker as male parent to male child, as commanding officer to enlisted soldier. Hierarchy was not only natural, it was essential and desirable. The success of the team depended upon it. 'Be as business-like as a parent or a commanding officer should be. Being business-like is the essence of being human, of understanding human needs and development, and that is the greatest tribute in our language to industry.'[13] Line cautioned his listeners to avoid the piecemeal approach of 'applying psychology to the details' – and then concentrating on rooting out pathologies rather than cultivating the healthy adjustment of 'normal' personalities – and not at the level of overall policy. 'You have asked psychology to come in only at the detail level – when you have a stutterer, or a recalcitrant worker, or a delinquent.' The point was to interweave psychology throughout all educational policy, to entrench the principles of psychological technique directly within the recruitment and training process. In the end, the worker ought to feel pride in his company and his employer. 'Can you intrigue him to become a member of your corporation – to accept your corporation as his society?' It was up to employers to invite the returning soldier to join the enterprise as an 'active partnership.' 'If you can, he will dignify your enterprise,' Line advised. 'If you cannot, he will be a constant rebel.'[14]

This, then, was the approach Line intended to adopt for all rehabilitation programming falling to his department: 'In so far as these cases can
be got at within the Service before they come out, it is our intention to
see that every individual soldier gets to thinking about an appraisal of
himself in terms of what he needs to know.'[15] Too many recruits had
faced so many obstacles – everything from 'broken homes' to unemployment – yet they remained 'fine specimens of personality,' in Line's
assessment. Hope for a meaningful future was as powerful a motivation
for the adult as it was for the young child. 'No matter what pain and grief
and squalor he endures,' a belief in better times ahead, the hope that
life would be pleasant, the opportunity for personal development –
these were all indicative of what Line defined as the 'learning instinct.' If
private enterprise took that as its starting point, industrial peace, prosperity, and a flourishing citizenship would result, collective benefits in
which all could share. The potential economic boost for industry was
incalculable, provided employers knew how to avail themselves of this
opportunity. And, of course, few would dispute the notion that a benefit
to industry was in equal proportion a gain for the rest of society.

'Back to Civvy Street': Rehabilitation and the
Veterans' Counselling Program

The Veterans' Welfare Division was established by Order-in-Council
6282 in 1941. At that time, civil re-establishment was clearly defined as
re-employment. As deputy minister of veterans' affairs, Walter Woods
oversaw an operation that had been in the planning stages since the
opening days of the conflict.[16] Woods took a hard line approach, a
reflection of the nineteenth-century liberal discourse of individual responsibility in which the principle of 'less eligibility' was also anchored.[17]
According to this view, the government service was 'in no sense a guarantee to provide a job for every man who has been in the Service.'[18] In the
event, government officials would continue to counter any perception
that returning men would be automatically entitled to a job as direct
compensation for military service. The Post-Discharge Re-establishment
Order was designed to overcome any 'economic hardship' caused by
time away on military service, or 'dislocation from private life.' While the
order was not to be administered in a 'narrow or parsimonious manner,'
neither was it intended to provide indefinite support to any person –
principally, any male person – who had worn a uniform. Out-of-work
benefits were subject to stringent eligibility criteria. To qualify, a person

had to be both capable of and available for work. Those unable to find a job were to enrol in training as assigned, 'to fit him or to keep him fit for employment or for re-employment.' 'It is not the intention of the Government to subsidize idleness and in so far as such idleness is encouraged, the war effort is impeded.'[19] As the legislation made clear, entitlement was not among the design principles informing re-establishment programming. The problem to be averted if at all possible was 'dependency' – the obverse of employability – permitting out-of-work benefits provided under the re-establishment order to 'degenerate' into a form of 'dole' or a 'relief measure.' 'The longer they [ex-service personnel] are permitted to rest on out of work benefits,' according to an internal policy document listed as Confidential Letter 11, 'the more difficult it will be to handle them later on.' Aptitude testing was highlighted in clause 30 of the confidential memorandum as a promising administrative assessment tool. Should any doubt exist as to the best placement for the individual in question, welfare officers were told to order an aptitude test 'as a matter of course.' Occupational history forms accompanied each person as she or he journeyed through the post-discharge process. If any evidence turned up suggesting that the person had been a 'social problem case' before the war, staff were to permit such 'cases' to revert to 'their former status' as a 'charge upon the municipality.'[20]

Rehabilitation training was provided under Privy Council Order (PCO) 7633 of the Post-Discharge Re-establishment Order, to assist the veteran in securing any position he or she might have attained 'if his [*sic*] career had not been interrupted by service.' Suitable occupation was defined according to need, abilities, and 'personal characteristics of the individual.' The interest of the state 'from an economic and social point of view' was to assist the veteran to return to 'the pre-war occupation or the position the person might reasonably have expected to have occupied.'[21] Skill was the only guarantee to 'preference in employment,' not government, nor legislation, nor prior right or entitlement. Training was in no way to be regarded as a right or reward for 'service to the state.' Finally, rehabilitation officials were advised, 'it should always be remembered that training grants are intended for those who are willing to help themselves.' In this way, rehabilitation policy drew on masculinist discourses of employability, chiefly that of the skilled male breadwinner of British origin whose location in the labour market was unquestioned; whose employment rights and ownership of his 'skill' formed the basis of his citizenship entitlements; and whose wage-earning capacities, articulated to the 'family wage' system, precluded the autonomous wage-earning and household formation capacities of women as always already wife-dependent. Rehabilitation programming also continued to draw on the moral regulatory discourse of 'honest labour' rooted in the principle of 'less eligibility,' as well as discourses of gender and racialized citizenship, which cumulatively positioned the ideal citizen as skilled, white, male, and of British descent.

From its Ottawa headquarters, the Department of Veterans' Affairs directed the massive service operation for demobilized service personnel. By 1946, the Veterans' Welfare Division had absorbed the Social Services Directorate, transferred from Departmental Administration to Rehabilitation Services, providing services at rehabilitation centres under the auspices of a rehabilitation review board. The majority of services were devoted to vocational counselling, directing veterans into appropriate training and education programs.[22] The work could not have succeeded without the aid of local citizens' rehabilitation committees, the Department of Labour through its training program, Canadian Vocational Training (CVT), and the now jointly administered National Selective Service/National Employment Service apparatus. A veterans' welfare officer was placed at every NES office. Similarly, the Department of Labour stationed veterans' employment advisers at all district rehabilitation centres. Out-of-work benefit payments were administered through the Unemployment Insurance Commission (UIC). An undertaking such as this could only work through a state public sector infrastructure capable of processing a flood of people who were understandably weary of government red tape. It had to be well organized, since every woman and man had to register at a DVA Rehabilitation Centre within the first month of discharge to qualify for rehabilitation credits. The largest of these centres were located in Winnipeg, Toronto, and Montreal. The heaviest volume was recorded between the late autumn and early winter of 1945–6, with activity winding down considerably by the spring of 1947. A total of 553,431 people had been discharged from the services by the end of March 1946, leaving another 184,838 still to be discharged.[23] Hitting the labour market during the seasonal low of winter, many veterans experienced problems locating a job. Where only 824 were recorded as receiving out-of-work benefits in April 1945, the number climbed to 43,524 in March 1946.[24] Honourably discharged veterans qualified for out-of-work benefits for up to twelve months, if the benefits had been applied for and approved within eighteen months of discharge. Ex-service personnel – in particular, men, whose access to insured employment through insurable occupations greatly exceeded women's – were provided with an additional incentive of finding a job in one of the insured occupations covered by the Unemployment Insurance Act. Those able to find work in an insured position and remain there for a minimum period of fifteen weeks within a twelve-month period – worked consecutively or not – were deemed to have been in insurable employment from the time of enlistment to the date of discharge. These provisions, for the purposes of UI eligibility, were a considerable bonus for those too young to have gained any work experience before enlistment. Personnel selection and placement proceeded within rehabilitation programming according to the same sets of knowledge practices as had informed military recruitment and personnel selection. Woods later described the new approach in his memoirs, explaining how DVA training was intended either to achieve immediate 're-establishment in civil life' or to direct the veteran into 'a new occupation *better suited to his physical and mental capacities* and his economic needs.'[25] Assessment standards, because objective, were more reliable in their predictive and administrative capacity. Veterans had been torn from their communities, in some cases for several years, and, for many, well before they had had the opportunity to establish an employment record. The only way to surmount this 'handicap of the lack of associational and neighbourhood influence' was through a modern placement service guided by a program of objective testing and counselling. In this way, the most suitable applicant would get the job 'irrespective of whether the employer happens to know his uncle or not.'[26]

'The Best Adjustment Plan Is a Job'

The rehabilitation program was fully operational in 1945 under the command of NCMH associate S.N.F. Chant, director general of rehabilitation. Chant felt that the program should concentrate on bolstering the confidence of returning veterans, since there was nothing to be gained in 'minimizing the very real difficulties they will have to face.'[27] Better 'to quiet the fears and concerns' of veterans by addressing the challenges they could expect to confront. 'You have all wondered what will happen when the one-time elevator boy or filing clerk returns to you as a major or squadron leader,' DND Director of Personnel Selection William Line told a McGill audience of industrial relations experts. How would industry – indeed how would society – cope? According to Col. Line, 40 per cent of soldiers in the Canadian military suffered from maladjustment and, he continued, 'I would also say that this, by and large, reflects poor vocational adjustment as the main contributing cause.'[28] All military recruiting had begun with the medical examination, psychological testing, and intensive interviewing to assemble individual profiles and case histories. But the more important phase, Line observed, was that of reception 'in which the recruit is now a partner.'[29] The experience of the military was directly transferable to private enterprise. Indeed, it had to be. Discontinuity in experience, as would inevitably follow if the squadron leader was shunted into the back room to once again take up his position as a filing clerk, was the gravest danger of all. The veteran both wanted rationally and longed emotionally to return to civilian life. Successful rehabilitation meant that employers – and any other civilian agents with whom the veteran would have contact – had to make 'his' needs their starting point. 'It is not enough for you to build up team work within the factory itself; the factory has to become part of his own life – of his conception of himself and his team.' Accommodation was the first phase: 'You start with him as he is and try to gauge, not what you want him to know, but what he himself needs to know – how he needs to develop. He must first be accommodated to you, and he wants so to be, in that *he is seeking his vocational expression through you*.'[30] The conditions of learning, in other words, took precedence over the content to be learned.

Canadians, civilian and enlisted personnel alike, absorbed the principles of rehabilitation through a barrage of print and broadcast media as part of a public education campaign overseen by the Rehabilitation Information Committee (RIC).[31] The RIC coordinated the information activities of all government departments connected with veterans' demobilization, rehabilitation, and civil re-establishment. While applied educational psychology was acknowledged as a useful and important part of rehabilitation work, however, not all agreed with its near-exclusive concentration on the 'psychology of the individual' as the proper focus of rehabilitation policy.[32] The debate broke when the RIC met on 6 December 1944 to consider the CBC radio broadcast 'The Soldier's Return.' The series had been prepared by the National Committee for Mental Hygiene, many of whose members now ran the personnel and rehabilitation operations within DND and DVD. Discussion revolved around the merits of psychological reconditioning versus those of 'honest labour,' signalling a profound shift in contemporary understandings of employability. Critics expressed alarm that the NCMH series might 'leave the impression that men returning from active service would generally need psychiatric treatment.'[33] Demobilization, argued these proponents of the 'honest labour' approach, was a matter of civil re-establishment through work, not social and psychological adjustment. Analysing 'the psychological aspects of civil re-establishment' was all well and good, but normal adjustment could best be facilitated by placing (male) veterans directly into jobs as quickly as possible. A good job would go much further towards benefiting the veteran by equipping 'him' to re-enter civilian life than any amount of dabbling in the murky interstices of 'personality,' suggesting as it did a psychological 'reconditioning' of (a man's) mind.

The armed forces representatives to the RIC were articulating a clear position that drew directly on the experiences of the last war. Many First World War veterans had become isolated, standing in potential opposition to former friends, family, co-workers, and communities, as a result of having lived through traumas few could begin to understand let alone directly confront. There was an important difference between the veterans of the Canadian Expeditionary Force who had fought in the First World War and the group of veterans now awaiting discharge. New psychological and psychiatric knowledges and the technologies developed in their name had created a new form of soldier. The modern 'fighting man' gained a distinct identity in psyche-based discourses as one whose capacities and aptitudes were calculable, honed, and directed into the best possible application within the modern military apparatus. This, at least, was the thoughtful opinion of Robert England, executive secretary of the General Advisory Committee on Demobilization and Rehabilitation (GACDR).[34] The GACDR Subcommittee on Employment took up the more critical challenges surrounding the job placement of ex-service personnel, in part through a program of vocational training and counselling. In a confidential submission to GACDR tabled in 1942, England contrasted the problems confronted in the aftermath of the First World War to the very different conditions obtaining now. It was, he contended, a very different, very modern war. Where the First World War had been fought by recent 'immigrants,' this was a war being conducted by Canadians, prosecuted by men 'born and educated' in Canada.[35]

England's assertions of the 'superiority' of the Second World War veteran drew upon a range of discursive constructions of 'intelligence,' 'scientific objectivity,' and the alleged neutrality of mental testing technologies. In part, such arguments were informed by the exclusionary practices of army recruiters, as evidenced by the 'pure European descent' or 'pure white race' practices of military selection.[36] At the same time, England's comments reflected experiences of the interwar period, revealing the influence of racialized conceptions of the intelligence of so-called inferior races that had resulted from mass testing by the U.S. Army during the First World War. Now even the most junior member of the modern army was well-acquainted with the 'modern techniques of personnel selection,' having been put through a rigorous process of aptitude and IQ testing. The army had changed since the First World War. Soldiers were now serving in a 'modern mechanized armed force.' Industrialized war was more effective, its technology more efficient, replacing the mindless slaughter, mud, and disease that had confronted the previous generation of fighting men. Psychological screening was not invasive. On the contrary, psyche-based techniques were to be welcomed by the modern soldier as useful both in helping him to survive in the theatre of war and in guiding him towards rehabilitation training and, by inference, employment security upon demobilization. In his summary presentation, England also drew on the civil service admission interview, suggesting that its checklist might serve a useful purpose in the work of rehabilitation counselling. The checklist included an assessment and ranking of the following: appearance, bearing, social and moral qualities, alertness and judgment, presentation of ideas, and vocabulary and general speech. Whatever the merits of the current compromise, the Dominion Civil Service Commission made extensive use of intelligence and related tests, and if it was good enough for the civil service then surely it was good enough for DVA. In this way, England drew upon work already well underway within the Directorate of Personnel Selection, to which I now turn.

From Elevator Boy to Squadron Leader ... and Back?

The confidence invested in the testing program was as profound as it was absolute: here was an administrative tool that could be deployed with ease and efficiency, provided always that it remained in the hands of a trained technician. In his review of mental testing procedure, England was particularly excited by the new perspective these techniques offered for resolving the vexing question of reinstatement in civil employment. Like so many others who contemplated the possible applications of modern personnel selection methods to industry, England looked to the obvious benefits of objective testing and personnel selection procedures. These procedures explicitly opened up the interior of the policy subject to techniques of governance, a way of mapping populations within the modern labour force according to new grids of intelligibility, constituting emotional stability, suitability, and interests as effects of discursive categories around which employability would be organized – aptitude, intelligence, and capacity. The military had proved the efficacy of such methods. The point now was to encourage employers and government to adopt them. According to England, here was an objective, scientific method by which to sidestep the pressures of nepotism and eradicate the role of personal networks – conventional and clearly inefficient methods of job placement favoured primarily by those having all the right connections. The view held by some uninformed individuals in business and community that military service created problems, that it 'unfits the man for civil life,' would have to give way in the face of what England described as 'a new concept' of the 'carefully selected group,' habituated to the rigours of psychological testing. Test results were seen to generate objective documentary evidence – empirical proof – that these individuals were 'better men that [sic] those who remained at home.' The patriotic contribution these veterans had made to the defence of their nation was unquestioned. Now evidence of their psychological stability provided an additional dimension to the 'sentimental appeal of having fought for the country in which they now seek employment.'[37] As England's comments made clear, there was little to be gained in possibly alarming prospective employers, family members, and communities at large by suggesting that veterans might have become psychologically impaired as a result of their wartime experiences.

The CBC/NCMH series 'The Soldier's Return' went off without a hitch. It was, by all accounts, remarkably successful. As a who's who of the mental hygiene community, a line-up featured 'outstanding Canadian authorities' such as Clarence Hincks, director of the National Committee for Mental Hygiene (Canada); Col. William Line, director of personnel selection at DND and formerly from the University of Toronto Department of Psychology; Roger Myers, from the University of Toronto Department of Psychology; William Blatz, director of the Institute of Child Study, University of Toronto; Joy Maines, president of the Canadian Association of Social Workers and secretary of Community Chests, Ottawa; J.D. Ketchum, director of reports, Wartime Information Board, 'on loan' from University of Toronto Department of Psychology; Col. J.D. (Jack) Griffin, consultant psychiatrist at the Royal Canadian Army Medical Corps (RCAMC) Directorate of Medical Services, DND, and medical director of NCMH; and Brig. J. Rees, consulting psychiatrist to the British Army and head of the Tavistock Clinic, London, England. Speakers from industrial personnel selection departments also appeared, notably Grace Hyndman, wartime director of women personnel for the General Engineering Company, and G.A.S. Nairn, president of Lever Brothers.[38] Whatever the concerns of the RIC, the series revealed a close adherence to the mental hygiene program for rehabilitation as a process of 'adjustment,' psychologically, emotionally, domestically, and vocationally.

On 17 January 1945, G.A.S. Nairn, president of Lever Brothers (Canada), delivered his talk in the series, 'Speaking for Industry.' Nairn praised the tremendous gains of the military in applying human psychology to the work of personnel selection and placement. It would be a considerable step backward were private industry to revert to the flawed methods of the 'old-fashioned employment office.' For that matter, the civil re-establishment order, with its promise of re-employment in former jobs, was probably just as flawed as the haphazard method of employment office or plant gate hiring. Military reports such as those provided by Col. William Line for the McGill lecture series had made it clear that far too much wasted human potential and social disorder followed in the wake of these self-selecting and unscientific methods of personnel placement. Nairn used Line's research to argue that, as service psychologists demonstrated, upwards of 40 per cent of those in the workforce, or at least the male workforce, were poorly matched in their jobs. With the looming prospect of peaceably integrating the former elevator boy-turned-squadron leader back into the workplace, here was an outstanding opportunity for employers in private industry to reap the benefits of the military investment in human potential. Like England, Nairn also explained that the armed services had developed systematic psychological profiles of its enlisted personnel. Would employers not stand to gain from such a well-organized, well-documented system of personnel assessment? Consider, Nairn told his national audience, the 'psychological wonders' in which the nation might share if the labour force were organized to the same standard as the military. A system of psychological testing, assessment, and job placement would work as both a preventive and a productive strategy. Society would avoid the symptoms of occupational maladjustment – the 'square peg in the round hole' phenomenon – which included unemployment, union agitation, antisocial acts in the workplace, chronic absenteeism, and high turnover rates. On the positive side of the balance sheet, industry stood to benefit from the new ground broken by the military in developing a comprehensive system of personnel assessment, identifying and deploying human resources in the most productive and efficient locations across its vast apparatus. Full employment had 'social as well as psychological importance.' Cultivating human capacities in this way could 'shape the whole course of social development in the postwar era.' Social unrest would be reduced and wealth and prosperity increased in direct proportion to the development of 'contented and productive citizens.'[39]

'Am I Intelligent Enough to Do This Job?'

For the returning veteran, the route to civil re-establishment would be a long one. Finding a job was only one of the many hurdles that lay ahead, but it was surely a top priority. Officials at Veterans' Affairs were well versed in the best techniques, and not only because of the difficult experiences, some would say blunders, of the last war. Indeed, the popular adage in military circles – that the wars of the present were generally fought on the basis of the last one – applied equally to the demobilization of armies. In the months to follow, DVA would closely follow the advice of staff psychologists, launching perhaps the first mass experiment based on the principles of self-help. Veterans were inducted into the rehabilitation program through a series of self-help guides intended to advise and educate demobilized personnel, prospective employers, and community members about the Veterans' Charter.

Self-help guides followed a question-and-answer format, encouraging women and men to consider their future employment as a function of personal aptitudes, capacities, and interests. Royal Canadian Air Force (RCAF) personnel were told that 'An aptitude test is in *your* best interest.'[40] The test was the best way to decide one's proper vocation. The popular 1945 guide *What Happens Now? A Veterans' Guide* put the matter in the following way: 'What is the level of intelligence of people who "go places" in this field? Can I measure up to that level? Does the occupation require any special skills or aptitudes? How do I rate in this respect?'[41] Equipped with the proper tools, every veteran would find her or his path back to 'civvy street,' accompanied at every step by assistance and direction from a raft of professionally trained and knowledgeable practitioners. Simultaneously, in a booklet issued for employers, unions, and citizen rehabilitation committees, readers were encouraged to find out all they could about employment provisions, including reinstatement in former jobs; training; job creation; industry, union, and government cooperation; and finally, the following: 'personnel management, with particular relation to the study of the abilities, skills, personal qualities and problems of veterans.'[42] In the end, successful rehabilitation lay within the grasp of the individual veteran, a theme reinforced in all of the guidebooks. The best thing a veteran could do was consult the DVA counsellor. Veterans were invited to enter the counselling process even before they were issued with discharge papers. Testing was the ticket to future success, not just in a job but in a lifetime career – code for security and future prosperity of self and family.[43] Finding a new job was as much a matter of psychological matching as it was an economic necessity.

The guides promoted a lifestyle of responsible consumption, and of success, security and stability in work, community, and home life. But none of this was obtainable without a job. Who wanted to return to the insecurity of unemployment? And men were the primary wage earners, the primary actors in the market for jobs. The belief that personal success was determined by tapping the psychological resources inherent in each individual transformed the employment relation – that is, successful labour market attachment – into a psychological relation guided by expert intervention and diagnosis. For example, a booklet developed for the RCAF, 'Procedure for Personnel Counselling,' presented aptitude testing as the first and most important step along the way to a successful, rewarding, and exciting career.[44] The illustrations in the booklet told the story of the successful path to civilian readjustment. All characters in this narrative were male and white. One such illustration denoted a series of walls posed as potential barriers. At the base of each was an open door through which passed the initially perplexed but increasingly informed and relaxed ex-serviceman, arm-in-arm with the trusted male counsellor. The 'procedure for personnel counselling' in this masculinist depiction was implicitly organized into four phases: assessment, revelation, selection, and placement, each coinciding with the discovery of inner personal capacity, matching to the appropriate jobs, finding the right opportunities, and securing expert assistance.

Identifying the 'person' was represented through four constituent components, depicted through a series of panels, each representing a distinct area of knowledge about the individual job seeker. Science, personified by the expert diagnostician, remained outside the frame, unseen but clearly present, guiding the individual candidate through an exercise that would produce revelatory knowledge of the self. The subject of the first panel was aptitude, represented in the form of a human head (white, male). Intelligence was symbolized by a calliper positioned at the side, a hand holding a magnifying glass, and, at the bottom, the ubiquitous square peg/hole and round peg/hole, signifying the correct fit. The next panel depicted a young person (also white and male) surrounded by the interests of childhood: paints, books, mechanical tools, cars, cannons, beakers, aeroplanes, and, a hint at the relevance of the other images, money. In other words, interests developed early in childhood as 'play' held the secrets to adult work capacities, an untapped lode of potential knowledge about true character and employment capacity. The adult realization of these childhood interests was signified by the militarized images of the final two panels: service experience and civil experience, each representing identical figures in military and work uniform, respectively. Security was the unifying theme in this cartoon, security in employment through a career for which the individual was already ideally suited, his personal interests having been discovered, confirmed, and made intelligible and rational by scientific technique. The dream of security could be manifested only through stable employment. The veteran who landed a stable perch in the workforce would enjoy the personal satisfaction of a rewarding job and, better yet, all the consumer goods to follow. By the end of the booklet, the now happy ex-serviceman is seen rolling up his shirt-sleeves, eager to rejoin civilian life, while, unknown to him, an equally keen bespectacled 'president' of industry is seen leaning over his desk, fixing an excited sight line directly on the veteran. The key to such a happy ending lay in unlocking the inner capacities for learning, the aptitudes of skill in a given occupation, and commitment to the occupational programming developed by DVA and NES.

Back to Civilian Life: Rehabilitation for Ex-Servicewomen

On 4 January 1945, Dr Olive Ruth Russell was appointed executive assistant to the director at Veterans' Affairs, S.N.F. Chant; her role was to specialize in women's rehabilitation.[45] In the news release announcing her appointment as the first senior woman to join DVA, Russell was presented as an expert in vocational guidance, an educational psychologist whose postgraduate and professional work had proved a tremendous asset to the women's armed services. Russell's pre-war work found a far more receptive audience in the postwar period of rehabilitation planning than it had during the tumultuous Depression years. The June 1945 issue of *Saturday Night* magazine carried a lengthy article promoting her research as part of a broader strategy of publicizing the work of veterans' rehabilitation generally. Russell was an ideal emissary for the scientific remedial work of rehabilitation, given her extensive academic credentials and background as an educational and employment expert. Throughout the period, Russell was featured in press reports and magazine articles, her photograph accompanying nearly every story. Her views of women and waged work were revealed in each of these accounts as consonant with those of her counterparts at the NSS Women's Division: some women would work for pay and would be directed into occupations thought suitable for them, while others would resume their domestic posts. Russell went one step farther in her advocacy on behalf of women much like herself: university educated and 'professional.' In the main, however, Russell, too, would experience at first hand the challenge of disturbing the received 'naturalness' of a racially and sexually divided labour market underpinning the social order.

Like her professional colleagues, Russell saw that rehabilitation involved more than demilitarization and civil re-establishment. The postwar project could potentially redefine the values and practices of democratic and responsible citizenship, beginning with the attributes and capacities of individual citizens themselves. The *Saturday Night* article recounted Russell's advocacy of systematic vocational guidance for all individuals at all ages. In 1938, Russell had drafted a petition that was presented to Prime Minister Mackenzie King by the Ontario Vocational Guidance Association. In it, she had argued for a system of comprehensive personnel assessment, which, if implemented, would resolve the multitude of social problems that inevitably trailed in the path of the maladjusted individual. This was the promise of rehabilitation. The article was written by Lieut. F.E. Whyard of the Women's Royal Canadian Navy Service (WRCNS) Naval Information service. In her correspondence with Whyard, Russell lamented the obstacles she and her mental hygiene colleagues confronted at virtually every turn in their work. Her own career development had suffered, simply because she was a woman, something she attributed not to gender but to ignorance of advanced educational policy. For example, she was compelled, after doing graduate research in Europe, to accept a teaching position that paid less than the job she had left in order to take up graduate studies in the first place. 'Yes, I was a victim not only of the Depression but of the fact that Canada lagged so far behind in developing Psychology and Guidance. Perhaps that experience has only added to my desire to see to it that young people get the encouragement, opportunities and help needed to develop their talents most effectively.'[46] The experiment in public policy now underway promised to change all that. For perhaps the first time, government was committed to scrutinizing the conditions of civil formation, monitoring the progress of civilian adjustment, and investing in the development of responsible citizens, happy homes, and healthy communities. So much of juvenile delinquency – including the sexual improprieties of dissolute youthful leisure activities, unemployment, family discord, and social conflict manifested in political agitation – was caused by malformed and misdirected personality. The magazine article reconstructed Russell as a leader in the movement to remedy such ills, one who brought her expertise to bear in a constructive program of rational guidance.[47]

Russell's job was largely concerned with carrying the work of rehabilitation into a network of community, service, and related governmental relations and thus linking women's organizations to the day-to-day operations of both the DVA and the NES. She spoke regularly at national conferences of the National Council of Women of Canada (NCWC), working closely with the leadership of the Canadian Association for Adult Education, the YWCA, the Canadian Welfare Council, and the Community Chest and related civic organizations across the country. At every turn, she encouraged closer liaison with local citizens' committees and social and state agencies in a comprehensive effort to secure the successful reintegration of all citizens through the work of rehabilitation. At the same time, in conjunction with the Research Division of the Department of Labour, she continued the work of developing a body of vocational expertise and consistent and comprehensive tools to aid this work, focusing on techniques for the systematic assessment of occupations and required vocational skills.[48] In 1945, soon after V-E Day, the Training Division of DVA joined the Department of Labour in establishing an Occupational Information section and a three-digit coded classification of all occupational skills, based on the U.S. Dictionary of Occupational Titles.[49] This material was supplemented during 1946–7 by a survey of seventy selected occupations. Information about occupational trends and vocational training requirements provided a foundation for regular bulletins and reports by which counsellors were intended to organize their work and advise veterans. By 1949 the Occupational Information Service was transferred as a regular service to the Department of Labour. This work complemented the findings of the Royal Commission on Veterans' Qualifications, the so-called Bovey Commission, appointed in 1945, in part to review the training received by enlisted personnel within the services and to recommend a systematic method for accrediting such training in civilian employment.

To each of these policy locations Russell carried a consistent message:

women had demonstrated their employment capacity throughout the war in both military and civilian roles, and educated, skilled, and professional women could no longer be denied equal access to the labour market. At the same time, Russell, like her colleagues at the Department of Labour, worked to restore and secure the racial and sexual division of labour within the household and the formal waged economy. As proof that these efforts were effective, Russell reported that by the end of 1947, 24 per cent of all ex-servicewomen (11,685 women) had claimed training benefits, a much higher proportion than men. Of these, 9,205 had enrolled in some form of vocational training in more than 100 occupations.[50] What she did not indicate was that the vast majority of these women were concentrated in some 30 occupations that were conventionally designated as women's occupations. Employment of ex-servicewomen was not viewed as a problem – even though 5.3 per cent were registered as receiving out-of-work benefits as at 31 March 1947. If this had been viewed as an official unemployment rate, it was certainly higher than the national average for the period – a position that became a well-entrenched claim in the official narratives produced in the ensuing postwar period. Equal pay, however, remained a serious concern, a vestige of the sex discrimination against which Russell and some of her colleagues continued to agitate, with limited success. Even before the process was completed, the rehabilitation program was judged an outstanding success, due in large part to the enthusiasm and commitment of servicewomen themselves and their adaptability and discipline in readjusting to civilian endeavours. Notwithstanding such a stellar record, Russell remained deeply concerned for the prospects of ongoing discriminatory practices, fearing a backlash that would most certainly threaten these hard-won gains.

Russell was a lead instructor at the DVA Counsellors' Training courses starting in 1945. All counselling staff were sent to Ottawa for a one-month training course in vocational counselling. Women were seen to present a unique and particular set of challenges, enough to justify specially designated services and personnel equipped with the correct knowledge and expertise to attend to the need for 'personal attention and follow-up.' However, at the time Russell joined the department, there were no designated women welfare officers within DND. The National Selective Service was not equipped to address the special rehabilitation needs of servicewomen, nor was the Department of Pensions and National Health. Russell had begun calling for the appointment of officers specifically assigned to and responsible for personal intervention with and supervision of discharged personnel in 1944. The NSS was ill equipped to address the 'peculiar needs of our service women,' she reported, and so was incapable of providing the personalized service so necessary to their successful rehabilitation. This work was not limited to service referrals but was directly implicated in the formation of responsible citizens. As Russell wrote, it was the responsibility of the women's welfare officer, should any be appointed, to 'do the follow-up needed for persons who have proved unable or unwilling to accept the responsibilities of citizenship in the army or in civilian life.'[51]

Even before moving over to DVA, Russell had wondered when and how, if at all, the rehabilitation needs of servicewomen discharged from the services would be addressed in policy. This was a pressing matter during her tenure at the Canadian Women's Army Corps, concerned as she was that 'unsuitable personnel' not be permitted to slip back into civilian life where they might resurface as 'problems' after the war. Certainly, welfare agencies were not up to the task of dealing with the problems presented by 'persons who have proved unable or unwilling to accept the responsibilities of citizenship in the army or in civilian life.' Rehabilitation was more than a matter of ensuring satisfactory individual adjustment. It was a crucial policy challenge for a liberal state emerging from total war. Rehabilitation was about securing the welfare of democratic society by ensuring that each and all took up their responsibilities of citizenship, as self-governing and self-regulating subjects. Russell instructed counsellors that their role was to ensure that women received full counselling services, including the regular use of intelligence tests to avoid the employment problems associated with the 'square peg in a round hole' phenomenon. Women had equal access with men to all rehabilitation services, including vocational assessment, counselling, and, if necessary, training, all of which included referral to appropriate employment through the NES. Nonetheless, as I discuss in the next chapter, training for women was restricted at every turn to a limited range of occupations that were deemed 'suitable' for women. The home and household were considered women's primary location. Word did not appear to be getting through, however. At a meeting of citizens' rehabilitation committees held in North Bay in July 1946, the woman representative responsible for ex-servicewomen's rehabilitation in that area claimed that she was entirely unaware of any legislated training provisions for women.

The Canadian Veterans' Publishing Company published *What Happens Now? A Veterans' Guide.* Servicewomen, according to the guide, would have full access to rehabilitation credits. Women were entitled to everything, 'from soup to nuts,' including a clothing allowance and a rehabilitation cash grant upon discharge, medical care and pension credit, dependant's care, and a training and education allowance. A woman would also have preference in employment, provided she was not married. The Veterans' Charter testified to the new gender equality. However, marital status undermined such claims, as women veterans would soon find out. For example, all veterans were entitled to a parcel of land under the Veterans' Land Grant Act. In effect, however, a married ex-servicewoman could not apply for a land grant, although title would be readily conferred on her ex-serviceman husband. The re-establishment credit would not be affected, however. Women found the helpful advice that the re-establishment cash credits could be used 'to help furnish their home.' Home was the goal, despite the reassuring tone and confident message of veterans' manuals such as *What Happens Now?*: 'In short, girls, you have just about the same rights and privileges in your rehabilitation as have the ex-servicemen.'[52] Clearly, however, women did not and, under a male family wage and citizenship entitlement structure, would not enjoy the same eligibility as men.

In the seventy-nine pages of *What Happens Now?*, only a brief one-and-a-half-page section specifically addressed the concerns of women veterans. 'What about the Service Woman?' was a chatty guide to the minimum provisions available under the Charter. The white male veteran was depicted in military dress, a business suit, or, occasionally, coveralls. Advertisements abounded, denoting the seamless business-community-government reconstruction effort. The only female representation portrayed the ex-servicewoman in a decidedly non-military, stylish (though tailored), feminine garb, complete with a decorative nosegay. Servicewomen's pensions, the manual explained, were on the same scale as men's, although 'for obvious reasons, a dependent wife or pensioned widow of an ex-serviceman is not eligible for out-of-work benefits.' 'Frequently one hears the remark,' the guide continued, 'that the rehabilitation problems of the ex-servicewomen can be summed up in a single word – marriage.' Of course, there was 'a grain of truth' in this exaggeration, but no one really questioned 'that all servicewomen by their wonderful contribution to victory have earned, in their own right, the honours and privileges of those who have served.'[53] *Back to Civil Life* carried the same message, that rehabilitation services were equally available to both women and men. However, the theme of equal access was significantly undermined by the theme of domesticity that pervaded the guides. There was no question about it: science established that women and men had different aptitudes. The sexual division of labour was constituted as not only natural, as the way things are, but also rational. Through the self-help guides, recent employment trends were described as a temporary aberration in the normal state of affairs, despite the fact that so many women had moved into the skilled trades and occupations in the industrial – and military – labour force. Service personnel were now counselled that this phenomenon was behind them, a signal to male veterans that they need not fear permanent displacement from the workforce by the wartime labours of either civilian women or servicewomen.

By January 1946, concerns about the differential access to rehabilitation services and programs had reached the office of E.L.M. Burns, director general of rehabilitation for DVA. In a strongly worded circular, Burns insisted that services for women become more closely integrated into the rehabilitation apparatus. Far too many women were not receiving access to training that 'would be desirable for their most effective rehabilitation into civilian employment,' he directed. Criticisms of the program were now wending their way through the official apparatus, leading to the suggestion that a separate division ought to be established for the female veteran. Women were the best counsellors of other women. The idea that ex-servicewomen had to jostle their way through throngs of men in public spaces such as veterans' centres or employment offices was unacceptable. After a brief round of official bickering, welfare officers and occupational counsellors for women veterans were finally appointed late in 1946, in the hope that the women's section of the now-combined NSS/NES would be able to handle ex-servicewomen's needs. In part responding to Burns's allegations that women were not receiving the full benefits due to them, Russell acknowledged that there would be no separate women's branch within the DVA rehabilitation apparatus. Instead, women veterans would be channelled through the same apparatus that was handling the redeployment of civilian workers. Furthermore, the practice of determining the availability of training options as the preliminary step towards placement – in either domestic or waged labour – was reversed. Burns was sharply critical of the direction policy had taken in the matter of women's training, of channelling women through available training first, and from there into employment. That practice, he stated, must stop.[54] This approach reflected the decentralized and localized planning procedures related to employment policy for women that were already underway at the NSS Women's Division. Employment officers made referrals within a set range of 'suitable' occupations for women, geared to local employment levels within these occupations. The final decision was made based on whether or not training was available. 'The Counselling should be directed primarily toward choice of occupation rather than toward training as such,' Burns stated, echoing the approach taken by Fraudena Eaton.

Like so many of her colleagues, Russell was certain that, once capricious practices of 'sex discrimination' had been reversed through the legislative provisions of the rehabilitation program, women who deserved greater opportunity in new professions and emerging occupations would actually break new ground. This made it all the more important to safeguard the integrity of the professions by not referring into training any whose capacities, abilities and suitability might be considered 'doubtful.'[55] Vocational counselling, that is, also worked in reverse: it opened up opportunities and actualized equality claims, securing the legitimate equality claims of those meriting such advancement – in a word, gate-keeping. 'Women of below average general ability' seeking jobs 'for which their intelligence ill-equips them' were in no position to break new occupational ground. Counsellors were to be 'on the alert' against the 'square peg in the round hole,' since *No one remains happy long in work that is either too easy or too difficult for his or her general level of ability.*'[56]

DVA women's counselling staff had exclusive authority to determine an appropriate training referral. The servicewoman would be counselled about her occupational 'choice' based on individual suitability 'in light of her own wishes, her past training and experience, her ability to absorb further training, and last but by no means least, with a view to the employment trends for women in the community in which she intends to live.'[57] Again, the language of 'individual choice' and 'individual desires' closely informed the operation of counselling discourse. Women were to be made to feel, and hopefully accept, that the decisions taken were their own and, therefore, were in their own best interests. The approach was consistent with the principles of educational psychology discourses, in which the agency of the counselled subject held the key to success. Rehabilitation counselling would have succeeded where its results had been equally decided upon by the ex-servicewoman together with the counsellor. Women worked with counselling staff, learning to appraise 'their own capacities and suitability for certain types of training and work' under the guidance of staff 'skilled in the best psychological techniques.' Testing and the relations mobilized through such practice were equitable because they were objective. However, interpretation of

its results, through which the knowledge of the individual was constituted as 'appraisal,' was subjective, according to Russell – it was an art. 'It
is true that tests may be dangerous in the hands of unskilled counsellors
and caution must be taken to safeguard any misuse that could easily be
made of them,' she argued. The counsellor could no more attempt to
conduct a thorough appraisal without the aid of testing instruments
than a medical practitioner could read the condition of a body without a
standardized gauge or tool – stethoscope or thermometer – capable of
penetrating the body's surface. The counsellor had to be fully conver-
sant with the 'unique' aspects of women's employment and training, a
gesture towards the ongoing tension between CVT and the NES so
pointedly criticized in the Burns memorandum.

Like her colleagues at the NSS Women's Division, Russell instructed
the counselling staff to encourage women veterans into domestic employment, still a viable solution to the problem of finding suitable waged
work for those with less developed skills or education. Compulsion
would not work in this case, but would instead drive away the 'desired
type' of woman, leaving only the 'least employable pool' available as
potential domestic workers. There was no point in 'trying to force
unwilling, untrained and incompetent young women into household
employment.' And so, Russell joined her counterparts at the NSS
Women's Division in the effort to find 'ways and means of raising the
status of this occupation so as to attract intelligent willing workers to
want training for this important work.'[58] The challenges, she thought,
were far from insurmountable.

Problems encountered in rehabilitation counselling were invariably
cast as a function of personal maladjustment. The DVA publication
Veterans' Affairs carried a feature article in its May 1947 issue about the
considerable contribution made by mental hygiene clinics in the work of
the Veterans' Administration in the United States. Although reflecting a
stronger Freudian approach than was apparent in much of the work
conducted by mental hygiene practitioners in Canada, the message was
the same. Problems were common, whether derived from poor adjustment, insecurity, or 'the unconscious mind': 'it doesn't mean you are
crazy or wacky but just darned unhappy with your life.'[59] To illustrate,
the two case studies examined below (both presented by Edna M.
Whinney, chief women's counsellor for DVA) reconstruct the leading
aspects of counselling work and its ultimate success in the satisfactory
adjustment made by the individual. In the first, a clearly qualified and
stable young woman was able to satisfy her ambition to take up post-

graduate studies in home economics at Columbia. Her chosen career was appropriate, and her pre-enlistment service as a dietician at a hospital and then a department store reflected the steady pursuit of a stable and promising career in this feminine profession. Her 'outstanding service and personality' made her a fine officer, reflecting diligence, discipline, and good deportment: everything a professional 'girl' needed to succeed. Case number two, on the other hand, told a different but regrettably all too common tale. In this case, the thirty-six-year-old woman had worked as a music instructor, assisting her mother. This was her 'pre-enlistment' history, the first entry in the case study that Whinney presented to her attentive audience. She began to train as a registered nurse, but stopped after eighteen months because she had a 'nervous breakdown.' Following that, she worked 'at numerous hospitals' as a practical nurse. In these few lines, the woman was constructed as unmarried, largely under her mother's care, unable to complete skilled training in a professional capacity, perhaps artistic but decidedly emotionally unstable – with the artistry and the instability possibly being connected – and incapable of maintaining steady employment, even at a less skilled vocation within the same field of nursing. Her service and post-discharge history were formed in much the same terms:

> Service Experience:
> 1 year service as Sick Berth Attendant in Wrens. Discharged 'unsuitable' because of nervous breakdown. Psychiatrist's report made at time of discharge, confirmed a neurosis largely due to insecurity. Mother, father and grandparent who lived with the family, all died within a few months of each other. Only brother left home and there was no close contact.
> Post-discharge experience:
> A summer fruit picking on a friend's farm. A few weeks demonstrating and selling sheet music in a chain store, replacing a girl on holidays. Six months clerk in Civil Service.

The counsellor in charge of the case advised a return to nursing and suggested that the woman should accept a temporary work assignment to determine her 'suitability and interest.' However, the experience proved too 'strenuous,' and she returned and asked to be trained in stenography. She was then referred to the DVA psychiatrist, who thought further training was unnecessary since it was only 'a further search for security.' The intrepid counsellor, after four interview sessions, concluded that the best options were piano teaching, clerical work, and, once again, practical nursing. The assessment included a visit to the music store where the woman had worked before the war demonstrating popular musical scores. This and a visit to another store led the counsellor to conclude that a career in music sales was unlikely to yield employment. Instead, and against the psychiatrist's considered judgment, the counsellor prepared an application for review by the Training Board, on the rationale that occupational training as a clerical typist would have a stabilizing and remediating effect and was sure to lead to security in both employment and personality. The veteran would be happiest and most efficient in a routine job that would allow some scope for her imaginative talents.

1. Her skill as a pianist would assist her in learning typing.
2. Additional skills would promote self-confidence.
3. Applicant was obviously conscientious and sincere, although immature for her years.[60]

Piano playing surely facilitated technical typing skills, an occupation that would provide personal satisfaction, artistic expression, and employment stability until marriage brought her working career to a satisfactory conclusion.

As the official in charge of women's rehabilitation, and the key educator of DVA counselling staff, Russell worked to expand rehabilitation policy by incorporating the principles of mental hygiene in all counselling assessments of women veterans. She turned to reports from American surveys of military personnel for evidence. The problem was far more widespread than many wanted to believe: 45 per cent of all discharges on medical grounds were the result of 'emotional instability,' 'psychoneurosis,' or 'other psychiatric conditions.' The fact that there was no physical evidence of interior instability or illness contributed to the tendency of most to regard these persons with aversion and fear, or at least incomprehension. Russell sought to normalize the conditions surrounding maladjustment to encourage an enlightened community response to the suffering encountered among fellow citizens, civilian or veteran. After all, every individual had his or her 'breaking point,' so that 'the sturdiest personalities can break under strain beyond human endurance.' Sympathy was good, but referral to experts was better. The knowledge that even the most 'normal' individual might break under the strain of daily life was a central preoccupation of postwar society – and understandably so, given the difficult times just past.

Talk about healthy adjustment was becoming much more popular, meeting with particular success in a CBC radio lecture and advice show 'In Search of Ourselves.' The mental health drama was launched in 1949 fuelled by the outstanding success of the pilot series, 'The Soldier's Return,' broadcast throughout 1947–8. 'In Search of Ourselves' drew upon the same themes and strategies that had been organized through the earlier NCMH-CBC collaborative series, only now the focus was extended beyond the civil re-establishment of veterans to investigate everyday life and its problems. Listeners were invited to scrutinize the problems in daily life through the dimension of personality adjustment, that is to say, the discourse of mental health. The program opened a new door into daily experience, promising relief from personal troubles, dissatisfaction, conflict, and insecurities. Across the country, radio listeners could identify with the dramatized scenarios beamed into their kitchens and living rooms, as actors struggled to meet the seemingly prosaic but obviously unsettling conflicts of family, work, and personal life. The show promised happiness and personal growth, each episode ending with the resolution of marital, family, or personal conflict through the intervention of the psyche-based techniques and friendly counsel of Dr Jack Griffin. Although a few listeners wrote in to complain that they found 'some of the case histories too sad,' far more indicated how strongly the dramas resonated with them, since they had 'encountered similar problems in their own or other people's lives.' Griffin's advice was described as 'of great help in understanding why people sometimes act and talk so strangely.'[61] Each instalment in the series dramatized the details of a particular 'case study' by steadily charting the breakdown of an individual, thus examining in careful detail the deterioration of normal and healthy adjustment. 'In Search of Ourselves' took off as a national problem-solving event, transforming the listening audience into active participants through the venue of 'listening clubs,' 'discussion groups,' and letter writing. As an educational initiative, the series told listeners what to look for and how to identify markers and interpret clues as early warning signs. The sympathetic and compassionate friend, family member, teacher, employer, and co-worker learned to search vigilantly for similar indicators in themselves and those around them. As a new programming feature on the CBC, the mental health drama carried the same message as individual counselling: maintaining one's mental health was a regular feature of healthy living, as important to a wholesome life as were proper nutrition and daily exercise.

'I Trust You Will Not Think I Am a Feminist': Equality Rights for the Postwar Woman?

Russell argued consistently throughout her tenure with DVA that the legislative acts that collectively made up 'the Veterans' Charter' were more consistent with the principles of women's equality than any other area of Dominion legislation. She considered that women's equality claims were best assured through the rehabilitation program, embedded within which was the recognition that women were entitled to full access to all governmental services and programs on an equal basis with men. In her many speeches to women's organizations, citizens' committees, and service organizations, Russell actively constructed a narrative of equality as something achieved by women steadily throughout the war. As an example of the significance of these gains, she pointed out how women who enlisted in the newly established women's divisions of the services had initially received only two-thirds of the equivalent male wage and had been denied access to benefits for dependants. Russell felt that the status of all women in society would improve on the basis of the considerable achievements of women in the services. As proof, she pointed out that women were eligible for all benefits and credits legislated through the 'Veterans' Charter.'[62]

Women were accorded formal equality with men in every area of rehabilitation legislation – but with the significant exception of married women. Robert England's recently published compendium detailing the principles and purpose of rehabilitation programming, *Discharged* (1944), concluded that the best route to successful reintegration into civilian life was through secure employment at a reasonable – male breadwinner/ family – wage.[63] The same held true for women, Russell contended. This was the best way to ensure that wartime gains became the foundation for advancement and prosperity well into the future. This 'hard-won economic independence' brought with it the recognition that women needed to work. In an analysis that closely adhered to liberal choice theory, rational economic choice saw women and men as equal citizens actively contributing to social and economic production, and as equal consumers freely participating in the rationalized space of free markets. Freedom of choice was the central unifying principle making such markets democratic and, therefore, defensible, something women alongside men had fought a war to defend. The prospect of returning to the pre-war era of entrenched sex discrimination was a troubling one to be resisted, even if that meant risking political challenge from those predisposed to misinterpret Russell's position. This was not an unabashed declaration of feminism, something she repeatedly eschewed as a narrow political tendency promoting only women's self-interest. As she put it, 'I trust you will not think me a feminist thinking only of advantages for women.'[64] On the contrary, women's freedom of choice had to be defended since without this there could be no happy home or healthy democracy. Russell's interest in rehabilitation programming, therefore, lay in using that legislative base to mark out a new brand of citizenship, one that included 'protecting women's freedom of choice in regard to her home life and occupation.'[65]

Russell was intent on advancing the equality of choice that largely informed her understanding of the origins and irrationality of 'sex discrimination.' Access to and pay in employment ought to be limited only by capacity, ability, and suitability, each of which could be determined through the judicious application of psychological personnel selection and placement techniques. The denial of employment opportunities to women not only ran counter to the tenets of liberal democracy: sex discrimination in employment consigned thousands of women to poverty and, as depression, war, and totalitarianism had already demonstrated, 'poverty anywhere in the world constitutes a danger to prosperity everywhere.'[66] Those who ignored the tremendous contributions of service and civilian women to the war effort, arguing that women ought now to cede their place in the labour market to men, advanced a straw argument against the growing movement for full employment. She made newspaper headlines following an address in Vancouver in March 1946 in which she claimed that there was little to be gained by attempting to force ex-servicewomen into domestic work. They simply would not comply, nor should they. These women had consistently exceeded the level of most women in civilian society by every standard, Russell argued: IQ tests, level of education, percentage of skilled tradeswomen – whatever the measure, ex-servicewomen surpassed it and merited better than household employment in their postwar career. But there was more than merit at stake: there was also desire. Veteran women needed jobs that not only matched their qualifications but also permitted them to 'realize their desires,' and, as she told the Vancouver Council of Women, this was the challenge facing women's organizations.[67] Those few 'unfortunate persons' who had managed to get into the services and damage the otherwise excellent reputation of the women's divisions in no way disproved the overall superiority of the ex-servicewomen who had served so well. Russell acknowledged the consistent support of local councils and other women's organizations in assisting the women's services through the very difficult and trying period of breaking this new ground.[68]

In this way, Russell joined in an emerging narrative that constructed the postwar woman as a signifier of all that women had gained during the Second World War. Her public speeches and policy advocacy actively constructed the postwar world as one inhabited by women who were now fully integrated in legislation, in the labour force, and in their own households. The 'women of tomorrow' had 'invaded man's last domain' by going to war. According to this narrative, 'Winnie the welder' and 'Rosie the riveter' had replaced the 'shop-girl'; their overalls, lunch pails, and production charts had replaced 'bridges' and 'teas.' The question was, was this a permanent trend? 'The housewife who has stayed at home is war's "forgotten woman,"' according to Russell.[69] The postwar woman of this world was gaining financial independence and, more important, a psychological identity grounded in newfound 'self-esteem.' She was secure in her identity as feminine, as mother, and as skilled and/or professional. There were less positive changes, too. 'Standards regarding sex relations' had altered, prompting fears of an apparent escalation of venereal disease and illegitimacy. The 'increased tempo of money and fast living' were cited to support claims for greater vigilance to ensure that the heedless materialism and excessive individualism of the pre-war period did not return.[70] The massive changes wrought by the war had opened up the labour market to women, and that, in Russell's view, was the sure route to women's equality. At the same time, women were characterized as 'vitally important' in the work of homemaking and as 'rearers of the Nation's children,' a task she characterized as both science and art.[71] The science lay in the work of understanding human nature, a sphere in which women excelled if properly trained. Workers in the household were also critical, a task that Russell had already made clear did not include the woman of tomorrow, the postwar woman. Nonetheless, there was no disputing women's right to work 'on the basis of merit,' free of 'sex discrimination.'

Dependence upon government was to be studiously avoided, particularly in the context of a program positioning counselling staff to screen and decide the assistance they could offer in the remediation of legitimate needs. If the services of 'specialists' were called for, then such would be provided, but only to ensure that the individual would, as a process of self-development, come to recognize that both the source of 'need' and its remediation lay within – to 'help Johnny see Johnny through.' Civil society would be enlisted in a generalized effort to make good the objectives of reintegration, through housing assistance, personal shopping advice, even the correct and satisfactory use of leisure time (all with a strong emphasis on responsible citizenship), delivered by service clubs, women's organizations, the church, independent business, psychologists, and social agencies. Such a program was best achieved through the public education system. In an echo of the mental hygiene program worked out by Griffin, Laycock, and Line, Russell told her audiences that it was more than time that education be expanded to its fullest potential, addressing human needs through psychological development. In a *Globe and Mail* report of one such address, she referred to the nation's investment in medicine in pursuit of national health or in the psychical sciences for the cultivation of national resources, and asked why a similar investment was not made in teachers so that they could take on the vital and challenging task of cultivating the nation's human resources? If 'billions of dollars' could be committed to the physical sciences, then why 'quibble over a few hundred dollars,' as boards of education were so inclined to do? Echoing the horror of her generation at the prospect of nuclear devastation, Russell counselled an enlightened program for cultivating full human capacity and creativity. Education, psychology, and the social sciences, after all, saw to 'the welfare of mankind rather than its destruction.'[72]

The war had strengthened community and national identity, opening up the opportunity for social reconstruction on the secure footing of psychological science, a society committed to the recognition and satisfaction of human need. Her speeches and correspondence repeatedly pointed to the 'sociological changes' that had stripped away regional, cultural, and class barriers. Canada was poised to take its place in the emerging international order and to participate in the expansion of markets through organized international trade and cooperation agreements. Ensuring prosperity and democratic security through models of Westernized economic development was a far more effective strategy than the 'thunderous declarations of the rights of man.' That is, Russell was now turning to a cooperative model for 'world' economic development, under the leadership and on the model of the U.S.-dominated United Nations. 'Development' in this model truly was a civilizing mission of the West. For example, the slogan of the U.N.'s Relief and Rehabilitation Agency, 'a pint of milk for every Hottentot,' summarized the postwar reconstruction (development) programs initiated under U.N. auspices. It also presaged a model of Western development and political security that undermined independence movements more interested in pursuing autonomous routes to cultural, economic, and political self-determination.

World conditions had a direct bearing on national security and prosperity. In Russell's view, Canada was the 'land of milk and honey,' a land of promise looked upon by 'the hungry millions of Europe and Asia with longing eyes.'[73] The West held the promise of democratic growth and prosperity against the 'backwardness' and the potential threat posed by the impoverished world. Russell supported the popular Wendell Willkie, looking to the leadership of the United States in 'freeing' the world politically and economically. National problems could only be resolved through the international order. Russell's hopes for gender equality were firmly anchored by the cultural, political, and economic superiority of the 'West,' signified by the United States. Through the Western model of free market production, consumption, and economic prosperity in the postwar world, employment in the domestic economy really had no predetermined limit. Full employment planning, therefore, must include (white) women equally with men. As Russell confidently explained, 'as long as there is human need in the world there is work to be done,' and women would surely find their rightful place in such a world.[74]

Conclusion

Russell's brand of feminist thought was a tenuous balance between domesticity and the principles of liberalism. The subject of both was that universalized category of woman as presumptively white, educated, and heterosexual. The interests and aspirations of the 'postwar woman' were co-extensive with the interests of nation and the organizing precepts of the postwar international order, itself constituted as the collective security interests of Western industrial states. The citizenship claims and equality rights of the postwar woman were firmly ensconced in a shared national and cultural identity. Her reproductive and productive capacities were legitimately practised, but only through domesticity or work in a skilled occupation, profession, or business. Poverty, delinquency, racialized difference, inferior capacity, and illegitimate need were the obverse of this universal liberal female subject whose equality claims Russell sought to articulate. The purpose and the tremendous potential of rehabilitation programming, according to Russell and her colleagues, lay in its capacity to forge responsible forms of citizenship: this was the essence of the social security state.

Russell shared her views with many of her colleagues in both DVA and Labour, women who, like her, had reached senior positions overseeing policy programming for women. Their efforts to advance equality claims within the state directly challenged their own position as senior policy practitioners presiding over the emerging policy regime of a social security/welfare state in which domesticity discourses were deeply entrenched. These women promoted policy discourses that destabilized and fragmented gender-based equality claims, even as they argued that equality of position and access should be enjoyed by all women. In the next chapter, I examine the policies and deliberations surrounding postwar rehabilitation training for women. The gains of the 'postwar woman' would not be – nor were they necessarily intended to be – shared by all women. As a liberal equality claim, the universalized articulation of women's right to choose was firmly anchored within the postwar liberal and imperialist world order. Russell's ideas about the citizenship rights of this new category of woman were grounded in ideas about 'collective' security and the democratic responsibilities of citizenship that purportedly faced all women in the emerging postwar world. But the women leading this universalized democratic reconstruction of the postwar social, political, cultural, and economic order were more at home among the upper ranks of the NCWC, the YWCA, and the newly formed groups of business and professional women: middle-class, white, educated, and heterosexual. This was the ideal postwar woman, eager to take up her new position in the postwar world.

chapter six

The Return to Domesticity: Canada's Womanhood in Training

From her post at the helm of the federal government's Second World War 'manpower' agency, the National Selective Service Women's Division (NSSWD), Fraudena Eaton would make sure that the disruption of women's 'normal' employment wrought by the move to wartime production was temporary and even minimal, and that the pre-war occupational distribution and domestic status of women would once again be restored, and soon. Of the 4 million women registered in 1946 as being of 'gainful occupational age' at fourteen years or older, Eaton thought it was most appropriate that 2.4 million were now re-engaged in 'home-making.'[1] This high figure could only mean that life was well on its way to resuming its regular course across the war-weary Dominion. Of the 1,300,500 women not seen to be 'homemakers,' Eaton calculated that about 700,000 were in gainful occupation. That left only 650,000 to be accounted for. These women were not be to considered unemployed, Eaton hastened to add, since only 100,000 of them were actually looking for work.

Who made up the other 500,000 women? 'Slack.' Young women and girls who under normal circumstances ought to remain at home among their families of moderate income. Apart from a few in cities, most were young women from farms, villages, and small towns for whom no 'vocational opportunity' was apparent. The alleged 'slack' were women who had been rapidly drawn into war industries, escalating the number of women registered in a 'gainful occupation' by 1946. But Canada, Eaton asserted, was more than capable of withstanding this 'intensive invasion of the home' experienced by all of the countries making up the Allied Forces, England most of all. Beginning in 1944, thousands of married women were returning to their domestic stations. Women's war experience in the formal waged economy was viewed as a temporary interruption of the regular economic and social order. Moreover, it was an epiphenomenal policy event, motivated as much by the desire to perhaps earn some extra money and/or supplement their husband's incomes as by patriotic spirit. Fraudena Eaton joined her women colleagues in the federal bureaucracy in confidently promoting the notion that changes in labour force composition were merely temporary adjustments and not the early marker of a deepening, much less permanent, trend. Seven out of every ten women would respond to the 'tugs of home life' and take up homemaking or 'just living at home,' leaving only a handful to seek paid work in the postwar economy. Many of these would find their place in the newer electrical, chemical, and radio industries – or with those traditional female employers of last resort, garment manufacturing and domestic service: industries, that is, that 'prefer the dexterity, cleanliness and painstaking patience of women workers.'

The transition from war to peace, like that from peace to war, ushered in a new brand of female bureaucrat. Women such as Fraudena Eaton at the Department of Labour, or Mary Salter and Olive Ruth Russell at the Department of Veterans' Affairs (DVA), shared a common objective: to entrench women's employment and training as a distinct policy stream in the federal state. They hoped the attention devoted to women would continue, perhaps through a women's branch within an Industrial Welfare Bureau. As a reading of their plans for women's training and employment within the immediate postwar administration indicates, many feared that the access to public policy planning they had lobbied for might easily be lost once the wartime planning administration was dismantled. When R.F. Thompson was appointed to head the postwar training agency, Canadian Vocational Training (CVT), Eaton pressed the deputy minister of labour, Arthur MacNamara, to appoint a woman at least to the position of assistant to the CVT federal training director. This arrangement would have replicated what Eaton and MacNamara had put in place during the war at National Selective Service. Eaton's proposal was easily justified on the grounds that women's unique status within the labour market, the labour force, and the workplace required specialized knowledge that was best provided – and directed – by other women. Failing such an appointment, at the very least an advisory structure should be established, much like the bipartite advisory committee at the Unemployment Insurance Commission (UIC) representing the particular positions on policy matters of business and labour. 'There is no reason,' she advised MacNamara, 'why the advice of women should not be sought' as a feature of labour policy administration. In fact, she concluded, any training director or policy official 'should be pleased' to have the opportunity to secure regular and sound advice from representative women. The number of women registering with NES was dropping at a time when, if anything, it should be growing, prompting Eaton to renew her calls for a publicity campaign and out-reach through local advisory committees, maintaining the supervision and monitoring capacity of the NES to ensure that women would be directed into 'appropriate' employment. Maintaining a comprehensive statistical record and profile was also a good way of assuring that the expertise of the Women's Division would continue to be recognized.

Returning to Civilian Life: Servicewomen and the Veterans' Rehabilitation Program

Senior defence staff anticipated that demobilization of servicewomen would be delayed, in part because so many were assigned to clerical work where the demand for their services would continue until the machinery of war was fully dismantled. Of the 15,769 women still awaiting discharge in 1946, most would continue to be employed in clerical work until demobilization was completed. Certainly, the view from the War Cabinet Office in Britain was that the timing of the demobilization of women depended at least in part on 'whether women should be employed after the war' in either a civilian or a military capacity.[2] As these officials made clear, there was far less urgency in the matter of discharging service-women since, in the anticipated rush for jobs, in all likelihood women would resume their pre-war domestic status. According to Walter Woods, deputy minister of veterans' affairs, no account was to be taken of additional money received by the veteran or his 'dependants' from so-called 'casual earnings or outside employment that did not adversely affect the training program,' again on the principle that vocational training would be the veteran's main activity until he was finally placed.[3] The equality principle was at least partially undermined by yet another directive instructing veterans' welfare officers to determine benefit en-titlements according to the wage-earning status of the veteran's female spouse. If the female spouse was found to be 'self-supporting,' the veteran was to be registered and benefits rated 'on the basis of a single man and not on the basis of a married man.'[4] Meanwhile, marital benefit entitlements were calculated to include costs associated with a house-hold and dependants, reflecting the principle of the family wage. Such provisions would have significant repercussions for ex-servicewomen, and for women employed in the civilian economy generally, in the two-tiered occupational welfare program that was beginning to take shape.

What were the postwar intentions of ex-servicewomen? One of the few women senior officials, Marion Graham, supervisor of women's rehabilitation training for CVT, tried to find out. Graham asked the three women's services to survey their members about postwar plans. At a time when so many assumed that women's top priority was to return to home and domesticity, the surveys suggested otherwise. The Canadian Women's Army Corps (CWAC) reported that only 17 per cent intended to return to/enter marriage and therefore withdraw from paid employment. Another 11 per cent were uncertain of their future plans. That left 72 per cent who planned to return to former employment and/or seek training and another job somewhere else, probably somewhere better. Similarly, the survey conducted among the Women's Royal Canadian Navy Service (WRCNS) indicated that 6 per cent planned to return to their homes, while another 13 per cent had no firm plans as yet. The remaining 81 per cent wanted training and/or paid employment. The Royal Canadian Air Force (RCAF) women's service showed the same pattern: only 11 per cent of their members would enter marriage and not seek paid employment, while 12 per cent were uncertain about their future activities. Fully 77 per cent planned to get a postwar job, with or without the assistance a training course might bring them.[5] Certainly, each of the women's services argued, it would be essential for training and related services to remain available to their members. Overall, at least 30 per cent of women awaiting discharge were prepared to take some form of vocational training, with the rest indicating academic or on-the-job training. In all of the survey reports, many of the women gave as their main reason for uncertainty the possibility that their male partners would likely object if they wanted to enter training or an educational program. Several also indicated that they did not have enough information about the services available to them, a point that was echoed by the community citizens' rehabilitation committees, which also complained about the lack of publicity.[6]

Rehabilitation officials concluded that the best adjustment plan was a job. Training would equip the veteran for a 'suitable' occupation as a civil readjustment measure, ensuring against the risk of unemployment should there be another economic recession. The principle of means testing was formally expunged from employment-related rehabilitation policy, placing all benefits on the footing of universal entitlement within an insurance-based program of income support. The state had an interest in ensuring that the veteran found a place in the postwar economy, in a stable job that paid a reasonable living wage. Although the Post-Discharge Re-establishment Order applied to only 35 per cent of total enlisted service personnel, a massive training effort was soon underway across Canada.[7] To qualify for training, a veteran had to apply within one year of discharge and, in any case, before 31 December 1947.[8] In all, approximately 130,000 men and women received training in one of over 60,000 university courses and 85,000 approved vocational training courses, most passing through during November 1946, when enrolment peaked at 34,806. By 31 March 1946, 23,618 women and men had signed up for vocational training. Of the nearly 50,000 women who had enlisted in the armed services, 36,000 had been discharged by the end of the 1946 fiscal year. Approximately 3,500 women were engaged in vocational training during the same period. By March 1947, this number shot up to 11,685, or 24 per cent, considerably exceeding the proportion of men enrolled in training, a fact that did not pass unnoticed by DVA officials.[9] Another 55 per cent were employed in the formal waged economy, while 20 per cent had withdrawn from the labour market altogether. The rate of unemployment among enlisted women for the end of the 1946 fiscal year was 2 per cent, lower than the average for civilian women and for enlisted men. By March 1947, a total of 2,625 women had registered for and received out-of-work benefits for varying periods – 5.3 per cent of all enlisted women. DVA also encouraged training on the job, for which the government did not offer any financial assistance, and by January 1947 approximately 22 per cent of DVA-approved training was delivered by this method, while 69.7 per cent was delivered as full-time training through a school or institute.[10]

Servicewomen readily signed up. Of the nearly 50,000 women in the services, approximately 25 per cent activated their rehabilitation training and education benefits, the majority, 10,000 women in all, in CVT vocational training. However, as Pierson and Cohen demonstrated in their study, by 1947, 85 per cent of these women were concentrated into the top five of a possible ninety-one occupations for which CVT-approved vocational training was available. Nearly 50 per cent were enrolled in commercial training in the clerical group of occupations, while the remainder were distributed across hairdressing, dressmaking, nursing, and pre-matriculation.[11] Under the terms of the Post-Discharge Re-establishment Order, all rehabilitation credits were equally available to women and men. How, then, was the treatment of women veterans so stringently curtailed? As an examination of policy deliberations among key senior officials reveals, government departments actively participated in a combined effort to limit training and employment opportunities, based on what was commonly accepted practice, conditioned by a view of occupations – and of the criteria for economic citizenship – shaped by a racialized and gendered typology. As a result, policies governing postwar re-establishment, in the main, sought to reinstate the 'natural' (pre-war) social order within both the labour market and occupational structures. Labour market access, firmly anchored in the male 'family wage,' would be closely monitored through employment and training policy.

In February 1946, the supervisors of women's training gathered for a national conference in Ottawa to review the national program. In his opening address, CVT head R.F. Thompson explained that the conference had been pulled together to make sure that the terms of re-establishment were being met in all regions across the country. Specifically, Thompson wanted to impress upon delegates that women and men enjoyed 'equal rights and equal privileges' in all federally sponsored training. Lest anyone misunderstand what this meant, the rest of the conference agenda carefully reviewed all of Ottawa's objectives for training and employment policy, based on pre-war employment patterns. National Council of Women of Canada (NCWC) president Mrs Edgar Hardy, who on Eaton's recommendation had been appointed chair of the advisory subcommittee to guide CVT in the development of training 'suitable for women,' did not disagree. In the run-up to demobilization during 1944, CVT's approach to women veterans was clearly outlined to the newly appointed Hardy. Thompson explained that the advisory committee was not to consider courses of academic education or occupational training. While training should relate to jobs, he pointed out, CVT had no purview over employment placement: 'Our programme is not responsible for the placing in employment of men or women discharged from the Forces, but only with their preliminary training.'[12] The former fell to the NSS and NES – specifically, Eaton's Women's Division. The government's position, as it was developed in the postwar planning exercises in 1944, was to promote pre-employment training as a method for directing women into 'suitable' occupations, thus restoring the gendered structure of the labour market as a social institution. As Thompson explained to Hardy, 'equality' was subject to two limitations: suitability, and the prospect of a job at the end.[13]

Economic and employment research generated objective empirical proof that the labour market conformed to predictable trends, closely monitored by government and academic experts. Federal employment policy was to facilitate existing trends, not to disrupt or challenge them. It was for this reason, conference delegates were told, that all training was developed to reflect and complement local labour market conditions, to respond to local needs, and to mirror the organization of community and region as closely as possible. Conference delegates were treated to lengthy presentations about the occupations identified as ideal for women, including home service training, practical nursing, dressmaking, and commercial training in office work for the clerical group of occupations, and, finally, hairdressing. These were the areas of employment thought appropriate for ex-servicewomen. Although demand continued to be highest in commercial and hairdressing courses, CVT and NSS/NES were discouraging further enrolment, delegates were advised, for fear that these occupations were becoming overcrowded. It is also likely that CVT wanted to fill other courses, particularly household service.[14]

By 1947, a total of 334 were enrolled in dressmaking, the leading choice for trades training – and the only one promoted – among ex-servicewomen. According to the Department of Labour, dressmaking and design were promoted so that women would 'be better equipped to undertake the sewing required in the general round of Homemaking or with the idea of supplementing their husbands [sic] salaries.'[15] While household labour and homemaking were the clear priority of this program, placement in the formal waged economy – an ancillary objective – was possible, but not encouraged. Another 371 women were listed as taking CVT-sponsored pre-matriculation training; departmental reports also indicated that 1,200 women veterans overall engaged in this program to raise their academic standing for university enrolment or to prepare for trades training.[16] Few women wanted training on the job, preferring direct referral into employment – there, presumably, to learn from co-workers. This form of training was, as indicated earlier, favoured by government, since any associated training costs would be absorbed by the employer or, what was more likely, assumed by the workers. Hairdressing courses drew an enrolment of 194 women, a number that led officials at CVT and in the Women's Division to conclude that the occupation was 'overcrowded.' The hotel, restaurant, and the domestic group of occupations showed 121 women in training. The largest concentration by far remained in the home service program, promoting placement in household employment. Home service training centres were opened in Vancouver, Calgary, Saskatoon, Winnipeg, Toronto, Montreal, and Quebec City for ex-servicewomen. The Calgary, Saskatoon, Toronto, and Vancouver schools were also open to civilian women. NES was directly responsible for 'screening' applicants for the program. Still, despite the 'all out' effort, by 1947 CVT was arguing that the numbers did not justify continuation. 'It was most disappointing,' CVT officials complained, 'that more veterans did not make application for training in this field,' particularly given the redoubling of efforts to make the program 'attractive and beneficial.'[17] By now, labour officials were convinced that if the occupation was to be preserved, and they took note of the 'paramount interest' expressed in this goal by 'various women's organizations across Canada,' it would have to be covered under workers' compensation legislation and the Unemployment Insurance Act. While note was made that submissions to that effect had proceeded through local women's councils to various provincial governments, there was no move by the federal government to amend the act.

Enrolment in training was one thing. But how many women actually completed their courses, going on to employment? Although records on this question were not as readily available, in April 1946, Marion Graham included a breakdown in her regular report to Thompson. By the spring of 1946, 36,558 women had been discharged from the services, of whom 3,702 had been enrolled in CVT courses between 1 April 1945 and 31 March 1946. A total of 180 were engaged in on-the-job training, 3,188 were in institutional training, and 334 were taking pre-matriculation or correspondence courses. In addition to the 10 per cent taking CVT, another 54 per cent were in commercial training, 11.5 per cent were taking professional training including pre-matriculation, 17.4 per cent were in personal service, 11.5 per cent were in semi-skilled and skilled occupations, and 4.7 per cent were in so-called semi-professional work. Of the 3,702 women in CVT-sponsored training, 782 (21 per cent) had graduated. However, 679 or fully 18 per cent were listed as having 'withdrawn' for a 'multiplicity of reasons, personal and circumstantial.'[18] Applications for training were also, it appeared, regionally concentrated and therefore likely subject to considerable fluctuation based on regionally variant local economies. For example, 44 per cent of women discharged in the North Bay, Ontario, region in May 1946 applied for training.[19] This high percentage suggests that CVT was dragging its feet when it came to establishing courses for ex-servicewomen, a concern that likely prompted the earlier survey of women's services. Despite the survey effort, CVT officials concluded that the Pre-employment Training

Survey (PTS) results were not so far off after all. In April 1946, Thompson communicated to all regional directors within the system that the following types of training were to be made available: business and commercial, hairdressing, dressmaking and designing, practical nursing, merchandising, and 'salesmanship,' the latter two of which might just as readily be provided through on-the-job training. Home service training would remain within the existing centres already identified, even if few expressed any interest in it.[20] Courses were limited on a regional basis. For example, Salter investigated the situation in Edmonton and found that, apart from hairdressing, the only other course available in the city and therefore the region was homemaking.[21] Approval for out-of-province training was difficult to obtain, and poor coordination between CVT and NES left women with little support once they had completed training. In Vancouver, pre-matriculation courses were filled beyond capacity, and women were turned away unless such training was applied for preparatory to university enrolment.[22] Hairdressing had a long waiting list.[23] The majority of training was otherwise concentrated in the areas of commercial, dressmaking, and power-machine operating for garment manufacture.

Rehabilitation policy for ex-servicewomen was organized through vocational counselling discourse. Women hoping to qualify for job training were assessed on the basis of physical condition, previous education, occupational experience prior to enlistment or while in service, preferences and aptitudes, and tangible employment opportunities. Each of these criteria was grounded in gendered, class-based, and racialized conceptions of employability, defined as aptitude and suitability. 'Personal choice' was a key term in the counselling exercise, since cooperation of the subject legitimized the final outcome as the product of individual choice. Edna Whinney, chief women's counsellor at DVA in Ottawa, aptly summarized the approach, explaining that the important feature of occupational counselling was 'that the ex-servicewomen [sic] herself must make the final decision about her future. We never influence a veteran towards a particular type of employment or training. It is our job to give all information possible to enable her to make her own decision.'[24] Problems in civilian re-establishment, including vocal or even passive resistance expressed through a refusal to sign up for courses such as household training, were portrayed as the product of an unrealistic or uncooperative attitude on the part of women themselves. Many women had moved to the Ottawa area during the war and, according to Whinney, had 'grown to like our city and plan to seek employment here.' A large number were now awaiting discharge, but few would want to return to the jobs they had held before the war. Unemployment was less of an issue than unrealistic expectations. For example, officers and senior NCOs who had 'become accustomed to wielding authority' were likely to encounter the greatest difficulty, faced with the probability of civilian employment 'where they may be relegated to comparatively unimportant duties.'[25] The problem of readjustment, then, was more a matter of attitude adjustment than material re-establishment, a view echoed at a DVA meeting held in Montreal in April, 1947. By this time, approximately 50,000 women had been discharged and, based on a follow-up survey conducted by Helen Hunt, now supervisor of women's rehabilitation, and her colleague, Marion Graham, almost 50 per cent of all servicewomen had married and withdrawn from the formal waged labour market. While the tendency among employers to favour 'youth and pulchritude' above maturity and experience was roundly deplored, conference delegates overall deemed that the rehabilitation program for women was proceeding swimmingly, there was little if any unemployment, and women were gaining access to training and suitable employment. *Veterans' Affairs*, DVA's mouthpiece, commented that, while there might be the occasional 'problem' with the 'odd ex-service woman,' it was generally found that 'these veterans had been problems prior to enlistment.'[26] That being the case, DVA was not responsible if it could be demonstrated that service work had in no way contributed to 'their present difficulties.'

Officials at both DVA and CVT argued that the real measure of rehabilitation was civilian readjustment and, in this, their expertise as counsellors and placement officers would guide the personal or subjective preferences articulated by women veterans. That is, while the best adjustment plan for a male veteran was a job, for the woman veteran, 'personal adjustment' was the more important determinant of success. Employment, while significant, was also personally variable. Dr Mary Salter, superintendent of women's rehabilitation for DVA, emphasized that the most important aspect of rehabilitation was not employment but civil re-establishment, defined as reintegration into the community, there to resume a normal and stable home life.[27] Every effort ought to be made to ensure that each individual ex-service person be reintegrated into the community as an 'effective, happy and well-adjusted citizen.' Of course, girls seemed to prefer taking up hairdressing. Still, home service was a viable option also. Although few had availed themselves of domestic training, perhaps, Salter speculated, once all training centres were up and running, more might be prepared to apply. Determining 'suitability' for employment and occupation was the most important criterion employment and training counsellors were told to address: suitability defined as the interest and capacity of the individual and the needs of the community. The objective of rehabilitation, framed in this way, was not a 'search for what is available' so much as it was a 'determination of what a veteran needs.' 'Need,' in rehabilitation discourse, overlooked material condition and concentrated instead on the psyche-based register of personality.[28] Needs-based determination, that is, was the principal organizing technique of the federal government's vocational training and employment policy for women. Salter's directive illustrates how rehabilitation discourses worked at positioning the female subject – the woman veteran – in relation to domesticity and community. Individual interest and community need had after all to be brought into alignment if successful reintegration were to occur. The social order, and the middle-class household, would be stabilized and the labour market restored to its predictable patterns, reflected in the trends charted by the employment experts at the Department of Labour.

What were the job prospects for ex-servicewomen seeking a place in the postwar economy? Here again, Graham conducted an informal survey of employment opportunities for ex-servicewomen, a study that confirmed the diminished opportunities for employment in the postwar period. By 1946, ex-servicewomen had begun to move in large numbers back into what was now an employers' labour market. Job requirements had increased, and now applicants were facing rejection because they lacked the 'necessary qualifications.' For example, the Pacific Regional Advisory Board, where unemployed ex-servicewomen were concentrated in the clerical group of occupations, reported that women in both Victoria and Vancouver were being turned away by employers on the claim that they lacked the necessary qualifications or did not have a 'regular background.' The criterion among employers, with which the NES agreed, was the 'suitability' of the applicant.[29] Alberta Crandall, women's supervisor for the Maritimes, indicated that ex-servicewomen would likely find little awaiting them in that region. On-the-job training had little to offer. Crandall canvassed several manufacturing firms in the region, including textiles, boot, shoe, and leather, and related light manufacturing industries believed appropriate for female employment. An expert chocolate dipper required at least two years' experience to reach the peak wage of $25 per week.[30] A machine operator in the textiles industry might make $40 per week as a weaver, but took up to three years to reach that wage on the piece-rate system. In any case, women who had formerly been employed in domestic and factory labour were making it quite clear that they did not want to return to these low-wage pre-war jobs. Employers acknowledged that very few women were returning to their plants. Crandall was particularly perplexed by the 'apathy' of ex-servicewomen concerning the rehabilitation project. Perhaps the reality was sinking in that finding a job with wages and working conditions comparable to those during the war was unlikely at best. W.K. Tibert, director of vocational education for New Brunswick, was more candid on the matter of women's employment opportunities in New Brunswick. As he explained to the CVT director in Ottawa, with 7,000 unemployed men looking for work, 'industry will be able to secure all the men they require' and would, therefore, have no need to tap the female reserve.[31] Home service training was always an option, although Tibert doubted that there would be any demand for training 'unless the attitude of the girls being discharged changes materially in the near future.'[32] In the interim, he assured Thompson that Miss Crandall would continue to pursue the possibility of practical nursing training as an alternative. The rank order of priority was now patent: preference in employment extended first to male veterans, then to civilian men, and after that, perhaps, to ex-service and civilian women.

Like their sisters in uniform, civilian women also encountered barriers in the postwar labour market. The prospects for job training remained limited at best, since the only game in town was the short list of courses available through CVT. All CVT courses were open to civilians, provided the applicant qualified for unemployment insurance. However, this first required that each provincial government sign Schedule M of the federal-provincial Re-establishment Training Agreement, a provision that extended federally sponsored training to civilians. In March 1946, with thousands of civilian women now out of work, Toronto regional CVT director R.H. Kerr suggested opening up to civilian women courses currently reserved for women veterans. It was becoming difficult to fill these classes, which nonetheless had to be kept open for ex-servicewomen.[33] Why not supplement the still low numbers of ex-servicewomen, at least until the balance of female veterans received their discharge papers? Unless this could be done, Kerr indicated, it would be very difficult to justify maintaining these special training courses.[34] All three of the women's services indicated that the number of women wanting to register for training would soon increase. But Ontario, where most of the training was needed, had yet to sign the Schedule M agreement. Even Thompson was moved to observe that the recalcitrance of that province denied laid-off civilian women much-needed access to training. Thompson responded to Kerr that, while Ontario had agreed to veterans' training, Schedule M was 'definitely excluded.' 'Personally,' Thompson confided to Kerr, the position taken by the Ontario government – and shared by Manitoba – was 'a mistake particularly insofar as the training of women is concerned.' The province, he continued, should sign the agreement so that the large numbers of unemployed women could be trained and directed to industries that were experiencing critical labour shortages, specifically the needle trades, home service, and practical nursing, thereby 'utilizing the classes which have been set up for discharged members of the Forces if and when the enrolment of ex-servicewomen is not sufficient to fill these classes.'[35] Until Ontario agreed to sign a federal-provincial training agreement, there was nothing Ottawa could do about training laid-off civilian war workers.

As federal wartime policies wound down, civilian workers faced other obstacles as well. By V-E Day, plans to dismantle the federal Wartime Day Nurseries Service were well underway. Providing day nurseries had made sense during the war, as part of the national objective to free up as much of the female 'labour reserve' as possible. With the arrival of the armistice, that federal prerogative ended. A sound postwar labour policy framework did not include federal programming to provide childcare services to working women. Officials at the NSS were well aware that the news of the program's termination would not go over well. The anticipated closure of day nurseries was met by petitions to the National Selective Service and the federal Department of Day Nurseries from women who clearly wanted and needed these services, based in part on their intention to continue working in the postwar economy. One such petition, addressed to the Ministry of Health and Social Welfare, made its way to the desk of NSS Women's Division head Fraudena Eaton. The petition came from a group of Toronto women, who appealed to the federal minister of health in the hope that their wartime day nursery would be kept open at least during the 'necessarily unsettled postwar period.'[36] Petitioners used exactly the same arguments that had been offered by the prime minister just a few short years before to entice Canada's women into joining the war effort. Access to childcare benefited the home, these working mothers argued, by strengthening the family as a social and psychological unit. Facilities staffed by trained child experts constituted a vital national resource and service, educating parents on issues of childhood development and healthy living. Daycare increased the standard of child mental and physical health. Young children could be educated in habits of per-

sonal cleanliness, behaviour, and 'care of self' through healthy relationships with other children. Far from destabilizing home and family, these
women stated, the nurseries strengthened the bond between parent and
child, not least because parents had more patience with and apprecia-
tion of their children 'if they are not with them the whole day.' Clearly,
too, accessible and reliable childcare enabled women to work, even if
only in low-wage jobs. As mothers and as workers, women had played a
strategic role in fighting and winning the war. Such identities would not
be so easily set aside now that the war was done.

Knowing the resistance the withdrawal of federal support for daycare
would provoke, Eaton and MacNamara pondered the most appropriate
date for its termination, especially with regard to Ontario. The longer
the federal government postponed the move, the longer the provinces
would procrastinate over assuming any responsibility. Eaton proposed
June 1946 for the federal termination and hoped that the provinces
would agree to assume full responsibility for the program's continuation. By February 1946, there was still no agreement in place, and
MacNamara wrote to W.A. Goodfellow, the Ontario minister of public
welfare. 'As you know,' MacNamara told the minister, 'the Dominion
share of financing this project was undertaken as a war measure for the
reason that women whose children were in day care centres were engaged in work of national importance.' Now that the designation of
essential war worker no longer existed, Ottawa had no choice but to
withdraw, leaving it to the provinces to take over. Goodfellow agreed
that the program might be continued on a cost-shared basis with municipalities, asking only that the federal government extend the program
until June, the end of the school term.[37] There was, in other words, a
chance that the public purse might fund a day nursery program.

Meanwhile, applications for day nurseries continued to come in. The
situation in Toronto was especially trying, so much so that when associate director Margaret Grier was sent by Eaton to investigate, the former
could only report that the majority of women using the nursery program
had to work outside the home. Many, it seemed, had been deserted by
enlisted husbands. Who better to qualify for the assistance a public day
nursery was meant to provide? Even the Report on the Post-War Problems of Women recognized this unique category of woman whom the
state had a duty to assist. Individual need notwithstanding, Eaton knew
the limits of her portfolio, accepting that 'sound' public policy' could
only be built on the solid foundation of the family wage. There was only
so far government was prepared to go. The NSSWD authorized system-

atic disqualification, based on the rationale that only essential war workers could qualify for subsidy. During the war, women applying for daycare
had been required to produce the NSS permit showing employment in a
designated essential war industry, a requirement that was revised following considerable opposition, thereby opening the nursery program to all
civilian women workers.[38] Grier found it impossible to determine who
had, and who had not, duly qualified, at least in the nurseries she visited.
With this in mind, Eaton instructed that, effective 30 June 1946, all
daycare provided to Ontario children by federal-provincial agreement
would be terminated, although registration of children of employed
women would continue to be accepted until that date. Perhaps most
telling of all, the federal government would no longer collect any registration statistics 'except by request.' Not collecting statistics on the
number of women requiring access to childcare meant that the childcare
needs of working women were effectively erased from the policy agenda.[39]

The employment bar against married women was another area in
which formal equality statements directly contradicted actual public
policy. On the one hand, the NSS had worked closely with employers
during the war, encouraging them to institutionalize the practice of part-
time employment through the 'housewife's shift.' Here again, Eaton
found herself compelled to block recognition of married women's
employment rights, despite its recommendation in the McWilliams
committee's Report on the Post-War Problems of Women. The place for
the married woman was clearly in the home. The Women's Division even
considered home-based production as a way of balancing the policy
directive of encouraging women to withdraw from the paid labour force,
without, as Eaton described it, 'involving the Government in harsh
discriminatory policies which will create injustices.' Perhaps, through
the National Employment Service, it would be possible 'to influence
married women with home responsibilities to refuse employment' by
encouraging them to take up home-based work? Such a proposal neatly
avoided policy that was overtly discriminatory, since it was based not on
the 'right of married women to work but rather the responsibility towards home.' Of course, primary responsibility towards the home was
one thing; working from the home for remuneration was another.
'There is always the practical argument that a woman has to earn a good
income before it pays financially to take paid employment,' Eaton
thought, noting that, 'Counselling on self-employment, sales commission work, etc., should be reviewed as possible advice for married
women.'[40] Promoting work from the home was the answer, and women's

organizations were keenly in support. The proposal permitted Ottawa to appear supportive of women's need of a second income without having to endorse stable labour market access or, worse, the embarrassment of appearing opposed to the employment rights of married women. This option was promoted in particular to support the growing handicrafts and related tourism industry.

Two program proposals to the NSSWD and CVT illustrate the direction this approach would take. The first concerned a 'Tentative Outline for Vocational Training Programme in Arts and Crafts, under the Department of Extension of the University of Alberta.' The program was described as having potentially salutary aesthetic as well as economic effects, not least of which was a 'citizenship development' component aimed at instilling cultural respectability while at the same time encouraging cultural cohesion within a given community.[41] Handicraft production, it seemed, was all the rage among sociologists. Souvenir manufacture was envisaged as economic development, contributing to the growth of what would become a thriving tourism trade, with profound implications for national and cultural identity – not least of which would be the deepening commercial appropriation of Aboriginal cultures. The second proposal came under the title 'Rehabilitation of Female War Workers Originally from Rural Districts.'[42] In it, women's employment specialist Renée Morin proposed that the federal government could encourage the revival of handicrafts in Quebec as a strategy to secure the cultural and economic future of rural Québécoises. Les Ecoles ménagères provinciales were leading the way, cultivating indigenous skills consistent with their civilizing mission to protect and preserve local cultural integrity. The 'possibility of selling these goods at their door to American tourists' was drawing 'village women' back into handicraft production, Morin observed. The point then to secure and deepen potential markets in order to create viable employment across rural Quebec for women artisans working within the household. As a strategy for gender-based cultural and economic production, for Morin the future lay in home-based artisanal handicraft production.

'Finding the Right Girl': Domestic Service, Hospital Service, and the Needle Trades

Training policy operated as a vehicle for the gendered regulation of labour market structures. As a central feature of employability discourse, vocational training was the answer to deficiencies of skill, attitude, and aptitude. Women workers responded to inadequate wages, unsafe working conditions, and placement in low-wage or unwanted employment, in particular domestic labour, much as they always had, usually through individual acts of resistance: leaving a job, staying away from work, or refusing a job referral. Whatever the rationale for an individual worker, such reasons became lost to view once interpreted through the lens of employability discourse, dominated by concerns about absenteeism, 'unsuitable' work attitude, deficient skill, low intelligence, or unrealistically high wage expectations. Problems associated with insecure or unstable labour force attachment could easily be solved by improving the employability of the individual. This, at least, was how UIC officials saw the matter. NES staff were having trouble finding suitable employment for unemployed women. But the cause was not structural unemployment among women but rather a lack of training courses.[43] At the same time, CVT training was broached separately from employment placement, fragmenting training within employment policy, while even further undermining any relevance it might have as a viable response to work reorganization and redistribution, new production technologies and management techniques, and new occupational skill requirements, all of which were constant changes confronted by working people. Such fragmentation intensified the individualizing effects of pre-employment vocational training deployed to 'upgrade' occupations deemed suitable for women by upgrading individual workers. Specifically, this chapter ends with a closer look at the programs advanced by policy bureaucrats to provide for women seeking their place in postwar Canada: training for the household, hospital services, and the garment trade.

The Home Aide Project

The shortage of domestic household workers was the product of economic and social changes that were likely to be permanent. Women were turning away from the occupation, joining an exodus already noted in the well-circulated special report on the subject in the September 1946 report from the U.S. Women's Bureau and the November 1946 issue of the *U.S. Employment Service Review*.[44] Women would consider any alternative to domestic service. This was, of course, common knowledge, an observation shared by virtually any (Western) country studying women's occupational trends. On the demand side, it was clear that those middle- and lower-income households that might have hired domestic workers in the past now enjoyed access to labour-saving devices that dramatically redesigned and restructured household labour.[45] The trend was clear. Women looking for work through the National Employment Service, when asked to identify their occupation, invariably named a sector other than domestic service, even when advised that jobs in their chosen sector were scarce. The pattern held at NES offices across the country. Women preferred to hold on for the possibility of paid work in their occupation of choice over the certainty of employment in domestic service. As evidence of this trend, Margaret Grier at the Women's Division pointed to the clerical group of occupations, where applicants outnumbered vacancies by a margin of two to one nationally: that is, 10,500 applicants going after a total of 5,000 jobs. A three-to-one ratio existed in textiles.

Household work, most agreed, was viewed as the lowest rung in the ladder of economic evolution. Occupations involving some measure of domestic labour were similarly cast as inherently unskilled and therefore most suitable for women lacking in education, or aptitude, or whose employment capacities were dubbed inferior. In the main, that was the standard characterization of working-class women and those whose racialized or ethnic identities marked them as 'other.' Women resisted the occupation at every turn, frustrating Women's Division officials and NES officers alike. When Eaton addressed the National Rehabilitation Conference held in 1946, she adopted a new approach to domestic labour, this time locating it within the civilizing discourse of Western industrialized democracies. As a member of the club of Western powers, Canada could rightly assume its place as a superior modern power. The new lexicon advanced the modern household as similarly progressive, but those labouring there for pay, however meagre, were now cast as 'primitive' and subordinate. In the so-called primitive organization of production, women engaged in 'housewifery' as an occupation. Those who transferred this labour into the market, working in the homes of others, were culturally, socially, and economically 'underdeveloped.' Some moved ahead into 'public housekeeping' in hotels and institutions as a natural extension. The next step in this cone of increasing diversity was personal services, followed by business services, and so on.[46] Household training, therefore, normalized the subordinated status and marginality of such labour in public policy planning and programming. As a normal feature of any modern society's cultural and economic development – in fact, as an elaboration of that development – such labour secured the respectable bourgeois household. Suitable employment for women began with the relationship between household and the formal waged economy. All of the organizations involved in the business of redirecting women after the war thought the same way, from the National Council of Women of Canada (NCWC) to the YWCA and related women's service organizations. Household employment had always been and would remain the first and last choice for women's employment policy, a position Eaton and her colleagues vigorously defended. The challenge was to persuade women to accept the work as the most realistic option.

In March 1945, several months before the results of the Pre-employment Training Survey – the planning exercise that would determine postwar policy – began to arrive in her office, Eaton commiserated with MacNamara on the challenge of making the occupation acceptable to working women. 'It has always seemed such a sad thing to me,' she wrote, 'that domestic work with its endless possibilities for women has never been put on an acceptable basis either socially or with regard to conditions of work.'[47] The domestic shortage could not be resolved through unofficial, voluntary channels. That approach had been tried through the pre-war domestic service program under the Dominion-Provincial Youth Training Plan. It had failed, quite miserably. If the NES could take on the work of 'maintaining standards through placements' and, even better, if the provincial governments could see their way clear to cooperating with the federal department by revising their labour standards legislation, then perhaps, just perhaps, women might be enticed into this most suitable of female vocations. But this was still so much wishful thinking. The Women's Division took on the task with diligence, acting on behalf of the elite women's organizations whose lobbying for household labour continued unabated. Women would have to take up this vocation, especially if the occupation could be reformed – an appropriate task for the federal government in formulating its response to women's postwar employment needs.

Reservations notwithstanding, the Home Aide project was pushed through, named to distinguish it from the pre-war household service training program administered on the recommendations of the Women's Advisory Committee of the National Employment Commission. Unlike the pre-war program, the Home Aide program did not include a residential component. Local employment offices were instructed to encourage ex-servicewomen, later joined by women laid off from war industries, to sign up. Policy officials at NSS now wanted to see a short training course followed by immediate placement. The hope was that training would ligitimize household labour as an occupation. In the absence of improved provincial labour standards, the program would give the impression of occupational security and status. As Eaton put it, limiting the course length 'would not impose too much upon the applicant and would serve to introduce the idea of training being a necessity.'[48]

There was debate within the Department of Labour and organizations such as the NCWC about whether domestic labour was the best remedy for female unemployment, and some officials decided to investigate the reasons behind women's persistent refusal to enter such employment. Sharp class divisions quickly emerged. Margaret Grier studied the matter and soon reached the only possible conclusion: the program was of benefit mainly to its more prominent advocates, namely middle- and upper-class women. As the main political agents with whom government consulted on policies concerning women, their organizations were the most avid proponents of household service training. Grier was among the few senior policy staff to question the appropriateness of committing public funding to what was clearly a class-based program of benefit only to 'wealthy homes.' Perhaps it was more appropriate to leave such training and placement to commercial agencies? Designing an urban solution to attend to the needs of wealthy urban women was not an exercise to which Grier wanted to devote much time, despite the lobbying by local councils of women and their national umbrella, the NCWC. 'The women's organizations do, after all, represent the women and homes of "better than average income" on the whole,' Grier mused.[49] Channelling public funds into a special training program exclusively designed to meet the needs of this group was sure to generate a public outcry. 'Raising standards' through 'expensive training' might seem reasonable to the women of higher income groups, but it was not appropriate to design public policy based on the exclusive urban views of 'the city woman.' Farm and rural women gained nothing from the plan. Ottawa could ill afford to overlook the fact that 'real hardship has been caused all across Canada by its attraction of competent help away from the farm and low income home.'[50] Instead, the department's efforts would be better spent in encouraging young women to exchange their low-paying factory jobs for a wholesome life with cash and good living accommodation in a town or suburb, those 'small homes with children where really a "hired girl" is needed.' If Ottawa encouraged women's employment in the industrial, commercial, and retail sectors, the available pool of labour would become even more inelastic, making domestic assistance more inaccessible than it already was.[51] The 'family type of girl' was easily lured by a 'high-powered city training unit.'

These comments opened up a new way of approaching domestic service within public policy. Women required assistance in the productive and reproductive labour of the household, and the scope of state policy in this area ought to be extended. As Grier presented to MacNamara, rather than dither around with yet another training and placement program that would do little to redress the real problem – urban female unemployment – the department should commit itself to the study of labour market supply and demand in the rural economy, extending to agricultural regions the same attention habitually accorded to urban economies and examining need in relation to household income.[52] Government might encourage Women's Institutes to develop programming to assist farm households. Practical training, assisted by the network of Women's Institutes and provincial education departments, would surely do the job better, given closer links to the rural home. Community agencies could address the household labour needs of low-income urban homes through a program of community home visiting, sponsored by welfare services, family agencies, and even women in trade unions, rather than spend vast sums of money to supply wealthy households with 'the right type of girl.' Instead, perhaps the Home Aide program could assist in the provision of day workers and part-time helpers for the 'stable income home of the business and professional group.' All of these plans lay in the future, but in the interim, Grier counselled patience. Women's unemployment levels were rising, but there was as yet 'little heavy pressure or urgency on thousands of women workers ... unskilled and semi-skilled workers [who] are still hopeful of getting back to the factory or office openings that are just not going to open.'[53] Until things changed, women would not accept 'reality' (as the Department of Labour saw it), that is, retrain, accept lower wages, or even 'enter housework or train for it.' Until the tide of women's expectations began to turn, it was best to wait and prepare the domestic service program for the time when women would turn to it. Here was a position, clearly articulated, with which Eaton could finally agree. Of course, wealthy city women required assistance in the household, but a better public service would be to reach precisely the groups identified by Grier – rural women and low-income households. Behind the scenes, officials counted on the certainty that diminishing employment opportunities would eventually compel both ex-service and civilian women alike into household employment.

The plan was delayed at the outset because training agreements were still not in place in each province, thus preventing CVT from moving ahead immediately on training programs for displaced industrial workers. Predictably, when the program was rolled out to women veterans, the uproar could be heard all the way back to Ottawa. Employment officials complained that women refused to cooperate, while ex-servicewomen simply refused to participate. For example, CVT staff in Alberta were reluctant to list the course. CVT was supposed to be in the business of providing relevant vocational training leading to regular employment, and household service simply did not fall within that category. Promoting household service in the roster of CVT courses might effectively disallow other options and in that way deny women, in particular ex-servicewomen, access to longer-term vocational training in other occupations.[54] Moreover, the Alberta officials feared that the proposal would stir up resentment among women. The Home Aide program could not operate successfully even as a reserve to which women could be referred if their personality, appearance, or limited experience made them unsuitable for other occupations.[55] Calgary officials did try to implement the program on a 'reserve' basis, in the expectation that some women might just be desperate enough to enrol. According to Miss E. Clark of the Calgary office, screening and classification reflected the growing trend towards credentialism that required training, experience, and qualifications as criteria for an NESWD referral. A 'considerable number of girls asking for employment for which they have no qualifications' might just make a good pool for referrals into the Home Aide course.[56] Few women in Vancouver would sign up for the program either, although E.S. Morley, supervisor of the Vancouver NSSWD office, remained confident of its long-term success: 'There seemed to be some misunderstanding that these women are replacing charwomen,' she observed of potential employers. 'They do not seem to realize that these women are qualified workers.'[57] Lobbying for the Home Aide program intensified, however, whatever the intended targets of the plan thought.

In contrast, Olive Ruth Russell proposed the Home Service program as more appropriate for ex-servicewomen. In a well-developed home, women might find fulfilment and satisfaction. Russell designed what she regarded as a program to encourage women to face up to the challenges of domestic home life, bringing public policy to bear on the household as a social unit while at the same time promoting the objective of settling women safely back into the domestic sphere. I now turn to a discussion of the Home Service program.

'The Mental Hygiene Aspects of Homemaking': Home Service Training for Women Veterans

While Russell was at the DVA, one of her first major projects concerned the development of a 'home service' training course for (soon to be) married heterosexual couples. The innocuous course launched intense debate within the Departments of Labour and Veterans' Affairs over the purpose of CVT training and the breadth of government responsibility for women's rehabilitation. The Home Service program was designed to accommodate ex-servicewomen as a pro-natalist policy promoting domesticity and citizenship, not employment, but CVT and NSS/NES had no interest in a program that did not lead, or at least contribute, to employability. Resistance to the program is worth examining in detail, since it illustrates the multiple rationales operating during the period as state officials attempted to compel women to withdraw from formal waged employment while at the same time – in a gesture towards formal equality – promoting government-sponsored training. The Home Service program in part took up themes addressed in the NCMH-CBC broadcast series 'The Soldier's Return.' Russell likewise believed that rehabilitation was more than an economic matter of reassimilating discharged military personnel into the civilian community through appropriate occupation in the labour force or the household. Life had changed because of the war, and it was folly to anticipate that women and men would settle down quietly into their former lives as though the events of 1939–45 had never happened. For that matter, many commentators feared a return of the 'evils' that had characterized Canadian life in 1939, of which unemployment was only the most obvious. For example, although marriage rates had climbed from a steady 9.7 per 1,000 between 1941 and 1945 to reach 10.9 per 1,000 population in 1946, divorce rates had more than tripled since the war began, rising from 2,068 in 1939 to 7,683 in 1946.[58]

In an address to the Ottawa Business and Professional Women's Club on 13 March 1945, among the first of many similar speeches she would deliver as part of her work with the DVA, Russell enjoined her audience to adopt a broader understanding of the real tasks and challenges lying ahead. While thousands of civilians eagerly anticipated the return of family, friends, and community members from military service, many, and particularly many women, looked upon such reunions with some trepidation. Some women feared the return of male family members, Russell acknowledged, and for good reason.[59] It must seem ironic, she told the business women, to think that, in the midst of tearful reunions and the flurry of planning for victory celebrations, 'the joys of homecoming may easily be turned to quarrels and bitterness.' Nonetheless, substantive changes would have occurred among all the partners in the household, in relations both outside the home and within it. Marriage and parenting might be natural roles, the knowledge for which could be acquired solely through experience, but women and men needed expert guidance to help them develop a comprehensive understanding of their respective roles and responsibilities in an equal and healthy partnership.[60] Conventional 'feminine' attributes of nurturing, love, and patience would be the most appropriate response to the challenges and unexpected behaviours presented by returning men. But should conventional responses fail, it was time to call in the expert counsel of psychology. The Home Service course would instruct women – and men – in a mental hygiene program for sustaining healthy heterosexual marriage and home life, in keeping with the notion that happy homes were vital to liberal governance.

The family-living component of the Home Service program represented a direct extension of the NCMH campaign for an improved national standard of mental hygiene, linking parenting and child development as twin themes of personal psychological adjustment and responsible citizenship. The family and its conduct were simply too important to democratic citizenship to be left to muddle through the challenges of growth, development, discord, and challenge among and between parents, child, community, and employment. When Russell was approached by members of the Etobicoke Board of Education – specifically, by the principal of Etobicoke High School, Gordon Kidd – following her address there to the Women Teachers' Federation in November 1946, she immediately agreed to assist Kidd in developing a course for parents and teachers on child guidance. She wrote to her former boss at the DND, William Line, now back at his post in the Department of Psychology at the University of Toronto, asking that he consider leading the course. At the same time, she activated the NCMH network, proposing Mrs Clarence Hincks, Dr Jack Griffin or Dr William Blatz as additional resources. Russell returned to this theme throughout her work as a policy analyst and advocate in the DVA, advancing the principles espoused by the NCMH. Conventional psychological and psychiatric practice in Canada was limited as long as it remained fixated on avoiding mental ill health by promoting individual conformity. 'I have been deeply concerned over the recurring setbacks that psychology and mental hygiene have received, particularly in Canada,' she confided.[61] Most

Canadians shunned the issue, and the psychiatric profession did not help. The common message was repressive and stifling, Russell observed, following the thinking that the best way 'to avoid mental ill health is to obey one's every impulse and conform to the mores, rather than risk being inhibited or different.' By contrast, the mental hygiene program advocated by the NCMH sought to inculcate healthy attitudes and interests, working through the internal environment of the individual to promote healthy adjustment to social obligations and responsibilities. The difference lay in constituting the notion of individual interests as consonant with the responsibilities accruing to social location. As she explained to Line, mental hygiene encouraged the development of attitudes that would give young and old alike 'the drive to strive to adjust the environment and the mores (and themselves) to conform to what Plato describes as the highest good.' Conformity amounted to regulation and discipline, stifling the individual by positing only the choice to resist or obey. 'Wanting to be good' was an entirely separate act from 'trying to be good' and perhaps failing in the attempt.

The original outline for the course investigated the minutiae of family history, including historical approaches to family and social change, the modern family, and contemporary problems. In fact, Russell proposed a comprehensive look at the family as primary social unit, as democratic institution, and as integral to community, friendship, and the healthy formation and adjustment of personality. The family was the foundation of democratic and responsible citizenship and, moreover, the first line of prevention and diagnosis in a national standard for mental hygiene. Allegedly unemployable individuals were seen as the psychological products of maladjusted families. The division of labour within the household, the allocation of decision-making roles, budgeting, the growth and development of the family as a viable unit – Russell proposed to cover them all. In addition, candidates would learn about proper nutrition and food preparation, clothing needs, and household management, the latter consisting of a detailed study of the household as a site of labour reorganized according to the principles of scientific management. Curriculum for these sections was to be developed by Doris Runciman of the Canadian Home Economics Association.[62]

The greatest concern was that the course would be altered from instruction in family living to a course in 'homemaking' of the type proposed by the Canadian Legion Educational Services (CLES). For this reason, Russell asked Dr Jack Griffin to develop the 'Mental Hygiene Aspects of Homemaking' module. 'In order to ensure continuity, integrity and uniformity of point of view in the mental hygiene part of the proposed course,' Russell and Griffin insisted that the module be led by a mental hygiene expert.[63] The course was organized into five topics: Out of Uniform – the transition to civilian life; People and Personalities – understanding human relationships; What Makes a Good Marriage; Childcare and Training; and finally, Understanding the Adolescent. Griffin outlined the central precepts of individual psychology according to the NCMH: heredity, environment, satisfaction of basic needs, adjustment, desire for approval and success, and 'desire to be like others.' Human relationships were characterized as the interaction, sometimes smooth but often not, of personalities. Women would explore how personality developed as the natural and healthy, if fragile, process of satisfying basic needs and of healthy adjustment to one's fellow citizens, community, home, and responsibilities. The challenge for Griffin was instructing those of 'indifferent' educational background in the complexities and intricacies (what he called the 'cardinal principles') of mental hygiene.

Relations of class, race, gender, and sexuality informed a curriculum that investigated the origins of deviance, delinquency, and threat. Here was a golden opportunity to instruct young women whose mental capacities had been thoroughly vetted by the work of people like Russell and who were, or would soon be, wives and mothers, responsible for rearing future citizens who might otherwise succumb to juvenile delinquency. But how to reduce the complexities of educational and human psychology to what Griffin dubbed the 'simplicity and practicality' required by the general population? The initial proposal included a film, short filmstrips, and a series of four-hour lectures delivered over ten to twelve sessions. According to Griffin's draft curriculum, 'Mental Hygiene Aspects of Homemaking,' the mechanics of household work might well be left to pictorial representation, but the 'more subtle social, emotive and psychological components of home and family living' were far too important to be left to mere passive display through film. 'The emphasis,' read the proposal, 'is on attitudes and feelings, rather than mechanical rules and recipes.' The interior of the educational subject constituted the true matter to be addressed, thus requiring the active intervention of the psychological expert as instructional intermediary. Griffin proposed a list of possible instructors: Mrs F. Johnstone, director of parent education at the Institute for Child Study, University of Toronto; Mrs R. Davis, psychiatric social worker, Toronto; and NCMH associate S.R. Laycock, professor of educational psychology at the University of Saskatchewan.[64]

Marriage was constructed as a rational extension of healthy and successful adjustment, provided one understood the importance of being suitably matched with one's mate in personality and character. In Topic Three of the course, women – and men – were to receive a series of six lectures covering such topics as 'What Makes a Good Marriage? – Social, Emotional and Physical Aspects of Marriage.' The psychological description of the marital state transformed popular notions about romance, jealousy, and bliss into psychological conditions such as 'romantic infantalism,' 'disillusioned cynicism,' or even 'determined idealism.'[65] Compatibility between partners ensured a healthy union. Compatibility involved the areas of personality and character; background – that is, class location expressed as education, occupation, activities of parents, and so on; aims, interests, and careers; and religion and race. The course included a component on family planning, information and practices associated with conception, pregnancy, and childbirth, and, in the same module, 'psychological differences between the sexes.' That is, in each area of heterosexual marital and familial organization and practice, 'common' knowledge and comprehension was disrupted and transformed, calibrated to the psychological dimension.

Russell intended that the Home Service program would be jointly sponsored by CVT and DVA. From the start, CVT had only one question: Where was the employment component? Undeterred by such opposition, Russell floated the proposal as a 'special information project,' a collaborative effort involving the Wartime Information Board (WIB), the National Film Board, the Department of Veterans' Affairs, Canadian Vocational Training, the armed services, and the Department of Health and Welfare. She brought the Canadian Association for Adult Education (CAAE) on board, a natural alliance given the organizational cooperation agreement between the CAAE and the NCMH, whereby each provided access to the other's institutional and community networks, academic and governmental contacts, and research. The course would draw on a variety of multimedia technologies and methods of instruction; would be delivered by a rotating series of lecturers; and would continually expand by enlisting participants from households and organizations in the surrounding community, identifying new problems and areas for remedial instruction and expert advice.

The course was intended to supplement the work of rehabilitation counselling, not to substitute for rehabilitation training through CVT. Russell outlined this caveat in her proposal to J. Andrew, chair of the Rehabilitation Information Committee (RIC) of the WIB, pointing out that there was no intention of allowing the Home Service course to be used to pressure women into household training for domestic service and so disentitle them from other occupational training and/or labour market access to the formal waged economy. Women should be encouraged both to oversee healthy households and to participate in the waged economy if that was their choice, subject always to their 'suitability.'[66]

In any event, at the meeting of the RIC on 9 July 1945, the full committee reviewed and provisionally approved Russell's proposal. The DVA liked the idea, especially given the uproar over the Home Aide program, which CVT seemed intent on foisting upon women veterans. While women opposed household service, they seemed genuinely interested in homemaking. Citizens' Rehabilitation Committees across the country also supported the plan. Promoting career options in other areas was fine, but everyone knew that the home would be women's principal domain. Perhaps, argued the DVA, there was a compelling need for such a sensible course of instruction after all? The federal Department of Health and Welfare lent its strong endorsement as well, and from an equally strategic standpoint: at a time when considerable public expenditures were flowing into private households through the new family allowance program, what assurance did government have that this money was being used wisely, let alone efficiently? On this rationale, Health and Welfare staked out its own regulatory and disciplinary interests, suggesting only that the course be opened to the general civilian population.[67] From the RIC, the proposal was turned over to a working committee (including representatives from the armed services, Labour, Health and Welfare, DVA, CBC, and NFB) to take it through to the next phase. In a further meeting, held on 21 August, DVA, Health and Welfare, and Russell agreed to enlist Griffin, NCMH, and Doris Runciman of the Canadian Home Economics Association to prepare their respective segments of the course. As Russell explained to Thompson of CVT, Griffin had been invited expressly by Health and Welfare to advise on the 'psychological aspects of family living.'

By October, DVA appeared ready to turn the whole issue over to CVT since most servicewomen would soon be under its umbrella, and CVT intended to focus only on programs with a clear employment component. That meant, if anything, domestic service training. Health and Welfare, meanwhile, intended to proceed with a general film project, given its concerns about regulating family allowance transfers to the household. At the same time, a household science course and text were being developed by CLES. This curriculum, which was sent to Russell for review, contained no mental hygiene content at all, prompting her to reject it on the grounds that it was precisely the mental hygiene content that had been 'repeatedly emphasized as desired by the service women who have been requesting the course.'[68] Russell drafted a letter to Thompson, signed by DVA training director W.R. Wees, which, while it was never sent, clearly reflected her exasperation with the entire matter and with CVT's persistent opposition. Whatever the final outcome, by the time a decision was taken one way or the other, demand among servicewomen would have considerably diminished from a peak of between one and two thousand, she pointed out.[69] Certainly there was evidence to suggest that women were not interested in such a course. A survey of CWAC in September 1945 turned up only 133 potential applicants, although among the reasons listed for not pursuing this option were insufficient information about the course and concern that male partners would 'accept no further separation while the wife is on course.'[70] On the other hand, Edith Scott, matron and women's rehabilitation supervisor with the WRCNS, took an entirely different view, suggesting that the course was precisely what servicewomen stated they wanted. She felt it would contribute to the stability of peacetime society. Women were specifically interested in learning of the 'practical and psychological aspects of the care of home and family,' Scott reported to Marion Graham. The women's air force division was similarly eager to see a course on the successful establishment of a home, although there was no mention that such a home might include a psychological dimension in need of careful attention.[71] Scott also seemed ready to concede that women could sign up instead for household training in lieu of a more comprehensive program in home and family living.

By early 1946, concern about the Home Service course had reached its peak at the Department of Labour. At the most senior level, Eric Stangroom expressed his serious reservations, sharing with MacNamara the suspicion that 'pressure from DVA and various women's organizations [had] forced CVT' to take on a course 'which contributes little to the employment picture.'[72] MacNamara doubted that the plan would 'prove attractive to young ladies,' and similarly did not support the federal government's involvement. The Home Aide program, alternatively, was more in line with where CVT and Labour might commit resources, if only young women would agree to give it a try.[73] Family development and marital harmony were simply not arenas in which state policy had any business – unless there was a breakdown, in which case it was up to Health and Welfare to step in. Margaret Grier communicated as much to MacNamara in March 1946. She had never been 'sold' on a class that was just a 'very expensive method of training a small number of girls and women from the Services as housewives.' She was quite prepared to toss the ball over to the Department of Labour, however, on the off chance that the program might 'bring a greater stability and happiness in home life, if such is its function.'[74]

Such, as Eaton well knew, was not the Department of Labour's function. In Eaton's view, promoting happier homes was not the business of the state and was better left to the YWCA, adult education groups such as the CAAE, and university extension courses. The Department of Labour looked after the stability of the labour market, not the stability of the household. She acknowledged herself to be an obstructionist, albeit a very well-intentioned one.[75] Russell had pressed ahead with the course despite her own reservations and the objections of others, meeting with and securing approval from the WIB, consulting with 'eminent' household economists and other experts in the development of course materials, and even ignoring Eaton's advice that a one-year course was entirely too long for the subject matter. In this regard, Eaton prevailed, and the course was revamped into a short program of instruction in household economics. Men would not be encouraged in any way to enrol. The residential component was dropped as a seeming 'extravagance to those who find it is not open to their own daughters.'

By the time the program was finally launched in Toronto on 18 February 1946, its content had been scaled back considerably to conform to the curriculum originally proposed in the CLES home economics program. Women received instruction in budgeting, interior redecorating and design, shopping for the home, and meal preparation and nutrition – all delivered at 'the laboratory' at 216 Huron Street, site of the Training and Re-establishment Institute Annex. All was not lost, however, as students would attend one lecture each week in 'Family Relations.'[76] The press release issued to promote the program singled out the study of childcare scheduled to proceed in a specially prepared 'pink and blue nursery' – should there have been any doubt that children tended to arrive in one of two quite distinct genders. The course description, signed on behalf of Labour by Vince Phelan, indicated that qualification included both the suitability of applicants and an intention to use the training either in one's own home or 'as a means of livelihood in someone else's household,' an accommodation to CVT employment criteria that considerably altered the original purpose of the program.[77] But the problem simply would not go away. In Ontario, the course included a residential component not unlike the model adopted for pre-war domestic service training, adding to the inevitable confusion over how it was to be distinguished from the NES Home Aide program. The Department of Labour had already issued a clarification distinguishing among the two household training courses: Home Aide and Home Service. To add to the general chaos, the Home Aide program was run from the same location.

The Ward Aide Program

Like the Home Aide program, the Ward Aide course seemed an appropriate occupational training program that would accomplish the Women's Division's dual objectives: moving women into areas where there was a severe labour shortage, and ensuring that CVT programs met the training requirements of ex-service and civilian workers alike. Once again, the shortage of labour was characterized as a shortage of 'suitable workers' and not a structural issue of an economy in which women exercised rational choice, seeking higher paying jobs under safer and more favourable working conditions while avoiding low-wage work in less desirable conditions. In the event, the training program followed the strategy of upgrading the occupation by upgrading the worker.

Ward aides were among the lowest-paid staff in hospitals and sanatoriums. Few women willingly took on this type of work, contributing to a chronic shortage of available labour. Nursing staff objected to having to assume tasks more in keeping with domestic work than the skilled labour for which they had been so extensively trained.[78] Nurses and other hospital workers left the sector in droves during the war, eager to take jobs that paid more and offered better conditions and, perhaps, a less hierarchical work environment. Now that layoffs from the war industries were well underway, it was reasonable to anticipate increased employment applications among the hospitals. But hospital workers were not coming back. Even the Canadian Hospital Council (CHC), fretting over increased union organizing in the sector, was forced to admit that 'old conditions of employment' were no longer acceptable to many workers. The discussion made its way to the floor of the council's annual meeting in 1945, suggesting that personnel planning officers might 'carry on the employment work more efficiently' than overworked administrators, and perhaps prove a bulwark against trade unionism. The Mother Superior presiding over the Sherbrooke Sanatorium took a decidedly astringent view of the problems confronting the hospital administrator. In her opinion, the problem with ward aides was not a structural one of low wages, poor working conditions, and better options elsewhere. On the contrary, the problem derived from 'lack of competency and skill' among the girls who ended up in the occupation. The inefficiency of ward aides had exacted far too great a cost in her institution. The views of the Mother Superior were widely shared among those who customarily approached wages and working conditions as an accurate reflection of individual efficiency and social worth.

For all of these reasons, the occupation was ideally suited to the policy objectives of the pre-employment training program envisaged by Eaton and her colleagues in the Women's Division. At the same time, the ward aide vocation reflected considerable changes occurring throughout the nursing group of occupations. As part of the recommendations of the Royal Commission on Veterans' Qualifications (the Bovey Commission), the category of practical nursing was created to respond to the shortage. Practical nursing would provide a good outlet for trained ex-servicewomen, without drawing opposition from the Canadian Nurses' Association (CNA).[79] The CNA was invited to design the CVT practical nursing course.[80] Once again, whether the goal was to improve the efficiency of workers or compel women to accept work they manifestly did not want to do, policy planners expected women to come round in the absence of better alternatives.

The plan was developed at the Regina Employment and Selective Service Office, based on an extensive training course that set about to reform the 'character' of the trainee. The 'better type of girl' was seen to have left this work for more interesting and more 'remunerative' employment elsewhere. Those entering the occupation lacked appropriate education, leaving them unprepared for and largely 'disillusioned' by the work. That is, the problems thought to beset this category of worker manifested themselves in a poor attitude, unruly behaviour, and unrealistic expectations, deficits that could be easily corrected through the new remedial strategy. The successful trainee would understand and accept her (subordinate) place, developing a stable work identity as a result of the training discourse.[81] In the production of the ideal-typical pedagogical subject, the attitude of the trainee towards her fellow workers and future employers was as much a focus for instruction as the curriculum content. But it is the articulation of this approach to the interiority of the training subject that is of particular interest here. Instruction modules outlined the particulars of cleaning, changing linens, arranging flowers, and feeding patients. Integrated throughout were techniques emphasizing the character of the ideal ward aide as an exemplar of compliant femininity, competence, and attentiveness. The ideal employee, modelled on notions of female subordination and respectability cumulatively assessed as personality, in effect defined the prescriptive occupation requirements and conditions of employment. Managerial technique was in this way integrated into the training program, while character formation – a clear objective of the course specified in modules addressing personal hygiene, ethics, deportment, and cheerfulness – enumerated the requirements of attitude and aptitude for this inherently feminized occupation. Trainees were taught to respect authority, remain courteous, maintain an appropriate attitude towards co-workers, and, most important of all, adopt a 'business-like attitude' at all times.[82]

Organizations such the YWCA, the NCWC, and the Big Sisters expressed considerable interest in and support for the course and appeared pleased by its results. Women trained through this program were reportedly 'conscientious' and 'dependable,' according to their new employer. When the Weston, Ontario, employment office decided to run a three-month course for 'nurses' aides,' officials there asserted that the fact of training was itself sufficient to convince 'the girls' that they were 'learning something worthwhile.'[83] Overall, the experience of training was alleged to have instilled a new sense of 'self-confidence' and interest, a clear indication of character reformation and rehabilitation that was productive of a more appropriate feminine worker identity now invested with an internalized sense of obedience and compliance – of self-government. Training of this kind, that is, was seen to facilitate the capacity to be taught, integrating the managerial techniques that would position the future employee within the routines and rituals of the workplace, as the following testimony to the allegedly positive effects of courses of this type suggested: 'Such pre-employment training seems to have a definitely stabilizing effect on the girls, as well as providing a foundation for training on the job later.'[84]

The Needle Trades

The needle-trades sector confronted chronic and persistent labour shortages throughout the war, in large part because of the conditions of employment as a low-wage industry. Industry representatives, with the support and participation of the craft and industrial unions in the sector, seeking to organize a sectoral strategy, drew upon pre-employment training as a labour stabilization scheme. As the steps taken to organize a Winnipeg Needle Trades Training Institute suggest, the employer organization and unions within the sector deployed the pre-employment training strategy as a vehicle for achieving stability within the industry. In so doing, both parties focused upon improvement of labour quality as the route for occupational upgrading. In July 1945, the Garment Manufacturers' Association of Western Canada (GMAWC) presented a proposal to the NSS/NES for a sectoral strategy of government-sponsored pre-employment training for workers in the industry. The apparent shortage of 'trained experienced help,' argued the GMAWC, meant that garment manufacturers could not fill production orders from the Department of Munitions and Supply, or lucrative orders from the United Nations Relief and Rehabilitation Agency and expanding domestic consumer markets.[85] The labour-intensive garment industry was a large employer in the region. The GMAWC claimed to represent twenty-four plants. In the Greater Winnipeg area alone, the sector employed 4,000 industrial sewing-machine operators. According to the association's president, S.B. Nitikman, another 1,500 workers could readily find full-time permanent work as power sewing-machine operators. And yet, Nitikman continued, consultation with the newly formed Employer Relations section of the NSS had failed to secure suitable workers. The NSS claimed that it could not supply girls and women to the industry and, even when it was able to do so, many moved on after a short period of employment.

The association proposed a three-point program to deal with the problem consisting of (1) a publicity program through the Consumer Branch of the Wartime Prices and Trade Board, the NFB, the CBC, and the Canadian Press to emphasize the strategic importance of the sector for the national economy; (2) a publicity campaign tying the clothing shortage to the chronic shortage of labour and promoting the sector as a large employer in a peacetime economy; and (3) establishment of a training institute in Winnipeg, with government taking responsibility for finding and training workers. According to the proposal, training would 'condition [entrants] psychologically' as part of a pre-employment program that would carefully screen each entrant.[86] The industry contribution to the proposed institute would consist of a committee appointed to work with a jointly appointed board of directors to develop curriculum and supply equipment and materials for instructional purposes. Trainees would receive income support from government during the six weeks of instruction; industry would provide subsidized work placements with an hourly wage floor of thirty cents, for a forty-four-hour week, and 'the possibility of earning even more on our piece work incentive.' At the end of a six-month probationary training period, trainees would receive a $50 bonus paid by the Dominion government as an incentive to complete the program and commit to remaining in the position. This inducement, the employer organization argued, would have a pronounced 'stabilizing effect,' thus resolving the original problem of high turnover rates. Further, the bonus would actually increase the wage rate by five cents over two successive eight-week periods, suggesting that it would be paid out by employers as an hourly increase every two months and not as a lump sum.

The proposal sat with the NSS for another year while piecemeal plans were attempted and the federal Department of Labour haggled with the Manitoba government over signing on to the cost-sharing agreement for the labour market training of civilian workers who did not qualify for UI. In August 1946, plans were ready to launch a major industry training effort in the form of a jobs 'contest' to attract workers into the sector. The meeting, sponsored by the NES, was organized by the Winnipeg Needle Trades Training Institute, chaired by N. Neaman, the employer representative. The rest of the council comprised S. Herbst, representing the unions organized in the sector – the International Ladies' Garment Workers (American Federation of Labor [AFL]), the Fur and Leather Workers (Congress of Industrial Organizations [CIO]), the Amalgamated Garment Workers (CIO), the United Hatters, Cap and Millinery Workers (AFL) – and H. Stephens, secretary, representing the NES.[87] The *Winnipeg Free Press* made its boardroom available for this well-publicized 'contest' to draw workers into the industry. The meeting was well attended, with representatives of eighty-four employers, the four labour unions from both the industrial and craft sides, the provincial department of education, the provincial minister of labour, the Winnipeg School Board, the NFB, and the NES. Everyone hoped the 'sweat shop' label would recede into the past. 'No one,' reported the NES, was 'more concerned than the employer and his [*sic*] union about maintaining and even improving this present high standard' of employment and production.[88] Once the sweatshop 'fallacy' was eradicated, NES could work full time on 'dispatching workers to jobs, instead of acting as a selling agency.'[89] Employers were encouraged to cede their right to hire to the NES, the latter to work in close association with the Employer Relations branch of the UIC. The model had worked well in the Montreal garment trade, where the Montreal Needle Trades Institute maintained strong institutional link with the Quebec UIC. Montreal manufacturers had expressed 'alarm' at the costs of high turnover, estimating that the costs associated with training new employees ran as high as $75 per worker.[90]

The model used for the Quebec construction trades, while perhaps designed to undercut the hiring-hall system of the unionized building trades, sparked the enthusiasm of the architects of the Winnipeg Institute. The system would function like a closed hiring hall operated by the federal employment service, with selection and referral at the sole discretion of the NES in collaboration with the employer and the director of the training program. 'Suitability' could be determined almost exclusively on the basis of employer demand.

As the plan began to take shape, interest increased among the various parties. The proposal allied economic development with employment development policy objectives: Winnipeg had a large and growing garment sector. Instead of competing against Montreal and Toronto, the Winnipeg sector saw itself as a gateway to western markets, shifting production from work clothing to the broader market of consumer fashions as part of a modernization and development strategy. NES looked forward to directing unemployed workers, particularly women, through the proposed institute and into the sector, starting with unemployed workers who were UI-eligible. Employers would have access to government-provided training, wage subsidies, and employment referral – that is, the NES would assume full responsibility for labour supply. For its part, the NES would establish its credibility as an employment agency working in the direct interests of capital through its Employer Relations Branch. As part of a sectoral adjustment program, workers who successfully completed their training would be recognized by all garment employers in the region, a design feature intended to offset competitive 'poaching' among employers, while harmonizing standards for employment conditions and encouraging flexibility in the labour supply. Employers would be assured of the 'quality' and credentials carried by centrally trained workers. Moreover, workers would be taught consistent production methods and work routines through a standardized industry curriculum that reflected employers' priorities for work design and competitive work performance. And what was in it for the unions? Jobs. And recognition of unions, by employers and government, as the legitimate bargaining agents for the industry.

The proposal carried some urgency since the chronic shortage of labour was likely to intensify in the wake of pending amendments to the Income Tax Act. During the war, the income of married women was tax exempt up to $660 per year, a move designed to draw more women into the labour force. In 1946, that exemption was to be lowered to $250, prompting employers to argue that they were likely to lose between 80 and 90 per cent of the 1,500 married women then working in garment plants in the Winnipeg area.[91] NES officials confidently asserted that a strategy of vocational guidance and pre-employment training, backed up by a program of careful screening, would help in stabilizing the workforce: 'We feel that more success will be obtained by placing an applicant who has chosen the needle trades work as a vocation in preference to having been converted.'[92] The training council received the assurances of the minister of education, J.H. Dryden, that needle-trades training would be included in the provincially funded Manitoba Technical Institute. However, the council wanted an institute of its own. Dryden appointed the director of technical training for the Manitoba Department of Education, R.J. Johns, to conduct a survey of technical and vocational training for the council. The survey began in January 1947, when a committee of the council travelled to Ontario and New York City to study the joint labour-management training activities conducted in a variety of programs, plants, vocational institutes, and schools. NES representative Stephens, the employer relations officer with the NES Winnipeg office, accompanied Johns and the employer and union representatives, Neaman and Herbst. After visiting companies, schools, unions, and training institutes in Woodstock, Toronto, and Hamilton, Ontario, the committee proceeded to New York City. Committee members were pleased that the business people interviewed demonstrated interest in Winnipeg, although one New Yorker was said to have commented, 'Winnipeg. That's in Australia, isn't it?'[93] The New York Fashion Institute of Technology was a model of personnel planning and efficiency. One of the institute instructors, a Mrs Kapt – who professed to have a 'Canadian background' – described the Canadian industry as a 'vocational dumping ground.' Conditions were gradually improving, provided her Canadian colleagues might 'get our Canadian girls to realize the future that lies ahead of them in this industry.'[94]

Committee members promoted education as a 'common meeting ground' upon which labour and management could jointly work to achieve industrial stability and workplace harmony. For its part, labour sought to improve the educational status of its members and was prepared to provide them with both 'moral' and financial backing. Employers shared the 'moral' and financial commitment to training, while contributing their managerial 'expertise' based on 'practical experience' in the area of personnel management. As a vehicle for securing, improving, and consolidating the gains education might bring to labour-management relations, the survey committee recommended the estab-

lishment of industrial advisory committees composed of three representatives each from the labour and management side and one from the
public education sector. The NES would assume the role of 'impartial
public body' on the committee, contributing its expertise in analysing
and predicting employment trends and acting as a liaison among labour,
management, and education. Students would be recruited into the industry through the public education system and the NES on a cooperative placement basis. Finally, all assessment, hiring, and placement
functions would be assumed by the NES, which was deemed 'well equipped
to relieve industry of this burden.'[95]

The 1947 report of the Needle Trades Training Council Educational
Survey Committee is noteworthy not only as a study of industrial training
within the sector, but also for how training was mobilized through key
knowledge practices of managerial technique: namely, mental testing,
vocational training, and 'human resource management.' The survey set
out to determine the root cause of high labour turnover and proceeded
from there to the key features of personnel planning: applicant induction (personnel interviews), training, human relations, working conditions, personal conveniences, and wages. Material conditions – likely
determinants of job safety, security, and satisfaction – found no place in
the analysis. Wages and working conditions were 'reasonably favourable'
and therefore unlikely to contribute to 'excessive turnover' in the industry. This could only leave issues of labour force quality, with special
accommodation to the needs of a female workforce – 'personal conveniences' such as a lunch room, rest area, appropriate washroom facilities, and the like. But the more serious matter was 'deficiencies in
applicant induction, applicant training' and 'human relations.'[96] The
best modernization plan was, in fact, a continuation of the techniques
applied during the war through joint productivity committees and the
industrial welfare program: educational films, a training school for be-
ginners, re-education of workers, part-time training on the job for students, and plant visits for school students.

The first stop on the survey tour had been the York Knitting Mills in
Woodstock, Ontario. There the committee had met with Dr H.A. Grant,
production engineer; Ralph Pasgrave, industrial engineer; H. Woods,
manager; and Miss M. Robinson, personnel manager, presiding over the
largely female workforce. York Knitting Mills had learned well the lessons of employment and personnel experts and outlined a full program
of personnel assessment, scientific management, mental testing, and
strategic deployment of 'human resources' according to the most mod-

ern methods of work design, just-in-time training, and work distribution. 'Before entering company service,' every applicant was subjected to and had to pass a series of tests: '(a) General Health, (b) Eye, (c) General Knowledge, (d) I.Q. rating, and (e) Manual Dexterity.' The test of general health was 'visual.' Any doubts revealed there would be followed up by a complete medical examination. The company team did not indicate who paid for the examination, although no doubt refusal by the applicant to pay or cooperate would likely have ended the 'applicant induction' process right then. The eye test was to determine 'visual efficiency' in short-range vision and horizontal and vertical focusing, all using equipment provided by the Visual Engineering Institute of Guelph, Ontario. Again, costs were not alluded to. The general knowledge test did not warrant any comment, given its 'elementary' nature; failing it would also eliminate the applicant. There followed a review of 'general knowledge' tests then in circulation in Ontario that assessed for literacy, in linguistic as well as cultural and 'moral' codes, to screen systematically and systemically for prescriptive and proscriptive racialized, cultural, class, and gender-based criteria. If and when the applicant passed that hurdle, it was on to an IQ test. Applicants were asked to identify misplaced or missing items in a picture of 'a well known piece of merchandise,' a practice that assumed familiarity with an item bounded by culturally specific knowledge. The manual dexterity test required agility in both left and right hands, separately and simultaneously. Women, of course, were thought to have a particular proclivity for such dexterity. Testing apparatus was designed explicitly to screen for productivity. All results – 'ratings' – were interpreted by an outside firm of industrial engineers, specialists in the field. As evidence of their success, company representatives claimed to have conducted an experiment in which 350 applicants were hired 'irrespective of their rating.' Company records were produced to demonstrate that, had the company used the rating system, it would have saved $6,200 in wages paid out to workers who were incapable of reaching even the lowest production quota.[97]

Unfortunately, some Department of Labour officials were sceptical of the claims made by the training council. The industry had already received considerable funding from the federal government during the war to help meet its labour requirements, particularly through direct wage subsidies. Plant schools had been established under the War Emergency Training program in at least six Winnipeg plants under contract to the Department of Munitions and Supply. The experience, according to CVT director Thompson, had been neither a happy nor an entirely satisfactory one. There were distinct indications of employer abuse of the wage subsidy program. That is, companies readily took on new trainees and used the workers as long as they remained on government subsidy throughout the training period, only to dismiss that group and move on to the next lot. Seeing no appreciable growth in the size of the labour force, Thompson axed the program.[98] As far as Thompson was concerned, industry turnover could not be accurately assessed on the basis of a cursory review of global statistics alone. Certainly the Department of Labour was by now more than adept at scrutinizing and classifying the activities of workers; perhaps it was now time to consider employer practices more rigorously as well, particularly in cases where employer councils wanted public funds to continue to provide them with a trained, stable labour force.

Conclusion

Women bureaucrats oversaw the demobilization of servicewomen and civilians alike. At virtually every turn, they faced the reality that preference in the postwar economy went to men, notwithstanding the formal equality provisions of the Veterans' Charter. In his postwar narrative *Rehabilitation: A Combined Operation,* Walter Woods, deputy minister of veterans' affairs, made note of the 'considerable resentment' against the discrimination experienced by the ex-servicewoman. The gesture taken to correct this discriminatory practice in the name of formal equality was, however, just that – a gesture. Woods reflected conventional understandings of women's occupations. There was no real discrepancy in the shorter training periods approved for women as compared to those approved for male veterans since 'there was a great demand for female help in all industries which did not require much skill other than dextrous fingers.'[99] The sexual division of labour was simply a reflection of the natural order of things, even if recent experience suggested otherwise. Neither was female unemployment an issue in postwar Canada. A 'test check' conducted in December 1947 had indicated that of the 'few hundred' women so registered by the Unemployment Insurance Commission, 'ninety per cent were without skills and consequently were hard to place in jobs that were acceptable to them.'[100] Woods's account survives as an authoritative official narrative about rehabilitation policy, testifying to the gender-based equality measures contained within the Veterans' Charter – at least formally. Women veterans were not even eligible for rehabilitation training benefits until 1944, a reflection of the attitude shared at the highest levels of government.

The occupations open to women in the years following the Second World War were few. Most of those who worked for pay would have to find their place in low-waged industries like the textile, garment, and related needle trades, along with cleaning and personal services. Across all of these sectors, pre-employment vocational training followed a strategy for the occupational 'upgrading' of primarily working-class women – cast now as an 'unskilled reserve.' At the same time, pro-natalist domesticity discourses promoted a national standard of improved mental hygiene, melding well with new ideas about social security programming and citizenship formation. All eyes were directed at fortifying the middle-class home as a central plank of the program for postwar reconstruction. When attention turned once again to issues like rising levels of juvenile delinquency, mental hygiene advocates such as Russell pointed out that women could not possibly fulfil both parenting roles equally well. Moreover, the idea of combining motherhood and paid work threatened the stability, indeed the viability, of the middle- and working-class home. The family was an integral social unit of community and nation – one of the cornerstones of liberal democracy. Arguments such as these demonstrated that achieving domestic stability was the goal of public policy, specifically of pro-natalist policy planning for middle-class, white, heterosexual women in the postwar world. Motherhood-as-occupation ran through employment and training policy as an integral, if implicit, theme. Domesticity discourse worked through two channels. Pro-natalist discourse secured and stabilized women's identities as the middle-class, white mothers of the nation's future citizens. In anti-natalist discourse, working-class women and women racialized as 'other' were viewed as mothers who were also labourers, or as single women who would find a place in domestic service or in the rural agricultural economy. Working-class women, women of colour, and ethnically diverse women were understood to enter paid employment through economic necessity, but only in the absence of a responsible male provider. In this way, waged work signified the failure of home and household. These were the women absorbed into the category of the 'reserve of unskilled women' – the possible source of disruption, deviance, and challenge in the social: women in need of expert intervention and regulation. Their presence posed a challenge to the stability of the formal waged economy and the workplace. Vocational training, in this way, promised to restore stability and order.

Russell's homemaking program best exemplified the pro- and anti-natalist discourses of citizenship and domesticity around which the mental hygiene program was organized, a prescriptive social universe grounded in class, race, gender, and sexual order, which, if it could be achieved, would assure the stability and health of the national character. Marriage, therefore, would be subject to scrutiny as a domain of governance, to ensure the reproductive, social, and economic consonance of hetero-sexual partners. Compatibility was transformed through mental hygiene discourse as an index for differential aptitude, intelligence, and capacity – cumulatively represented as personality and character. There were clear racial, class, and gender dimensions by which difference and dis-cord, sameness and harmony could be readily apprehended. Basic physi-ological needs, if addressed and satisfied, translated into mental health; if neglected or denied they became manifest in deviance, unhappiness, and delinquency, or worse. Here was the new terrain of citizenship formation in the home, the domain of marriage, parenting, and home-making. The 'family living' component of the course reflected the desire of the NCMH to institute a national standard for mental hygiene – or mental health, as it became known by the 1950s. For too long, the mental hygiene of citizens had been neglected as a critical component of public policy and human relations. Problems of the social were taken up through tropes of deviance and disruption, as incorrigibility among girls, as juvenile delinquency, unemployment, criminality, and sexual devi-ance, including prostitution and homosexuality – psychological manifes-tations of mental ill health. Mental illness need not be feared, as the popular mental hygiene dramas broadcast by the CBC counselled. As part of the rehabilitation program, the Home Service course was a course in practical instruction for newlyweds. It presented an excellent opportunity to show how problems of maladjustment could be rem-edied, if not prevented, by early detection through the expertise of the psyche-practitioner. Instruction in citizenship, parenting, and the con-duct of a healthy home life provided a considerable opportunity for these experts and their desire to implement a comprehensive program to reshape the home, and women as wives and mothers. That it did not succeed is testimony to the single-minded objective of postwar policy, for women veterans and civilians alike. Clearly, 'training housewives' – as it was characterized by senior staff – was not the responsibility of the Department of Labour, or, for that matter, the point of rehabilitation planning. If the best adjustment plan for men was a job, then marriage (with or without employment), was best for women. Marriage, a natural enough state, was all the adjustment women required.

Conclusion

As early as 1941, senior officials in the federal government (the 'Ottawa men'), aware that Canada would face serious problems meeting military production quotas to supply the Allied Forces in Europe, asked, *Is the individual a national asset worth developing?* The answer, as Canada's leading psychologists well knew, was a resounding yes! Psychological experts played a key role in forging policies that would guide Canada through the war, while simultaneously laying the foundation for the postwar social security state. The cream of Canada's intelligence men and women, leading experts affiliated with the elite National Committee for Mental Hygiene (Canada) (NCMH), saw an opportunity to realize their long-held ambition to establish a national standard for mental health. Economic prosperity and domestic stability began with the individual. Sound social and economic planning mattered little if individual citizens remained maladjusted, their potential productive capacities undeveloped. The proper focus of government, according to these experts, lay in cultivating the *employability* of its citizens, a key insight that brought psychological expertise into the service of achievable economic objectives.

The Second World War witnessed an unprecedented level of economic and social planning and was, as such, a critical period in the formation of the Canadian welfare state. Officials liked to think of themselves as being in charge of a command economy, giving policy practitioners access to far-ranging experimental interventionary powers across an array of areas of social and economic life.[1] Recollections just after the war describe the period as one of tremendous experimentation. The infusion of new ideas and new challenges presented unparalleled opportunities for policy practitioners and agencies to develop new and different forms of state regulation and to expand the activities of government into new areas of civilian life, social services, and economic activity. For example, John J. Deutsch, of the Bank of Canada, later recalled his sense of personal challenge and excitement as he looked upon the possibilities for governmental experimentation in the trying days of the war. Noting that it had become 'necessary over a very short period of time to mobilize the entire resources of the country under the direction of a highly centralized administrative machine,' he stressed that a sense of 'overriding national necessity' made it possible 'to make short cuts, to experiment, to adopt expedients, to undertake on a large scale programs that had never been tried before.'[2]

Certainly the Department of Labour expanded throughout the war to become a massive bureaucracy of considerable complexity and authority, however fraught its administrative capacity and competence may have appeared as policy practitioners struggled to meet their new responsibilities. Viewed in this way, the Labour Supply Investigation Project (LSIP) was a significant policy event, an exercise in defining the economy – now including the labour force – as a rational and discrete administrative space as well as a legitimate domain of governance. The labour market was conceptualized as national in scope. Committee members approached cultural diversity as difference, a potential source of social and regional barriers in the movement of labour. This was particularly the case in descriptions of agricultural communities and of Quebec as a site of profound cultural difference. Gender was explicitly mobilized to illustrate the multiple challenges ethnicity and racialized difference were thought to pose to labour mobility. That is, mobilizing women would launch culture on a collision course with economy, producing endless social problems, needs, and challenges that government would have to address. The constellation of relations linking economy, culture, and the social was in this way problematized as a further site of governance. The policy agenda would be very full indeed.

The Ottawa men carefully considered the implications of mobilizing Canada's womanpower. For perhaps the first time, women would be foregrounded as subjects in employment policy. This construction was accomplished in multiple ways. How were the unique challenges posed by women workers described? How would these problems be taken up? Answers to these questions reveal policy attempts to measure, with the intent of administering, the quality and calibre of the labour force as part of the project of the state. This was an exercise of governance in which each and all had a role to play: employers, organized labour, women, various levels of government, communities, and men. This exercise would have transformative effects, and at the same time evoke resistance from a variety of quarters. The 'manpower shortage' was approached as the product of challenges originating in five distinct areas. Heading the list was the vexing yet all-too familiar challenge in the Canadian federation: lack of comprehensive federal-provincial policy, funding, and responsibility for effective labour force deployment. All levels of government were criticized for their lack of statistical knowledge about the labour force and any potential reserves available for recruitment into the market. Women would now be ushered into the machinations of public employment policy: conceptualized and assessed, valued and counted for their productive capacities as subjects of employment discourse, albeit in ways that did not substantively – or permanently – alter their status identities with respect to domesticity.

Prime Minister Mackenzie King described the steps that were being taken to ensure the capable administration of the new-found supply of female labour, in part to allay fears about the indiscriminate intermingling of male and female workers and also to create the impression of order in directing women from the household into industry with minimal disruption. The program operationalized the findings and recommendations of the LSIP through an extensive array of social and economic measures, all designed to move women into military-industrial and essential civilian production. The significance of policy responses to the 'manpower problem' lies in part in how the labour market was constituted through policy discourses as an object of regulation by masculinist state power. Groups of women were universally constituted as 'female labour,' a category of potential labour that was positioned as always already marginal to the regular labour force. An important policy effect of this work lay in constituting the identity of the ideal typical worker, who was seen to occupy the economic space circumscribed by a national labour market. The key figure constituted and mobilized through this policy discourse was signified through the identity of the white, male subject, the worker-citizen whose rights were articulated to his capacity to assert ownership of his labouring capacity, itself calibrated as an index of efficiency and productivity.

Policy practitioners sought to develop measures that would overcome and/or remediate such deficiencies, expressed as obstacles to mobility, to facilitate regional, sectoral, and occupational movement in response to national priorities. Policy measures adopted to recruit the 'female labour reserve' worked in such a way as to intensify the gendering of the bodies and minds of groups of women workers, constituted anew as 'female labour.' Occupational skill was taken up through employability discourse as a strategy through which the body of the woman war worker was conceptualized as 'female' within the production process and within the social environment of the modern production facility, whether in the industrial or the service sector. In the gendered and racialized bodies of the female labour reserve resided inherent limitations of skill and aptitude and, therefore, productive capacity as efficient and employable workers. Culture, ethnicity, social and geographic location, educational background, and language – while operating as code for relations grounded in class, gender, and racialized subjugation and marginality – were constituted as potential hindrances to the otherwise smooth flow of labour. At the same time, policy practitioners worked within what was coming to be understood and apprehended as a market that was national in scope. The still greater challenge lay within the mind: addressing the attitudes of women towards their status as workers would be variously taken up in ways reflective of the anticipated class and racial identity of those women were alleged to be. Cultural location produced women who resided principally in middle-class homes and whose main occupation was mother and wife, whether actual or potential; young single women lured to the city, leaving behind the ordered security of home and community; immigrant women deemed out of place in the routines and practices of industrial and urban society; and farm women to whose own farm duties were added the work of handicraft production and assisting their farmer husbands.

'Employability' would become a central theme in federal policy, propelling wartime mobilization and postwar rehabilitation alike, but now it would take on a much more complex meaning than its Victorian predecessor, the 'work test' principle that informed relief measures. Manpower policy became a matter of strategic national significance. Armed with the apparatus of scientific personnel planning, the newly arrived employment experts argued that effective employment policy should seek out and correct industrial inefficiencies. Industrial inefficiency was understood as 'maladjustment' – 'the square peg in a round hole,' according to the popular phrase, leading invariably to occupational maladjustment, chronic absenteeism, even worker sabotage. Looked at in this way, maladjustment could be easily corrected through the sound scientific techniques of personnel planning, the apparatus of intelligence tests and aptitude assessment, and training and vocational counselling. The strategy was applied first to women recruited for the war effort. But, argued experts such as Dr Olive Ruth Russell of the Canadian

Women's Army Corps (CWAC), this same strategy could be used – and was – with even greater effect when applied to the problem of unemployment. And so, unemployment could be seen as a deficiency of the individual – the maladjusted worker who lacked adequate skill, capacity, training, or all three. Unemployment thus appeared both in actuarial terms (i.e., potential liability to the Unemployment Insurance program) and individual terms in a very new light, as a managerial and psychological problem rather than merely the malfunction of the economy.

Experts were convinced that these techniques could be readily applied through postwar rehabilitation and reconstruction planning. Planning for the war also meant planning for the postwar period in the same measure, an approach that permits the historian to highlight how women were understood differently at these distinct historical moments. During the Depression, women were for the most part not considered unemployed even when they desired and could not find waged work. According to the common sense of the interwar period, no domestic worker need ever be unemployed. Indeed, any woman found to be unemployed was deemed *unemployable*. By the Second World War, these same women were considered employable, provided they were properly trained, and it was here that officials in the federal Departments of Labour and National Defence turned to the expertise of educational psychologists and other employment experts, who in turn gained considerable influence in the wartime administration. These new approaches to employment policy would become a regular feature of managerial technique, institutionalized in that hallmark of the modern corporation, the personnel department.

Postwar planning was also about creating happy homes for a happy democracy. Everyone shared in the task of creating stable and well-adjusted households and families, and nothing was more integral to this exercise than motherhood and jobs for returning soldiers. Most people anticipated, indeed dreaded, that the pre-war unemployment crisis would return – from senior officials right through to business, community organizations, veterans' organizations, and individual women and men. Certainly, senior women bureaucrats attempted to balance postwar equality objectives against this fear. Women's postwar employment was a politically charged matter, reinforced by pointed allusions to sexual danger, immorality, and excessive and unwholesome leisure activities among women whose taste for such activities had been unhealthily whetted by their inflated wartime incomes. The postwar state accelerated the use of vocational training, often considered the benevolent arm of the welfare state, to shore up the boundaries of a racially and sexually divided labour market. When officials turned to postwar planning, it was assumed that women would be uninterested in paid work, despite considerable evidence to the contrary. 'I want to get a post-war job' was a familiar refrain by 1944, but such aspirations found little accommodation in the male breadwinner regime of the postwar Canadian welfare state. And so throughout the postwar period, government officials carefully balanced liberal rights alongside other discourses of citizenship, domesticity, and employability.

What began as a question of directing labour flows into essential industries and areas of priority economic activity during the early years of the war soon became a matter of redirecting labour to prevent anticipated unemployment in the postwar period. Full employment was now understood as an achievable economic phenomenon. After all, the war had produced economic activity at a level never before experienced in the Dominion, boosting productivity and ushering in a new era of personnel planning into the bargain. War, while it might leave a devastating path of destruction, was also good for business and for the economies of at least some of the victors. But not all would find their place in the postwar economy. The experience of full employment during the war, while it did not abruptly transform ideas about employability,[3] involved the state more directly in the regulation and day-to-day administration of the labour market. Among the policy officials whose work is considered here, administration of employment policies, and therefore questions concerning the employability of individual citizens, became a matter of intense national interest. A risk-management approach to employment – embodied in the 1940 passage of the Unemployment Insurance Act, along with the actuarial management of the unemployment insurance fund – could now be realized by improving the employability of the labour force.

But this was not to be, nor could it be, an exercise for the state alone. As the experience of the war demonstrated, productive efficiency was a national objective in which each and all had an important part to play. Efficiency was a social as well as an economic objective, one that could not only mitigate but also potentially eliminate altogether the social instability associated with unemployment. Everyone feared the return to high unemployment once the war was finally over. In fact, most expected it. Not only that, but many also recalled the poor treatment accorded to veterans of the First World War. And above all, few doubted the politically charged significance of high male unemployment, for organized labour, for the organized left, or for the male veterans' associations.

The combined experience of full employment during the Second

World War brought hundreds of thousands of new entrants into the paid workforce and profoundly transformed relations surrounding employment, unemployment, citizens, and the state. The personnel department of the modern corporation and the public employment office emerged as important sites through which the state and the community engaged with individual women and men, through the activities of personnel screening, intelligence testing, training, referral, and placement. These interactions constituted new terrain for social research and investigation, remediation, and adjustment. The 'maladjusted worker' gained a new identity in the form of the irregularly employed working man or the female unskilled casual labourer.

This study has traced, on the one hand, the work, analyses, and knowledge practices of policy officials who were responsible for managing women and, on the other, the administrative category of 'female labour.' Both official categories of administration and individual women were profoundly transformed through state policy – specifically, through the discourses of employability and domesticity that so closely informed the purpose and direction of public policy. Policy discourses describe historically contingent social regimes that regulate and reproduce citizenship entitlements. As regulatory procedures, policies of state collectively characterize forms of treatment and conditions of access within the national social body. Policy effects are real, borne out in the lived experiences, opportunities, and deprivations to which people are subject within a state regime. Welfare state policy regimes similarly constitute and organize conceptions of the 'social' and the pathological, as features of state formation generally and, in the case of Canada, as an extension of the Dominion as white settler colony. The postwar consensus – considered an exercise in social bargaining – was very much a reflection of the formative articulation of 'the social' within welfare state formation. The postwar settlement, then, was an extension of such nation-making practices, located within the broader historical context of welfare state formation and the production of historical and theoretical knowledge about nation states. As such, the materiality of race and the racialization of gendered knowledges and class-based relations are all to be found within economic and social forms, taken up and administered through economic and political/cultural rationalities and through policy regimes that are deeply embedded within welfare state formations.

This is also a study of the multiple ways in which labour markets are historically constituted as social as well as economic institutions, an imagining of 'nation,' as well as a series of economic relations and events. Measures of the national labour market also trace the boundaries of nation and nationhood. Just as national boundaries constitute a perimeter – the possibility as well as the limits – of nation, so too the contours of the formal waged economy enable and delimit citizenship capacities: deciding, for example, who is really unemployed, who is really a citizen, and who is creating social problems that in turn become pathologized as individual deficiencies. This, too, has been an accomplishment of the Canadian welfare state.

When Canada entered the Second World War in September 1939, its role as a major supplier of the Allied Forces would soon test the limits of the Dominion's labour force capacities. The strategic economic rationality of war profoundly transformed the business of government, of production, and of household and community. Despite the persistent efforts of employment policy practitioners and experts, Canada entered the war and a range of military industrial production commitments without a comprehensive national 'manpower policy.' The pressures of military industrial production soon exposed deep fault lines within the labour market as it was understood and framed by policy practitioners. At the same time, regional and interprovincial barriers to labour mobility, recalcitrant employers, and profound regionalized poverty in areas devastated by the recent Depression further confounded the efforts of the Department of Labour to meet labour supply requirements.

The confidential report of the Labour Supply Investigation Project was completed in October 1941, as federal officials at the Department of Labour grappled with the deepening crisis of labour shortages in critical production areas. The LSIP was a substantive investigation of the national labour market and supply, of the quality of that supply, of employment practices and labour-management relations, and of the policy interventions needed to identify and then mobilize human resources for total war. As such, the report was deeply critical of the existing disjointed system of training and employment placement, of private employment agencies, and of the fractious climate of industrial relations. The report was particularly critical of employer opposition to hiring women workers. Researchers proposed a comprehensive program of personnel management on the one hand and a national employment and training system on the other. A key recommendation of this report was that the federal government should deploy what many saw as a massive reserve of untapped female labour. But there was a problem. How were policy officials to go about measuring, let alone recruiting, a supply of labour the existence of which had been structurally elided and systematically denied as a matter of federal policy? Government planners authorized broader and more far-reaching techniques by which to identify, recruit, train, and deploy the female 'labour reserve.' The labour market was conceptualized as national in scope. The quality of the labour supply, moreover, was foregrounded as a concern of government and an object of governance, both within state agencies and among community, social agencies, individual workers, and employers. Techniques of management replaced the 'invisible hand' as the regulatory principle around which the national labour market was organized.

Winning the war was a business in which each and all had a role to play. Nowhere was this more crucial than among women – first young, single women and, by 1943, married women as well, all of whom were the targets of National Selective Service (NSS) Women's Division recruiting efforts. From counting the potential supply of women workers, the attention of the federal Department of Labour turned to outlining the steps thought necessary to enable the federal state to implement a comprehensive and coherent employment policy. A range of supporting regulatory measures was envisaged, positioning the public employment office as a linchpin within a national employment service. Skill was a central organizing principle and strategy in employment policy discourse, a category that positioned the ideal-typical subject of employment rights discourse as male, white, able-bodied, and of British origin.

Women were foregrounded for the first time as central subjects of employment policy discourse, thought to present unique challenges within the labour market and the workplace. The labour supply was approached through the lens of employability discourse, through a new grid of intelligibility that opened up the interior of the subject as a legitimate domain of governance and a site of intervention. The 'scientific' assessment of labour-force quality drew upon a range of discursive techniques of mental testing, techniques that were part of the regular apparatus of personnel management. Aptitude testing was held up as the signifier of the modern economic enterprise, a practice employers were enjoined to adopt within their own internal organization in order to improve the efficiency of personnel and, what was after all the main objective, the productive capacity of the national economy mobilized for total war. Deficiencies in labour-force quality were conceived of as originating in and manifested through gender, class, and race and articulated through culture-as-difference. Problems of labour force attachment were similarly approached as originating in the psychology of the individual, as deficiencies of skill and capacity.

Populations were singled out for particular scrutiny, constituted as potential 'problems' on the basis of ethnicity, national origin, culture, and education – code for class, gender, and racialized subjugation and marginalization. Similarly, departmental officials constituted the recruiting practices of the NSS along racialized lines. For white men and women of British origin, the NSS prevailed upon patriotic duty, positioning women in particular as serving home and nation through their selfless identification of the national interest as coextensive with their own desires as wives, mothers, and daughters, and above all as citizens rallying to the fight for democracy and national security. The war also foregrounded race and ethnicity as the state classified women and men according to apparent country of origin and descent. Those not meeting the criterion of British descent were singled out for intensive regulatory intervention, including incarceration. Compulsory practices of recruiting and deployment in low-wage industries were reserved in particular for men excluded from military mobilization orders, including those of Chinese, Japanese, or East Indian 'racial origin.' The disciplinary powers of the state were invoked without hesitation, as department officials proposed RCMP surveillance and investigation of specified national groups.

Vocational training and personnel programming were central to policy work at the National Selective Service. These techniques were key to the administrative work transacted through the official space of the public employment office as strategies to rationalize the flow of labour within the national labour market. NSS director Arthur MacNamara, NSS Women's Division associate director Fraudena Eaton, and their colleagues drew upon the expertise of management consultants, educational psychologists, employment researchers, and policy experts to assist them in the formidable challenges of full labour force mobilization, training, and employment placement. Throughout the period of the Second World War, the number of women in the labour force more than doubled from 600,000 in 1939 to 1,300,500 by 1945. Notwithstanding the massive presence of women within the formal waged economy, the patriarchal bedrock upon which conceptualizations of work, employability, and domesticity were based remained undisturbed. Policy officials remained clear that the 'full employment' policies of the postwar period would not include women.

Industrial and domestic strategies adopted by the NSS Women's Division structured and also modified relations of work and household through the twin rationales underpinning the policy regime of the

Canadian welfare state during this period: the national enterprise of winning the war and the domestic enterprise of securing the peaceful withdrawal of women from the formal waged economy at war's end. Training for women war workers was rooted in differential notions of women's skill and aptitude. The design and allocation of job tasks reified gender essentialism, mapping the minds and the bodies of women as always already female within the production process and therefore marginalized within the rational space of the modern industrial enterprise. As subjects of training policies, women were positioned as out of place in, unfamiliar with, and requiring habituation to the disciplines and routines of economic modernity.

Employment experts from the Montreal management consulting firm Stevenson and Kellogg joined forces with industrial psychiatry, proposing work reorganization schemes that promised to improve efficiency and output. They saw 'absenteeism' and labour turnover as problems of worker instability, problems to which women were particularly prone, and that directly implicated the rationalizing and regulatory possibilities of comprehensive personnel programming. On the strength of these expert studies, the NSS Women's Division devised a program of industrial welfare, in contradistinction to the masculinist program of industrial relations, designing a gender-based strategy for personnel programming in which women workers were positioned as the subjects of moral investigation and regulation. Industrial welfare was intended to place women in wartime employment and then to keep them there for the duration. But it also operated as a program of moral regulatory intervention, organizing the social relations of war workers as the subject of sexualized investigation and supervision. As moral regulatory subjects, women war workers were seen as requiring careful and close supervision by women personnel practitioners.

This was not an exercise for the state alone, however, notwithstanding that the NSS had temporarily assumed the role of overseer of the national labour market. Policy officials worked diligently to counter mounting criticism of government handling of the 'manpower crisis,' projecting an image of the state at the helm of the well-oiled NSS machine, capable of identifying and remedying problems in even the remotest corners of the national economy. Their best efforts were challenged at every turn, not least by women war workers. Managing women war workers proved to be a daunting task. The NSS Women's Division investigated complaints that would today be identified as sexual and other forms of harassment. Such investigations cast women as agents of disruption. Resistance of varying forms met with intensified scrutiny and programmatic attempts to structure and regulate women's relations and interactions during leisure as well as working hours.

The majority of women and men both anticipated and dreaded the return of high unemployment once the war was finally ended. Many women, moreover, needed and wanted to remain in waged work and seemed unprepared to abide by the prescriptive designs of the NSS Women's Division to move them into low-waged industries, if not out of the labour market altogether. By 1944, women began to turn their sights towards the postwar period. 'I want to get a postwar job' became a familiar refrain, as employment officers at the NSS employment office took up the task of directing women out of wartime employment and into either a narrow and narrowly prescriptive range of occupations designated as 'suitable' for women or out of waged employment.

Planning for the transition to the postwar economy was well underway by 1943. Statistics became a tool of governance in this planning exercise. They were also a site of contention, as officials deliberated over how many women workers were likely to be found in an economy operating under 'normal' conditions. All agreed on the need to dampen expectations of federal responsibility for female employment and to downplay awareness of the high numbers of laid-off women war workers who might now be classified as officially unemployed. In this exercise, the labour market for women was conceptualized as local and decentralized, subject to highly regionalized variance. Strategies for the redeployment of women in the peacetime economy followed suit, with employment policy developed and implemented through a network of local employment advisory committees made up of volunteer representatives of business and women's organizations, in a move that further marginalized women's access to and location within the formal waged economy.

When NSS regulatory controls over the movement of labour were revoked in May 1945, the employment office took on a new significance as an administrative site for redirecting women from the strategic economic rationality of an economy mobilized for war to the domestic passivity of peace. The 'problem' of postwar employment was approached through the techniques of vocational guidance, most clearly exemplified in the strategy of pre-employment vocational training, a program designed to redirect women war workers into a handful of occupations. What began as a question of jobs in the postwar economy was now a matter of employment preparedness and occupational upgrading.

The NSS Women's Division Pre-employment Training Survey was a survey of occupations rather than of postwar employment opportunities for women, and as such it instituted and entrenched a two-tiered training system as a formative feature of the Canadian welfare state. Occupational aptitude and skill became critical determinants of future employability in a strategy that sought to upgrade 'female' occupations by upgrading women as subjects of remedial training policy discourses. The survey was a formative strategy for the development of postwar employment policy for women, one that entrenched the sexual and racial division of labour while at the same time constituting women's employment capacities as a function of class, gender, sexuality, and race. As workers, women were constituted as marginal to the formal waged economy, only partially capable of achieving desired levels of productivity and skilled capacity. While women might have an innate aptitude for various forms of work, psyche-based practitioners and policy experts alike argued that skilled work was beyond the capacity of the average, 'normal' woman worker. As subjects of domesticity discourses, women were redirected into the postwar household, there to take up their proper vocation as mothers, as consumers, or as labourers in the households of other women. These discourses articulated the boundaries of nation, reifying the national labour market as the prescriptive domain of men, the site of national security and strength, while asserting the differential citizenship capacities of women, those who only a few short years before had been enjoined to secure the interests of the nation on the home front.

By V-E Day on 8 May 1945, peace in Europe was finally at hand. Most people anticipated that the Japanese capitulation would not be far behind. The work of rehabilitation and national reconstruction was well underway, following a program that enlisted the full participation of employers', community, women's, and business organizations, trade unions, veterans' organizations, and individual women and men, along with a host of state officials and policy experts. Rehabilitation policy involved the mutually constitutive interests of nation, citizenry, and industry in a process that consolidated and sought to stabilize civil society through a smooth transition to the social order of peace. Rehabilitating ex-servicewomen and -servicemen was accomplished through a series of discourses that centrally positioned home and family on the one hand and employment stability, consumption, and national security on the other.

Rehabilitation deployed the full range of psyche-based knowledge practices developed and implemented through the unprecedented opportunities for research and practice made possible by the war. Practitioners associated with the NCMH were integral to this work, strategically positioned throughout the services and, for the postwar period, state agencies concerned with overseeing the transition to peace. Mental hygiene discourses broadened the scope of rehabilitation work, opening up the application of psyche-based concepts such as security and adjustment as largely unrecognized dimensions of civil rehabilitation and social reconstruction. Aptitude and intelligence testing, these expert practitioners claimed, were objective and transparent methods by which to screen, calibrate, and organize the labour force.

Work conducted by the Directorate of Personnel Selection at the Department of National Defence was directed by mental hygiene experts. There, the systematic deployment of mental testing was argued to have brought substantive gains to both the military and the nation, rationalizing recruitment and military deployment through scientific assessment, calibration, and regulation of military personnel. Practitioners envisaged similar gains for the civilian population, especially in industry, schools, and even the home. As a function of individual psychology, intelligence and aptitude were made visible through objective scientific techniques of observation. They were, in this way, discursive categories constituting the interior of the subject as a site for regulatory intervention.

The organizing precepts of scientific racism and sexism lay deeply embedded within the techniques and technologies of mental testing. The racial and gender-based typology of intelligence constituted through mental testing technologies dated back to the First World War, when mental testing techniques were developed for mass application in the U.S. Army. At the University of Toronto, leading educational psychologist Peter Sandiford was instrumental in deepening the racializing practice of mental testing within educational practice. Dr Olive Ruth Russell worked with Sandiford as a graduate student and research associate at the Ontario College of Education before the war. Her work as a CWAC army examiner and later director of women's rehabilitation for the Department of Veterans' Affairs (DVA) drew upon racialized, gender, and class-based precepts, conditioning her assessments of who was a legitimate mother, worker, citizen, or suitable candidate for acceptance into the women's armed services. Forms of resistance, of sexual agency – indeed, any behaviour held to defy standards of acceptable and 'suitable' feminine identity – were pathologized in Russell's work for the Canadian Women's Army Corps, signifying the likely presence of incorrigibility, sex deviance, dependency, delinquency, even criminality. As an educational psychologist, Russell was deeply immersed in the formative principles and knowledge-making practices of the mental hygiene program. Vocational counselling provided a crucial point of convergence, a conduit through which the mental hygiene program joined with the liberalist project of education to promote good citizenship and social order. Associates of the NCMH hoped to instil a national standard of mental health and to promote mental health and prevent mental ill-health. Happy democracy depended upon happy homes. Much of Russell's work as an educational psychologist during the Depression gained far greater strategic significance during and after the war. The formation of good citizens – of self-governing subjects, as suggested in the phrase 'helping Johnny to see Johnny through' – gained considerable resonance and relevance as part of the postwar work of rehabilitation and civil reconstruction.

Self-help guides distributed to ex-service personnel emphasized the importance of avoiding the 'square peg in a round hole' phenomenon, a mismatch between individual and vocation thought to signify individual and therefore social maladjustment. That road ended in unemployment, individual unhappiness, and even family breakdown. Intelligence, personality, ability, and aptitude: these were the secrets, the truths of the self awaiting discovery, but only with the aid of the expert practitioner. As ex-service personnel were advised, 'an aptitude test is in *your* best interest.' Participation in and stable attachment to the labour market were as much a matter of uncovering and utilizing psychological resources – the hidden but discoverable truths of the self – as they were a function of economic conditions. And that was not all. Satisfaction and fulfilment of personal desire, of individual potential, were every bit as important as the mere meeting of basic needs – or so the psyche-experts and personnel officers claimed. The model of male wage earner/female dependant stood at the core of rehabilitation and reconstruction programming, rendering the notion of individual choice little more than a rhetorical position. DVA officials repeatedly argued that rehabilitation counselling, training, employment placement, and related services were not imposed upon ex-service personnel but were rather the product of the individual's choice. Veterans' counsellors were advised regularly to include the individual counselled subject as a full participant in the counselling exercise. In this way, the individual agency and subjectivity of ex-servicewomen constituted the vehicle for counselling discourse.

DVA policy worked within the framework of, and effectively reinforced, the fixed parameters of the racially and sexually divided labour market. The individualizing effects of liberal choice discourses worked through the interior of the subject to actively form self-governing subjects who would take up their positions as responsible citizens in postwar society. For men, DVA policy revolved around one central point: the best adjustment program was a job. This was a clear articulation of the employment rights accorded to men within the model of the family wage system. The ideal citizen was one whose sights were firmly set on peace, prosperity, and consumerism. Full employment meant stable employment and income for men, while women were residual, much as they were within the income and related policies of the emerging social security state, positioned as dependants of male wage earners.

Even as rehabilitation legislation formalized the equality rights of women, training and employment policy followed similar paths for ex-service and civilian women: a narrow range of occupations considered suitable for specified groups of women, while the preferred location was the allegedly natural one of motherhood, child rearing, domesticity, and community service. Freedom of choice made markets and society in general democratic and therefore defensible. In this way, Russell joined with an emerging narrative of the postwar woman as the universalized signifier of all that women had gained during the Second World War. This was a model of Western superiority – of democracy and prosperity set within an emerging international order that was presided over by the United Nations.

Such a model for social order was premised upon the racialized cultural, political, and economic superiority of the West as signified by the United States, most notably in the form of free market production, consumption, and economic prosperity in the postwar world. In this world, women's citizenship rights were constituted through gendered, class-based, and racialized knowledge practices that foregrounded a universalized category of woman as presumptively white, educated, and heterosexual, a group whose interests and aspirations were coextensive with those of nation, whose citizenship capacities were legitimated in the context of a shared national and cultural identity, and whose reproductive and productive capacities were legitimately practised through domesticity or 'suitable' occupation. Poverty, delinquency, racialized difference, deficient and inferior capacity, illegitimate need, and pathologized dependency were the obverse of the universal liberal female subject embodied by the 'postwar woman.'

The final report of the advisory committee to investigate the Post-War

Problems of Women, issued in 1943, mobilized a similar trope of the postwar woman as a universalizing figure of Western progress produced through liberal democratic choice. This report and the 1945 Pre-employment Training Survey conducted by the NSS Women's Division worked together as key policy events, constituting a cumulative body of evidence signifying the problems women were alleged to confront in the postwar period. Both documents, and the knowledge practices mobilized in their development, contained prescriptive policy responses to the realities the reports were alleged to convey and the problems they were held to identify and remedy. Both documents, moreover, provided a critical institutional organizing pretext and context, drawing organizations of white, middle-class, educated, and professional women, such as the National Council of Women of Canada (NCWC), local councils of women, and the Young Women's Christian Association (YWCA), within the ambit of state formation activities and practices of governance.

Policy and social planners, community agencies, and voluntary organizations were preparing to address the prospect of hundreds of thousands of women who would be laid off from essential war industries. Certainly, the spectre of thousands of young women trooping along urban streets in search of work, housing, and amusement held little appeal for policy practitioners at the NSS Women's Division, let alone among the ranks of respectable citizens eager to facilitate the transition to domestic peace. Programs and practices deployed by the NSS Women's Division effectively screened out as many women from the formal waged economy as possible. The range of training options offered to civilian women through the Canadian Vocational Training Program was explicitly narrow, localized, and fragmented, on the rationale that women were to be discouraged from seeking employment in city-based factories. Stabilizing the household and averting postwar unemployment among men were the twin priorities governing the design and implementation of postwar employment policy. From a strategic economic asset and viable source of labour – a human resource – women were transformed in postwar employment and training policy into a disruptive force capable of destabilizing the wage-setting mechanism of the labour market and a residue of largely unskilled 'female labour.'

Pre-employment vocational training constituted and then regulated the differential employment needs of women in the postwar economy. Throughout, the 'quality' of the labour supply was the central problem to be addressed, screening for 'suitable' women and girls through pre-employment training. Training strategy was designed to stabilize labour supplies across low-wage industries and sectors that were subject to chronic labour shortages, particularly domestic service, the needle trades, and hospital service. Training was also a strategy to suppress worker resistance. As a moral regulatory practice, pre-employment training was intended to direct women into jobs they might not otherwise choose. Screening for the 'right type of womanhood' was at the same time a technique of psyche-based knowledge practices, eliding material conditions and social relations by taking up manifestations of racism, sexism, and class-based oppression as indices of individual employability.

Domestic service was considered the most viable outlet for female employment, despite the repeated opposition expressed by women and by employment officers charged with the task of directing women into this occupation. Plans for household service training were pushed ahead nonetheless, a move that sparked increasing opposition on all sides and ultimately exposed the sharp class division separating the promoters and the intended targets of the program. In an alternative proposal, Olive Ruth Russell developed the Home Service program for ex-servicewomen. Russell's program was a product of mental hygiene discourse, an example of pro-natalist policy designed to promote domesticity, partnership, and good citizenship rather than employment. The program was not implemented, however, as the Department of Labour baulked at the idea of instituting a course for which there was no employment component. It was not the business of the federal government to train women to become 'housewives,' however much the Department of Pensions and National Health welcomed the course as an opportunity to monitor and extend its regulatory capacities over women who were recipients of the family allowance. In the end, home economics replaced the mental hygiene component of the Home Service course in a blended program for household service training.

Domestic stability was a central design principle underlying postwar employment policy. Stability and respectability closely informed pro-natalist planning for white, middle-class, heterosexual women within a policy regime that took up motherhood as the integral, if implicit, policy objective. Domesticity discourse in this context worked through two channels. Pro-natalist discourse secured and stabilized white, middle-class, and heterosexual identity of women as mothers and rearers of future citizens. Anti-natalist discourse positioned working-class women, Native women, and women racialized as 'other' as mothers who were at the same time labourers, understood to work out of economic necessity but only in the absence of a male provider. Work for an hourly wage that was 'unskilled' signified a threat to household, home, and motherhood. This 'reserve of unskilled female labour' was a potential source of disruption and deviance. Resistance to low wages and hazardous working conditions, whether expressed through turnover, absenteeism, or in other ways, was taken up as further evidence of the need to instil appropriate work habits and closer adherence to gender, class, and racialized norms, as employers and policy practitioners, backed up by community organizations such as the NCWC, emphasized the need for 'good workers' and improved labour quality.

Domesticity and liberal equality discourses were balanced through a strategic accommodation, mobilizing racialized and class-based interests while at the same time seeking the gender-based aspirations embodied within the postwar vision of white, bourgeois, liberal maternalism. Categorical knowledge practices generated through these intersecting discourses mobilized a series of identities within public policy: mothers/wives, actual or potential, who were or would be employers of household workers; professional or business women in whom the state had invested and whose potential economic and social contributions were accorded greater recognition and value; professional nurturers in emerging occupational sectors of the social security state; purportedly unskilled or semi-skilled workers within a limited range of manufacturing and service industries; and, finally, workers in the homes of white middle- and upper-class women of British origin.

Women thought to be 'unsuitable' would be directed into low-wage industries as part of a broader strategy of low-wage competition. At the same time, women racialized as 'other' were the explicit focus of anti-natalist domesticity strategies, to be drawn into the domestic labour force. In this way, pre-employment training was positioned as a strategy for the assessment and calibration of potential women workers, a way of screening out those deemed 'unsuitable' and a program through which the practices of vocational guidance might be used to direct women into the occupation for which their particular aptitude apparently indicated they were best suited. Pre-employment training was therefore a strategy to upgrade the occupation by upgrading the worker. Training was deployed in this exercise of governance to facilitate the formation of self-governing and self-regulating subjects, workers who knew and accepted their responsibilities within the routines and rituals of work, women who had 'freely chosen' their vocation.

Working through discourses of employability and domesticity, the training and employment policies devised for women operated cumulatively as a strategy for decentralization, shifting the deliberation and implementation of a limited range of policy options to the local level and thus dispersing responsibility for postwar women's employment across a diverse range of local advisory committees. From a labour market that was conceptualized as national in scope during the Second World War, the market for women's labour was now approached as a matter of local diversity and highly regionalized variance. This was the government strategy for regrouping female labour and channelling it into a considerably narrowed range of employment options, under the guise of a comprehensive program of vocational guidance and training. As women would soon discover, while their brothers, fathers, and sons might be positioned as allegedly 'free agents,' able to move with some autonomy and capacity to mobilize their rights in their own labour through the 'free labour market,' women were the subjects of a considerably straitened employment policy. For them, the labour market was anything but 'free.'

Notes

Introduction

1 Ruth Roach Pierson, *'They're Still Women after All': The Second World War and Canadian Womanhood.*

2 See, for example, J.L. Granatstein and Peter Neary, eds, *The Good Fight: Canadians and World War II;* and Peter Neary and J.L. Granatstein, eds, *The Veterans Charter and Post-World War II Canada.* See also J.L. Granatstein, *Canada's War: The Politics of the Mackenzie King Government, 1939–1945.*

3 See, for example, Dean F. Oliver, 'Public Opinion and Public Policy in Canada: Federal Legislation on War Veterans, 1939–1946.' The postwar period saw renewed concern about juvenile delinquency, which, when the subject concerned girls and young women, invariably implicated sexuality and sexualizing discourse. See, for example, Franca Iacovetta, 'Gossip, Contest, and Power in the Making of Suburban Bad Girls: Toronto, 1945–1960.' For comprehensive historical studies of the deployment of discourses of sexuality in Canadian history, see Gary Kinsman, *The Regulation of Desire: Homo and Hetero Sexualities.* For postwar policies concerning domestic workers, see Christiane Harzig, 'The Stork Story: Regulating Female Sexuality in Canada's Post World War Two Recruitment of Domestics'; and Franca Iacovetta, 'The Sexual Politics of Moral Citizenship and Containing Dangerous Foreign Men in Cold War Canada, 1950s–1960s.'

4 Peter Neary and Shaun Brown, 'The Veteran's Charter and Canadian Women Veterans of World War II.'

5 See James Struthers, 'Family Allowances, Old Age Security, and the Construction of Entitlement in the Canadian Welfare State, 1943–1951,' 198.

6 The principle of 'less eligibility' maintains that any form of income replacement would always remain below the lowest notional labour market wage.

See James Struthers, *No Fault of Their Own: Unemployment and the Canadian Welfare State, 1914–1941*. For studies of welfare programming, see also James Struthers, *The Limits of Affluence: Welfare in Ontario, 1920–1970*. For a study of the regulation of women through social welfare programming by both state and community agencies, see Margaret Little, *No Car, No Radio, No Liquor Permit: The Moral Regulation of Single Mothers in Ontario, 1920–1997*.

7 Joan Scott, 'Experience,' 28.

8 See, for example, Franca Iacovetta, 'Making Model Citizens: Gender, Corrupted Democracy, and Immigrant and Refugee Reception Work in Cold War Canada.' See also Guard, 'Women Worth Watching: Radical Housewives in Cold War Canada.' For a study of postwar state policing of women engaged in consumer activism, see Guard, 'Canadian Citizens or Dangerous Foreign Women? Canada's Radical Consumer Movement, 1947–1950.' For the later Cold War period, see Iacovetta, 'Freedom Lovers, Sex Deviates, and Damaged Women: Iron Curtain Refugees in Early Cold War Canada.'

9 Ruth Roach Pierson with Marjorie Cohen, 'Government Job-Training Programmes for Women, 1937–1947,' 79–80. Conversely, Diane Forestell and others have attempted to salvage the perception that the Canadian government was not equivocating on the matter of gender-based equality but that instead any significant move in that direction would have to await more congenial times. See, for example, Forestell, 'The Necessity of Sacrifice for the Nation at War: Women's Labour Force Participation, 1939–1946.' Forestell argues that in fact public opinion was weighted very much in favour of women's withdrawal from the formal waged economy, a view that disallows analysis of how 'public' is formed through the deployment of opinion polling as a technique of governance. In contrast to Forestell's positivist approach to opinion poll results as historical source material, Robinson's recent study of the use of polling and market research by the federal government from 1930 to 1945 closely documents the activities of psyche-based practitioners in the conduct of polling and the deeply inegalitarian foundation of this commercialized technique. See Robinson, *The Measure of Democracy*.

10 See Riley, *'Am I That Name?' Feminism and the Category of 'Women' in History*.

11 Peter Miller and Nikolas Rose summarize this view as follows: 'Personal autonomy is not the antithesis of political power, but a key term in its exercise, the more so because individuals are not merely subjects of power but play a part in its operations.' See Rose and Miller, 'Political Power beyond the State: Problematics of Government,' 174. For a critical analysis of the general tendency among some governmentality theorists to overemphasize the state/government as the sole site/field of governance and thus

underemphasize the operation of agencies conceptualized as 'ou
beyond the periphery of the state, including oppositional movem
O'Malley, Weir, and Shearing, 'Governmentality, Criticism, Politics.' For a
study of the limits of rights discourse and the future capacities of liberalist
discourse in the postmodern democratic polity, see Wendy Brown, *Politics
Out of History.*

12 See Sefton MacDowell, 'The Formation of the Canadian Industrial Relations
System during World War II.' For a recent examination of the historical
implications of trade union participation in tripartism, in particular the
impetus towards institutionalizing a 'split-level' economy that had the effect
of privileging high-waged, unionized, skilled male workers and of deepening
red-baiting tactics in the ensuing era of Cold War political rationality, see
McInnis, 'Teamwork for Harmony: Labour–Management Production
Committees and the Postwar Settlement in Canada.'

13 Sefton MacDowell, 'Formation of the Canadian Industrial Relations System,'
10.

14 Stevenson, 'National Selective Service and Employment and Seniority Rights
for Veterans, 1943–1946,' 96. See also, Stevenson, *Canada's Greatest Wartime
Muddle: National Selective Service and the Mobilization of Human Resources during
World War II.*

15 See, for example, Boyer and Drache, eds, *States against Markets: The limits of
globalization.*

16 See Ruth Pierson, 'Gender and the Unemployment Insurance Debates in
Canada, 1934–1940'; and Porter, 'Women and Income Security in the
Postwar Period: The Case of Unemployment Insurance, 1945–1962.' For
the Depression era, see Hobbs, 'Gendering Work and Welfare: Women's
Relationship to Wage-Work and Social Policy in Canada during the Great
Depression.' For the social construction of skill and of labour markets
generally, see Gaskell, 'Conceptions of Skill and the Work of Women: Some
Historical and Political Issues'; Crompton, Gallie, and Purcell, 'Work,
Economic Restructuring and Social Regulation'; Kaye, '"No Skill beyond
Manual Dexterity Involved": Gender and the Construction of Skill in the
East London Clothing Industry'; and Creese, *Constructing Masculinity: Gender,
Class, and Race in a White-Collar Union, 1944–1994.* Yet another dimension in
the historical analysis of how labour markets come to be constituted as such
involves the study of variance and continuity in labour market 'space' and
scope. As George Grantham and Mary MacKinnon put it, 'economists study
how given market structures produce specific outcomes. To historians,
however, the question is how that structure came to be what it is.' Immigration policy and labour 'standards' combine with broader regulatory prac-

tices including recognition of unions as collective bargaining agents, occupational health and safety, and other 'employment standards' policy. Finally, the regionalization of labour markets – a theme addressed in this study – is identified as 'most obvious in the sphere of social regulation in the conditions of employment ... [which] impose national or cultural definitions on labour markets.' See Grantham and MacKinnon, *Labour Market Evolution: The Economic History of Market Integration, Wage Flexibility, and the Employment Relation*, 4, 5.

17 See Bowles and Gintis, *Democracy and Capitalism: Property, Community and the Contradictions of Modern Social Thought*, 111 and 227 (ch. 4, n40). Joan Sangster's historical study of women production workers in Peterborough shares a similar finding with respect to the organization of work and ideologies of domesticity in shaping women's identities as women and as workers, with tremendous implications for both. See Sangster, *Earning Respect: The Lives of Working Women in Small-Town Ontario, 1920–1960*.

18 Hobbs, 'Gendering Work and Welfare.'

19 Lewis, 'Introduction: Women, Work, Family and Social Policies in Europe'; Lewis, 'Gender and the Development of Welfare Regime'; and Lewis, *Should We Care about Family Change?*

20 For a study of the Canadian mental hygiene movement during the postwar period, see Gleason, *Normalizing the Ideal: Psychology, Schooling, and the Family in Postwar Canada.*

21 Douglas and Greenhous, *Out of the Shadows: Canada and the Second World War*, 259. For an intriguing study of the development of psychiatry as a regular component of work within the Armed Services, see Copp, 'From Neurasthemia to Post-traumatic Stress Disorder.' See also Copp and McAndrew, *Battle Exhaustion: Soldiers and Psychiatrists in the Canadian Army, 1939–1945.*

22 For an excellent study of the intersection of psyche-discourses with postwar educational policy in the history of sexuality, see Adams, *The Trouble with Normal: Postwar Youth and the Making of Heterosexuality.*

23 For a discussion of the emergence of the psychological register as the prevailing discourse in social policy regimes across welfare states, see Fraser and Gordon, 'Toward a Genealogy of Dependency: Tracing a Keyword of the U.S. Welfare State,'

1: 'I Want You to Pick One Intelligent Girl': Mobilizing Canada's Womanpower

1 Library and Archives Canada (LAC), RG 27, Vol. 897, File 8-9-74, pt 3. Report of the Labour Supply Investigation Committee to the Labour Co-

ordination Committee, October 1941. The Labour Supply Investigation
Project (LSIP) was established by Order-in-Council PC 14/5484 and issued
its final confidential report to the War Cabinet the following October.

2 Ibid., 3–4. Rather than attempting a global estimate of available labour
reserves, the Committee concentrated on conducting what it described as a
'survey of informed opinion' combined with detailed case studies of strategic industries and geographic regions.

3 LAC, RG 27, Vol. 897, File 8-9-74 pt 3. Report of the Labour Supply Investigation Committee to the Labour Co-ordination Committee, October 1941:
157.

4 Ibid., 141. For a study of the implementation of labour-management productivity committees initiated during the Second World War as part of a
broader program to consolidate state intervention in industrial relations
and to broker the postwar compromise of productivity bargaining and
material consumption, see McInnis, 'Teamwork for Harmony: Labour-
Management Production Committees and the Postwar Settlement in
Canada.'

5 LAC, RG 27, Vol. 897, File 8-9-74, pt 3. Report of the Labour Supply Investigation Committee to the Labour Co-ordination Committee, October 1941,
57. The lack of trained managers who might have some knowledge of
modern personnel practices was finally addressed through a training program launched by the Department of Labour and delivered at the University
of Toronto. Plant forepersons, both women and men, learned detailed
managerial techniques of job analysis and efficiency in workforce organization. In the words of one observer, students of personnel management, even
some appreciative employers, were actually coming to regard 'labour relations in terms of human relations.' Clearly, more personnel management
training was needed, a measure that reflected the rationale underpinning
the employment strategy overall.

6 LAC, RG 27, Vol. 897, File 8-9-74, pt 3. Report of the Labour Supply Investigation Committee to the Labour Co-ordination Committee, October 1941:
161.

7 As part of its research, the LSIP sampled eighty-four firms, most of which
argued that labour quality was diminishing even faster than quantity. As a
narrative device, the report encapsulated the litany of problems faced by
employers in the experience of a single (perhaps fictitious) company in
order to expose the inefficiency of all conventional hiring methods.
Ethnicity and racialized difference – signified in this example by the dubious
'foreign names' – was a clear marker of potential deficiency, positioning
such workers as counter to the ideal-typical worker as male, skilled, white,

and of British origin. That said, it is interesting to note that the employer in question appeared to have been sceptical of fully 100 per cent of the applicants who appeared at his plant gate: 'One Toronto machinery company employer estimated that 50 per cent of the persons seeking work at his gate carried foreign names, and were not employed by him, that 25 per cent were physically unfit, 15 per cent were employed and shopping around for another job, and another 10 per cent were unemployed persons of Anglo-Saxon extraction' (ibid., 77–8). With examples like this, surely there could be no rational reason beyond that of routine convention to explain why employers would not avail themselves of modern personnel techniques.

8 Ibid., 78.
9 LAC, RG 27, Vol. 968, File 4, NSS Field Organization and Activities of Employment Services Division, Speech by Minister of Labour Hon. Humphrey Mitchell, 18 February 1944: 3–4.
10 LAC, RG 27, Vol. 605, File 6-24-1, pt 1. NSS Employment of Women, 'Ten Points in Prime Minister's Speech,' 24 March 1942.
11 Wilson, 'Manpower,' 6–7.
12 Ibid., 6.
13 Stevenson, 'National Selective Service and the Mobilization of Human Resources in Canada during the Second World War.'
14 Ibid., 50.
15 Shortages were reportedly concentrated in Quebec and Ontario in essential industries as follows:

Textile products	4,075 (36%)
Iron and products	5,032 (45%)
Vegetable products (other than food)	1,838 (16%)
Chemical	275 (2%)
Total	11,220

LAC, RG 27, Vol. 605, File 6-24-1, pt 1. Employment of Women – General. Report on the Registration of Women, 13 October 1942: 1–2.
16 Ibid., 3.
17 LAC, RG 27, Vol. 605, File 6-24-1, pt 1. Employment of Women – General. Department of Labour News Release, Address of Mrs Rex Eaton, Assistant Director of National Selective Service to National Council of Women, 17 June 1943: 1.
18 LAC, RG 27, Vol. 605, File 6-24-1, pt 1. Employment of Women – General. Report on the Registration of Women, 13 October 1942: 3.
19 Ibid., n3, Table VIII: 27c.
20 See Parr, 'Shopping for a Good Stove: A Parable about Gender, Design, and

the Market'; and Owram, *Born at the Right Time: A History of the Baby Boom Generation.*

21 LAC, RG 27, Vol. 897, File 8-9-74, pt 3. Report of the Labour Supply Investigation Committee to the Labour Co-ordination Committee, October 1941, n6, Table VIII: 28c.

22 LAC, RG 27, vol. 605, File 6-24-1, pt 1. Employment of Women – General. Eaton to Little, 3 July 1942.

23 LAC, RG 27, Vol. 3384, File 2. Binder, 'Vocational Training and Wartime Bureau of Technical Personnel,' 1.

24 LAC, RG 27, Vol. 3384, File 2. Binder, 'Vocational Training and Wartime Bureau of Technical Personnel,' 8–9.

25 Whyte, 'Psychologists Go to War,' 12. The Canadian Psychological Association was formed in April 1939, an act that has since been characterized as a necessary step taken in anticipation of impending war and the need to 'provide psychologists with a unified and coherent voice in guiding psychology's contributions to the anticipated war.' See Ferguson, 'Psychology in Canada, 1939–1945,' 697.

26 RG 27, Vol. 1524, File NSS Manpower Surveys of Canadian Industry. Stevenson and Kellogg, 'Proposed Procedures for Manpower Survey of a Canadian Industry,' 9.

27 Ibid., 11–12.

28 Ibid., 'Exhibit VIII. Job Analysis,' 32–50.

2: The National Selective Services Women's Division and the Management of Women War Workers

1 Library and Archives Canada (LAC), RG 27, Vol. 605, File 6–23. Employment. Health, Welfare and Recreation for Workers. Eaton to Hon. Humphrey Mitchell, Minister of Labour, 'Situations existing in certain war industries,' 26 August 1942.

2 McInnis, 'Teamwork for Harmony: Labour–Management Production Committees and the Postwar Settlement in Canada,' 319. A measure of underemployment and forced withdrawal from the formal waged economy would no doubt have yielded a higher count.

3 Ibid., 113.

4 Ruth Pierson, *'They're Still Women After All,'* 117.

5 Porter, 'Women and Income Security in the Postwar Period: The Case of Unemployment Insurance, 1945–1962,' 113. Porter characterizes this as a movement from domestic service 'and unskilled occupations' to 'higher-paid, skilled positions' in manufacturing. See n10 at 113.

6 Brandt, '"Pigeon-Holed and Forgotten": The Work of the Subcommittee on the Post-War Problems of Women, 1943,' 241–2.

7 Stevenson, 'National Selective Service and the Mobilization of Human Resources in Canada during the Second World War.'

8 McInnis, 'Teamwork for Harmony.' As McIinnis states, Paul Martin, parliamentary assistant to the minister of labour, described the emerging industrial relations climate as the harbinger of a 'new democratic citizenship' for the postwar industrial era. McInnis, 322.

9 See Irving Abella's classic study, *Nationalism, Communism, and Canadian Labour*. See also Wells, 'The Impact of the Postwar Compromise on Canadian Unionism: The Formation of an Auto Worker Local in the 1950s'; and Carew, 'Charles Millard, A Canadian in the International Labour Movement: A Case Study of the ICFTU, 1955–1961.'

10 LAC, RG 27, Vol. 605, File 6-23. Employment. Health, Welfare and Recreation for Workers. Eaton to Hon. Humphrey Mitchell, Minister of Labour, 'Situations existing in certain war industries,' 26 August 1942.

11 LAC, RG 27, Vol. 605, File 6-24-1, pt 1. NSS Employment of Women. Fraudena Eaton to Mme Paul Martel, 12 March 1943.

12 LAC, RG 27, Vol. 605, File 6-24-1, pt 1. NSS Employment of Women. Alfred Charpentier, 'Women's Work.' Confederation of Catholic Workers, 11 May 1942.

13 LAC, RG 27, Vol. 605, File 6-24-1, pt 1. NSS Employment of Women. U.N. Information Centre, 'The Employment of Women in Germany' (typescript).

14 LAC, RG 27, Vol. 605, File 6-24-1, pt 1. NSS Employment of Women. Eaton to A. MacNamara, 9 March 1943; Eaton to A. Mitchell, 'Employment situation (women) in Province of Quebec,' 20 February 1943.

15 LAC, RG 27, Vol. 605, File 6-24-1, pt 1. NSS Employment of Women. Renée Morin, letter marked 'Confidential' to Mr L.J. Trottier, Chief Commissioner, UIC, 15 March 1943.

16 Ibid.

17 LAC, RG 27, Vol. 605, File 6-24-1, pt 1. 'NSS Employment of Women – General. Morin to Eaton, 'Report on Industrial Relations Conference, Bureau of Industrial Relations, Dalhousie University, June 25,' 7 July 1943: 2.

18 LAC, RG 27, Vol. 605, File 6-23. Employment. Health, Welfare and Recreation for Workers. Eaton to Hon. Humphrey Mitchell, Minister of Labour, 'Situations existing in certain war industries,' 26 August 1942.

19 LAC, RG 27, Vol. 36. Department of Labour. Report on National Selective Service Operations for Civilian Employment. Section III, 'Employment of Women – Textiles.' September 1943.

20 LAC, RG 27, Vol. 605, File 6-23. NSS Employment. Health, Welfare and

Recreation for Workers, Department of Labour press release, Ottawa, 5 September 1942.

21 LAC, RG 27, Vol. 605, File 6-18. Memorandum from V. Phelan, Director of Information, Office of War Information, to Dr Allan Peebles, Deputy Minister of Labour, 1 February 1943.

22 LAC, RG 27, Vol. 605, File 6-23. Employment of Women. Report on Industrial Welfare Conference, Ottawa, 8–9 February 1943.

23 See Strange, *Toronto's Girl Problem.* See also Rose, *Governing the Soul: The Shaping of the Private Self.*

24 LAC, RG 27, Vol. 605, File 6-18. 'Absenteeism.' S. Wyatt, R. Marriott, and D.E.R. Hughes, Medical Research Council Industrial Health Research Board, Emergency Report No. 4, 'A Study of Absenteeism among Women,' London, 1943.

25 LAC, RG 27, Vol. 897, File 1–10–1. NSS – Administration. 'Employment of Stevenson and Kellogg.' Letter from Ministry of Labour to Stevenson and Kellogg, Industrial Engineers, Montreal, 11 September 1942.

26 LAC, RG 27, Vol. 605, File 6-18. Absenteeism. A. MacNamara, memorandum to Dr Howland, 24 August 1943, and John Grierson, WIB Office of the General Manager to A. MacNamara, Deputy Minister of Labour, 8 September 1943; Report of Informal Meeting of Advisory Committee on Absenteeism Studies, 3 September 1943. The recorded minutes of the meeting noted the poor attendance of committee members, all claiming absence due to the pressures of work. See also LAC, RG 27, Vol. 897, File 1-10-1. NSS – Administration. 'Employment of Stevenson and Kellogg.' Memorandum from T.H. Robinson to MacNamara, 18 December 1942.

27 LAC, RG 27, Vol. 897, File 1-10-1. NSS – Administration. 'Employment of Stevenson and Kellogg.' 'Report of Investigation into Manpower Situation within the City of Welland 1942' (typescript), 1.

28 The move to contract the outside expertise of the consulting firm initially in 1942 had prompted another department official, T.H. Robinson, to comment that he for one looked 'forward to the time when any of the work Stevenson and Kellogg can do for us could be done by members of our own staff.' LAC, RG 27, Vol. 897, File 1-10-1. NSS – Administration. 'Employment of Stevenson and Kellogg.' Memorandum from T.H. Robinson to MacNamara, 18 December 1942.

29 LAC, RG 27, Vol. 605, File 6-18. Absenteeism. A. MacNamara, memorandum to Dr Howland, 24 August 1943, and John Grierson, WIB Office of the General Manager, to A. MacNamara, Deputy Minister of Labour, 8 September 1943; Report of Informal Meeting of Advisory Committee on Absenteeism Studies, 3 September 1943.

30 These results were compiled from a census of eighteen war plants. Again, married women were found to have the highest number of absences, followed by single men, single women, and married men. 'New residents of a community' were absent more frequently than 'regular residents.' The study problematized women according to marital status in an attempt to draw out any difference between the attendance patterns of single woman and married woman, thereby bringing attention to bear on the effect of marriage and childbearing on women's capacity to be reliable workers. Management was enjoined to reassure women, assisting them that they might overcome their handicaps as women through appeals to self-confidence and community assistance. Organizing results by gender and marital status opened up both dimensions as categories for regulatory intervention, while allowing for the more obvious identification of factors such as daycare and assistance with domestic chores including shopping and food preparation, to free women to at least some extent from the burden of the double day.

31 LAC, RG 27, Vol. 1524, File NSS Manpower Surveys of Canadian Industry. Stevenson and Kellogg, 'Proposed Procedures for Manpower Survey of a Canadian Industry.'

32 LAC, RG 27, Vol. 605, File 6-18. Absenteeism. Office of War Information, 'OWI Advance Release 1822 for Monday Morning Papers,' 17 May 1943, 3.

33 LAC, RG 27, Vol. 605, File 6-24-1, pt 1. NSS Employment of Women – General. Minutes of a Personnel Conference by the National Selective Service (Women's and Welfare Division) for Female Personnel Officers and Welfare Workers in War Industries, held at the Windsor Hotel, Montreal, 15 December 1942: 3.

34 LAC, RG 27, Vol. 605, File 6-24-1, pt 1. NSS Employment of Women – General. Eaton to J.A. Ward Bell, Trade–Schools Regulation Administration Office, Vancouver, B.C., 4 August 1942.

35 LAC, RG 27, Vol. 968, File 17. NSS Statistics and Correspondence on Labour Supply. 'Army Course on Veteran's Rehabilitation. The Employment Service and the Veteran,' W.K. Rutherford, Associate Director, Employment, 25 September 1944.

36 LAC, RG 27, Vol. 605, File 6-24-1, pt 1. Eadie to Eaton, 22 May 1943.

37 LAC, RG 27, Vol. 605, File 6-24-1, pt 1. NSS Employment of Women – General. Fraudena Eaton to Mary Anderson, Director of U.S. Department of Labor Women's Bureau, 23 January 1943.

38 LAC, RG 27, Vol. 605, File 6-24-1, pt 1. NSS Employment of Women – General. Eaton to Laura Smith, War Department HQ Services and Supply, 26 January 1943. Smith to Eaton, 17 February 1943.

39 LAC, RG 27, Vol. 1524, File NSS Manpower Surveys of Canadian Industry.

Stevenson and Kellogg, 'Proposed Procedures for Manpower Survey of a Canadian Industry,' 1943: 26.

40 LAC, RG 27, Vol. 605, File 6-24-1, pt. 1. NSS Employment of Women – General. Sara Southall, Personnel Department, International Harvester Company Chicago, to Eaton, 1 February 1943, 2.

41 LAC, RG 27, Vol. 605, File 6-24-1, pt 1. NSS Employment of Women – General. Eaton to MacNamara, 2 February 1943.

42 LAC, RG 27, Vol. 605, File 6-24-1, pt 1. NSS Employment of Women – General. Fraudena Eaton to Mary Anderson, Director of U.S. Department of Labor Women's Bureau, 23 January 1943. Eaton to Laura Smith, War Department HQ Services and Supply, 26 January 1943. Smith to Eaton, 17 February 1943.

43 For an account of the VD scare during this period, see Ruth Pierson, *'They're Still Women After All.'*

44 LAC, RG 27, Vol. 605, File 6-24-1, pt 1. NSS Employment of Women – General. Eaton to Mary Eadie, Supervisor, Women's Division Employment and Selective Service Office, Toronto, 8 June 1943.

45 LAC, RG 27, Vol. 605, File 6-24-1, pt 1. NSS Employment of Women – General. B.G. Sullivan to Eaton, 'Re: Women's Personnel Group of Toronto,' 21 June 1943.

46 Thelma LeCocq, 'Woman Power,' 40.

47 LAC, RG 27, Vol. 3384, File 2. Binder, 'Vocational Training and Wartime Bureau of Technical Personnel,' 2.

48 Ibid., 40.

49 Training was carried out under this program in four classifications: war industry training; 'upgrading' of supervisors and forepersons; pre-enlistment training of RCAF personnel; and army trades training of enlisted men.

50 LAC, RG 27, Vol. 8-9-74, v. 1. A.W. Crawford, 'Memorandum for Labour Co-ordination Committee Re: Training of Industrial Workers,' 24 July 1941: 27.

51 LAC, RG 27, Vol. 728, File 12-2-1. Letter from McLarty, 27 November 1941. For the period 1941–2, McLarty authorized the transfer of $4.76 million to the provinces for the training of war workers.

52 LAC, RG 27, Vol. 3533, File 3-26-41, pt 1. Administration: Suggestions and Representations re: Training – General Correspondence. McLarty to Ian Mackenzie, Minister of Pensions and National Health, 2 May 1941.

53 Canada, Department of Labour, *Labour Gazette*, March 1941: 271.

54 LAC, RG 27, Vol. 605, File 6-24-1, pt 1. NSS Employment of Women – General. 'Training of Women for War Industries in the War Emergency Training Program' (nd, na), 1–2; Report from Department of Education,

Technical Education Branch, F.H. Sexton, Director of Technical Education, to T.D.A. Purves, Deputy Minister of Labour, Nova Scotia, 30 April 1943.

55 See Phillips and Taylor, 'Sex and Skill.' See also Creese, *Constructing Masculinity: Gender, Class and Race in a White–Collar Union, 1944–1994.* As Creese argues in her study, 'to define a job as technical was to define it as masculine.' Creese, 113.

56 LAC, RG 27, Vol. 605, File 6-424-1, pt 1. NSS Employment of Women – General. Report from Department of Education, Technical Education Branch, F.H. Sexton, Director of Technical Education, to T.D.A. Purves, Deputy Minister of Labour, Nova Scotia, 30 April 1943.

57 Oliver, 'A Wartime Schoolroom,' 90.

58 Ibid.

59 LAC, RG 27, Vol. 36. 'Report on National Selective Service Operations for Civilian Employment. 21st Report, December 1944.' Memorandum. Eaton to MacNamara, Great Western Garment Company, Edmonton.

60 Edwards, 'Night-and-Day School.'

61 Ibid., 17.

62 Ibid., 22..

63 LeCocq, 'Woman Power,' 11.

64 Ibid., 10.

65 For a discussion of the campaign to increase part-time war workers, see Ruth Pierson, *'They're Still Women After All.'*

66 LAC, RG 27, Vol. 605, File 6-24-1, pt 2. NSS Employment of Women – General. Department of Labour Employment Service and UI Branch, Ottawa, 24 August 1943. NSS Circular Number 277, 'Part Time Workers,' Allan Mitchell, Director of Employment Service and UI. 'Planning for Part-time Workers,' by Miss E.R. Cornell, Regional Adviser, Montreal, 3–4.

67 Ibid., 3–5.

68 Ibid., 5.

69 Dressage in this context references the third of Foucault's three functions of labour: productive, symbolic, and dressage, denoting the management of work as taming, performance, and discipline. Labour as dressage addresses the performative character of work, a normative although not necessarily productive and economically functional dimension of managerial technique. See Jackson and Carter, 'Labour as Dressage.'

70 LAC, RG 27, Vol. 1516, File 0-14.2, pt 1. Wartime Information Board, Minutes of Meeting of Committee on Industrial Morale, Friday, 11 June 1943. The issue of 'absenteeism' constituted the subject of a labour-management discussion segment for the CBC 'Labour Forum' series that spring in which both groups took issue with the Department of Munitions and Supply's

allegations that workers were largely to blame. In contrast, labour – and management – representatives to the Committee on Industrial Morale pointed to the following causes: lack of a 'comprehensive survey' investigating cause and effect; illness, accident, strain, and lengthy shifts; 'indifference to the war' prompted by fear of postwar economic insecurity; problems stemming from housing and transportation; married women with 'housekeeping responsibilities,' inadequate time to shop for basic necessities, and problems with child care.' The committee, on the basis of these arguments, therefore recommended a government survey 'to get at the facts of absenteeism.' See Minutes of Committee on Industrial Morale, 11 June 1943: 2.

On the basis of this work, the Department of Labour's Labour-Management Co-operation Section of the Industrial Relations Branch issued the brochure 'Absenteeism' suggesting that the Labour-Management Productivity Committees could take on the problem and work towards its resolution. A Labour Management Productivity Committee study, the pamphlet read, 'can change the negative "absentee" into a positive work attendant.' LAC, RG 27, Vol. 605, File 6-18. Department of Labour Labour-Management Co-operation Section of the Industrial Relations Branch. 'Absenteeism' (nd; likely 1943).

3: The Psychologist Goes to War: Assessing and Recruiting for the Canadian Women's Army Corps

1 For a discussion about the differential moral standard set for CWAC personnel and the anti-VD campaign conducted during the Second World War as an instance of sexual regulation, see Ruth Pierson, *'They're Still Women After All.'*

2 The fallacy of the tests, one that even Brigham eventually acknowledged, was the unreliability, if not the absurdity, of the army test data on two counts. First, the Alpha and Beta could not be combined into a single score as they each measured different things and were in any case internally inconsistent. Second, the tests did not measure supposedly innate intelligence, as Yerkes and his colleagues alleged, but instead assessed familiarity with American language and culture. See Gould, *The Mismeasure of Man*, 222–33.

3 Terman, *The Measurement of Intelligence*, 6–7. By 1919, Terman had finalized the Stanford-Binet scale of intelligence, the prototype for all intelligence tests to follow in the massive testing industry, and he proceeded to circulate his views from his post as professor of psychology at Stanford University. From the outset, Terman's target was population screening to identify and segregate the allegedly 'feeble-minded' population from the apparently normal. The policy recommendations accompanying this program were

republished verbatim – indicating acceptance of their authenticity and
veracity – in a 1944 guide to the Stanford Revision of the Binet-Simon
Intelligence Scale. Foremost among them was the call to apply the test more
systematically in order to segregate out 'dull' and 'border-line' adults from
those who were truly 'feeble-minded.'

4 Ibid., 65.

5 'Educationist Urges Need of Selective Immigration,' *The Daily Mail and
Empire*, 25 February 1928: 5.

6 Sandiford, *Educational Psychology: An Objective Study*, 49.

7 Ibid., 49.

8 Sandiford remained loyal to his eugenic roots, arguing that in the battle
between biology and environment, biology would always remain paramount.
Education policy clearly had its limits: 'Education can and does produce
wonders in one generation; its effects, however, are mostly limited to one
generation. To improve human stock permanently, it must first be bred and
then educated' (ibid., 49). Furthermore, not all education subjects would
benefit from a standardized strategy, given the disparate capacities of people
generally, a disparity that could be traced back to its genetic source. 'So far
as education is concerned, intelligence and capacity to learn are practically
synonymous ... but the learning is easy if there is good nerve material to
work with' (ibid., 143).

9 Blatz, *Understanding the Young Child*, 54.

10 Ibid., 36.

11 Terman, *Measurement of Intelligence*, 71–2.

12 Blatz, *Understanding the Young Child*, 235.

13 Sandiford, *Educational Psychology*, 163–4.

14 Ibid., 164.

15 The intelligence men were anxious to distance themselves from the work of
phrenologists such as Lombroso. Protestations aside, much of this work took
a leaf from the measurement of skull size. Among the foundational principles of racial typologies, the most 'scientific' of which was the cephalic
index, the empirical basis for anthropological studies throughout much of
the first two decades of the century. See Barkan, *The Retreat of Scientific
Racism*.

16 Sandiford, *Educational Psychology*, 27–8.

17 Gregor Mendel, an Austrian monk, is credited with researching and documenting the transfer of characteristics from one generation of garden peas
to the next, classified as dominant and recessive genes. This group of
insights – described as Mendelianism – was recorded and circulated in the
1860s and was 'rediscovered' or rehabilitated as part of eugenic discourses.

See Barkan, *The Retreat of Scientific Racism*. See also Keller and Lloyd, *Keywords in Evolutionary Biology*. Mendelians also drew upon the work of August Weisman, whose theories of germ plasm also stressed the continuity of inheritance over the longer term. This approach stood in direct contrast to that of the more orthodox Darwinian evolutionists, whose stance stressed sudden breaks, chance, contingency, and discontinuity.

18 Sandiford, *Educational Psychology*, 39.

19 The methodology of intelligence testing has generated considerable debate, not least because of the slippage between application of mathematical technique leading to the subsequent 'discovery' of biological fact. Factor analysis was a prime tool in the arsenal of the mental testing practitioner. According to Gould, 'Spearman invented factor analysis to study the correlation matrix of mental tests and then reified his principal component as g or innate, general intelligence. Factor analysis may help us to understand causes by directing us to information beyond the mathematics of correlation. But factors, by themselves, are neither things nor causes; they are mathematical abstractions.' Gould, *Mismeasure of Man*, 245–6. Cyril L. Burt, official psychologist for the London County Council from 1913 to 1932 (where he spent most of his time measuring and ranking school children), whom Gould calls the 'greatest reifier of them all,' went so far as to attempt to fix in the brain the physical location for mathematical factors that he had drawn from his 'correlational matrix of mental tests' (Gould, 290). Even as Spearman's g was refuted by later work, specifically that of Thurston and the concept of multiple factors of intelligence, the fundamentals of testing – reification and hereditarianism – survived virtually unchallenged. Some children were good at some things, others not. Identity was still seen to be rooted in intellectual capacities, which collectively defined the essence of the individual, and these essences were still seen to be subject to calibration, manifested in relation to averages and norms, deviations and maladjustments. Again, as Gould has argued, 'To the statistician's dictum that whatever exists can be measured, the factorist has added the assumption that whatever can be "measured" must exist. But the relation may not be reversible, and the assumption may even be false' (Juddenham 1962, as cited in Gould, 310). Among the oldest prejudices stemming from modernist discourses, upon which discourses of intelligence have drawn are the ladder of progress as a model for the organization of life and the reification of abstraction as a criterion for ranking. As Gould puts it, '[e]volution then becomes a march up the ladder to realms of more and more g' (318).

20 Library and Archives Canada (LAC), MG 31, K13, Vol. 2, File 13. Olive R. Russell, letter to the editor, 'Co-operation in Cause of Education Urged on

School, Home and Community,' press clipping, nd. According to Russell, it was absurd to criticize (as many were doing) the educational reforms introduced under the auspices of the 'new education' or the 'Haddow method' of permitting greater freedom of selection in academic curricula if these changes had been introduced without any additional training for the teachers whose job it would be to implement, oversee, and monitor the outcomes of the new method. One should no more criticize a new educational philosophy more than one would 'condemn Packard cars because some people run them into the ditch' or even 'a Steinway piano because a novice plays it hopelessly.'

21 LAC, MG 31, K13, Vol. 1, File 12. Olive Ruth Russell, 'A Study of the Factors underlying the Inter-correlations of "Verbal," "Mathematical" and "Form Perceptive" Tests.' PhD diss., University of Edinburgh, 1934: 6.

22 Russell's dissertation was an attempt to develop a viable testing technique, one that addressed the perceived weaknesses of the single measure of intelligence proposed by Spearman, the so-called g factor for general ability.

23 This approach drew on the research program of William Blatz, whose work at the University of Toronto-based Institute for Child Study informed the training of this new generation of psychologists. Blatz worked alongside Hincks and Bott at the psychology department at the University of Toronto, before moving over to direct the Institute for Child Study on a multi-year grant from the Laura Spelman Rockefeller Memorial Foundation, remaining at the institute until 1960. He finally retired from academe in 1963. Adjustment to the surrounding environment – including the psychological causes of maladjustment – was a central focus of Blatz's research. As Richardson has observed in her study of the mental hygiene movement in both Canada and the United States, Blatz exemplified the individualization of psychological practice. 'While the specifics of the generalization about developmental processes have changed, more important than the specific content of the message about normality and abnormality was the institutionalization of the idea that we can scientifically validate standards of normal physical and mental functioning.' See Richardson, *The Century of the Child*, 127. Blatz, as one researcher, used this criterion in a very contemporary sense to individualize education as a form of self-development.

24 Blatz and Bott, *Parents and the Pre-School Child*, 7.

25 For a discussion of the intervention of the experts into practices of mothering, see Riley, *War in the Nursery*.

26 Blatz and Bott, *Parents and the Pre-School Child*, 7. Blatz, Bott, and their colleagues generated vast quantities of data through mass-based and longitudinal studies, the earliest of which was the study of 'normal' children at the

Regal Road Public School in Toronto launched in the early 1920s under Hincks's direction. The final phase of this study – Phase 4 – was only recently launched over 1997–8, by Dr Richard Volpe at the Institute for Child Study. Only empirical data were deemed capable of providing the foundation for theoretical insights into the development of human personality, based on the emergent notion of a life cycle comprising a series of developmental stages. This research strategy actively constituted the 'normal,' organized into a series of phases to be monitored and administered through schooling and into the appropriate vocational activity. Freudian psychoanalysis was viewed with a scepticism bordering on ridicule, as the following by Blatz to the adherents to Freud's methods suggests: 'If one does not arrive at their findings or conclusions, it is said to be because one is not fully initiated into the proper technique, or perhaps because one first requires to be analysed oneself.' Blatz and Bott, 11.

27 LAC, MG 31, K13, Vol. 1, File 11. Olive Russell, 'The Philosophy of the New Education,' *The Torch: A Magazine for Leaders of Canadian Girls in Training* 12, no. 1 (January-February 1936): 4.

28 LAC, MG 31, K13, Vol. 1, File 11. Olive Ruth Russell, 'The Vocational Guidance Movement in Germany Prior to Hitler's Regime,' *Ontario Vocational Guidance Association Bulletin Number 24* (December 1936): 2.

29 As it turned out, the Toronto Board of Education began to implement vocational guidance programming in collegiate institutes under its jurisdiction. Students were instructed in how to select a vocation, assessing their own and others' personality characteristics, researching occupations, identifying their own interests and abilities, assessing their own failures, and conducting interviews, all in relation to occupational choice. Teachers were instructed in the importance of administering and interpreting mental tests, including tests of IQ. Students and teachers staged 'playettes' on themes of vocational guidance, organized student groups including one called the 'progress club,' and compiled resources for the school library and scrapbooks for classroom use. See Toronto Board of Education Archives and Records Centre, Manuscript Collection, Reports by Board Officials, 1937–1962: Report by Dr Cecil Goldring, Director of Education for Toronto, on the Vocational Guidance Program in Secondary Schools, 8 March 1943. For a slightly different examination of Goldring's work in relation to his growing concern over the delinquency of young women in particular, see Mariana Valverde, 'Building Anti-Delinquent Communities.'

30 LAC, MG 31, K13, Vol. 1, File 11. Olive Russell, 'Is Vocational Guidance Feasible?' *The School* (March 1939): 566.

31 LAC, MG 31, K13, Vol. 1 File 1. 'Too Much Stress on Skill, Not Enough on Personality, Claims Dr Olive Russell,' *Globe and Mail*, 29 January 1938.

32   See Stephen, 'The "bad", the "incorrigible," and the "immoral."'

33   Ibid., 80–1.

34   LAC, MG 31, K13, Vol. 1, File 11. Olive Russell, 'Is Vocational Guidance Feasible?' *The School* (March 1939): 567. For a discussion of the rise of fascist organizing in Canada see Robin, *Shades of Right: Nativist and Fascist Politics in Canada: 1920–1940*, and Principe, 'A Tangled Knot: Prelude to 10 June 1940.' For a fascinating contemporary study, a review of 'ethnic' press conducted by a former agent of the federal Department of Justice charged with the 'handling of interned aliens' during the First World War, see Kirkconnell, *Canada, Europe and Hitler.* Kirkconnell advised against viewing all 'foreign' residents in Canada as de facto sympathizers with either the Nazi regime or the fascist regime of Mussolini.

35   LAC MG 31, K13, Vol. 2, File 14. Department of National Defence, 1942–1947. Edward T. Folliard, 'The Psychiatrist at War,' *Washington Post* 1942 (news clipping, np).

36   Griffin, Laycock, and Line, *Mental Hygiene: A Manual for Teachers*, 73.

37   Ibid., 103–4.

38   Ibid., 120.

39   Ibid., 184–5.

40   LAC, MG 31, K13, Vol. 2, File 13. 'Personnel Selection and The "M" Test: Policy' (typescript, nd), 1.

41   See Copp, 'From Neurasthemia to Post-Traumatic Stress Disorder'; and Copp and McAndrew, *Battle Exhaustion.*

42   The six tiers were as follows:
     GROUP I (total score 175 or better). Very superior intelligence and learning capacity (within the top 6% of the recruit population).
     GROUP II (total score 160–174). High ability, though not up to the standard of group I. Learning capacity sufficient to enable them to assimilate Officer training (if qualities of leadership are present).
     GROUP III (total score 130–159). Above average intelligence. Able to undertake most work of a complicated sort, or to learn all but the most technical of Army trades.
     GROUP IV (total score 100–129). Average intelligence. Able to carry out ordinary duties with minimum of supervision.
     GROUP V (total score 70–99). Limited ability. Able to perform simple routine tasks under supervision.
     GROUP VI (total score 0–69). Definitely below normal; falls within lowest 8% of recruit population. (Some of the men scoring in this group will be feeble-minded).
     LAC, MG 31, K13, Vol. 2, File 13. 'Personnel Selection and The "M" Test:

Policy' (typescript, nd), 2. According to instructions to technicians charged with administering the 'M' test, examiners were to occupy two positions: that of educator, drawing a tested subject's attention to errors in completion 'in a most quiet and kindly manner'; and that of state official admonished to 'Remember the note at the top of the booklet that it is an offence under the Official Secret's [*sic*] Act to communicate any of the subject matter of these tests to any person, either in or out of the army.' See also LAC, MG 31, K13, Vol. 1, 'Information for N.C.O.'s Regarding the "M" Test,' 2.

43 LAC, MG 31, K13, Vol. 2, File 13. 'Personnel Selection and the "M" Test: Policy' (typescript, nd), 2.

44 LAC, MG 31, K13, Vol. 1, File 11. Olive Russell, 'Is Vocational Guidance Feasible?' *The School* (March 1939): 561.

45 From the behaviourist camp came the confident assertion that all behaviour was capable of quantification as well as reduction to biological causes. However, this was not an uncontroversial or uncontested claim. For example, a 1935 text by David Wechsler challenged the prodigious ability of science to measure any human capacity based on two central propositions: (1) all human capacities are either physical or 'psychophysical' quantities and, therefore, (2) as such, all are capable of measurement. Conversely, Wechsler argued that there were multiple capacities distributed across a broad continuum that were not reducible to the status of discrete entities. The real issue, then, lay in the validity of statistical methods that attempted to transmute 'scales of relative position' into gradations of equal units. Mental testing, of course, measures only the degree of deviation from the performance average of the group, a point lost on many of its avid proponents, then as now. The significance of such deviance was invariably taken up as racialized (or gender, or class-based) difference. And difference lay at the other end of the exercise of assessing and quantifying human capacities: in sum, difference and the significance of deviation from the statistical norm or average. Wechsler was among the minority in the United States who, from within the discourse of mental testing, questioned its veracity and, indeed, purpose: 'The facts which we have gathered to show the range of human capacities ... should do much to make us suspicious of those who, in order to glorify some of the selected members of our species, find it necessary to misinterpret the facts altogether.' Wechsler, *The Range of Human Capacities*, 126.

46 LAC, MG 31, K13, Vol. 1. Olive Ruth Russell. Directorate of Personnel Selection. Proforma no. 2. CWAC Recruits Rejected by O.C., 29 April 1943.

47 Ibid.
48 Binet and Simon, 'The Development of Intelligence in the Child,' 44.
49 LAC, MG 31, K13, Vol. 1, File 11. Olive Russell, 'The Philosophy of the New Education,' *The Torch: A Magazine for Leaders of Canadian Girls in Training* 12, no. 1 (January–February 1936): 5. See also 'Persistent Human Needs: An Address Given at the Parent-Teacher Meeting on Fathers' Night, Moulton College, February 16, 1942 (Day after fall of Singapore).'
50 LAC, MG 31, K13, Vol. 1, File 11. Olive Ruth Russell, 'Persistent Human Needs.'
51 For an intriguing study of the natalist education campaigns in Ontario up to the Second World War, see Comacchio, *Nations Are Built of Babies: Saving Ontario's Mothers and Children, 1900–1940.* See Comacchio's chapter 6, 'A Healthy Programme for Life: The Management of Childhood,' for a discussion of the transition to the technique of discipline through regulation in parent-education programs and child-rearing advice literature. See also Blatz and Bott, *Parents and the Pre-School Child.*
52 See Strange, *Toronto's Girl Problem: The Perils and Pleasures of the City, 1880–1930*; and Stephen, 'The "bad," the "incorrigible," and the "immoral."'
53 Ruth Pierson, *'They're Still Women After All,'* chapters 5 and 6.
54 Kunzel, 'White Neurosis, Black Pathology: Constructing Out-of-Wedlock Pregnancy in the Wartime and Postwar United States.'
55 LAC, MG 31, K13, Vol. 1. Olive Ruth Russell. Directorate of Personnel Selection. Proforma no. 2, Capt. Olive R. Russell, Type of Personnel, CWAC Recruits Rejected by O.C., Report to Maj. J.W. Grimmon, District Army Examiner M.D. 1, London, Ontario, 28 April 1943: 2.
56 Ibid.
57 Ibid., 1.
58 Ibid., 2.
59 LAC, MG 31, K13, Vol. 1. Olive Ruth Russell. Directorate of Personnel Selection. Progress Report, Halifax, Nova Scotia, M.D. 6, 13 September 1943 – 29 September 1943: 2.
60 For a discussion of the racism characterizing the mental hygiene movement generally in this era, see McLaren, *Our Own Master Race: Eugenics in Canada, 1885–1945.*
61 LAC, MG 31, K13, Vol. 2, File 14. Personal letter to Marion Needler, Good Friday, 1943: 4.
62 Ibid., 10.
63 LAC, MG 31, K13, Vol. 2, File 13. CWAC Report no. 4 by Olive R. Russell, Lt, Toronto, Ont., 11 December 1942, to the Director of Personnel Selection, National Defence Headquarters: 'Some Observation [*sic*] and Recommen-

dations regarding CWAC Personnel Selection Work. Policy in Regard to Unsuitable Personnel for CWAC,' 2.

64 Ibid.

65 Ibid.

66 LAC, MG 31, K13, Vol. 1. Olive Ruth Russell. Directorate of Personnel Selection. Salter to Russell, 8 January 1943.

67 The practice of compiling case files to produce longitudinal case histories of individuals and populations – an outgrowth of this work – would have important implications for the postwar period and echoed a similar call for the longitudinal referencing of case files processed through local employment offices. Certainly, the Toronto Social Service Index operated as a central clearing house of information generated through the Toronto social work/social service agency network, geared towards what its directors claimed was the general welfare of the individual in whose name such information was compiled in the form of an individual and familial 'history.' Confidentiality became an issue of increasing concern in transferring information of such a personal and intimate nature over to an outside agency, even to the armed services, although, as Jean Walker, executive secretary of the index acknowledged, 'the only real protection is in the judgement and integrity of those who use the Index.'

Russell was adamant that the confidential nature of the records generated in work of this kind be protected as an indication of the professional integrity she was anxious to secure for her profession overall. For example, she noted in one of her reports, in a hand-written addendum, a situation recounted to her by a 'civilian' in which a unnamed male 'A[rmy] E[xaminer]' had gone out of his way to look up a man's A. card [in which were recorded all examination and interview results, diagnosis, and recommendations] and had talked about it very freely and disparagingly with a group of civilian friends.' LAC, MG 31, K13, Vol. 2, File 13. CWAC Report no. 4 by Olive R. Russell, Lt, Toronto, Ont., 11 December 1942, to the Director of Personnel Selection, National Defence Headquarters, 'Some Observation [sic] and Recommendations regarding CWAC Personnel Selection Work. Policy in Regard to Unsuitable Personnel for CWAC,' 4.

Where the interests and remediating intent of the index and its users were driven by the formative principles of professional social work, there could be no question but that the highest principles of integrity would ultimately redound to the benefit of the 'client.' The information lodged at the index could do as much potential harm as good to the individual client; however, such concerns were allayed in the confident assertion that the trained professional social worker could be depended upon to discern the longer-term effect of such dissemination and weigh any danger against the best interests of the alleged individual client. Embarrassment and 'immediate disappointment' were often the price to be paid at the level of the individual, Walker explained, necessary sacrifices to the 'ultimate good of the individual and the community – as we social workers have learned, too!' LAC, MG 31, K13, Vol. 2, File 13. C. Jean Walker, Executive Secretary, Social Service Index (Member of the Federation for Community Service), Toronto, to Lt O.R. Russell, 16 December 1942.

No single agency, even an agency of the state, could address itself to all 'phases of a client's life,' although such an all-encompassing gaze or net could eventually be achieved where all agencies and, more importantly, those working within such agencies, understood themselves to be working as part of the broader network. This is what the index was intended to symbolize and to activate: it was a unifying and consolidating repository and an active agent that received and transmitted information from a variety of disparate points and cumulatively organized and presented a composite documentary representation – a profile – of the individual client. Knowledge produced there represented the professionalizing effects of social work: 'any community servant will feel that his or her work is not isolated but part of a closely interwoven network. It is to assist in making this network an effective community support, rather than an entanglement that the Index exists.' Such a central agency greatly facilitated the regulatory project of the welfare state.

68 LAC, MG 31, K13, Vol. 1. Olive Ruth Russell. Directorate of Personnel Selection. Russell to Maj. J.W. Grimmon, 28 April 1943.
69 Ibid.
70 LAC, MG 31, K13, Vol. 2, File 13. Report to Brig. R.D. Sutherland, Atlantic Command Headquarters, Halifax, N.S., 24 July 1944: 2. Interview detailing work of CWAC army examiner, typescript, nd, probably 1944. In her letter to Sutherland, marked 'Personal,' Russell explained the purpose of her report as follows: 'On the occasion of my interview with the Officer Appraisal Board, you did me the honour of requesting that certain remarks which I made at that time [be] embodied in a memorandum for your personal use.' She acknowledged moving far beyond her purview as army examiner to comment on an important subject related to the welfare of the CWAC, namely, the importance of personnel work to preparing women for their citizenship duties in the postwar world.
71 LAC, MG 31, K13, Vol. 2, File 14. Dr Olive Ruth Russell, DND 1942–1947. Correspondence. Dr Mary Salter, Lt, Directorate of Personnel Selection, NDHQ Ottawa, to Russell, 8 January 1943. The record referred to was

M.F.M. 196. All confidential information, Salter avowed, was better recorded on M.F.M. 238. See Salter to Russell, 12 January 1943, n72 below.

72 LAC, MG 31, K13, Vol. 1. Salter to Russell, Ottawa, 12 January 1943. At issue was the question of whether the customary M.F.M. 196 should be expanded to include notations of a more detailed nature, including a psychological assessment report completed on women thought to embody potential difficulties, or whether such information was best left off the report and only included where the more detailed and more confidential M.F.M. 238 was requested by an individual officer.

73 See in particular chapter 5, 'Ladies or "Loose" Women' and chapter 6, 'VD Control and the CWAC,' in Ruth Pierson, *They're Still Women After All.*

74 LAC, MG 31, K13, Vol. 2, File 13. CWAC Report no. 4, by Olive Ruth Russell, Lt, Toronto, Ont., 11 December 1942, to the Director of Personnel Selection, National Defence Headquarters, 'Some Observation [*sic*] and Recommendations Regarding CWAC Personnel Selection Work. Policy in Regard to Unsuitable Personnel for CWAC,' 20.

75 LAC, MG 31, K13, Vol. 2, File 14. Salter to Russell, 13 May 1943.

76 Ibid.

77 LAC, MG 31, K13, Vol. 1. Olive Ruth Russell Papers. Personal. Brig. R.D. Sutherland, Atlantic Command Headquarters, Halifax, N.S., 24 July 1944: 2.

4: Preparing for the Peace: The Demobilization of Women Workers

1 Library and Archives Canada (LAC), RG 27, Vol. 605, File 6-24-1, pt 2. NSS Employment of Women – General. Mrs E.W. Gerry, Supervisor of the Women's Division, UIC, Winnipeg, to Eaton, 1 March 1944; Eaton to Gerry, 14 March 1944.

2 LAC, RG 27, Vol. 605, File 6-24-1, pt 2. NSS Employment of Women – General. Peebles to MacNamara, 18 February 1944.

3 LAC, RG 27, Vol. 605, File 6-24-1, pt 2. NSS Employment of Women – General. Peebles to MacNamara, 18 February 1944: 2. The new table was based on the 1941 census 'and other sources.' Estimates of 'women gainfully occupied' showed an increase from August 1939 to 30 January 1943 of 347,000. The old table showed an increase over the same period of 402,000.

4 LAC, RG 27, Vol. 605, File 6-24-1, pt 2. NSS Employment of Women – General. Eaton to MacNamara, 9 May 1944.

5 LAC, RG 27, Vol. 605, File 6-24-1, pt 1. NSS Employment of Women – General. Memorandum to MacNamara from J.S.M. of I.R.O., 7 October 1942. Letter to Peter Heenan, Chair of the Regional War Labour Board for Ontario, from A. Mitchell, 9 October 1942.

6 LAC, RG 27, Vol. 605, File 6-24-1, pt 2. NSS Employment of Women – General. Eadie to Eaton, 'Report on Labour Trends,' 20 September 1944.

7 For an account of the postwar return to domesticity in Britain, see Riley, *War in the Nursery.*

8 LAC, RG 27, Vol. 605, File 6-24-1, pt 1. NSS Employment of Women – General. B.G. Sullivan, UIC, to Eaton, 8 April 1943. 'Questionnaire to Married Female Applicants', dated 30 March 1943.

9 LAC, RG 27, Vol. 605, File 6-24-1, pt 1. NSS Employment of Women – General. Department of Labour News Release, Address of Mrs Rex Eaton, Assistant Director of National Selective Service, to National Council of Women, 17 June 1943: 4–5.

10 Canada, Advisory Committee on Reconstruction VI, 'Post-War Problems of Women,' 1. Hereafter PWPW. For a complete account of members and their activities on the subcommittee, see Brandt, '"Pigeon-Holed and Forgotten": The Work of the Subcommittee on the Post-War Problems of Women, 1943.'

11 Where women were compelled to work, their economic status derived from the inability to select marriage as an option. Marriage, nonetheless, was the natural state: 'We believe that the right to choose is not going to operate to make every woman, or even much larger groups of women, want to leave their homes for the labour market. It is the right to choose which is demanded. Happier homes, and, therefore, a happier democracy, will result from the recognition that woman [*sic*] choose or do not choose marriage as their vocation. It must be remembered that for many single women marriage will be an impossibility because of the casualties of the war.' PWPW, 9.

12 Ibid., 16.

13 Ibid., 5

14 For a discussion of the introduction of family allowances in Ontario before the Second World War, see Comacchio, *Nations Are Built of Babies: Saving Ontario's Mothers and Children, 1900–1940.* For the postwar period, see Struthers, 'Family Allowances, Old Age Security, and the Construction of Entitlement in the Canadian Welfare State, 1943–1951.'

15 PWPW, 1.

16 Ibid., 11.

17 Ibid., 7. Here was a good case of upgrading the occupation by upgrading the worker. Trainees would first be carefully screened for suitability and reliability and then put through a program of training provided on a part-time as well as a full-time basis, together with a program of short-term evening instruction and a continuation course for the experienced household worker. The focus of training, an apparent improvement over the pre-war

training provided under the Dominion Youth Training program, was an emphasis on the proficiency and accreditation of the trainee on the one hand and the training of employers on the other. Government-sponsored training – and there was no doubt that this proposal would be integrated into the broader postwar training strategy – would conform to a 'uniform standard of proficiency' just like the standardized outcomes achieved through other apprenticed skilled trades. As for employers, the implication was that if women – that is, those whose middle-class households were not only the anchors of democracy, happy or otherwise, but also the future workplaces of this 'reserve of unskilled woman-power' – took a dim view of the value of their own household work, then how could they convince their potential employees to look upon their own labours with 'craft pride' and as a true, skilled vocation. How, moreover, could they provide the guiding hand of citizenship education to their social inferiors? This was held to be the true reason for the failure of pre-war training efforts; it was also believed to be the reason so many women shunned domestic service as the employment of last resort: 'A necessary condition for success in the rehabilitation of the household worker and the raising of her social status to a place commensurate with the vital importance of her vocation is a change in the attitude of employers. Unwillingness to recognize the value of the house worker's service and to give her adequate remuneration both in the form of wages and good working conditions has been the stumbling block in the way of improvement in this field.' Ibid., 8.

18 LAC, RG 27, Vol. 605, File 6-24-1, pt 1. NSS Employment of Women – General. Mary Eadie to B.G. Sullivan 'Employment of Women – Circular E17,' 7 May 1943: 2.
19 Ibid., 6.
20 Ibid., 4.
21 Ibid., 12.
22 Ibid., 13.
23 Ibid., 20.
24 Keith, 'Situations Wanted: Female,' 75.
25 Ibid., 154.
26 LAC, RG 27, Vol. 3044, File 153. Rehabilitation – General 1943–1946. Allan Peebles and George Luxton, 'Suggestions Regarding Research on Postwar Employment,' 9 March 1944: 1–3. The proposal tabled by Luxton and Peebles was to make recommendations to the NSS Administrative Board on the 'scope and technique of a survey to obtain information on the probable postwar employment situation.'
27 Ibid., 2–3.

28 LAC, RG 27, Vol. 897, File 8-9-74, vol. 1. A.W. Crawford, 'Memorandum for Labour Co-ordination Committee Re: Training of Industrial Workers,' 24 July 1941: 32–3.

29 LAC, RG 27, Vol. 897, File 8-9-74, vol. 1. Memorandum R.F. Thompson to Dr Bryce M. Stewart, Chair, Interdepartmental Committee on Labour Co-ordination, 'Recommendations Regarding Training Programme,' 19 July 1941: 8.

30 LAC, RG 27, Vol. 605, File 6-24-1, vol. 3. NSS Employment of Women – General. Eaton to Miss E.S. Morley, Superintendent of Women's Division, Vancouver, 14 May 1945.

31 LAC, RG 27, Vol. 605, File 6-24-1, vol. 3. NSS Employment of Women – General. Confidential Circular 379, 11 May 1945: 1.

32 LAC, RG 27, Vol. 605, File 6-24-1, vol. 3. NSS Employment of Women – General. Eaton to Miss E.S. Morley, Superintendent of Women's Division, Vancouver, 14 May 1945: 2.

33 LAC, RG 27, Vol. 605, File 6-24-1, vol. 3. NSS Employment of Women – General. J.S. Brown, Supervisor, Women's Division, to Gordon Anderson, Manager, Employment and Selective Service Office, Hamilton, 'New Regulations Affecting Women,' 18 May 1945.

34 LAC, RG 27, Vol. 605, File 6-24-1, vol. 3. NSS Employment of Women – General. Confidential Circular 379, 11 May 1945, 'NSS Relaxation of Controls,' and NSS Circular No. 379-2, '1. Women. 2. Relaxation of Controls. 3. Separation Notice. 4. Issuance of Permits,' 25 May 1945.

35 LAC, RG 27, Vol. 1516, file 0-26-1. NSS Correspondence with UIC Re: Vocational Training Pre-Employment Courses. Toronto – Junction Report, 2–3.

36 See, for example, LAC, RG 27, Vol. 1516, file 0-26-1. S.B. Nitikman, President, Garment Manufacturers Association of Western Canada, Winnipeg, Manitoba, to Mrs Gerry, NSS, Winnipeg, 11 July 1945. This view constituted a key theme in the organization of postwar vocational training in the case studies discussed below.

37 The following regions sent back reports in response to the survey:
    Pacific Region: Vancouver, Victoria
    Prairie Region: Edmonton, Calgary, Regina, Saskatoon, Winnipeg, Fort William
    Quebec: Montreal, Sherbrooke, Quebec City
    Maritimes: Saint John, Moncton, New Glasgow, Sydney, Halifax
    Ontario Region: Windsor, Welland, Galt, Kingston, Peterborough, St Catharines, Hamilton, Brantford, Guelph, Kitchener, London, Woodstock, North Bay, Weston, Toronto, Toronto Junction, Ottawa

38 LAC, RG 27, Vol. 748, file 12-15-5, pt 1. Department of Labour NSS – Training Branch, Schools and Courses – Household Workers. Associate Director Fraudena Eaton. Circular from Department of Labour Employment Service and Unemployment Insurance Branch, Ontario Region – To Managers Ontario. From B.S. Sullivan, O.R.S.

39 LAC, RG 27, Vol. 1516, file 0-26-1. NSS Correspondence with UIC Re: Vocational Training Pre-Employment Courses. Pre-Employment Vocational Training for Women Survey – May 1945. Memo to Arthur MacNamara from Fraudena Eaton, 19 May 1945. Department of Labour. Employment Service and Unemployment Insurance Branch. Employment Circular, 17 May 1945. As Ruth Pierson and Marjorie Cohen have observed, a list of [30] occupations was provided, to ensure that 'continuous employment' was understood to mean employment in the narrow band of designated 'female occupations.' Pierson and Cohen, 'Government Job-Training Programmes for Women, 1939–1947.'

40 LAC, RG 27, Vol. 1516, file 0-26-1. NSS Correspondence with UIC Re: Vocational Training Pre-Employment Courses. New Glasgow Report, from Manager, Employment and Selective Service, Moncton, NB, 27 June 1945, Doris M. Merry for WAD Trent manager.

41 LAC, RG 27, Vol. 1516, file 0-26-1. NSS Correspondence with UIC Re: Vocational Training Pre-Employment Courses. Saskatoon Report, [July 1945?]: 1.

42 LAC, RG 27, Vol. 1516, file 0-26-1. NSS Correspondence with UIC Re: Vocational Training Pre-Employment Courses. Annette E. Coderre, Sherbrooke, 5 July 1945: 1–2.

43 LAC, RG 27, Vol. 1516, file 0-26-1. NSS Correspondence with UIC Re: Vocational Training Pre-Employment Courses. Winnipeg, 11 July 1945: 4.

44 LAC, RG 27, Vol. 1516, file 0-26-1. NSS Correspondence with UIC Re: Vocational Training Pre-Employment Courses. London Report, [July 1945?]: 2.

45 LAC, RG 27, Vol. 1516, file 0-26-1. NSS Correspondence with UIC Re: Vocational Training Pre-Employment Courses. K. Keenan, 'Report on the Survey of Opportunities for Training for Women Workers,' Kingston, 13 July 1945.

46 LAC, RG 27, Vol. 748, file 12-15-5, pt 1A. 'Vocational Training for Women' (typescript, nd), 2.

47 LAC, RG 27, Vol. 1516, file 0-26-1. NSS Correspondence with UIC Re: Vocational Training Pre-Employment Courses. Ottawa Report, [Ms] M.K. Marsden, Supervisor of Women's Employment, 11 July 1945: 1–2.

48 LAC, RG 27, Vol. 1516, file 0-26-1. NSS Correspondence with UIC Re:

Vocational Training Pre-Employment Courses. 'National Selective Service – Guidance Department, Board of Education,' St Catharines Report, [July 1945?]: 2–3. Sections 1 to 7 included space for personal information, health, and 'occupational handicaps,' and information thought pertinent to a construction of character: 'activities, talents, interests, hobbies.' Examiners were to rate the subject as excellent, above average, average, below average, or poor in assessed abilities and aptitudes. Learning capacities were segregated into 'school learning,' mechanical aptitude, and clerical aptitude, a gender-based differential. 'Personality development' comprised a ranking of the individual's 'industry,' 'reliability,' and 'accuracy.' Finally, a small section of the form provided space for the construction of an employment history, including place of employment, nature of the work, job name and tasks, and 'follow-up visits.' At the bottom was a space for 'remarks' by the examiner.

49 LAC, RG 27, Vol. 1516, file 0-26-1. NSS Correspondence with UIC Re: Vocational Training Pre-Employment Courses. Winnipeg, Mrs E.W. Gerry Supervisor, Female Employment Division, 11 July 1945: 3.

50 LAC, RG 27, Vol. 1516, file 0-26-1. NSS Correspondence with UIC Re: Vocational Training Pre-Employment Courses. Kitchener, 'Report on Pre-Employment Vocational Training of Women,' 28 June 1945: 1.

51 LAC, RG 27, Vol. 748, file 12-15-5, pt 1. Department of Labour NSS – Training Branch, Schools and Courses – Household Workers. Associate Director Fraudena Eaton. London Report, nd: 2–3.

52 LAC, RG 27, Vol. 748, file 12-15-5, pt 1. Department of Labour NSS – Training Branch, Schools and Courses – Household Workers. Associate Director Fraudena Eaton. Mrs Kate Lyons, Supervisor, Edmonton Women's Division, 13 July 1945: 2.

53 LAC, RG 27, Vol. 748, file 12-15-5, pt 1. Department of Labour NSS – Training Branch, Schools and Courses – Household Workers. Associate Director Fraudena Eaton. Maritimes Report, Miss E.L. Caldwell, Women's Supervisor, Halifax. From Miss A.M.S. Ward, General Secretary, YWCA, nd.

54 LAC, RG 27, Vol. 748, file 12-15-5, pt 1. Department of Labour NSS – Training Branch, Schools and Courses – Household Workers. Associate Director Fraudena Eaton. Winnipeg. To Mr J.F. White, Regional Superintendent, from Mrs E.W. Gerry, Supervisor, Female Employment Division. Re: Employment Circular No. 10 – Pre-Employment Vocational Training, 11 July 1945: 2. This usage of origins makes clear the racist exclusion of 'Japanese' from the concept of Canadianness, as 'race' and the racialization of difference superseded all other identity signifiers.

55 LAC, RG 27, Vol. 605, file 6-24-1, pt 1. Employment of Women – General. Eaton to MacNamara, 27 August 1945.

56 LAC, RG 27, Vol. 748, file 12-15-5, vol. 1. Thompson to Miss Isobel Robson, 18 November 1944.

57 LAC, RG 27, Vol. 748, file 12-15-5, pt 1A. Speech delivered by Mrs Rex Eaton, National Conference, organized by Mary Salter, February 1946: 5.

58 Public Archives of Ontario (PAO), RG 7, VII–1, Vol. 9. Marion Findlay Papers. Reconstitution of Postwar Reconstruction Advisory Committees, 'Report on the Post-War Problems of Women,' nd.

59 For the final summary of the Pre-employment Training Survey, see LAC, RG 27, Vol. 605, file 6-24-1, pt 1. Employment of Women – General. Eaton to MacNamara, 27 August 1945.

5: 'An Aptitude Test Is in *Your* Best Interest': Canada's Employment Charter for Women Veterans

1 Neary and Brown, 'The Veteran's Charter and Canadian Women Veterans of World War II,' 393.

2 Library and Archives Canada (LAC), RG 27, Vol. 3575, File 11-8-9-9, vol. 1. Rehabilitation Information Committee. 'The Role of Information in the Re-Establishment of Veterans in Civilian Life,' 4.

3 LAC, MG 31, K13, Vol. 2, File 14. Line to Russell, 27 April 1944.

4 LAC, MG 31, K13, Vol. 2, File 14. Personal letter to Line, 3 January 1944.

5 Also on the organizing committee were Hincks, Blatz, J.C. Meakins of McGill University, and G. Humphrey of Queen's University. The second Inter-Service conference was held in 1945, organised by J.D. Griffin, Brock Chisholm, and Ewen Cameron, professor of industrial psychiatry at McGill University. That same year, the psychiatry section of the Canadian Medical Association (CMA) was organized. Line was a member of the U.S.-based Group for the Advancement of Psychiatry, an exclusive 150-member body devoted to advancing the application of psychiatric knowledge practices. The Canadian Psychiatric Association was formed on 1 June 1951. See Richardson, *The Century of the Child*, 164.

6 Cameron and Ross, *Studies in Supervision*.

7 F. Cyril James, 'Preface,' v.

8 In this argument, Line revisited many of the points articulated in the earlier *Mental Hygiene Manual for Teachers*.

9 Line, 'The Learning Process,' 81.

10 Ibid., 77.

11 Ibid., 92–3.

12 Ibid., 90.

13 Ibid., 94.

14 Ibid., 95.
15 Ibid., 92.
16 LAC, RG 38, Vol. 184. Department of Veterans' Affairs – Rehabilitation File Confidential Letters, vol. 1. Confidential letter 1, from W.S. Woods, Associate Deputy Minister, Department of Pensions and National Health, 22 July 1941: 2–4. Contrary to Woods's desire, an atmosphere of harmony and cooperation did not always prevail in relations between DVA welfare officers and DES/UIC staff. The objectives of the DES were closely informed by the necessity of placing the most suitable applicant, while those of the DVA were to execute the terms of the Re-instatement in Civil Employment Order. Numerous disputes appeared to plague the work of both groups, prompting a flurry of circulars and reviews of the respective jobs and responsibilities of the two staff groups.
17 I would like to thank James Struthers for clarifying this point.
18 LAC, RG 38, Vol. 184, File 1. Department of Veterans' Affairs – Rehabilitation File Confidential Letters. From W.S. Woods, Associate Deputy Minister, Department of Pensions and National Health. Confidential Letter no. 1 to District Welfare Officers, 22 July 1941: 5. For a discussion of this aspect of civilian re-establishment, see Don Ives, 'The Veterans Charter: The Compensation Principle.'
19 LAC, RG 38, Vol. 184, File 1. Department of Veterans' Affairs – Rehabilitation File Confidential Letters. Confidential Letter no. 11 to District Administrators and Welfare Officers, 24 January 1942: 1–2.
20 Ibid., 2–4.
21 LAC, RG 38, Vol. 184, File 1. Department of Veterans' Affairs – Rehabilitation File Confidential Letters. Office Manual on Vocational Training Provided under the Post Discharge Re-Establishment Order, P.C. 7633, as amended by P.C. 775, 1 March 1944. P.R. 14.674: 2.
22 Canada, Department of Veterans' Affairs, 'Counselling Procedures,' in *Annual Report*, 1948: 24.
23 Canada, Department of Veterans' Affairs, *Annual Report*, 1947: 19.
24 Ibid., 15.
25 Walter S. Woods, *Rehabilitation: A Combined Operation*, 73 (my emphasis).
26 LAC, RG 38, Vol. 186, File 'Committee on Demobilization and Re-Establishment, Subcommittee on Employment and Post-Discharge Pay.' Robert England, 'Confidential. Re: Minutes of Sub-Employment Committee,' 2 April 1942: 8.
27 LAC, RG 27, Vol. 3575, File 11-8-9-9, pt 2. Demobilization and Rehabilitation Information Committee – minutes. Subcommittee on Research, Item 6. Motion Pictures (b) Industrial Re-establishment, 7 February 1945: 2.

28 Ibid., 91. See also Jacques Donzelot, 'Pleasure in Work.'

29 Line, 'The Learning Process,' 86.

30 Ibid., 88 (my emphasis).

31 The Rehabilitation Information Committee was established by Order-in-Council P.C. on 17 October 1944.

32 LAC, RG 27, Vol. 3575, File 11-8-9-9, pt 2. Demobilization and Rehabilitation Information Committee – minutes. 'Progress Reports – Radio Programme Developments,' 6 December 1944.

33 For a description of the broadcasts, see LAC, RG 27, Vol. 3575, File 11-8-9-9, pt 1. Economics and Research Rehabilitation Information Committee. Andrew Cowan, 'Report to the Rehabilitation Information Committee on CBC Re-establishment Programmes,' 17 October 1945. For an overview of the broadcasts, see Canadian Broadcasting Corporation, *The Soldier's Return. A Digest of Talks Heard on the CBC Trans-Canada Network during the Winter of 1944–1945 on Wednesday Nights, after the National News Bulletin* (Toronto: CBC Publications Branch, 1945). For sound recordings of the summary of broadcasts series, see 'J.D. Ketchum of the Wartime Information Board comments on 20 talks,' CBC Archives, Accession and Item number 450502-01/00, Location number 450422-01, 2 May 1945.

34 The Advisory Committee on Demobilization and Re-Establishment, re-named the Advisory Committee on Demobilization and Rehabilitation (ACDR) – a telling shift – was chaired by Walter S. Woods, ADM at Pensions and National Health. In 1944 Pensions and National Health was reorganized into the two new ministries of Veterans' Affairs and National Health and Welfare. At this time, Woods was appointed deputy minister for the Department of Veterans' Affairs.

35 LAC, RG 38, Vol. 186, File 'Committee on Demobilization and Re-Establishment, Subcommittee on Employment and Post-Discharge Pay.' Robert England, 'Confidential. Re: Minutes of Sub-Employment Committee,' 2 April 1942: 4.

36 LAC, RG 27, Vol. 1486, File 2-162-9, 'NSS Exceptions to Regulations. Certain races not accepted to army for non-medical reasons.' Norman Robertson to Deputy Minister of National War Services, 15 December 1941. This question is discussed in chapter 4.

37 LAC, RG 38, Vol. 186, File 'Committee on Demobilization and Re-Establishment, Subcommittee on Employment and Post-Discharge Pay.' Robert England, 'Confidential. Re: Minutes of Sub-Employment Committee,' 2 April 1942: 5.

38 By this time, the NCMH (Canada) had merged into the U.S. umbrella, National Committee for Mental Hygiene, with Hincks at the helm. The

organization traversed the Canada-U.S. border as a single entity with a single program for legislative lobbying and organizing strategies and tactics. Joining the broadcast series, in illustration of the collaborative approach adopted more generally, was Dr A.H. Ruggles, superintendent of the Butler Hospital in Providence, Rhode Island, a member of the Surgeon General's Advisory Committee and a recognized expert on the mental hygiene concerns associated with veterans' re-establishment. Canadian Broadcasting Corporation, *The Soldier's Return. A Digest of Talks Heard on the CBC Trans-Canada Network during the Winter of 1944–1945 on Wednesday Nights, after the National News Bulletin* (Toronto: CBC Publications Branch, 1945), 48–9.

39 G.A.S. Nairn, 'Back to the Job: Speaking for Industry,' in *The Soldier's Return*, 37.

40 LAC, RG 27, Accession No. 71/98, Vol. 2, File 22-5-7-1. RCAF, *Personnel Counselling Programme ... in Brief.*

41 F.J. Picking, ed., *What Happens Now? A Veteran's Guide*, 29.

42 LAC, RG-27, Vol. 3575, File 11-8-9-9, vol. 1. Rehabilitation Information Committee, 'The Role of Information in the Re-Establishment of Veterans in Civilian Life,' 8.

43 Canada, Department of Pensions and National Health, *Back to Civil Life*, 9.

44 LAC, RG 27, Accession No. 71/98, Vol. 2, File 22-5-7-1. RCAF, *Personnel Counselling Programme ... in Brief.*

45 LAC, MG 31, K13, Vol. 1. Department of Veterans' Affairs. News Release 62, 4 January 1945.

46 LAC, MG 31, K13, Vol. 2, File 15. Russell to Lt F.E. Whyard, WRCNS, Naval Information, Ottawa, 19 June 1945.

47 LAC, MG 31, K13, Vol. 2, File 14. 'Article For Saturday Night' (typescript), 19 June 1945: 7. See also LAC, MG 31, K13, Vol. 1, File 7. 'Ontario Vocational Guidance Association to the Prime Minister of Canada.' The petition recognized that unemployment, labour turnover, and general worker inefficiency were symptomatic of deeper social problems and could therefore not be broached as temporary conditions derived from short-term economic causes.

48 LAC, MG 31, K 13, Vol. 2, File 15. 'Some Activities of the Executive Assistant, Rehabilitation Branch (Women's Rehabilitation),' 31 August 1945.

49 Canada, Department of Veterans' Affairs, *Annual Report*, 1948: 25.

50 LAC, MG 31, K13, Vol. 1. 'Women's Rehabilitation Annual Report,' 1946–7: 1.

51 LAC, MG 31, K13, Vol. 1. Personal. Brig. R.D. Sutherland, Atlantic Command Headquarters, Halifax, N.S., 24 July 1944: 6.

52 Ibid.

53 Ibid., 58–9.

54 Ibid.

55 LAC, MG 31, K13, Vol. 1. Russell, 'Rehabilitation of Women of the Armed Services.' Counsellors Training Course, Ottawa, 19 February 1945: 2.

56 Ibid., 7 (emphasis in original).

57 LAC, RG 38, Vol. 184. Department of Veterans' Affairs – Rehabilitation File Confidential Letters, vol. 1. Confidential Letter 179, 'Counselling and Liaison Regarding Vocational Training for Ex-Service Women,' 3 January 1946: 1.

58 Ibid., 3.

59 Greer Williams, 'Don't Try to Solve Conflicts with Fear of Going crazy,' 2.

60 Ontario Rehabilitation Committee, *Digest of Rehabilitation Conferences of Delegates of Ontario Community Committees*, Ottawa Conference, 225.

61 See 'Mental Health Dramas Draw a Big Response,' *CBC Times* (week of 20 February 1949).

62 'Veterans' Program Said Best of Lot – Dr Olive Russell Comments,' *Leader-Post* (Regina) 27 February 1946.

63 Robert England, *Discharged: A Commentary on Civil Re-establishment of Veterans in Canada*.

64 LAC MG 31, K13, Vol. 1. Russell, 'Rehabilitation of Women of the Armed Services.' Counsellors Training Course, Ottawa, 19 February 1945: 4.

65 LAC, MG 31, K13, Vol. 2, File 15. Letter to Marion Coffey, 24 July 1945.

66 LAC, MG 31, K13, Vol. 1, Russell, 'Rehabilitation of Women of the Armed Services.' Counsellors Training Course, Ottawa, 19 February 1945: 5.

67 'No Migration to Home or Housework for Majority of Women Veterans,' *Vancouver News-Herald*, 6 March 1946; 'Few Servicewomen Will Be Domestics Local Council Told,' *Vancouver Daily Province*, 6 March 1946.

68 LAC, MG 31, K13, Vol. 1. Russell, Address to Winnipeg Local Council of Women (nd), 3–4.

69 LAC, MG 31, K13, Vol. 1. Russell, 'Women Tomorrow': An Outline of an Address to Be Given at the University Women's Club, Halifax, 15 March 1944 (typescript).

70 Ibid.

71 Ibid.

72 'Cites Challenge of Education in Postwar World,' *Globe and Mail*, 5 November 1946; 'Education Stressed at Teachers' Meeting,' *Toronto Daily Star*, 5 November 1946.

73 LAC, MG 31, K13, Vol. 1. Russell, 'Women Tomorrow': An Outline of an Address to Be Given at the University Women's Club, Halifax, 15 March 1944 (typescript), 10.

74 LAC, MG 31, K13, Vol. 1. Russell, 'Rehabilitation of Women of the Armed
    Services.' Counsellors Training Course, Ottawa, 19 February 1945: 5.

6: The Return to Domesticity: Canada's Womanhood in Training

1 Library and Archives Canada (LAC), RG 27, Vol. 748, file 12-15-5, pt 1A.
   Speech delivered by Mrs Rex Eaton, National Conference, organized by
   Mary Salter, 3. See also Eaton to Grier, 22 February 1946, asking for summary of speech notes in preparation for same.
2 LAC, RG 38, Vol. 187. DVA – Rehabilitation. Strictly Confidential. Twelfth
   Meeting, 27 May 1941. Sir George Chrystal, War Cabinet Office, Great
   Britain, citing Brig. Pigott, Minutes, 2.
3 Woods, *Rehabilitation: A Combined Operation*, 73–96. See especially page 96 for
   a discussion of problems arising from means testing.
4 LAC, RG 38, Vol. 184. DVA – Rehabilitation. Confidential Letter 11 to
   District Administrators and Welfare Officers, 24 January 1942, 2. 'Where it is
   clear that the wife is self-supporting, any assistance granted should, in such
   circumstances, be on the basis of a single man and not on the basis of a
   married man.'
5 LAC, RG 27, Vol. 744, file 12-14-16-12, vol. 1. W.M. Taylor, Royal Canadian
   Air Force, to Marion Graham, 29 March 1946. D.I. Royal, Lt Col. Staff
   Officer, CWAC, to Graham, 18 March 1946; Adelaide Sinclair, Capt.,
   WRCNS, Department of National Defence Naval Service, to Graham,
   23 March 1946. The RCAF survey was conducted on a sample of 382 women
   stationed at Rockcliffe and at Toronto. The CWAC survey represented a
   sample of 350 women stationed in Ottawa. Figures for the WCRNS were not
   provided, although Sinclair indicated it was conducted on their largest
   representative unit stationed at Ottawa.
6 See, for example, Ontario Rehabilitation Committee, *Digest of Rehabilitation
   Conferences of Delegates of Ontario Community Committees*, North Bay Conference, 16 July 1946: 144.
7 For a discussion of the struggle surrounding veterans' right to re-establishment through a system of preferential hiring see Stevenson, 'National
   Selective Service and Employment and Seniority Rights for Veterans, 1943–
   1946,' 102. It is unclear, however, if this figure applies to ex-servicewomen as
   well.
8 The termination date for the war, for the purposes of the Veterans' Rehabilitation Act, was set at 31 December 1946, under the terms of Order-in-
   Council P.C. 5333. This meant that all applications for training benefits had

to be made within one year of discharge or within one year of the termination date, whichever was later. Canada, Department of Veterans' Affairs,
'Women's Rehabilitatio,' *Annual Report,* 1948: 22.

9. Ibid., 31. It is important to note that this figure covers only those in receipt
of training benefits for full-time enrolment in an approved school or training institute and does not include those placed in on-the-job training, for
which no financial assistance was allocated and therefore no benefits were
received.

10 Ibid., 22.

11 Pierson and Cohen, 'Government Job-Training Programmes for Women,
1937–1947,' 90.

12 LAC, RG 27, Vol. 744, file 12-14-16-12, vol. 1. Thompson to Hardy, 10 April
1944.

13 LAC, RG 27, Vol. 744, file 12-14-16-12, vol. 1. Thompson to Hardy, 19 October 1944.

14 LAC, RG 27, Vol. 748, file 12-15-5, pt 1A. Canadian Vocational Training,
Minutes of Conference of Supervisors of Women's Training, Ottawa,
11–13 February 1946: 1.

15 LAC, RG 27, vol. 744, file 12-14-16-12, vol. 1. Canadian Vocational Training
Program, Department of Labour for Women Veterans. Appendix B. April
1947: 4.

16 Ibid., 1.

17 Ibid., 2.

18 LAC, RG 27, Vol. 744, file 12-14-16-12, vol. 1. Graham to Thompson, 18 April
1946.

19 Ontario Rehabilitation Committee, *Digest of Rehabilitation Conference of
Delegates of Ontario Community Committees,* North Bay Conference, 16 July
1946: 144.

20 LAC, RG 27, Vol. 744, file 12-14-16-12, vol. 1. Crawford to All Regional
Directors, 'Provision of Training for Women Discharged from the Forces,'
3 April 1946.

21 LAC, RG 27, Vol. 744, file 12-14-16-12, vol. 1. Salter to Graham, 12 April 1946.
Report on Visit to Edmonton District, 5 March to 7 March 1946.

22 See also Pierson and Cohen, 'Government Job-Training Programmes for
Women, 1937–1947.'

23 LAC, RG 27, Vol. 744, file 12-14-16-12, vol. 1. Salter to Graham, 15 April 1946.
Visit of Superintendent of Women's Rehabilitation to Vancouver District,
9 March to 18 March 1946.

24 Ontario Rehabilitation Commission, *Digest of Rehabilitation Conferences of*

Delegates of Ontario Community Committees, Ottawa Conference, 23 July 1946, Mrs Edna M. Whinney, Chief Women's Counsellor, DVA, 'Counselling Procedure,' 223–5.

25 Ibid., 223.

26 Canada, Department of Veterans' Affairs, *Veterans' Affairs*, 2, no. 7 (15 April 1947): 6.

27 LAC, RG 27, Vol. 748, file 12-15-5, pt 1A. Canadian Vocational Training, Minutes of Conference of Supervisors of Women's Training, Ottawa, 11–13 February 1946: 3.

28 For a historical study tracking the rise of depending discourse in American social policy, see Fraser and Gordon, 'Toward a Genealogy of Dependency.'

29 LAC, RG 27, vol. 3533, file 3-26-41-1, pt 1. 'Confidential Unrevised Transcription. Minutes of Meeting,' Pacific Regional Advisory Board, Labour Department, Vancouver, B.C., 30 January 1946: 4.

30 LAC, RG 27, Vol. 744, file 12-14-16-12, vol. 1. Alberta Crandall, Maritime Supervisor, Women's Training, to Graham, 18 December 1945.

31 LAC, RG 27, Vol. 744, file 12-14-16-12, vol. 1. W.K. Tibert, Director, Vocational Education, Province of New Brunswick Educational Board, to Thompson, 4 December 1945.

32 Ibid.

33 LAC, RG 27, Vol. 744, file 12-14-16-12, vol. 1. Thompson to R.H. Kerr, Regional Director, CVT, Toronto, 20 March 1946.

34 LAC, RG 27, Vol. 744, file 12-14-16-12, vol. 1. Kerr to Thompson, 6 March 1946.

35 LAC, RG 27, Vol. 744, file 12-14-16-12, vol. 1. Thompson to Kerr, 20 March 1946.

36 LAC, RG 27, Vol. 609, file 6-52-1, pt 2. Petition to Ministry of Health and Social Welfare, Department of Day Nurseries, 20 April 1945. Signed Nora Gilhooly and twenty others. For a discussion of the day-nursery program see Light and Pierson, *No Easy Road*, and Comacchio, *Nations Are Built of Babies*.

37 LAC, RG 27, Vol. 609, file 6-52-1, pt 2. Eaton to MacNamara, 11 September 1945 and 19 February 1946. MacNamara to Goodfellow, 26 February 1946. Goodfellow to Mitchell, 7 March 1946.

38 Ruth Pierson, *'They're Still Women After All.'*

39 LAC, RG 27, Vol. 609, file 6-52-1, pt 2. Eaton to Grier, 4 April 1946.

40 LAC, RG 27, Vol. 605, file 6-24-1, pt 1. Employment of Women – General. Eaton to MacNamara, 27 August 1945.

41 LAC, RG 27, Volume 1516, file 0-6-21. NSS Correspondence with UIC Re: Vocational Training Pre-Employment Courses. Edmonton Report of Mrs

Kate Lyons, 13 July 1945. Donald Cameron, 'Tentative Outline for Vocational Training Programme in Arts and Crafts, under the Department of Extension of the University of Alberta.'

42 LAC, RG 27, Vol. 605, file 6-24-1, pt 3. Employment of Women – General. Renée Morin, NSS, 'Rehabilitation of Female War Workers Originally from Rural Districts.'

43 LAC, MG 28, I10, vol. 110, file 790. General Advisory Committee on Demobilization and Rehabilitation, Subcommittee on the Special Problems of Discharged Women, Minutes of Meeting, 17 May 1944.

44 United States Department of Labor, Women's Bureau. *Household Employment – A Digest of Current Information* (September 1946). United States Department of Labor, United States Employment Service, *Employment Service Review* (November 1946).

45 See Parr, 'Shopping for a Good Stove: A Parable about Gender, Design, and the Market.'

46 LAC, RG 27, Vol. 748, file 12-15-5, pt 1A. Speech delivered by Eaton to National Conference, Vancouver Region section, organized by Dr Mary Salter. See also Eaton to Grier, 22 February 1946, in the same file.

47 LAC, RG 27, Vol. 748, file 12-15-5, pt 1. Department of Labour NSS – Training Branch, Schools and Courses – Household Workers. Associate Director Fraudena Eaton. Eaton to MacNamara, 29 March 1945.

48 LAC, RG 27, Vol. 748, file 12-15-5, pt 1A. Eaton to MacNamara, 21 December 1945.

49 LAC, RG 27, Vol. 748, file 12-15-5, pt 1A. Margaret Grier, Assistant Associate Director, NSS, memorandum to MacNamara, 'Training of Women for Household Work,' 11 December 1946: 2.

50 Ibid., 3.

51 Ibid., 2.

52 Ibid.

53 Ibid.

54 LAC, RG 27, Vol. 748, file 12-15-5, pt 1A. Joe H. Ross, Regional Director, Alberta CVT, to Mr J. Smith, Manager, Calgary NES, 13 December 1945.

55 LAC, RG 27, Vol. 748, file 12-15-5 pt 1. Department of Labour NSS – Training Branch, Schools and Courses – Household Workers. Miss E. Clark for J.J. Smith, Acting Manager, UIC, Calgary, to Eaton, 11 May 1946.

56 Ibid.

57 LAC, RG 27, vol. 3533, file 3-26-41-1 pt 1. 'Confidential Unrevised Transcription. Minutes of Meeting,' Pacific Regional Advisory Board, Labour Department, Vancouver B.C., 30 January 1946, 4.

58 For a comprehensive study of the profound demographic changes underway

in the immediate postwar years, see Owram, *Born at the Right Time*, especially chapter 1.

59 LAC, MG 31, K13, Vol. 1. 'Rehabilitation of Persons from the Armed Forces with Special Reference to Ex-Service Women.' Address to the Business and Professional Women's Club, Ottawa, 13 March 1945: 4. J.D. Ketchum had raised the same issue at a meeting of the Rehabilitation Information Committee, as part of his report from the Subcommittee on Research, where it had been discussed with fellow committee members including Griffin and Line. The concern was that veterans and their families needed special services to assist them in dealing with what were euphemistically called 'domestic difficulties' (underscored in the minutes from the RIC meeting). If addressed early enough, such problems would not go on to become more 'serious troubles.' It is unclear from the minutes whether this matter was taken up in any substantive way. See LAC, RG 27, Vol. 3575, file 11-8-9-9, vol. 1. Demobilization and Rehabilitation Information Committee, 28 February 1945.

60 See also Gleason, 'Psychology and the Construction of the "Normal" Family in Postwar Canada, 1945–60.'

61 LAC, MG 31, K13, Vol. 2, file 14. Russell to Line, 9 November 1946.

62 LAC, RG 27, Vol. 748, file 12-15-5, vol. 1. Draft. Outline of Proposed Course as Sent to Specialists in Each Subject for Completion.

63 LAC, MG 31, K13, Vol. 2, file 14. 'Proposed Film Project and Training in Homemaking and Family Living,' 8.

64 LAC, RG 27, Vol. 748, file 12-15-5, vol. 1. Mental Hygiene Aspects of Homemaking, 1.

65 Ibid., 4. Topic 5 of the lecture series took up the category of adolescence, reorganizing the challenges thought to accompany this phase of development into the following sections: physical growth and development, which included the key terms of psychological, emotional, and social aspects as distinct dimensions of growth; mental development, divided into the slow and quick mind and ancillary educational implications; work and responsibility, the nascent phase of citizenship formation, including distribution of household chores, vocational interests and guidance, first job and responsible use of money, along with its obverse, the 'misuse' of money; leisure and recreation, divided into the phased progression from child to adult forms of play, commercial versus family recreation, and 'friends and companions' as areas of scrutiny. Finally, the module took up 'typical adolescent problems' through two main groups: evasion of 'reality,' and delinquency. The last section addressed 'attitudes towards sex' as a leading challenge meriting separate and careful scrutiny. This section was organized around three

themes: sex instruction; sex interests and questions; and 'social and family problems related to sex.' Regrettably, a full consideration of this component of the lecture series is beyond the scope of this chapter. Nonetheless, the principal and categorical knowledges around which the home and family living course was organized – responsible citizenship, domesticity, and the calibration of human capacities to achieve a higher standard of mental hygiene through the reorganization of the home – are equally compelling, in this case in the transformation of 'adolescence' through mental hygiene discourse and subsequent knowledge practices as a site for regulation and remediation.

66 LAC, MG 31, K13, Vol. 1. Russell to J. Andrew, Rehabilitation Information Committee, Wartime Information Board, 9 July 1945.

67 LAC, RG 27, Vol. 3575, file 11-8-9-9, pt 1. Economics and Research Rehabilitation Information Committee. Minutes of meeting of Rehabilitation Information Committee, Item 3, 'Homemaking and Family Living – Suggested course in for ex-servicewomen and men,' 11 July 1945: 2–3. The NCMH and its policy proposals were not lost on senior officials at the Department of Health and Welfare. In fact, the NCMH had long maintained a close relationship with officials at Health and Welfare. Hincks, Griffin, and their colleagues were called upon regularly in a consultative capacity with the department.

68 The CLES Planned Reading Series included a booklet entitled *Child Psychology* as a possible reference, although the topic was not integrated into the curriculum outline. LAC, MG 31, K13, Vol. 1. F.K. Stewart, Superintendent, Rehabilitation Courses, Canadian Legion Educational Services, Ottawa, to Russell, 5 October 1945.

69 LAC, MG 31, K13, Vol. 1. W.R. Wees, Director of Training, DVA, to R.F. Thompson, Director, CVT, 18 October 1945. Russell wrote on the letter that she had drafted the letter and, although it was never sent, did arrange for Graham to see it 'unofficially.'

70 LAC, RG 27, Vol. 748, file 12-15-5, vol. 1. Capt. H. Heather for Col. Line to Graham, 17 September 1945.

71 LAC, RG 27, Vol. 748, file 12-15-5, vol. 1. Edith Scott, Lt, WRCNS, Directorate of Rehabilitation, Naval Service, DND, to Graham, 20 August 1945; A.C.P. Clayton, Group Capt., Air Service, DND, to Graham, 20 August 1945.

72 LAC, RG 27, Vol. 748, file 12-15-5, vol. 1A. Morgan Haskett to Eric Stangroom, 28 November 1946.

73 LAC, RG 27, Vol. 748, file 12-15-5, vol. 1A. MacNamara to Stangroom, 29 November 1946.

74 LAC, RG 27, Vol. 748, file 12-15-5, vol. 1. Grier to MacNamara, 7 March 1946.

75 LAC, RG 27, Vol. 748, file 12-15-5, pt 1A. Eaton to MacNamara, 18 February 1946.

76 LAC, RG 27, Vol. 748, file 12-15-5, vol. 1A. 'Homemaking.' The only person identified in the release was its instructor, Miss B. Lucille Bridges, former RCAF officer and former director of home economics, Agricultural School, Kemptville, Ontario.

77 LAC, RG 27, Vol. 748, file 12-15-5, vol. 1A. Department of Labour, 'Homemaker's Course,' 18 February 1946.

78 LAC, RG 38, Vol. 184, Department of Veterans' Affairs – Rehabilitation. File Confidential Letters vol. 1. RNs' Association of Ontario (Education Committee). The proposed training course developed by the nurses' association included an aptitude test and a series of medical examinations, including a test for VD – the Wasserman Reaction. Psyche-testing included an assessment of 'personality.'

79 For a study of the closely integrated practices of occupational restructuring, work redesign, and immigration in nursing, see Calliste, 'Women of "Exceptional Merit": Immigration of Caribbean Nurses to Canada.'

80 Arthur MacNamara, 'Tells Training of Nurses' Aides,' 3. The Bovey Commission was the site of considerable contestation between unions and employers on the question of veterans' qualifications and preference in employment. The question of superior training, capacity, and suitability intensely politicized the question of employability and employment security. Labour centrals and individual unions argued instead for a shorter work week as the means to ensure full and stable employment. Employers, fearing the wage demands a trained and experienced workforce might legitimately make, disputed the relevance of the trades classification certificates issued by the service on the grounds that they inflated the skills of their bearers, giving 'an exaggerated idea' of their capacity. LAC, RG 27, vol. 3575, file 11-8-9-9, vol. 2. Rehabilitation Information Committee, Press Survey on Rehabilitation for January 1946.

81 LAC, RG 27, Vol. 1516, file 0-26-1. NSS Correspondence with UIC Re: Vocational Training Pre-Employment Courses. M.E. Cunning for L. Robinson, Manager, Employment and Selective Service Office, Regina, 12 July 1945, Section 3, Hospitals, subsection 1, Ward Aid [sic]: 1–5.

82 Ibid., 3.

83 LAC, RG 27, Vol. 1516, file 0-26-1. NSS Correspondence with UIC re: Vocational Training Pre-Employment Courses. Weston Report, 2.

84 LAC, RG 27, Vol. 1516, file 0-26-1. NSS Correspondence with UIC re: Vocational Training Pre-Employment Courses. M.E. Cunning for L. Robinson, Manager, Employment and Selective Service Office, Regina, 12 July 1945, Section 3, Hospitals, subsection 1, Ward Aid, 5.

85 LAC, RG 27, Vol. 1516, file 0-26-1. S.B. Nitikman, President, Garment Manufacturers Association of Western Canada, Winnipeg, Manitoba, to Mrs Gerry, NSS, Winnipeg, 11 July 1945.
86 Ibid.
87 LAC, RG 27, Vol. 742, file 12-14-7-2. Memorandum, E.N. Mitchell, Section Head, Vocational Training, UIC, Winnipeg, to Commissioner C.A.L. Murchison, UIC, 10 December 1947.
88 LAC, RG 27, Vol. 1521, file T7. NSS Needle Trades Industry, Report of industry meeting, 27 August 1946: 1.
89 Ibid., 5–6.
90 LAC, RG 27, Vol. 742, file 12-14-7-2. Vocational Training in Quebec. Letter to Regional Superintendent, Winnipeg. J.L. Lysecki and E.N. Mitchell from H.C. Hudson, Supervisor of Special Placements, 20 November 1947.
91 LAC, RG 27, Vol. 1521, file T7. NSS Needle Trades Industry, Report of industry meeting, 27 August 1946: 1.
92 Ibid., 2.
93 LAC, RG 27, Vol. 742, file 12-14-7-2. Needle Trades Training Council. Educational Survey Committee Report of Needle Trades Educational Survey Commencing 13 January 1947, Item 9, 'Impressions Gained While in New York.' The survey report described in considerable detail the operation of training institutes in New York, in particular the Central High School of Needle Trades. The visit to the Toronto meeting and visits to vocational schools all focused on trades in which men were employed and included none for women in this highly gendered division of labour. A description of the meeting is included in Item 5 of the report.
94 Ibid., Item 14.
95 Ibid., 'Executive Summary,' 1–2.
96 Ibid., 'Preamble.'
97 Ibid., Item 1, York Knitting Mills, Woodstock, Ontario.
98 LAC, RG 27, Vol. 742, file 12-14-7-2. Administration – Training and Education – Re-Establishment Training – Winnipeg Needle Trades Training Institute. Thompson to A. Brown, Solicitor, 'Training for Needle Trades – Winnipeg,' 18 December 1947.
99 Woods, *Rehabilitation*, 117.
100 Ibid., 257.

Conclusion

1 As historians such as Michael Stevenson have documented, the view that Ottawa was in complete charge of a 'command economy' during the

Second World War, at least with respect to the effectiveness and scope of NSS regulatory interventions, is in need of revision. See Stevenson, 'National Selective Service and the Mobilization of Human Resources in Canada during the Second World War.' See also Donaghy, ed., *Uncertain Horizons: Canadians and Their World in 1945.*

2 Deutsch, 'Some Thoughts on the Public Service,' 84.

3 Theda Skocpol has developed the concept of policy feedback to describe policy effects in the longer term and in particular their unintended effects across different electoral regimes, state formations, and, for that matter, industrial, market, and social formations. Skocpol included a most instructive discussion of her methodology in *Protecting Soldiers and Mothers: The Political Origins of Social Policy in the United States.*

Bibliography

Archival Sources

Archives of Ontario (AO)

Marion Findlay Papers.

Canadian Broadcasting Corporation Archives (CBC)

20 March 1942. 'Special – Discussion Group. Clarence Hincks, William Blatz, Stuart Jaffary Discuss the Effects of the Bombings and the War in Great Britain.'

3 June 1942. 'The Fight For a Free World.'

15 April 1943. 'Special – Women's Part in Labour Legislature [*sic*].' Interviewees: Margaret Bondfield, Frances Perkins, Mrs Rex Eaton.

22 March 1944. 'National Labour Forum. Labour Management Relations in B.C.'

6 March 1945. 'Special – Women's Canadian Club: Women's Help Wanted.'

2 May 1945. 'The Soldier's Return.'

8 May 1945. 'Special – Edgar McInnis Speaks on V-E Day.'

19 May, 1945. 'Eyes Front. Via the BBC in London, England, a Military Programme on Rehabilitation.'

October – 28 December 1945. 'Johnny Home Show.' Johnny Wayne and Frank Shuster,

22 October 1947. 'Guardians of Health.'

22 October 1947. Citizens Forum. 'Psychology vs. The Hairbrush.'

29 October 1948. 'Johnny Delinquent – Whose Responsibility?'

Library and Archives of Canada (LAC)

MG 28. National Council of Women of Canada Papers.
MG 31. Olive Ruth Russell Papers.
RG 24. Department of National Defence.
RG 27. Department of Labour.
RG 31. Dominion Bureau of Statistics.
RG 35. National Employment Service.
RG 38. Department of Veterans Affairs.
RG 50. Unemployment Insurance Commission.

University of Toronto Archives

Ontario College of Education, Department of Education Research, 1935–55.

Books, Articles, and Reports

Abella, Irving Martin. *Nationalism, Communism, and Canadian Labour.* Toronto: University of Toronto Press, 1973.
Abramovitz, Mimi. *Regulating the Lives of Women: Social Welfare Policy from Colonial Times to the Present.* Boston: South End Press, 1988.
Adams, Julia. 'Feminist Theory as Fifth Columnist or Discursive Vanguard? Some Contested Uses of Gender Analysis in Historical Sociology.' *Social Politics* 5, no. 1 (Spring 1998): 1–16.
Adams, Mary Louise. *The Trouble with Normal: Postwar Youth and the Making of Heterosexuality.* Toronto: University of Toronto Press, 1997.
Albo, Gregory. 'Competitive Austerity and the Impasse of Capitalist Employment Policy.' *Socialist Register* (1994): 144–70.
Albo, Gregory, David Langille, and Leo Panitch, eds. *A Different Kind of State? Popular Power and Democratic Administration.* Toronto: Oxford University Press, 1993.
American Statistical Association and the Social Science Research Council. *Government Statistics. A Report of the Committee on Government Statistics and Information Services.* Bulletin 26. New York: Social Science Research Council (April 1937).
Amos, Harry, and Charles G. Stogdill. *Canadian Intelligence Examination.* Toronto: Ryerson Press, 1940.
Anderson, Benedict. *Imagined Communities: Reflections on the Origin and Spread of Nationalism.* London: Verso, 1991.
Armstrong, Barbara Nachtrieb. *Insuring the Essentials: Minimum Wage Plus Social Insurance – A Living Wage Programme.* New York: Macmillan, 1932.

Armstrong, Pat, and Hugh Armstrong. *Theorizing Women's Work.* Toronto: Garamond Press, 1990.

Arnup, Katherine, Andrée Levesque, and Ruth Roach Pierson, with the assistance of Margaret Brennan. *Delivering Motherhood: Maternal Ideologies and Practices in the 19th and 20th Centuries.* New York: Routledge, 1990.

Ashforth, Adam. 'Reckoning Schemes of Legitimation: On Commissions of Inquiry as Power/Knowledge Forms.' *Journal of Historical Sociology* 3, no. 1 (March 1990): 1–22.

Atkinson, Raymond, Louise Odencrantz, and Ben Deming. *Public Employment Service in the United States.* Chicago: Public Administration Service, 1938.

Avery, Donald H. *Reluctant Host: Canada's Response to Immigrant Workers, 1896–1994.* Toronto: McClelland and Stewart, 1995.

Bakker, Isabella, ed. Rethinking Restructuring: Gender and Change in Canada. Toronto: University of Toronto Press, 1996.

Banting, Keith. *The Welfare State and Canadian Federalism.* 2nd ed. Kingston and Montreal: McGill-Queen's University Press, 1987.

Barkan, Elazar. *The Retreat of Scientific Racism: Changing Concepts of Race in Britain and the United States between the World Wars.* New York: Cambridge University Press, 1992.

Baron, Ava. 'Romancing the Field: The Marriage of Feminism and Historical Sociology.' *Social Politics* 5, no. 1 (Spring 1988): 17–37.

Barrett, Michele. *The Politics of Truth: From Marx to Foucault.* Stanford, CA: Stanford University Press, 1991.

Barry, Andrew, Thomas Osborne, and Nikolas Rose, eds. *Foucault and Political Reason: Liberalism, Neo-liberalism and Rationalities of Government.* Chicago: University of Chicago Press, 1996.

Baskerville, Peter, and Eric Sager. 'The First National Unemployment Survey: Unemployment and the Canadian Census of 1891.' *Labour/Le Travail* 23 (Spring 1989): 171–8.

– *Unwilling Idlers: The Urban Unemployed and Their Families in Late Victorian Canada.* Toronto: University of Toronto Press, 1988.

Beaud, Jean-Pierre, and Jean-Guy Prevost. 'The Politics of Measurable Precision: The Emergence of Sampling Techniques in Canada's Dominion Bureau of Statistics.' *Canadian Historical Review* 79, no. 4 (December 1998): 691–725.

Bellingham, Bruce, and Mary Pugh Mathis. 'Race, Citizenship, and the Bio-politics of the Maternalist Welfare State: "Traditional" Midwifery in the American South under the Sheppard-Towner Act, 1921–29.' *Social Politics* 1, no. 2 (Summer 1994): 157–89.

Bernier, Rachel. 'The Labour Force Survey: 50 Years Old!' *Canadian Economic Observer* (March 1996): 3.1–3.8.

Berrian, F.K. 'Jobs to Fit.' *Maclean's*, 15 May 1945, 12, 23–4.

Beveridge, William. *Full Employment in a Free Society*. London: George Allen and Unwin, 1945.

– *Unemployment: A Problem of Industry*. London: Longmans, 1930.

Binet, Alfred, and Theodore Simon. 'The Development of Intelligence in the Child,' L'Annee Psychologique, 1908; and 'New Methods for the Diagnosis of the Intellectual Level of Subnormals.' L'Annee Psychologique, 1905. In *The Development of Intelligence in Children*, 191–244. Nashville, TN: Williams Printing Company, 1980.

Bladen, Vince Wolf. 'The Population Problem.' *Canadian Journal of Economics and Political Science* 5 (1939): 528–47.

– 'Review of *Social Planning for Canada*.' *Canadian Journal of Economics and Political Science* 2 (1936): 240–1.

Blake, Raymond B., Penny E. Bryden, and J. Frank Strain, eds. *The Welfare State in Canada: Past, Present and Future*. Concord, ON: Irwin, 1997.

Blatz, William E. *Understanding the Young Child*. Toronto: Clarke, Irwin and Company, 1944.

Blatz, William E., and Helen MacMurchy Bott. *Parents and the Pre-School Child*. Toronto: J.M. Dent and Sons, 1928.

Boris, Eileen. 'The Racialized Gendered State: Constructions of Citizenship in the United States.' *Social Politics* 2, no. 2 (Summer 1995): 160–80.

– 'Mothers Are Not Workers: Homework Regulation and the Construction of Motherhood, 1948–1953.' In Evelyn Nakano Glenn, Grace Chang, and Linda Rennie Forcey, eds, *Mothering: Ideology, Experience, and Agency*, 161–80. New York: Routledge, 1994.

Bothwell, Robert, Ian Drummond, and John English. *Canada since 1945: Power, Politics, and Provincialism*. Toronto: University of Toronto Press, 1996.

Bott, E.A. 'Juvenile Employment in Relation to Public Schools and Industries in Toronto.' *Studies in Industrial Psychology* no. 2. University of Toronto Psychology Series, Vol. 4. Toronto: University Library, 1920.

Bowles, Samuel, and Herbert Gintis. *Democracy and Capitalism: Property, Community and the Contradictions of Modern Social Thought*. New York: Basic Books, 1986.

Boyer, Robert, and Daniel Drache, eds. *States against Markets: The Limits of Globalization*. New York: Routledge, 1996.

Brandt, Gail Cuthbert. 'Pigeon-Holed and Forgotten: The Work of the Subcommittee on the Post-War Problems of Women, 1943.' *Histoire sociale / Social History* 15, no. 29 (May 1982).

Bridges, J.W. 'A Study of a Group of Delinquent Girls.' *Pedagogical Seminary and Journal of Genetic Psychology* 34, no. 2 (June 1927): 187–204.

Briggs, Laura. 'Eugenics as Reform: The Case of Struggles over Maternal

Health, Tropical Medicine, and the New Deal in Puerto Rico, 1920–1942.'
    Paper presented at the Berkshire Conference, Rochester, NY, June 1999.
Brodie, Janine. 'Introduction: Canadian Women, Changing State Forms,
    and Public Policy.' In Janine Brodie, ed., *Women and Canadian Public Policy*,
    1–30. Toronto: Harcourt, Brace, 1996.
Brown, Shaun R.G. 'Re-establishment and Rehabilitation: Canadian Veteran
    Policy, 1933–1946.' PhD diss., University of Western Ontario, 1995.
Brown, Wendy. *Politics Out of History*. Princeton, NJ: Princeton University Press,
    2001.
– *States of Injury: Power and Freedom in Late Modernity*. Princeton, NJ: Princeton
    University Press, 1995.
Bruschett, Kevin. '"People and Government Travelling Together": Community
    Organization, The State and Post-War Reconstruction in Toronto, 1943–
    1953.' Paper presented at 76th Annual Conference of the Canadian Historical
    Association, St John's, NF, 1997.
Burchell, Graham, Colin Gordon, and Peter Millar, eds. *The Foucault Effect:
    Studies in Governmentality*. Chicago: University of Chicago Press, 1991.
Calliste, Agnes. 'Women of "Exceptional Merit": Immigration of Caribbean
    Nurses to Canada.' *Canadian Journal of Women and the Law* 6, no. 1 (1993):
    85–102.
Cameron, Barbara. 'Dualism or Solidarity? Reforming Canada's System of
    Labour Market Regulation.' In Cy Gonick, Paul Phillips, and Jesse Vorst, eds,
    Labour Gains, Labour Pains: 50 Years of PC 1003. Halifax: Fernwood, 1995.
Cameron, D. Ewen, and H. Graham Ross, eds. *Studies in Supervision. A Lecture
    Series Delivered at McGill University, Montreal. January 1945–March 1945*.
    Montreal: McGill University Press, 1945.
Campbell, Robert Malcolm. 'The Full Employment Objective in Canada, 1945–
    1985.' Ottawa: Economic Council of Canada, 1991.
– *Grand Illusions: The Politics of the Keynesian Experience, 1945–1975*. Peterborough:
    Broadview Press, 1987.
Canada, Advisory Committee on Reconstruction VI. *Post-War Problems of Women –
    Final Report of the Subcommittee, 30 November 1943*. Ottawa: King's Printer, 1944.
Canada, Department of Labour. *Dismiss ... but What of a Job?* Ottawa: King's
    Printer, 1945.
Canada, Department of National Defence. *Army Employment – Civilian Jobs: A
    Guide to Civilian Occupations Related to Army Employment*. Ottawa: King's Printer,
    1945.
Canada, Department of Pensions and National Health. *Back to Civil Life. Prepared
    to Inform Members of the Armed Forces and Canadians Generally of the Steps Taken for
    Civilian Rehabilitation of Those in Uniform*. Ottawa: King's Printer, 1944.

– *What Will I Do When the War Is Won?* Ottawa: King's Printer, nd.

Canada, Department of Reconstruction. *Employment and Income: With Special Reference to the Initial Period of Reconstruction.* Ottawa: King's Printer, 1945.

Canada, Department of Veterans' Affairs. *Annual Report.* 1947.

– *Annual Report.* 1948.

– *Veteran's Affairs.* 1947.

Canada, Dominion Bureau of Statistics. *Census Monograph No. 11: Unemployment. A Study Based on the Census of 1931 and Supplementary Data.* Ottawa: King's Printer, 1938.

Canada. *The Veteran's Charter: Acts of the Canadian Parliament to Assist Canadian Veterans.* Ottawa: King's Printer, 1946.

Canada, Wartime Information Board. *Looking Ahead: Our Next Job.* Canadian Post-War Affairs, Discussion Manual No. 3. Ottawa: King's Printer, 1945.

'Canada's Mentally Unemployable.' *Financial Post,* 11 December 1937, 11.

Canadian-American Women's Committee on International Relations. *International Co-operative Machinery. The International Labour Organization.* Proceedings of the Second Joint Conference. Montreal, 15–17 April 1943.

Canadian Broadcasting Corporation. *The Soldier's Return. A Digest of Talks Heard on the CBC Trans-Canada Network during the Winter of 1944–1945 on Wednesday Nights, after the National News Bulletin.* Toronto: CBC Publications Branch, 1945.

Canadian Conference on Social Work. *Proceedings of Canadian Conference on Social Work.* Eighth Biennial Conference. Montreal: 1942.

Canadian Medical Association. *The Canadian National Committee for Mental Hygiene: Report of a Survey Made of the Organization in 1932.* Ottawa: Metropolitan Life Insurance Company, 1932.

Canadian Welfare Council. *Dominion-Provincial Relations and Social Security.* Ottawa: Council House, 1946.

Carew, Anthony. 'Charles Millard, A Canadian in the International Labour Movement: A Case Study of the ICFTU, 1955–1961.' *Labour/Le Travail* 37 (Spring 1996): 121–48.

Cassidy, Harry. *Social Security and Reconstruction in Canada.* Toronto: Ryerson Press, 1943.

– *Unemployment and Relief in Ontario, 1929–1932: A Survey and Report under the Auspices of the Unemployment Research Committee of Ontario.* Toronto: J.M. Dent and Sons, 1932.

Cavell, Richard, ed. *Love, Hate, and Fear in the Cold War.* Toronto: University of Toronto Press, 2004.

Caves, Richard E., and Richard H. Holton. *The Canadian Economy: Prospect and Retrospect.* Cambridge, MA: Harvard University Press, 1950.

Chant, S.N.F. 'Review of *Occupational Abilities.' Canadian Journal of Economics and Political Science* 2 (February–November 1936): 233–5.

Chin, Christine B.N. *In Service and Servitude: Foreign Female Domestic Workers and the Malaysian 'Modernity' Project.* New York: Columbia University Press, 1998.

Chu, Paul. 'The Modern Approach to Industrial Welfare.' Originally published in *International Labour Review* 171, no. 6 (June 1955). In *International Labour Review: 75 Years of the International Labour Review: A Retrospective* 135, no. 3–4 (1996): 371–82.

'Cites Challenge of Education in Postwar World.' *Globe and Mail,* 5 November 1946.

Coats, R.H. 'Science and Society.' Presidential Address to the American Statistical Association, December 1938. Reprinted from the *Journal of the American Statistical Association,* March 1939. In *Canadian Journal of Economics and Political Science* 5, no. 2 (May 1939): 151–78.

Cobble, Dorothy Sue. 'Organizing the Post-Industrial Work Force: Lessons from the History of Waitress Unionism.' *Industrial and Labour Relations Review* 44, no. 3 (April 1991): 419–36.

Cockburn, Cynthia. *Brothers: Male Dominance and Technological Change.* London: Pluto Press, 1991.

Comacchio, Cynthia R. *The Intimate Bonds of Family: Domesticity in Canada, 1850–1940.* Toronto: University of Toronto Press, 1999.

– *Nations Are Built of Babies: Saving Ontario's Mothers and Children, 1900–1940.* Montreal and Kingston: McGill-Queen's University Press, 1993.

Connelly, M. Patricia, and Pat Armstrong. *Feminism in Action: Studies in Political Economy.* Toronto: Canadian Scholars Press, 1992.

Copp, Terry. 'From Neurasthenia to Post-Traumatic Stress Disorder: Canadian Veterans and the Problem of Persistent Emotional Disabilities.' In Neary and Granatstein, eds, *The Veterans Charter,* 149–59.

Copp, Terry, and Bill McAndrew. *Battle Exhaustion: Soldiers and Psychiatrists in the Canadian Army, 1939–1945.* Montreal and Kingston: McGill-Queen's University Press, 1990.

Corrigan, Philip. *Social Forms / Human Capacities: Essays in Authority and Difference.* New York: Routledge, 1990.

Corrigan, Philip, and Derek Sayer. *The Great Arch: English State Formation as Cultural Revolution.* New York: Basil Blackwell, 1985.

Creese, Gillian. *Constructing Masculinity: Gender, Class, and Race in a White-Collar Union, 1944–1994.* Toronto: Oxford University Press, 1999.

Crompton, Rosemary, Duncan Gallie, and Kate Purcell. 'Work, Economic Restructuring and Social Regulation.' In Rosemary Crompton, Duncan

Gallie, and Kate Purcell, eds, *Changing Forms of Employment: Organizations, Skills and Gender*, 1–20. London: Routledge, 1996.

Crowe, Cathy. 'Nurses' Experience of the Sexual Division of Labour and the Wartime Mobilization of Nurses during the 1930s and 1940s in Canada.' Unpublished paper, 1988.

Curtis, Bruce. *True Government by Choice Men.* Toronto: University of Toronto Press, 1992.

Davin, Anna. 'Imperialism and Motherhood.' In Frederick Cooper and Ann Laura Stoler, eds, *Tensions of Empire: Colonial Cultures in a Bourgeois World*, 87–151. Berkeley: University of California Press, 1997.

Dean, Mitchell. *The Constitution of Poverty: Toward a Genealogy of Liberal Governance.* New York: Routledge, 1991.

– *Critical and Effective Histories: Foucault's Methods and Historical Sociology.* London: Routledge, 1995.

Dehli, Kari. 'Fictions of the Scientific Imagination: Researching the Dionne Quintuplets.' *Journal of Canadian Studies* 29, no. 4 (Winter 1994–5): 86–110.

– '"Health Scouts" for the State? School and Public Health Nurses in Early Twentieth-Century Toronto.' *Historical Studies in Education* 2, no. 2 (Fall 1990): 247–64.

– 'Women and Class: The Social Organization of Mothers' Relations to Schools in Toronto, 1915–1940.' PhD diss., Ontario Institute for Studies in Education, University of Toronto, 1988.

Deutsch, John J. 'Some Thoughts on the Public Service.' *Canadian Journal of Economics and Political Science* 23, no. 1 (February 1957): 83–9.

Dickinson, James, and Bob Russell, eds. *Family, Economy and State: The Social Reproduction Process under Capitalism.* London: Croom Helm, 1986.

Dimand, Robert W. *The Origins of the Keynesian Revolution: The Development of Keynes' Theory of Employment and Output.* Stanford, CA: Stanford University Press, 1988.

Dobuzinskis, Laurent, Michael Howlett, and David Laycock, eds. *Policy Studies in Canada: The State of the Art.* Part 1. Toronto: University of Toronto Press, 1996.

Donaghy, Greg., ed. *Uncertain Horizons: Canadians and Their World in 1945.* Ottawa: Canadian Committee for the History of the Second World War, 1997.

Donzelot, Jacques. 'Pleasure in Work.' In Burchell, Gordon, and Millar, eds, *The Foucault Effect*, 251–80.

Douglas, W.A.B., and Brereton Greenhous. *Out of the Shadows: Canada and the Second World War.* Revised ed. Toronto: Dundurn Press, 1995.

Dubinsky, Karen. *The Second Greatest Disappointment: Honeymooning and Tourism at Niagara Falls.* Toronto: Between the Lines Press, 1999.

'Editorial: A Job to Be done.' *Financial Post*, 16 October 1936.

'Education Stressed at Teachers' Meeting.' *Toronto Daily Star*, 5 November 1946.

'Educationist Urges Need of Selective Immigration.' *Daily Mail and Empire*, 25 February 1928, 5.

Edwards, Frederick. 'Night-and-Day School.' *Maclean's*, 1 May 1942, 16–17, 22–4.

Emery, George. *Facts of Life: The Social Construction of Vital Statistics, Ontario 1869–1952*. Montreal and Kingston: McGill-Queen's University Press, 1993.

England, Robert. *Discharged: A Commentary on Civil Re-establishment of Veterans in Canada*. Toronto: Macmillan, 1944.

English, Allan. 'Canadian Psychologists and the Aerodrome of Democracy.' *Canadian Psychology* 33, no. 4 (October 1992): 663–72.

Epp, Marlene, Franca Iacovetta, and Frances Swyripa, eds. *Sisters or Strangers? Immigrant Women, Minority Women, and the Racialized 'Other' in Canadian History*. Toronto: University of Toronto Press, 2004.

Esping-Anderson, Gosta. *Politics against Markets: The Social Democratic Road to Power*. Princeton, NJ: Princeton University Press, 1985.

– *The Three Worlds of Welfare Capitalism*. London: Polity Press, 1990.

Ferguson, George A. 'Psychology in Canada, 1939–1945.' *Canadian Psychology* 33, no. 4 (October 1992): 697–704.

'Few Servicewomen Will Be Domestics Local Council Told.' *Vancouver Daily Province*, 6 March 1946.

Fisher, Allan G.B. *International Implications of Full Employment in Great Britain*. London: Oxford University Press, 1947.

Flax, Jane. 'Postmodernism and Gender Relations in Feminist Theory.' *Signs* 12, no. 4 (Summer 1987): 621–43.

Flugel, J.C. *A Hundred Years of Psychology, 1833–1933: With Additional Part on Developments, 1933–1947*. London: Gerald Duckworth, 1951.

Forestell, Diane G. 'The Necessity of Sacrifice for the Nation at War: Women's Labour Force Participation, 1939–1946.' *Histoire sociale/Social History* 22, no. 44 (November 1989): 333–48.

Foucault, Michel. *The Archaeology of Knowledge*. New York: Routledge, 1989.

– *The Birth of the Clinic: An Archaeology of Medical Perception*. New York: Vintage Books, 1975.

– *Discipline and Punish: The Birth of the Prison*. Harmondsworth, Middlesex: Penguin, 1977.

– *Power/Knowledge: Selected Interviews and Other Writings, 1972–1977*. New York: Pantheon Books, 1980.

Frader, Laura Levine. 'Social Citizens without Citizenship: Working-Class Women and Social Policy in Inter-War France.' *Social Politics* 3, no. 2–3 (Summer/Fall 1996): 111–35.

Frances, Raelene, Linda Kealey, and Joan Sangster. 'Women and Wage Labour in Australia and Canada Compared.' *Labour/Le Travail* 38 (Fall 1996): 54–89.

Fraser, Nancy, and Linda Gordon. 'Toward a Genealogy of Dependency: Tracing a Keyword of the U.S. Welfare State.' *Signs* (Winter 1994): 309–36.

Fudge, Judy, and Patricia McDermott, eds. *Just Wages: A Feminist Assessment of Pay Equity.* Toronto: University of Toronto Press, 1991.

Garraty, John. *Unemployment in History: Economic Thought and Public Policy.* New York: Harper and Row, 1978.

Gaskell, Jane. 'Conceptions of Skill and the Work of Women: Some Historical and Political Issues.' In Roberta Hamilton and Michele Barrett, eds, *The Politics of Diversity: Feminism, Marxism and Nationalism.* London: Verso Press, 1986.

Gettys, Luella. 'The Administration of Canadian Conditional Grants: A Study in Dominion-Provincial Relationships.' Committee on Public Administration, Social Science Research Association. *Studies in Administration* 3. Chicago: Public Administration Service, 1938.

Gibson-Graham, J.K. The End of Capitalism (as We Knew It): A Feminist Critique of Political Economy. Cambridge, MA: Basil Blackwell, 1996.

Gillespie, Richard. *Manufacturing Knowledge: A History of the Hawthorne Experiments.* New York: Cambridge, 1993.

Gleason, Mona. *Normalizing the Ideal: Psychology, Schooling, and the Family in Postwar Canada.* Toronto: University of Toronto Press, 1999.

– 'Psychology and the Construction of the "Normal" Family in Postwar Canada, 1945–60.' *Canadian Historical Review* 78, no. 3 (September 1997): 442–77.

Glucksmann, Miriam. *Women Assemble: Women Workers and the New Industries in Inter-War Britain.* New York: Routledge, 1990.

Gordon, Linda. 'Introduction: The New Feminist Scholarship on the Welfare State.' In Linda Gordon, ed., *Women, the State and Welfare.* Madison: University of Wisconsin Press, 1990.

– *Pitied but Not Entitled: Single Mothers and the History of Welfare.* Cambridge, MA: Harvard University Press, 1995.

Gossage, Carolyn. *Greatcoats and Glamour Boots: Canadian Women at War, 1939–1945.* Toronto: Dundurn Press, 1991.

Gould, Steven Jay. *The Mismeasure of Man.* New York: W.W. Norton, 1981.

– *Wonderful Life: The Burgess Shale and the Nature of History.* New York: W.W. Norton and Company, 1990.

Granatstein, J.L. *Canada's War: The Politics of the Mackenzie King Government, 1939–1945.* Toronto: Oxford University Press, 1975.

Granatstein, J.L., and Peter Neary, eds. *The Good Fight: Canadians and World War II.* Toronto: Copp Clark, 1995.

Grantham, George, and Mary MacKinnon. *Labour Market Evolution: The Economic History of Market Integration, Wage Flexibility, and the Employment Relation.* New York: Routledge, 1994.

Griffin, J.D.L., S.R. Laycock, and William Line. *Mental Hygiene: A Manual for Teachers.* Toronto: W.J. Gage, 1940.

Guard, Julie. 'Canadian Citizens or Dangerous Foreign Women? Canada's Radical Consumer Movement, 1947–1950.' In Epp, Iacovetta, and Swyripa, eds, *Sisters or Strangers?*, 161–89.

– 'Women Worth Watching: Radical Housewives in Cold War Canada.' In Kinsman, Buse, and Steedman, eds, *Whose National Security?*, 73–88.

Guest, Dennis. *The Emergence of Social Security in Canada.* Vancouver: University of British Columbia Press, 1980.

Gunderson, Morley. *Efficient Instruments for Labour Market Regulation.* Government and Competitiveness Project, School of Policy Studies, Queen's University, 1993.

Hacking, Ian. *The Taming of Chance.* New York: Cambridge University Press, 1991.

Hannant, Larry. *The Infernal Machine: Investigating the Loyalty of Canada's Citizens.* Toronto: University of Toronto Press, 1995.

Hanson, F. Allan. *Testing Testing: Social Consequences of the Examined Life.* Berkeley: University of California Press, 1993.

Hartstock, Nancy. 'Foucault on Power: A Theory for Women?' In Linda J. Nicholson, ed., *Feminism/Postmodernism*, 157–175. New York: Routledge, 1990.

Harzig, Christiane. 'The Stork Story: Regulating Female Sexuality in Canada's Post World War Two Recruitment of Domestics.' Paper presented at the Canadian Historical Association Annual Conference, Dalhousie University, Halifax, May 2002.

Hauser, Philip M., and William R. Leonard. *Government Statistics for Business Use.* New York: John Wiley and Sons, 1946.

Hennessy, Rosemary. *Materialist Feminism and the Politics of Discourse.* London: Routledge, 1993.

Higginbotham, Evelyn Brooks. 'African-American Women's History and the Metalanguage of Race.' *Signs* (Winter 1992): 251–74.

Hills, John, John Ditch, and Howard Glennerster, eds. *Beveridge and Social Security: An International Perspective.* London: Clarendon, 1994.

Hincks, Clarence Meredith. 'How Can We Promote Social Welfare in Canada?' In *Proceedings of the Canadian Conference on Social Work*, 8–10. Montreal: Canadian Conference on Social Work, 1930.

Hobbs, Margaret H. 'Gendering Work and Welfare: Women's Relationship to Wage-Work and Social Policy in Canada during the Great Depression.' PhD diss., University of Toronto, 1995.

Hobbs, Margaret, and Ruth Roach Pierson. '"A Kitchen That Wastes No Steps": Gender, Class and the Home Improvement Plan, 1936–1940.' *Histoire sociale/ Social History* 31 (May 1988): 9–37.

Hogan, Michael J. *The Marshall Plan: America, Britain, and the Reconstruction of Western Europe, 1947–1952.* New York: Cambridge University Press, 1995.

Hogben, Lancelot. *Nature and Nurture.* New York: W.W. Norton, 1933.

Hood, Jean Archibald. 'Some Behaviour Problems and Their Treatment.' MA thesis, University of British Columbia, 1937.

Iacovetta, Franca. 'Freedom Lovers, Sex Deviates, and Damaged Women: Iron Curtain Refugees in Early Cold War Canada.' In Cavell, ed., *Love, Hate and Fear in the Cold War,* 77–107.

– 'Gossip, Contest, and Power in the Making of Suburban Bad Girls: Toronto, 1945–1960.' *CHR* 80, no. 4 (December 1999): 585–623.

– 'Making Model Citizens: Gender, Corrupted Democracy, and Immigrant and Refugee Reception Work in Cold War Canada.' In Kinsman, Buse, and Steedman, eds, *Whose National Security?*, 154–67.

– 'The Sexual Politics of Moral Citizenship and Containing Dangerous Foreign Men in Cold War Canada, 1950s–1960s.' *Histoire sociale/Social History* 33, no. 66 (November 2000): 361–89.

Iacovetta, Franca, with Paula Draper and Robert Ventresca, eds. *A Nation of Immigrants: Women, Workers, and Communities in Canadian History, 1840s–1960s.* Toronto: University of Toronto Press, 1998.

Iacovetta, Franca, and Wendy Mitchinson, eds. *On the Case: Explorations in Social History.* Toronto: University of Toronto Press, 1998.

Iacovetta, Franca, Roberto Perin, and Angelo Principe. *Enemies Within: Italian and Other Internees in Canada and Abroad.* Toronto: University of Toronto Press, 2000.

'Ilsley Discloses Ottawa May Seek Wider Tax Scope.' *Montreal Gazette,* 16 January 1941.

Industrial Relations Counsellors, Inc. *Administration of Public Employment Offices with Unemployment Insurance: Canada, France, Sweden, Switzerland.* New York: J.J. Little and Ives Company, 1935.

International Labour Office. *Problems of Vocational Guidance.* Series J (Education), no. 4. London: Published in the United Kingdom for the International Labour Organization (League of Nations) by P.S. King and Son, 1935.

– *The War and Women's Employment: The Experience of the United Kingdom and the United States.* Montreal: International Labour Office, 1946.

Irving, Allan. *The Development of Income Security in Canada, Britain and the United States, 1908–1945.* Toronto: University of Toronto Faculty of Social Work, 1980.

Ismael, Jacqueline, ed. *Canadian Social Welfare Policy: Federal and Provincial Dimensions*. Kingston and Montreal: McGill-Queen's University Press, 1987.

Ives, Don. 'The Veterans Charter: The Compensation Principle and the Principle of Recognition for Service.' In Neary and Granatstein, eds, *The Veterans Charter*, 85–94.

Jackson, Nancy. 'Rethinking Vocational Learning.' In Rebecca P. Coulter and Ivor F. Goodson, eds, *Rethinking Vocationalism: Whose Life/Work Is It?*, 166–80. Toronto: Our Schools Our Selves Educational Foundation, 1993.

Jackson, Norman, and Pippa Carter. 'Labour as Dressage.' In McKinlay and Starkey, eds, *Foucault, Management and Organization Theory*, 49–64.

James, F. Cyril. 'Preface.' In Cameron and Ross, eds, *Studies in Supervision*, v.

Jenson, Jane. '"Different" but Not "Exceptional": Canada's Permeable Fordism.' *Canadian Review of Sociology and Anthropology* 26, no. 1 (1989): 69–94.

– 'Gender and Reproduction, or Babies and the State.' *Studies in Political Economy* 20 (Summer 1986): 43–72.

– 'Paradigms and Political Discourse: Protective Legislation in France and the United States before 1914.' *Canadian Journal of Political Science* 22, no. 2 (June 1989): 235–58.

Jenson, Jane, and Mariette Sineau, 'Family Policy and Women's Citizenship in Mitterand's France.' *Social Politics* (Fall 1995): 244–69.

Johnson, Andrew J., Stephen McBride, and Patrick J. Smith, eds. *Continuities and Discontinuities: The Political Economy of Social Welfare and Labour Market Policy in Canada. Part 3: Canadian Labour Market Policy.* Toronto: University of Toronto Press, 1994.

Johnson, Terry. 'Expertise and the State.' In Mike Gane and Terry Johnson, eds, *Foucault's New Domains*, 141–52. New York: Routledge, 1993.

Katz, Jonathan Ned. 'The Invention of Heterosexuality.' *Socialist Review* 21, no. 1 (1990): 7–34.

Kaye, Alison. '"No Skill beyond Manual Dexterity Involved": Gender and the Construction of Skill in the East London Clothing Industry.' In Audrey Kobayashi, ed., *Women, Work and Place*, 112–29. Montreal and Kingston: McGill-Queen's University Press, 1994.

Keith, Janet R. 'Situations Wanted: Female.' *Canadian Business* (November 1944): 72–5, 154.

Keller, Evelyn Fox, and Elisabeth A. Lloyd. *Keywords in Evolutionary Biology*. Cambridge, MA: Harvard University Press, 1994.

Kinsman, Gary. *The Regulation of Desire: Homo and Hetero Sexualities*. 2nd ed. Montreal: Black Rose, 1996.

Kinsman, Gary, Dieter K. Buse, and Mercedes Steedman, eds. *Whose National*

Security? Canadian State Surveillance and the Creation of Enemies. Toronto: Between the Lines, 2000.

Kirkconnell, Watson. *Canada, Europe and Hitler.* Toronto: Oxford University Press, 1939.

Kornbluh, Felicia. 'The New Literature on Gender and the Welfare State: The U.S. Case.' *Feminist Studies* 22, no. 1 (Spring 1996): 171–97.

Koven, Seth, and Sonya Michel, eds. *Mothers of the New World: Maternalist Politics and the Origins of Welfare States.* New York: Routledge, 1993.

Krashinsky, Michael. 'Putting the Poor to Work: Why "Workfare" Is an Idea Whose Time Has Come.' In John Richards, Aidan Vining, et al., *Helping the Poor: A Qualified Case for 'Workfare,'* 91–120. Toronto: C.D. Howe Institute, 1995.

Kumar, Krishan. 'From Work to Employment and Unemployment: The English Experience.' In R.E. Pahl, ed., *On Work: Historical, Comparative and Theoretical Approaches,* 138–66. New York, Basil Blackwell, 1989.

Kunzel, Regina G. *Fallen Women, Problem Girls: Unmarried Mothers and the Professionalization of Social Work, 1890–1945.* New Haven, CT: Yale University Press, 1993.

– 'White Neurosis, Black Pathology: Constructing Out-of-Wedlock Pregnancy in the Wartime and Postwar United States.' In Joanne Meyerowitz, ed., *Not June Cleaver: Women and Gender in Postwar America, 1945–1960,* 304–31. Philadelphia: Temple University Press, 1994.

Ladd-Taylor, Molly. *Mother-Work: Women, Child Welfare, and the State.* Urbana: University of Illinois Press, 1994.

– 'Saving Babies and Sterilizing Mothers: Eugenics and Welfare Politics in the Interwar United States.' *Social Politics* (Spring 1997): 136–53.

Laidler, David. *Fabricating the Keynesian Revolution: Studies in the Inter-War Literature of Money, the Cycle and Unemployment.* New York: Cambridge University Press, 1999.

LeCocq, Thelma. 'Woman Power.' *Maclean's,* 15 June 1942, 10–11, 40.

Lerner, A.P. 'Mr. Keynes' "General Theory of Employment, Interest and Money."' Originally published in *International Labour Review* 34, no. 4 (October 1936). *International Labour Review: 75 Years of the International Labour Review: A Retrospective* 135, no. 3–4 (1996): 337–46.

Lewis, Jane. 'Gender and the Development of Welfare Regimes.' *Journal of European Social Policy* 3, no. 3 (1992): 159–73.

— 'Gender and Welfare Regimes: Further Thoughts.' *Social Politics* 4, no. 2 (Summer 1997): 160–77.

– 'Introduction: Women, Work, Family and Social Policies in Europe.' In Lewis, ed., *Women and Social Policies in Europe.*

– *Should We Care about Family Change?* Toronto: University of Toronto Press, 2003.

Lewis, Jane, ed. *Women and Social Policies in Europe: Work, Family and the State.* London: Edward Elgar Publishing, 1993.

Lewis, Jane, and Gertrude Astrom. 'Equality, Difference, and State Welfare: Labour Market and Family Policies in Sweden.' *Feminist Studies* 18, no. 1 (Spring 1992): 59–87.

Light, Beth, and Ruth Roach Pierson. *No Easy Road: Women in Canada, 1920s to 1960s.* Toronto: New Hogtown Press, 1990.

Line, William. 'The Learning Process.' In Cameron and Ross, eds, *Studies in Supervision*, 77–95.

Little, Margaret. 'The Blurring of Boundaries: Private and Public Welfare for Single Mothers in Ontario.' *Studies in Political Economy* 47 (Summer 1995): 89–109.

– *No Car, No Radio, No Liquor Permit: The Moral Regulation of Single Mothers in Ontario, 1920–1997.* Toronto: Oxford University Press, 1997.

Logan, Harold A. *History of Trade Union Organization in Canada.* Chicago: University of Chicago Press, 1928.

– *Trade Unions in Canada: Their Development and Functioning.* Toronto: Macmillan Company of Canada, 1948.

Low, Ruth. 'The Unattached Woman in Canada: Who She Is and Some of Her Problems.' Paper presented at the National Conference of Social Work, Montreal, June 1935, to the National Travellers' Aid Society of the United States. Reprinted from *Child and Family Welfare*. Ottawa: Canadian Welfare Council, January 1936.

Mackenzie, Hon. Ian (Minister of Pensions and National Health). *Reconstruction, Social Security and Health Insurance.* Two complementary statements before Special Select Committees of the House of Commons. Ottawa: King's Printer, 1943.

Mackintosh, W.A. 'Canadian Economic Policy from 1945 to 1957 – Origins and Influences.' In Hugh G.J. Aikin, John J. Deutsch, et al., eds, *The American Economic Impact on Canada*, 50–68. Duke University Commonwealth Studies Centre. Durham, NC: Duke University Press, 1957.

– 'The White Paper on Employment and Income in Its 1945 Setting.' In Canadian Trade Committee, ed., *Canadian Economic Policy since the War*, 9–21. A series of six publications in commemoration of the 20th anniversary of the White Paper on Employment and Income. Ottawa: Carleton University, 1966.

McCallum, Margaret E. 'Keeping Women in Their Place: The Minimum Wage in Canada, 1910–1925.' *Labour/Le Travail* 17 (Spring 1986): 29–56.

McClintock, Anne. *Imperial Leather: Race, Gender and Sexuality in the Colonial Contest.* New York: Routledge, 1995.

McInnis, Peter S. 'Teamwork for Harmony: Labour-Management Production Committees and the Postwar Settlement in Canada.' *Canadian Historical Review* 77, no. 3 (September 1996): 317–52.

McIntosh, Mary. 'The State and the Oppression of Women.' In Annette Kuhn and AnnMarie Wolpe, eds, *Feminism and Materialism: Women and Modes of Production*, 254–89. London: Routledge and Kegan Paul, 1978.

McKinlay, Alan, and Ken Starkey, eds. *Foucault, Management and Organization Theory: From Panopticon to Technologies of Self.* London: Sage Publications, 1998.

McLaren, Angus. *Our Own Master Race: Eugenics in Canada, 1885–1945.* Toronto: McClelland and Stewart, 1990.

MacNamara, Arthur. 'Tells Training of Nurses' Aides.' *Veterans' Affairs* 2, no. 10 (1 June 1947): 3.

Maguinness, Olive Dickinson. *Environment and Heredity.* Toronto: Thomas Nelson and Sons, 1940.

Marsh, Leonard. *Canadians In and Out of Work.* Toronto: Oxford University Press, 1940.

– *Employment Research: An Introduction to the McGill Programme of Research in the Social Sciences.* Toronto: Oxford University Press, 1935.

– *Report on Social Security for Canada.* Report to the Advisory Committee on Reconstruction, Ottawa, 1943.

Marsh, Leonard, and O.J. Firestone. 'Will There Be Jobs?' Wartime Information Board, Canadian Affairs. Ottawa: King's Printer, 1944.

Marshall, Thomas Humphrey. *Citizenship and Social Class, and Other Essays.* Cambridge: Cambridge University Press, 1950.

Maxwell, W. Russell. 'Economic Theory and National Purpose.' *Canadian Journal of Economics and Political Science* 2, no. 2 (May 1936): 119–27.

Mayo, Elton. *The Social Problems of Industrial Civilization.* Boston: Division of Research, Graduate School of Business Administration, Harvard University, 1945.

Mehta, Uday S. 'Liberal Strategies of Exclusion.' In Frederick Cooper and Ann Laura Stoler, eds, *Tensions of Empire: Colonial Cultures in a Bourgeois World*, 59–86. Berkeley: University of California Press, 1997.

'Mental Health Dramas Draw a Big Response.' *CBC Times* (week of 20 February 1949): 5.

Metropolitan Life Insurance Company. *Unemployment Insurance: A Summary of Existing Governmental and Private Plans.* New York, 1931.

'Military District 10 Recalls Order in Drafting of Negroes.' *Montreal Gazette*, 30 December 1943.

Miller, Peter, and Nikolas Rose. 'Governing Economic Life.' *Economy and Society* 19, no. 1 (February 1990): 1–31.

Mink, Gwendolyn. 'Wage Work, Family Work, and Welfare Politics.' *Feminist Economics* 1, no. 2 (Summer 1995): 95–8.

– *The Wages of Motherhood: Inequality in the Welfare State, 1917–1942.* Ithaca, NY: Cornell University Press, 1995.

– 'Welfare Reform in Historical Perspective.' *Connecticut Law Review* 26, no. 3 (Spring 1994): 879–99.

Mohanty, Chandra Talpade, Ann Russ, and Lourdes Torres, eds. *Third World Women and the Politics of Feminism.* Bloomington: Indiana University Press, 1991.

Moraska, Eve. 'A Historical Turn in Feminism and Historical Sociology: Convergences and Differences.' *Social Politics* 5, no. 1 (Spring 1998): 38–47.

'More Work in Canada, but Relief Lists Are Longer.' *Ottawa Citizen*, 28 December 1936.

Morgan, Patricia. 'From Battered Wife to Program Client: The State's Shaping of Social Problems.' *Kapitaliste: Working Papers on the Capitalist State* no. 9 (1989): 17–39.

Morton, Desmond, and Glenn Wright. *Winning the Second Battle: Canadian Veterans and the Return to Civilian Life, 1915–1930.* Toronto: University of Toronto Press, 1987.

Morton, Nelson Whitman. *Individual Diagnosis: A Manual for the Employment Office.* McGill Social Research Series Number 6. Toronto: Oxford University Press, 1935.

– *Occupational Abilities: A Study of Unemployed Men.* McGill Social Research Series Number 3. Toronto: Oxford University Press, 1935.

Moscovitch, Allan, and Jim Albert, eds. *The Benevolent State: The Growth of Welfare in Canada.* Toronto: Garamond Press, 1987.

Mosse, George L. *Toward the Final Solution: A History of European Racism.* New York: Howard Ferlig, 1978.

Myers, Charles S., and Mary Cockett, eds. *Occupational Psychology.* Vol. 19. London: National Institute for Industrial Psychology, 1945.

– *Occupational Psychology.* Vol. 20. London: National Institute for Industrial Psychology, 1946.

Nakano Glenn, Evelyn. 'Citizenship, Gender and Race. Ethnicity and Nationality.' Paper presented at Internationalizing Women's Studies, Number 3: Comparative Research on Welfare States and Gender, University of Madison, Wisconsin, February 1997.

– 'From Service to Servitude: Historical Continuities in the Racial Division of Paid Reproductive Labour.' In Vicki L. Ruiz and Ellen Carol DuBois, eds,

Unequal Sisters: A Multi-Cultural Reader in U.S. Women's History, 405–35. New York: Routledge, 1994.

'Name Women's Committee on Employment.' *Winnipeg Free Press*, 6 November 1936.

Neary, Peter, and Shaun Brown. 'The Veteran's Charter and Canadian Women Veterans of World War II.' In Granatstein and Neary, eds, *The Good Fight: Canadians and World War II*, 387–415.

Neary, Peter, and J.L. Granatstein, eds. *The Veterans Charter and Post–World War II Canada*. Montreal and Kingston: McGill-Queen's University Press, 1998.

'Negroes Not Called Up.' *Montreal Star*, 29 December 1943.

Newkirk, Louis V., and Harry A. Greene. *Tests and Measurements in Industrial Education*. New York: John Wiley and Sons, 1935.

'No Migration to Home or Housework for Majority of Women Veterans.' *Vancouver News-Herald*, 6 March 1946.

O'Malley, Pat, Lorna Weir, and Clifford Shearing. 'Governmentality, Criticism, and Politics.' *Economy and Society* 26, no. 4 (November 1997): 501–17.

Oliver, Dean F. 'Public Opinion and Public Policy in Canada: Federal Legislation on War Veterans, 1939–1946.' In Raymond Blake, et al., eds, *The Welfare State in Canada: Past, Present and Future*, 193–214. Concord, ON: Irwin Publishing, 1997.

– 'When the Battle's Won: Military Demobilization in Canada, 1939–1946.' PhD diss., York University, 1996.

Oliver, Mary. 'A Wartime Schoolroom.' *Canadian Business* (January 1944): 69, 90.

Ontario Rehabilitation Commitee. *Digest of Rehabilitation Conferences of Delegates of Ontario Community Committees and Employer Interests – Permanent and Temporary along with Necessary Government Personnel.* Second series. Ottawa: 1946.

Ontario Teachers' Council. 'A Brief Presented by the Ontario Teachers' Council to the Royal Commission on Dominion-Provincial Relations.' April 1938.

Orloff, Ann Shola. 'Gender and the Social Rights of Citizenship: A Comparative Analysis of Gender Relations and Welfare States.' *American Sociological Review* 58, no. 3 (June 1993): 303–28.

– 'Gender in the Welfare State.' *Annual Review of Sociology* 22, no. 51 (1996): 51–78.

Ostner, Ilona, and Jane Lewis. 'Gender and the Evolution of European Social Policies.' In Stephen Liebfried and Paul Pierson, eds, *European Social Policy: Between Fragmentation and Integration*, 159–93. Washington, DC: Brookings Institution, 1995.

Owran, Doug. *Born at the Right Time: A History of the Baby Boom Generation.* Toronto: University of Toronto Press, 1996.

– 'Economic Thought in the 1930s: The Prelude to Keynesianism.' *Canadian Historical Review* 66, no. 3 (September 1985): 344–77.
– *The Government Generation: Canadian Intellectuals and the State, 1900–1945.* Toronto: University of Toronto Press, 1986.

Pahl, Leslie A. *State, Class, and Bureaucracy: Canadian Unemployment Insurance and Public Policy.* Kingston and Montreal: McGill-Queen's University Press, 1988.

Panitch, Leo. 'The Tripartite Experience.' In Keith Banting, ed., *The State and Economic Interests.* Royal Commission on the Economic Union and Development Prospects for Canada, Volume 32: 37–119. Toronto: University of Toronto Press, 1986.

Parr, Joy. *The Gender of Breadwinners: Women, Men and Change in Two Industrial Towns, 1880–1950.* Toronto: University of Toronto Press, 1990.
– 'Gender History and Historical Practice.' *Canadian Historical Review* 76, no. 3 (September 1995): 354–76.
– 'Shopping for a Good Stove: A Parable about Gender, Design, and the Market.' In Parr, ed., *A Diversity of Women*, 75–97.

Parr, Joy, ed. *A Diversity of Women: Ontario, 1945–1980.* Toronto: University of Toronto Press, 1995.

Pateman, Carol, ed. *The Disorder of Women.* Stanford, CA: Stanford University Press, 1989.

Paterson, Fiona M.S. 'Schooling the Family.' *Sociology* 22, no. 1 (February 1988): 65–88.

Peck, Jamie. *Work-Place: The Social Regulation of Labour Markets.* New York: Guilford Press, 1996.

Phillips, Ann, and Barbara Taylor. 'Sex and Skill.' In Feminist Review, ed., *Waged Work: A Reader*, 54–66. London: Virago, 1986.

Philpott, John, ed. *Working for Full Employment.* New York: Routledge, 1997.

Picking, F.J., ed. *What Happens Now? A Veteran's Guide.* Toronto: Canadian Veteran Publishing Company, 1945.

Pierson, Christopher. *Beyond the Welfare State? The New Political Economy of Welfare.* London: Polity Press, 1991.

Pierson, Ruth Roach. 'Gender and the Unemployment Insurance Debates in Canada, 1934–1940.' *Labour/Le Travail* 25 (Spring 1990): 77–103.
– *'They're Still Women after All': The Second World War and Canadian Womanhood.* Toronto: McClelland and Stewart, 1986.

Pierson, Ruth Roach, with Marjorie Cohen. 'Government Job-Training Programmes for Women, 1937–1947.' In Pierson, *'They're Still Women after All,'* 79–80.

Piess, Kathy. '"Charity Girls" and City Pleasures: Historical Notes on Working-Class Sexuality, 1880–1920.' In Kathy Piess and Christina Simmons, eds,

Passion and Power: Sexuality in History, 57–69. Philadelphia: Temple University Press, 1989.

Piven, Francis Fox. 'Women and the State: Ideology, Power and the Welfare State.' In Alice Rossi, ed., *Gender and the Life Course*, 265–87. New York: Aldine, 1985.

Piven, Francis Fox, and Richard Cloward. *Regulating the Poor: The Function of Public Welfare*. New York: Pantheon Books, 1971.

Pollard, Miranda. *Reign of Virtue: Mobilizing Gender in Vichy France*. Chicago: University of Chicago Press, 1997.

Poovey, Mary. *A History of the Modern Fact: Problems of Knowledge in the Sciences of Wealth and Society*. Chicago: University of Chicago Press, 1998.

– *Making a Social Body: British Cultural Formation, 1830–1864*. Chicago: University of Chicago Press, 1995.

Porter, Ann. 'Women and Income Security in the Post-War Period: The Case of Unemployment Insurance, 1945–1962.' *Labour/Le Travail* 31 (Spring 1993): 111–44.

Pressey, Sidney L., and J. Elliott Janney. *Casebook of Research in Educational Psychology*. New York: Harper and Brothers, 1937.

Principe, Angelo. 'A Tangled Knot: Prelude to 10 June 1940.' In Iacovetta, Perin, and Principe, *Enemies Within*, 27–51.

Pringle, Rosemary, and Sophie Watson. 'Women's Interests and the Post-Structuralist State.' In Michele Barrett and Anne Phillips, eds, *Destabilizing Theory: Contemporary Feminist Debates*, 53–73. Stanford, CA: Stanford University Press, 1992.

Rea, K.J. *The Prosperous Years: The Economic History of Ontario, 1939–1975*. Toronto: University of Toronto Press, 1985.

Richardson, Theresa. *The Century of the Child: The Mental Hygiene Movement and Social Policy in the United States and Canada*. New York: State University of New York Press, 1989.

Riley, Denise. *'Am I That Name?' Feminism and the Category of 'Women' in History*. Minneapolis: University of Minneapolis, 1988.

– *War in the Nursery: Theories of the Child and Mother*. London: Virago Press, 1983.

Roberts, Barbara. *Whence They Came: Deportation from Canada, 1900–1935*. Ottawa: University of Ottawa Press, 1988.

Robin, Martin. *Shades of Right: Nativist and Fascist Politics in Canada, 1920–1940*. Toronto: University of Toronto Press, 1992.

Robinson, Daniel J. *The Measure of Democracy: Polling, Market Research, and Public Life, 1930–1945*. Toronto: University of Toronto Press, 1999.

Rose, Nikolas. *Governing the Soul: The Shaping of the Private Self*. London: Routledge, 1991.

– *Inventing Ourselves: Psychology, Power and Personhood.* New York: Cambridge University Press, 1996.
– *Powers of Freedom: Reframing Political Thought.* New York: Cambridge University Press, 1999.
– *The Psychological Complex: Psychology, Politics and Society in England, 1869–1939.* London: Routledge and Kegan Paul, 1985.
Rose, Nikolas, and Peter Miller. 'Political Power beyond the State: Problematics of Government.' *British Journal of Sociology* 43, no. 2 (June 1992): 173–205.
Russell, Bob. 'A Fair or a Minimum Wage? Women Workers, the State, and the Origins of Wage Regulation in Western Canada.' *Labour/Le Travail* 28 (Fall 1991): 59–88.
Sainsbury, Diane. *Gender, Equality and Welfare States.* New York: Cambridge University Press, 1996.
Sandiford, Peter. *Educational Psychology: An Objective Study.* Toronto: Longmans, Green, 1938.
– *Foundations of Educational Psychology: Nature's Gift to Man.* Toronto: Longmans, Green, 1938.
Sangster, Joan. *Earning Respect: The Lives of Working Women in Small-Town Ontario, 1920–1960.* Toronto: University of Toronto Press, 1995.
Sassoon, Ann Showstack. 'Comment on Jane Lewis: Gender and Welfare Regimes: Further Thoughts.' *Social Politics* 4, no. 2 (Summer 1997): 178–81.
Sautter, Udo. 'The Origins of the Employment Service of Canada, 1900–1920.' *Labour/Le Travail* 6 (Autumn 1980): 89–112.
– *Three Cheers for the Unemployed : Government and Unemployment before the New Deal.* New York: Cambridge University Press, 1991.
– 'Unemployment and Government: American Labour Exchange before the New Deal.' *Histoire sociale / Social History* 18, no. 36 (November 1985): 335–58.
Schecter, Tanya. *Race, Class Women and the State: The Case of Domestic Labour in Canada.* Montreal: Black Rose Books, 1998.
Schumpeter, Joseph A. *Capitalism, Socialism, and Democracy.* New York: Harper and Brothers, 1950.
Scott, Ira D. *Manual of Advisement and Guidance. Prepared in Accordance with the Approved Policies of the Veterans' Administration.* Advisement and Guidance Division, Vocational Rehabilitation and Education Service. Washington, DC: United States Government Printing Office, 1945.
Scott, Joan Wallach. 'Deconstructing Equality-Versus-Difference: Or, the Uses of Poststructuralist Theory for Feminism.' *Feminist Studies* 14, no. 1 (Spring 1988): 33–50.
– 'Experience.' In Josephine Butler and Joan Scott, eds, *Feminists Theorize the Political*, 22–40. London: Routledge, 1992.

– *Gender and the Politics of History.* New York: Columbia University Press, 1989.
'Seek to Discover Jobs Unemployed Best Suited For, States Rogers.' *Regina Leader-Post*, 28 September 1937.
Sefton MacDowell, Laurel. 'The Formation of the Canadian Industrial Relations System during World War II.' In Granatstein, ed., *Canada's War*, 296–317.
'Separating the Unemployed.' *Winnipeg Free Press*, 26 November 1937.
Sharma, Nandita. 'Citizenship and the Social Organization of Migrant Labour in Canada during Late Capitalism.' Paper presented at the 'Women and Citizenship in the Era of Restructuring' session, Society for Socialist Studies, Learned Societies Conference, St John's, NF, June 1997.
Shore, Chris, and Susan Wright. 'Introduction.' In Chris Shore and Susan Wright, eds, *Anthropology of Power. Critical Perspectives on Government and Power*, 3–39. New York: Routledge, 1997.
Shore, Marlene. *The Science of Social Redemption: McGill, the Chicago School and the Origins of Social Research in Canada.* Toronto: University of Toronto Press, 1987.
Siim, Birte. 'The Scandinavian Welfare States – Towards Sexual Equality or a New Kind of Male Domination?' *Acta Sociologica* 30, no 3–4 (1987): 255–70
Skocpol, Theda. *Protecting Soldiers and Mothers: The Political Origins of Social Policy in the United States.* Cambridge, MA: Belknap Press of Harvard University Press, 1992.
– *Social Policy in the United States: Future Possibilities in Historical Perspective.* Princeton, NJ: Princeton University Press, 1995.
Smith-Rosenberg, Carroll. 'Discourses of Sexuality and Subjectivity: The New Woman, 1870–1936.' In M. Duberman, Martha Vicinus, and George Chauncy, Jr, *Hidden from History: Reclaiming the Gay and Lesbian Past*, 264–80. New York: Penguin Books, 1989.
Stacey, C.P. *Arms, Men and Governments: The War Politics of Canada, 1939–1945.* Ottawa: Queen's Printer, 1970.
Stage, Sarah, and Virginia B. Vincenti, eds. *Rethinking Home Economics: Women and the History of a Profession.* London: Cornell University Press, 1997.
Stephen, Jennifer. 'The "Bad," the "Incorrigible," and the "Immoral": Toronto's Factory Girls and the Work of the Toronto Psychiatric Clinic.' In Louis A. Knafla and Susan W.S. Binnie, eds, *Law, Society and the State: Essays in Modern Legal History*, 405–39. Toronto: University of Toronto Press, 1995.
Stevenson, Michael D. *Canada's Greatest Wartime Muddle: National Selective Service and the Mobilization of Human Resources during World War II.* Montreal and Kingston: McGill-Queen's University Press, 2001.
– 'The Industrial Selection and Release Plan, and the Premature Release of

Personnel from the Armed Forces, 1945–1946.' In Greg Donaghy, ed., *Uncertain Horizons: Canadians and Their World in 1945*. Ottawa: Canadian Committee for the History of the Second World War, 1997.

– 'National Selective Service and Employment and Seniority Rights for Veterans, 1943–1946.' In Neary and Granatstein, eds, *The Veterans Charter*, 95–109.

– 'National Selective Service and the Mobilization of Human Resources in Canada During the Second World War,' PhD diss., University of Western Ontario, 1996.

Stewart, Annabel Murray, and Bryce Stewart. *Statistical Procedures of Public Employment Offices*. New York: Russell Sage Foundation, 1933.

Stoddard, George D. *The Meaning of Intelligence*. New York: Macmillan Company, 1943.

Stoler, Ann Laura. 'Carnal Knowledge and Imperial Power: Gender, Race and Morality in Colonial Asia.' In Micaela di Leonardo, ed., *Gender at the Crossroads of Knowledge*, 55–101. Berkeley: University of California Press, 1991.

– *Race and the Education of Desire: Foucault's* History of Sexuality *and the Colonial Order of Things*. London: Duke University Press, 1995.

Stoler, Ann Laura, and Frederick Cooper, 'Between Metropole and Colony.' In Frederick Cooper and Ann Laura Stoler, eds, *Tensions of Empire: Colonial Cultures in a Bourgeois World*, 1–56. Berkeley: University of California Press, 1997.

Strange, Carolyn. *Toronto's Girl Problem: The Perils and Pleasures of the City, 1880–1930*. Toronto: University of Toronto Press, 1995.

Strange, Carolyn, and Tina Loo. *Making Good: Law and Moral Regulation in Canada, 1867–1939*. Toronto: University of Toronto Press, 1997.

Strong-Boag, Veronica. 'Home Dreams: Women and the Suburban Experiment in Canada, 1945–1960.' *Canadian Historical Review* 72 (December 1991): 471–504.

– *The New Day Recalled*. Markham, ON: Penguin Books, 1988.

Struthers, James. 'Building a Culture of Retirement: Pensions, Labour and the State in Post-World War II Ontario.' Paper presented at Canadian Historical Association Annual Meeting, St John's, NF, 1997.

– 'Family Allowances, Old Age Security, and the Construction of Entitlement in the Canadian Welfare State, 1943–1951.' In Neary and Granatstein, eds, *The Veterans Charter*, 179–204.

– *The Limits of Affluence: Welfare in Ontario, 1920–1970*. Toronto: University of Toronto Press, 1994.

– *No Fault of Their Own: Unemployment and the Canadian Welfare State, 1914–1941*. Toronto: University of Toronto Press, 1983.

Sugiman, Pamela. *Labour's Dilemma: The Gender Politics of Auto Workers in Canada, 1937–1979*. Toronto: University of Toronto Press, 1994.

Terman, Lewis M. *The Measurement of Intelligence. An Explanation of and a Complete Guide for the Use of the Stanford Revision and Extension of the Binet-Simon Intelligence Scale*. New York: Houghton Mifflin, Riverside Press Cambridge, 1944.

Thompson, Godfrey H. *The Factorial Analysis of Human Ability*. London: University of London Press, 1943.

Tillotson, Shirley. '"When Our Membership Awakens": Welfare Work and Canadian Union Activism, 1950–1965.' *Labour/Le Travail* 40 (Fall 1997): 137–70.

'Too Much Stress on Skill, Not Enough on Personality, Claims Dr Olive Russell.' *Globe and Mail*, 29 January 1938.

Trabue, M.R., and Frank Parker Stockbridge. *Measure Your Mind: The Mentimeter and How to Use It*. New York: Doubleday, Page and Company, 1920.

'Training for Post-War Employment.' *Labour Gazette* (April 1945): 523.

'Training: Post-War Training Programmes in Canada.' *Labour Gazette* (July 1945): 1023.

Turner, Bryan S., ed. *Citizenship and Social Theory*. London: Sage Publications, 1994.

United States Department of Labor, United States Employment Service. *Employment Service Review*. Washington, DC: United States Government Printer, November 1946.

United States Department of Labor, Women's Bureau. *Household Employment – A Digest of Current Information*. Washington, DC: United States Government Printer, September 1946.

Ursel, Jane. *Private Lives, Public Policy: 100 Years of State Intervention in the Family*. Toronto: Women's Press, 1992.

Valverde, Mariana. *The Age of Light, Soap and Water*. Toronto: McClelland and Stewart, 1991.

– 'Building Anti-Delinquent Communities.' In Parr, ed., *A Diversity of Women*, 19–45.

– '"When the Mother of the Race Is Free": Race, Reproduction, and Sexuality in First-Wave Feminism.' In Franca Iacovetta and Mariana Valverde, eds, *Gender Conflicts: New Essays in Women's History*, 3–26. Toronto: University of Toronto Press, 1992.

Vernon, Philip E. 'The Demise of the Stanford-Binet Scale.' *Canadian Psychology* 28, no. 3 (July 1987): 251–8.

Vernon, Philip E., and John B. Parry. *Personnel Selection in the British Forces*. London: University of London Press, 1949.

'Veterans' Program Said Best of Lot – Dr Olive Russell Comments.' *Regina Leader-Post*, 27 February 1946.

Walters, William Howard Charles. 'Decentering the Economy.' *Economy and Society* 28, no. 2 (May 1999): 312–22.

– 'The Fate of Unemployment: A Study in Governmentality.' PhD diss., York University, 1996.

Warren, Robert, Leo Wolman, and Henry Clay. *The State in Society: A Series of Public Lectures.* Toronto: Oxford University Press, 1940.

Wechsler, David. *The Range of Human Capacities.* Baltimore, MD: Williams and Wilkins, 1935.

Welland Public Schools. *A Programme of Citizenship: Experimental Edition.* Welland, ON, 1946.

Wells, Don. 'The Impact of the Postwar Compromise on Canadian Unionism: The Formation of an Auto Worker Local in the 1950s.' *Labour/Le Travail* 36 (Fall 1995): 147–73.

Whitton, Charlotte. *Behind the Headlines: Security for Canadians.* Vol. 3, no. 6. Ottawa: Canadian Institute of International Affairs and the Canadian Association for Adult Education, 1943.

– *The Dawn of Ampler Life: Some Aids to Social Security.* Toronto: Macmillan Company of Canada, 1943.

Whyte, A.P. Luscombe. 'Psychologists Go to War.' *National Home Monthly* 34, no. 11 (November 1943): 12–13, 22, 24.

Wilensky, Harold L. *The Welfare State and Equality: Structural and Ideological Roots of Public Expenditures.* Berkeley: University of California Press, 1975.

Williams, D.C. 'The Frustrating Fifties.' *Canadian Psychology* 33, no. 4 (October 1992): 705–9.

Williams, Fiona, 'Postmodernism, Feminism and the Question of Difference.' In N. Parton, ed., *Social Theory, Social Work and Social Change*, 61–76. London: Routledge, 1996.

– 'Race/Ethnicity, Gender, and Class in Welfare States: A Framework for Comparative Analysis.' *Social Politics* 2, no. 2 (Summer 1995): 127–59.

Williams, Fiona, and Jane Pillinger. 'New Thinking on Social Policy Research into Equality, Social Exclusion and Poverty.' In Jane Millar and Jonathan Bradshaw, eds, *Social Welfare Systems: Towards a Research Agenda.* University of Bath: Centre for the Analysis of Social Policy in Association with the Economic and Social Research Council, 1996.

Williams, Greer. 'Don't Try to Solve Conflicts with Fear of Going Crazy.' *Veterans' Affairs* 2, no. 9 (14 May 1947): 2.

Wills, Gale. *A Marriage of Convenience: Business and Social Work in Toronto, 1918–1957.* Toronto: University of Toronto Press, 1995.

Wilson, Kenneth R. 'Manpower.' *Maclean's* (1 September 1942): 5–7, 32–4.

Wolfe, Alan. 'Did Women Create the Welfare State? The Mothers of Invention.' *New Republic* (4–11 January 1993): 28–35.

Woods, Walter S. *Rehabilitation: A Combined Operation.* Ottawa: Edmund Cloutier, 1953.

Woytinsky, Wladimir. *Three Sources of Unemployment: The Combined Action of Population Changes, Technical Progress and Economic Development.* Geneva: International Labour Office Studies and Reports, Series C, no. 20, 1935.

Wright, Mary J. 'Women Ground-Breakers in Canadian Psychology: World War II and Its Aftermath.' *Canadian Psychology* 33, no. 4 (October 1992): 675–82.

Wright, Mary, and C. Roger Myers, eds. *History of Academic Psychology in Canada.* Toronto: C.J. Hogrefe, 1982.

Young, Charles H., and Helen R.Y. Reid. *The Japanese Canadians.* With a Second Part on Oriental Standards of Living by W.A. Carrothers. Edited by H.A. Innis. Published under the auspices of the Canadian National Committee for Mental Hygiene and the Canadian Institute for International Affairs. Toronto: University of Toronto Press, 1938.

Index

STUDIES IN GENDER AND HISTORY

General editors: Franca Iacovetta and Karen Dubinsky